A RESPONSE TO PROGRESSIVISM

A RESPONSE TO PROGRESSIVISM:

The Democratic Party and New York Politics, 1902–1918

ROBERT F. WESSER
State University of New York
at Albany

NEW YORK UNIVERSITY PRESS
NEW YORK AND LONDON

LIBRARY OF CONGRESS CATALOGING-IN-PUBLICATION DATA

Wesser, Robert F.
A response to progressivism.

Bibliography: p.
Includes index.
1. Democratic Party (N.Y.)—History—20th century.
2. New York (State)—Politics and government—1865–
1950. I. Title.
JK2318.N7W47   1986   324.2747′06′09   86–5415
ISBN 0–8147–9213–8

Book design by Ken Venezio

For Kathy, Bob, and Chris
with love

Contents

Preface

Historians have often pondered the question of what happened to the Democratic party in the period between the defeat of William Jennings Bryan for the presidency in 1896 and the election of Woodrow Wilson to that high office sixteen years later. It was a time when party leaders, frozen out of the councils of national power, had to content themselves with what successes they could muster in their states and localities. In places like the South, for example, Democrats assumed the major responsibility for accommodating the forces of change and implementing the policies and programs advanced by the more progressive elements of society. Here and there in other parts of the nation they acted in a similar fashion. But in many states—and the state of New York was a case in point—the Democracy seemingly did little to commend itself to the electorate; to contemporary observers; or, later, to historians who were usually cut from the same cloth as the elite critics of the first decade and a half of the twentieth century. The burden of criticism was that the Democrats were essentially obstructionists in their tactics, provincial in their outlook, and wrongheaded on the issues. The party was dominated by powerful political "machines"—in New York the much-maligned Tammany Hall—that depended for their sustenance on the ignorant masses huddled in the cities and the greedy business-financial interests seeking favors and special privileges. Thus it was that the "bosses" and their followers became the bête noir of the best citizens of the state and the chief objects of the reformers' wrath.

In the past two decades the image of the Democratic party in the heavily urban-industrial states during the progressive era has changed considerably. Thanks to the studies of J. Joseph Huthmacher, John D.

Buenker, and others, politicians who presumed to represent ethnic minorities and the so-called urban masses, in a sense, have been accorded redemption. Whatever their motives, they are now credited with having achieved a variety of reforms and, in many instances, contributed far more to the welfare of society as a whole than their much-heralded Republican middle-class and upper-class counterparts. In the process the machine-type Democrats of the 1900s and 1910s helped redefine and broaden progressivism so as to lay the foundations on the state level of Franklin D. Roosevelt's New Deal liberalism of the 1930s. They did these things not always acting alone but, as good pragmatists or realists, by joining with others to form coalitions that admittedly shifted from time to time and from issue to issue.

The present study, however, is not an attempt to flesh out the history of the New York Democratic party solely within the context of this revisionist interpretation. That political leaders Charlie Murphy, Al Smith, and Robert Wagner did play a key role in the transformation of their party as well as the nature and content of reform there is no question. One could even argue that by the time of World War I these Democrats were clearly on their way to establishing in New York the foundations of what would later be known as the welfare state. Important as this theme may be, and I give it considerable attention in my analysis, it constitutes only one part of a more complex, variegated story—the story of a group of political leaders who struggled, oftentimes among themselves, to formulate responses to a myriad of forces, most of which are subsumed under the label of progressive or progressivism, for the purpose of winning elections. They did so amid great social and economic change and within a certain defined environment—one could call it, broadly speaking, a political culture—that was multidimensional in character: a competitive two-party system with the GOP the dominant organization statewide; a polity divided along sectional and, to an extent, ethnocultural lines that became manifest in intraparty and interparty tensions; and an electorate that was fickle, changing, and withal skeptical of politicians in general and of major party spokesmen in particular. It is against such a background that I have sought to relate the history of the New York Democrats—their maneuverings, their strategies, and their performance—on the state level from the time of Murphy's rise to the leadership of Tammany

Hall in 1902 through the election of Al Smith to the governorship in 1918. Because of the competitive quality of the state's politics and the pressure this condition brought to bear on the Democrats, there is much in the pages that follow on the Republicans, Theodore Roosevelt's Progressives, and the Socialists. In addition, there is a good deal about presidential politics in 1912 and 1916—the first mainly to set the record straight on the factors behind Murphy's concern and strategy before and during the Baltimore nominating convention; the second to show, among other things, the impact of Wilson's efforts at renomination and reelection on the New York Democratic party. Finally, I have engaged in extensive electoral analysis largely to gauge the Democrats' success or failure in broadening the party's appeal through their persistent accommodation of reform. The sources of information and the methods used for this task together with the necessary illustrative data are presented in Appendix I and Appendix II.

It is always a pleasure for the historian to acknowledge the help that others gave during the course of researching and writing a scholarly project. I am very much indebted to the staffs of the many libraries I visited over the years for their kind consideration and unfailing courtesy. Although they are too numerous to mention by name, I am particularly grateful to the men and women in the manuscript divisions or departments of the following: the Library of Congress, the New York Public Library, the Franklin D. Roosevelt Library, the Cornell University Library, the Columbia University Library, the Syracuse University Library, the New York University Library, and the Yale University Library. Most of the basic research for this study—in published letter collections and memoirs, government documents, newspapers, contemporary magazines, and secondary books and periodicals—was done in the New York State Library in Albany and the Buffalo and Erie County Public Library. While the latter is nearly three hundred miles from my home, I often traveled there, especially in the early stages of the research, because it remains familiar and friendly ground. I am grateful to the personnel of these libraries. A special thanks goes to Lyall Squiar, who allowed me to read his collection of Clarence Parker Papers in his Syracuse home.

Agencies, societies, and other institutions aided in various ways. The Research Foundation of the State University of New York several years ago provided me with summer fellowships and travel grants to do essential research and to begin the writing phase of this project. Some of what I present here was first published elsewhere. Much of Chapter 5 appeared in *New York History*, LX (1979), 407–438; a portion of Chapter 8 dealing with woman suffrage and prohibition appeared in Milton Plesur, ed., *An American Historian: Essays to Honor Selig Adler* (Buffalo: State University of New York at Buffalo, 1980), pp. 140–148; and an essay summary of most of the book's conclusions was printed as part of the proceedings of the American-Italian Association Annual Conference held in 1983. I want to express my gratitude to Wendell Tripp at the New York State Historical Association in Cooperstown, to Milton Plesur at SUNY Buffalo, and to Francis X. Femminella at SUNY Albany for their permission to republish this material. Finally, I am thankful to a number of my colleagues in administration in Albany who made it possible for me to have two sabbatic leaves—one in 1976 and another in 1983–1984—that gave me time to research, think, write, and revise. The second one was particularly welcome because it came after three years in administration and afforded me the opportunity to put finishing touches on this study and to plunge ahead with a research project on Al Smith. I am especially grateful to Sung Bok Kim of the Department of History, Dean John Webb of the College of Social and Behavioral Sciences, and Vice-President Walter Gibson of Research and Graduate Studies for their success in obtaining financial assistance to help defray the cost of the book's publication.

Most of all, I should like to acknowledge the assistance and encouragement tendered by several people. The late J. Joseph Huthmacher gave me a detailed early draft of his manuscript on the New York career of Robert F. Wagner and graciously critiqued a preliminary version of this study. Bruce W. Dearstyne took time from his busy schedule to review the first few chapters. My friend and former colleague, Bernard K. Johnpoll, shared with me in numerous conversations his wealth of knowledge on radicalism and socialism and photocopied much of his material on these subjects for my use. Melvyn Dubofsky a long time ago kindly sent me a sheaf of worksheets on Socialist voting in New York City, 1900–1918. My former secretary, Michelle Carbonneau, typed the final draft in her usually efficient and good-natured fashion. I truly appreciate the efforts of all these people on my behalf.

Finally, I want to say a word of thanks to my wife, Helen W. Wesser, whose patience, understanding, and affection made the difficult times bearable and the good times even better. And to the children, now adults, my feeling is best expressed in the book's dedication.

Albany, New York   ROBERT F. WESSER

I

Economic, Social, and Political Backgrounds: 1880s–1910

By the early part of the twentieth century, America's dominant mood was one of optimism. These were the "confident years." The nation had just fought and won the "splendid little war" with Spain. The patriotism and enthusiasm of that triumph spilled over onto the domestic scene in the years that immediately followed. And why not? The nation's people were prosperous—at least by the standards of the Old World, and even by those of the preceding half-dozen years or so in this country. Factories were now booming; farm prices were rising; and foreign commerce was burgeoning. It was a time when most Americans—especially those who benefited from the material progress of the day—*could* look toward the future with unshaken confidence, even exuberance.

Such a mood of optimism could not mask the profound economic and social changes that occurred in America in the previous twenty years or so. The nation had been agrarian and rural; it entered the new century with a rapidly expanding industrial base and a growing urban population. In the thirty-year period from 1879 to 1909, the total capital invested in manufacturing establishments increased sixfold (from $2,693,238,000 to $17,210,365,000); the second-largest jump came in the ten-year period 1899 to 1909, which witnessed a rise of almost 100 percent. The value of products of manufacturing establishments showed a similar, if less dramatic, increase.[1] Accompanying this change was a tremendous leap in the nation's urban population. In 1880 fewer than 3 of 10 Americans lived in cities of 2,500 inhabitants or more; by 1910 the number was approaching 5 of 10. Equally impressive was the emergence of the large city: in these thirty years cities of 100,000 or more jumped from 20 to 38; those from 50,000 to 100,000 people rose from 15 to 59. Doubtless, much of this urban growth was due to a natural birth increase and internal migration, especially the movement of peoples from rural areas or villages to cities. But a substantial part of it was also the result of the heavy immigration to America in these decades. The 1880s saw over 5,000,000 newcomers arrive on the nation's shores, three quarters of whom came from northern and western Europe. While immigration would dip in the next decade because of the severe depression, it would reach flood tide in the early part of the new century: between 1901 and 1910 nearly 9,000,000 foreigners poured into America, a large percentage of whom now hailed from southern and eastern Europe.[2] And the flow would continue until World War I.

In these years America became a restive nation. As competition gave way to consolidation and the small business unit to the large corporation, sensitive citizens worried about the lost ideal of individualism. Following the "placid" 1880s, a decade that was actually fraught with great change, came the intense, bitter, depression-ridden 1890s. Here the problems of housing, sanitation, poverty, and unemployment plagued the expanding cities, while revolt in the farmland reached a crescendo. Never before were class fissures so deep and so unsettling in America. Coxey's Army, Homestead, Pullman, and Cripple Creek became symbols of working-class discontent. Less dramatic events after the return of prosperity and through the early part of the twentieth century signaled continuing divisions. Union membership jumped over four times between 1897 and 1910. The newborn Socialist party, with a membership of 10,000 in 1901, grew to 118,000 by 1912.[3]

New York's economic and social development mirrored the nation's. By the early years of the twentieth century, the state was an industrial-urban giant, which had fully earned her sobriquet, "Empire State." Not only was she first in nearly two thirds of the major industries in America, but the aggregate value of her manufactures probably surpassed that of every nation in the world except Great Britain, Germany, France, and perhaps Austria-Hungary and Italy. In finance and commerce New York's record was equally impressive. The center of much of this bustling activity was New York City, which, in all its diversity, by 1900 turned out over 60 percent of the manufactured goods in the state (and actually manufactured more than every other state in the Union but Pennsylvania). But the upstate cities were also burgeoning into major industrial centers, each with its own specialties. Buffalo's iron-and-steel industry, given impetus by its harnessing of electrical power in the 1890s, joined flour milling, chemical, and other lighter manufacturing as the city's leading endeavors. Rochester, already known for its great strides in the photographic and optical fields, actually employed a larger share of wage earners in the retail clothing industry from the turn of the century well past the first decade. And Syracuse, also with its clothing factories, its tanneries, and its carpenter shops, expanded greatly its foundries and machine shops.[4] Smaller urban centers like Utica, Troy, and Schenectady at least kept pace with the larger, more cosmopolitan cities.

The state as a whole underwent a substantial increase in population in these decades—from 5,082,900 in 1880 to 9,113,600 in 1910. Most of this upsurge came in the expanding cities. (By 1870 New York was considered an "urban" state by federal standards; the forty years after 1880 would witness both an absolute and a relative decline in rural population.) New York City alone grew from 1,911,698 to 4,766,883 in 1910[5] and, by this date, contained for the first time over one half of the inhabitants of the entire state. In the same years the population of Buffalo almost tripled; that of Rochester, Syracuse, and Utica more than doubled; that of Yonkers quadrupled; and that of Schenectady quintupled. As elsewhere, some of this increase stemmed from internal migration, but, in addition, these cities attracted newcomers from abroad in large numbers. Of course, none did so more than New York City. In 1910 New York City boasted over 3,000,000 foreign-born whites and children of foreign-born or mixed parentage, representing 70 percent of the total population. Equally important, New York's ethnic mix reflected the changing patterns of immigration in the period. While most of the city's foreign population in 1890 was of Irish and German origins, twenty years later Russian Jews were the largest single ethnocultural group, with Italian Catholics close behind the Germans

3

and the Irish. At the same time, most of the major interior cities also had a preponderance of immigrants and their children, but generally the older groups still prevailed. The sole exception was Utica, whose Italian population outstripped that of any other ethnic component in the city.[6]

New York State's work force had developed into a sizable, if divided, urban proletariat by the close of the first decade of the new century. The longer-established and stabler trades and crafts, themselves expanding in the period, gradually gave way in numbers to the semiskilled and unskilled laborers. Yet in terms of union membership, still a relatively small percentage of workmen by 1910, the craft unions remained dominant across the state. Most of these unionists—in the building, printing, brewing, and machine trades—were affiliated with the American Federation of Labor, usually through the city or town labor councils. Upstate urban centers, particularly Buffalo and Rochester, had strong central bodies. The most powerful union movement, however, was in New York City. In 1902 the margin of difference in membership between unions in the city and the upstate was 67,000 in favor of the former; by 1913 it had climbed to 318,000. Until the great organization thrust beginning in 1910, the large majority of these union members were either native-born or of Irish and German backgrounds. As a result of a series of bitter strikes over the next several years affecting mainly Jewish workers in New York City's garment industry, the character (as well as the aggregate) of union membership changed markedly. By 1913 unions in the needle trades, composed chiefly of Jewish workmen, expanded their membership some seven times; by 1912 they boasted one third of the total union membership in the entire state.[7]

Ethnocultural differences as well as occupational distinctions kept unionists apart from one another, a factor that surely helps explain why organized labor in New York was scarcely an effective political force throughout much of the progressive era. One manifestation of these divisions among workmen was the development and expansion of the socialist movement in the state during these years. Journalists, lawyers, and teachers joined workers in providing the national movement with a constructive, usually moderate leadership and following. Indeed, a New Yorker, Morris Hillquit, was a founding member in

1901 and a leading light thereafter of the Socialist Party of America. At the polls the Socialists were weak until well into the second decade of the century. It is true that Eugene V. Debs received his largest presidential vote in the Empire State in 1900 (running on the Social Democratic ticket) in 1904 and in 1908. But New York's percentage of Debs's national total declined markedly through 1912. Moreover, the state's Socialist party did not overtake Hearst's Independence League as New York's third party until 1910. Still, the preceding decade was a seedtime for socialism in both New York City and the upstate. The party recruited especially among the garment workers in the city's Jewish neighborhoods where it was warmly received, ran solid campaigns for office, and in general spread the leftist gospel. Upstate the movement was slow in taking hold. Cities like Buffalo and Rochester possessed a socialist movement long before the turn of the century, but the real organizational push in the interior centers did not occur until after the 1906 elections. Early the next year the New York State Socialist Quorum transformed itself into a state committee and, by that summer, was engaged in a sustained campaign to organize locals mainly in the industrial cities and towns. Soon foreign-language federations made their appearance. By the end of 1910, Socialist party membership was still only about 7,500 in all of New York; four years later it had climbed to almost 11,000 and was spread out among locals across the state. Among the most active were those in New York City, Schenectady, Buffalo, and Jamestown. The Socialist vote in these cities on state and local candidates remained uneven, however, with totals far exceeding membership and usually fluctuating with the intensity of protest against Democrats and Republicans. The most persistent gains in the decade were recorded in Schenectady where, in 1911, a Socialist mayor was elected.[8]

In the fullness of time, these profound developments in state and nation would have a great impact on major party politics. Both Republicans and Democrats were constrained to grapple with the powerfully new economic forces and the pains of economic dislocation; with the substantial population increases in the cities where social problems cried for solutions and where large numbers of new Americans year by year entered the electorate; and with an enlarged proletariat that heightened class consciousness amid continuing ethnocultural rivalries. The successes and failures of the politicians in adjusting older traditions and values to the modern exigencies would help determine which party, Democrats or Republicans, obtained the electoral edge.

I

In the early years of the period, both national political parties, each fearful of antagonizing disparate groups within its precarious coalition, evaded the growing restiveness and economic conflict across the land. But in New York State Democratic successes under Grover Cleveland, then David B. Hill, suggested that, by the late 1880s, the Democracy was adapting better to the changing environment than the Republicans. Specifically, the partisan Hill as governor developed a program favorable to laboring elements and new Americans, particularly Irish Catholics. Thus, he forged a winning combination of upstate urban organizations and downstate groups that seemed to presage a long-term advantage for the Democrats. Four years after Hill's second gubernatorial victory, Cleveland marched back to the White House with his home state solidly behind him. This triumph of 1892 was achieved mainly on the strength of a large urban vote all through the state.[9]

Then, however, the political tide in New York turned dramatically in the other direction. Renewed Democratic infighting between the Hill and Cleveland forces (though by now Hill had been replaced by Roswell Flower as governor), excesses of machine rule in New York City and in several interior cities in 1893 and 1894, and the severe economic depression of the 1890s set the stage for Republican ascendancy. While the Democratic administrations in Washington and Albany followed ineffective policies, GOP orators capitalized on traditional Republican appeals for protection, sound money, and business expansion—appeals that struck a responsive chord in this, a leading manufacturing state. And the Democrats' fate in New York was sealed in 1896 with the nomination of Nebraskan William Jennings Bryan for the presidency: neither businessmen nor farmers and workers could be persuaded that western "free silver" would restore prosperity to the Empire State. William McKinley's victory in New York, therefore, was sweeping. A badly divided Democracy was reduced to barebones in the state: even

New York City went Republican for the first time in a presidential contest in GOP history, and only the loyalty of Irish Catholics kept the Democrats respectable.[10] Whatever gains the Democrats had made in the late 1880s and early 1890s evaporated amid falling prices, growing unemployment, and declining profits. Now western- and southern-oriented, the national Democratic party seemed to offer little to urban-industrial New York.

For the next decade and a half, the Republicans dominated the politics of the Empire State. They won every presidential and gubernatorial election down through 1908, consistently controlled both houses of the legislature, and usually commanded substantial majorities in the state's congressional delegation. Impressive as these successes were, however, Republican pluralities were not always commanding, especially in state-wide contests in nonpresidential years, as symbolic appeals meant less to the voters in these than in national elections, as internal party conflicts developed or reappeared, and as new issues divided the electorate. Indeed, the New York Democrats made a quick recovery from the debacle of the mid-1890s: in 1897 they scored several victories across the state. And in the five gubernatorial elections between 1900 and 1908 they were at least moderately competitive with the Republicans, garnering on the average 46 percent of the aggregate vote statewide. Finally, in areas of proven Democratic strength—New York City in the downstate, Buffalo in the upstate—the party after the turn of the century was almost as successful as it had been in earlier days.[11]

During this time of Republican ascendancy, a fundamental characteristic of the political system in New York State remained its sectional and, to a degree, cultural underpinnings. The solid core of Republicanism lay in the upstate that, though declining in population relative to New York City, yet cast a larger total vote in general elections than the metropolis throughout the entire progressive era. Here native Protestant farmers, villagers, and small townsmen, whose origins dated back to the earlier New England migration or to the more recent immigration from the British Isles, Canada, and Scandinavia, were wedded to the GOP by ethnoreligious traditions and by the party's favorable economic program, most notably the protective tariff. With but one or two exceptions, the state's rural counties went consistently Republican all the way to 1910.[12] In addition, and more significantly,

7

the Republicans did well in the burgeoning interior cities—Buffalo, Rochester, Syracuse, Utica, Albany, and a half-dozen others—that by 1910 embraced nearly one half of the upstate population. In these urban centers entrenched GOP county organizations dominated by Yankee Protestant elites extended themselves to accommodate the growing numbers of new Americans while retaining their old-stock supporters, many of whom had flocked into the cities from the surrounding countryside. They cleverly exploited long-held animosities toward the downstate "colossus" on issues like taxation, transportation improvements, and representation and apportionment. Seizing on every opportunity to lambast New York City "machine" politics, they and their newspaper allies also trumpeted the virtues of Republicanism— virtues that rang truer in the wake of that "splendid little war" with Spain, renewed prosperity, and business expansion after 1900. They sometimes distributed the "spoils" of office among the newcomers and occasionally opened jobs in the party organization to them. In some instances they even joined forces with reformers, or they helped broaden reformism to embrace various proposals for social and economic betterment under the auspices of municipal government.[13]

While most of the upstate cities did produce Republican majorities in statewide elections throughout this era, it is difficult to ascertain the extent to which particular ethnic groups contributed to party victories. Among the older immigrants the Irish were lost to the Democrats, but predominantly German wards, at least late in the period, tended to divide their loyalties, probably on the basis of religious affiliation, with Protestants likely to be Republican and Catholics Democratic. Generally, however, German areas in the interior urban centers seemed to be moving more toward the GOP by 1910. The real problem in identifying ethnic voting preferences lies with the newer elements—mainly the Italians, the eastern European Jews, and the Poles—for this period was the very one during which the heaviest immigration took place, and the large percentage of these people did not become citizens until World War I and later. Moreover, only a small number of ethnic wards in the upstate cities encompassed the kind of single-group density that permits safe generalizations about voting patterns. Yet, given these limitations, a glance at the most homogeneous foreign districts in several urban centers for the years 1906–1910 does suggest that the Republicans were holding their own in areas filling up with the new arrivals, especially in Albany, Rochester, and Syracuse where GOP county organizations were exceptionally powerful. In cases where the Republicans apparently did less well with such voters—as, for example, in Buffalo and Utica—they were hard-pressed to win party victories, at least in gubernatorial elections.[14]

By contrast to Republican supremacy in the upstate, the Democratic party usually dominated the political life of New York City. Here two organizations, Tammany Hall in New York County and the Kings organization in Brooklyn, drew their strength from the hundreds of thousands of foreign-born and second-generation Americans that were crammed into the city's inadequate living quarters and constantly in need of aid and comfort to soften the harsh realities of life and work. While the New York "machines" cast their net widely among ethnic groups (including large numbers of German-Americans) in their pursuit of "neighborhood" politics, they relied most heavily on the support of Irish-Catholic voters. Beginning in the 1830s, the flow of Irish immigration to the United States continued steadily, though at a declining rate, all through the remainder of the century. By 1880, notes one historian, nearly 20 percent of the eligible voting males in New York City were Irish-born. In addition, 42.5 percent of the city's native Americans boasted at least partial Irish ancestry.[15] English-speaking and gregarious, eager to climb the success ladder, and excited by the hurly-burly of American politics, these newcomers quickly entered the political arena. Just as quickly they affiliated with the Democratic party. For the Whigs, then the Republicans fell prey to a nativism that dismissed Irish Catholics as the "uncompromising foe" in the cities. Nor could the Irish embrace Yankee reformism, which championed liquor control, immigration restriction, and abolitionism (with its threat of black labor competition). The flight of many a Yankee Protestant from the "party of rebellion" to the GOP further paved the way in the Democracy for politically and socially ambitious Irish-Americans. In New York City the rise of the Irish to prominence was symbolized by "Honest John" Kelly's capture of Tammany's leadership in 1872 and by William Grace's election to the mayoralty in the next decade.[16]

Just as the sons of Erin were gaining political supremacy in New York and Brooklyn, other groups, principally the Jews and the Italians, were flocking into Irish neighborhoods. By the early twentieth century, for example, the Lower East Side of Manhattan, earlier an Irish ghetto, now teemed with hundreds of thousands of Jews, constituting what Moses Rischin has called "an immigrant Jewish cosmopolis."[17] Italians were not quite so numerous, were less crowded in the ghettos, but were also concentrated in the southern tip of the island. Undoubtedly, racial and religious tensions developed between the better-established Irish and the invading newcomers, and sometimes these troubles erupted into ugly confrontations, even riots. Generally, however, Tammany district captains, in keeping with tradition, played the part of "the big brothers of everybody in the neighborhood" and, over the years, won for the Democratic organization an enlarged political following. Although Italians for a variety of reasons—their sense of transcience, their villagelike culture, and their strong family ties—were slow to enter the electorate, those who participated in the political process seemed to drift into the Tammany orbit by 1910. The Jews were another story. Surely a goodly number did respond favorably to the Tammany "welfare system," and the Hall gradually brought eastern European newcomers into the party's inner circles. But countless other Jews, driven by strong impulses for political and economic action to better their lot, repeatedly looked away from the Irish-dominated organization. All during the progressive era they remained susceptible to reformers of various stripes.[18] Certainly neither of these groups, nor for that matter the whole range of what are called new-stock Americans, realized anything like their full potential until much later. Meanwhile, however, Democratic strategists, in particular, had to take into account their needs and interests in planning political campaigns.

A major theme in the sectional politics of New York State was the conflict of cultures—with the Democratic, "foreign" downstate pitted against the Republican, Yankee upstate. But, of course, New York City was not exclusively foreign and Democratic, and the upstate was not all native and Republican. Each of the major parties, in fact, made claims in the other's territory. The GOP displayed some strength in New York City, garnering over 40 percent of the total vote in the three presidential elections and in all five of the gubernatorial contests in the years 1900–1908. This success, no doubt, was due partly to the Republican mystique and partly to the opposition's weaknesses, most notably the Democracy's identification with "Bryanism" and "Tammanyism." But, in addition, the Republicans in the city brought forward able, effective leadership and championed an enlightened program. In Manhattan they drew mainly upon the "better elements," native-born, middle-class, or wealthy Americans who resided in the "silk-stocking" districts through the center and along the Upper West Side of the island. Outside Manhattan, especially in Brooklyn, the GOP also commanded strong support from the "established citizenry." These better elements supplied the national party with much of its New York contingent—for example, Theodore Roosevelt, Henry L. Stimson, and Herbert Parsons—and they often joined independents and anti-machine Democrats in organizing fusion tickets to challenge Tammany Hall in municipal elections from the mid-1890s through the progressive era. In pursuit of good government and in campaigns against vice and corruption, fusion was successful in 1894, 1901, and 1913, each time after Tammany mismanagement in city or state. In such endeavors, and in others as well, the city Republicans made repeated attempts to win votes in the heavily ethnic, working-class districts of lower Manhattan.[19] Not surprisingly, these Republicans constituted the most progressive force in the state party and constantly challenged their more conservative brethren upstate on both program and party management.

In the upstate, the Democratic party, which had been strong in the days of Grover Cleveland but that fell into disarray following the Bryan defeat of 1896, underwent a rebuilding process for the next decade and a half. In Buffalo the pieces were picked up by the regular Irish- and German-Catholic leaders who would seek to add to their nucleus the large Polish and Italian immigration to the Queen City from the 1890s onward. Though divided among themselves, these regulars, having been closer to "Blue-Eyed Billy" Sheehan and David B. Hill than to Grover Cleveland, would gravitate once again to Tammany Hall in the early years of the twentieth century.[20] Doing battle with them in Buffalo as well as elsewhere in the upstate were scores of independent Democrats whose main support came from groups similar to those that made up the nucleus of Republican strength in the interior regions—native-born small-town and city manufacturers, bankers, merchants, lawyers, and even farmers. Legatees of the Cleveland tradition, these party rebels were more closely attuned culturally and politically to the good government fusionists in New York City than to their Democratic compatriots among Irish Catholics and other immigrant groups. Their major objective was to reorganize the state Democratic party by overturning the alliance of bosses and machines that to them represented all that was wrong and baleful in American politics.[21] To the independents, in fact, antibossism remained the cardinal feature of progressivism, and they would continue their forays against Tammany Hall and its upstate satellites well into the second decade of the twentieth century.

The complex sectional-cultural divisions in the New York polity, which oftentimes produced serious tensions within the major parties, also yielded overall a certain stability and equilibrium to the state in this era of great economic and social transformation. For in general elections each of the parties was obliged to make the necessary group accommodations to keep reasonably intact its geographic sphere of influence—the Republicans in the more heavily native upstate and the Democrats in the "foreign" downstate—and yet reach out to the other's home base. The Republicans held the electoral advantage until 1910 in statewide and national contests largely because they did consistently well in their domain and simultaneously garnered impressive support in Democratic New York City—support that was grounded on attractive symbolic appeals, effective leadership, and constructive programs as well as powerful attacks on the opposition's sins and weaknesses. By the same token, the party of "Bryanism" and "Tammanyism" retained a solid enough foundation in New York State so that if, and when, the GOP stumbled the Democracy could seize the opportunity at hand and march to victory. Such would be the case in 1910.

II

A key to the continued success of Republicanism in New York State was the party's great capacity to respond positively to the forces of change. Initially the process of accommodating reform agitation fell to the powerful boss of the GOP state organization, Thomas C. Platt. Platt was himself a practitioner of conventional nineteenth-century politics, and his machine was well financed by railroads, insurance companies, banks, and private utilities. Moreover, Platt's underlings in the state legislature served as willing "brokers" for the interests. But for reasons of survival, perhaps for the purpose of expanding his coalition, the "easy boss," after 1897, made a series of concessions to the growing number of political independents in the state's cities who advanced the first serious criticisms of the new urban-industrial conditions. These Yankee reformers, usually hailing from businesses and the professions, founded such organizations as the Citizens Union in New York City or swelled the ranks of good government clubs and municipal leagues in Buffalo, Rochester, Syracuse, Albany, and other upstate urban centers. Their assaults on the excesses of machine rule, together with their demands for structural changes in government and, in some instances, for economic and social reform were appealing enough in the elections of 1897 to force Platt and his organization to an accommodation. One concession by the Republican regulars was the adoption in 1898 of a primary law easing the way for party members to join municipal improvement clubs. Another was Platt's sponsorship later that year of Theodore Roosevelt's nomination for the governorship, a move, explained a GOP partisan, that would attract "many Democrats and Mugwumps" to the Republican party.[22]

As governor, Roosevelt was adept at satisfying the independent reformers and yet keeping orthodox Republicanism afloat. But TR's stay in Albany was brief, and his successors were not so astute—or so fortunate. For the shocking insurance investigation of 1905 brought under full-scale attack the entire New York Republican system, first under Platt's tutelage, then under the leadership of Benjamin B. Odell, Jr. Disclosures of influence-peddling involving public officials and party managers generated a popular outcry against both the corrupt politico-business alliance and the once indomitable Republican high command that suddenly looked as rapacious to critics as Tammany misrule in New York City in the 1890s. With the major New York leaders thoroughly discredited, the responsibility for restoring public confidence in the Republicans this time rested squarely with Theodore Roosevelt. Now ensconced in the White House, Roosevelt quickly moved into action. Concluding that the issue in New York related "to the bedrock principle of popular government . . . financial honesty and decency in public men," the president launched a program for the reorganization of the state party.[23] It began with a change in the leadership of the New

York County Republican Committee, where reform sentiment remained strong, and culminated with the gubernatorial nomination, in 1906, of Charles Evans Hughes, the very person who as chief counsel for the Armstrong committee had unearthed the Republican misdeeds. The Hughes selection—made against the wishes of many of the GOP state and county leaders—brought to the New York scene the fresh, untarnished figure of independence and probity Roosevelt and other reformers deemed essential for the future welfare of the party in the Empire State. In a bitter and unusually close election fought out on issues of reformism, Hughes defeated "radical" William Randolph Hearst for the governorship. The Republicans had thus prolonged their supremacy in New York on the note of progressivism.[24]

For nearly four years Charles Evans Hughes pursued a moderate reform program that purported to address the host of problems that the critics had long harped on—political misrule and corruption, the ravenous and grasping corporation, and social and economic deprivation. In so doing he came to rely on a loose coalition of supporters, including large numbers of independents and Cleveland-type Democrats ranging from political progressives such as Thomas Mott Osborne to newspaper editors like Louis Antisdale of Rochester and Oswald Garrison Villard and Joseph Pulitzer in New York City. These newspapermen, disgusted with both "Tammanyism" and Republican bossism, gave Hughes the best statewide press of any governor in years. In addition, there were the many and varied social welfare groups—social workers in the settlements, consumers' leagues and child labor committees, and even representatives of organized labor—attracted to one or more reforms within the broad spectrum of social amelioration and ever prepared to seize the opportunity at hand for specific legislative ends. Finally, there were the Republican lawmakers in Albany, seldom more than a small minority, who carried the burden of the Hughes program through the legislature. Well over half of these progressives hailed from New York City or its immediate environs, and nearly half of the rest originated from the larger upstate urban centers. The majority of those from New York City had been identified with the various municipal reform clubs from the mid-1890s past the turn of the century, and at least two had been active in the Citizens Union.[25] On the whole, these Yankee reformers continued on the state level their city campaigns for good government, business regulation, and social progressivism. In this sense, the Hughes program was municipal reformism writ large.

In due course, however, Hughes's progressivism placed severe strains on the New York Republican party. The program itself went beyond the limits acceptable to the GOP state leaders, many of whom were carryovers from the Platt-Odell days and certainly represented a more traditional version of Republicanism. It was one thing for William Barnes of Albany, Francis Hendricks of Onondaga, George Aldridge of Monroe, and the other nineteenth-century upstate conservatives to accommodate local pressures for reform to preserve the integrity of their county organizations; it was quite another for them to relent in the larger arena where they had less chance to control events and where change might alter fundamentally economic and political relationships. Thus, the leaders often resisted the governor's measures only to yield under pressure from Roosevelt's White House or out of mere party loyalty. Perhaps even more important in turning these standpatters away from Hughes was Hughes's mugwumpian qualities—his independence and aloofness, his unorthodox methods, and his palpable disdain for politics and politicians. (Roosevelt himself once complained that the governor was "selfish . . . to all considerations excepting his own welfare."[26]) Because Hughes lacked the desire to master the details of party management, he left the state organization in the hands of his opponents. Their mounting opposition to him and his brand of politics crystallized in the battle over enactment of a direct nominations bill in 1909–1910. To the Republican hierarchy, indeed, the direct primary came to symbolize a full-scale assault on the political system they held dear. In 1910 this issue mixed with others, including new revelations of corruption in the legislature, to produce deep divisions in the New York Republican party.

III

If Governor Hughes's progressivism and independence created serious tensions among Republicans in the Empire State, presidential politics completed the party rupture. Like politicians elsewhere, New Yorkers became embroiled in the deepening controversy between Theodore

Roosevelt and William Howard Taft in the summer of 1910. The curious fact about this episode in New York, however, was that the two national leaders were essentially on the same side and yet were unsuccessful in unifying the state party for the critical fall elections. Undoubtedly, this failure stemmed from Roosevelt's and Taft's own mistakes and misconceptions as well as from the growing stubbornness of the state and county leaders in resisting reform, whether directed by Hughes or Roosevelt.

For some fourteen months after his presidential term had concluded, Theodore Roosevelt was out of the country, first on an African safari, then on a grand tour of Europe. Meanwhile, President Taft, his designated successor, had followed policies that worsened already existing tensions between progressives and conservatives in the national Republican party. But midwestern insurgency never commanded much support in New York. On the matter of the tariff, for example, the state had benefited greatly, and New Yorkers remained contented with Taftian Republicanism. In addition, most of the state's progressive leaders, including Hughes, enjoyed warm personal relations with the president. For his part, Taft lent sympathy to their struggle for the direct primary and general party reform. Thus, when Roosevelt returned from abroad in June 1910, he felt free to accept Governor Hughes's appeal for help in the struggle against the county and state leaders. Indeed, the Colonel concluded that New York was just the right place for him to make his political reappearance: here he could bring together most Republicans, isolating the few intransigent Hughes opponents, and with proper deference to the Taft administration spur his party to victory in November.[27] New York, then, might serve as a springboard for GOP reunification in other parts of the country, where admittedly the task was more difficult.

Roosevelt's first gesture in the Empire State—a strong campaign for a modified version of Hughes's direct nominations legislation—was an abject failure, however. The bill went down to defeat in the legislature, and the standpatters gloated. "Teddy's licked to a frazzle," crowed Albany Boss William Barnes, adding, "We no longer worship the gods, we laugh at them."[28] In acting as he did, Roosevelt had overlooked two points: first, the deep resentment New York Republicans harbored toward outside interference, especially by the man who had earlier brandished the "big stick" at them; and second, the accumulated grievances against Governor Hughes. They could now show open defiance for Hughes had already accepted a nomination by Taft for the Supreme Court and would soon be out of the picture. But the Colonel *was* in the picture, and he would remain in it. In July he held private conferences at Oyster Bay with representatives of the two factions of the New York party for the obvious purpose of working out an accommodation. Hughes's direct primary opponents, State Republican Chairman Timothy L. Woodruff and Assembly Speaker James W. Wadsworth, Jr., each had a cordial session with Roosevelt. Compromise was out of the question, however, when Roosevelt made clear that the GOP gubernatorial nominee that fall would have to stand firmly on the Hughes reform program. To the organization faithful the Colonel's posture hurled a direct challenge at the party leadership. With some trepidation Woodruff was already expressing consternation at the "destruction of the Organization."[29]

From the beginning the New York standpatters had thought the worst of Roosevelt's intervention. His adoption of the Hughes cause, they suspected, was the first step of a cleverly worked-out scheme to seize control of the state party and use New York as a political base for grabbing the 1912 Republican presidential nomination. Stopping the Colonel now, they reasoned, would block his return to national power two years hence. "It would mean more than temporary defeat if we do not stand up," declared Vice-President James S. Sherman to a fellow New Yorker in late July.[30] For these conservatives the moderate Taft was far safer than the unpredictable, impetuous Roosevelt. They thus planned a course of action that would lead to undisputed conservative control of the New York Republican organization by means of a victory at the fall state convention. While plotting to close out Roosevelt, they tried to draw Taft in. To the old guard the president's earlier support of Hughes's direct primary had been only halfhearted. If apprised of Roosevelt's true intentions, and if then convinced of their genuine concern for the president's renomination, Taft, they apparently thought, would surely go along with them.

President Taft's attitude toward the complex New York situation remained ambivalent during the summer of 1910. He, too, feared and suspected Roosevelt. Yet knowing of Hughes's troubles with the state leaders, he could not trust them either. Perhaps aware of the need to find a back door to the president, Barnes, Woodruff, and the others persuaded Sherman, himself an upstate conservative and yet a member of the Taft team, to become a candidate for temporary chairman of the Republican state convention in Saratoga. Meanwhile, Roosevelt had acceded to the progressives' importunities to accept the position if offered to him—and he appeared to have Taft's support. Officially the president took no stance on the impending struggle. However, a careful evaluation of the evidence shows not only that he knew what the old guard was up to and could have stopped them but also that he deliberately chose not to do so. And on the day that the Republican state committee awarded Sherman the temporary chairmanship after a tough fight with the Roosevelt forces, both Taft and his private secretary, Archie Butt has recorded, laughed about the "defeated Theodore."[31]

Still, saner counsels prevailed on the two national leaders. Taft continued to resist pressures from Woodruff and Sherman to throw his support outright to the standpatters in New York. The president, reported Sherman in mid-August, "in his anxiety to avoid any break with Roosevelt . . . minimizes favorable considerations."[32] For his part, Roosevelt, though angry and disgusted with the administration, nonetheless kept quiet about Taft's "duplicity" in the state committee fiasco, then drew fram Taft a public confession of his innocence. Thereafter, the Colonel announced his determination to attend the Republican state convention and wage a floor fight for the progressive cause—not as a factional leader, of course, but as a spokesman for the vast majority of the party.[33]

Roosevelt's decision to wage the battle in his home state left him free in late August to make a much-heralded tour of the West, where he faced even more serious divisions within the GOP. Here he sought to heal the wounds between insurgents and conservatives by moving considerably left of center on the issues and yet mollifying the Taft wing in other ways. In Denver he attacked the nation's courts for declaring unconstitutional laws designed to regulate business and labor. Then in Osawatomie, Kansas, he delivered his now famous address advocating the community's right to regulate private property for the benefit of the general welfare. He went on to champion a program of reform that embraced the graduated income tax and the inheritance tax, a national workmen's compensation law, legislation tightening controls on woman and child labor, and a thorough revision of the tariff. Amid plaudits from the progressives and condemnation from the conservatives, Roosevelt proceeded during the same tour to pay homage to the Taft administration and carefully spread his endorsements of candidates for offices that fall. His total effort in the West, he believed all too optimistically, had the effect of reuniting the warring elements of the party. He hoped to do likewise back in the East.[34]

In New York State, however, Roosevelt's New Nationalism, the name given to his widely publicized program, had won little praise. Both conservative and progressive newspapers sorely condemned it more for its attack on the courts and its threatened concentration of federal power than its legislative proposals. The politicians reacted in like manner. For the recalcitrant state leaders the Colonel's "swing to the left" only confirmed their suspicions about him. Progressives were unhappy because the gap between Taft and Roosevelt now seemed wider than ever. (The president himself was deeply disturbed by the New Nationalism's "wild ideas.")[35] In the New York County Republican Committee, a nest of progressivism, a near showdown took place in mid-September between Taftites and Roosevelt supporters over the Colonel's program. So divided were the progressives here and elsewhere in the state that some proof of continued Taft-Roosevelt harmony became imperative. The "proof" came when New York County Republican Chairman Lloyd Griscom arranged a meeting between the two leaders at the home of a mutual friend in New Haven, Connecticut. Although the conference failed to improve their personal relations, Roosevelt and Taft agreed that the platform and the candidates at the Saratoga state convention should not be dictated by the conservatives. Unable to use the federal patronage to aid the progressive cause, the president nonetheless assured Roosevelt "the prestige of my support."[36]

"We're going to beat them to a frazzle," bellowed the expansive Roosevelt as he marshaled his forces for the state Republican convention.[37] He nearly did. After winning the hotly contested temporary chairmanship at Saratoga, Roosevelt drove through a progressive platform that heaped warm praise on the Hughes and Taft administrations. He also managed the gubernatorial nomination of Henry L. Stimson, successful U.S. Attorney for the Southern District of New York and a firm backer of the Colonel's principles. Friendly to Taft and Elihu Root (his law partner), close to Griscom and Herbert Parsons, and epitome of independent Republicanism to which Hughes had appealed, Stimson seemed the ideal man to head the state ticket. His own reluctance to run in what he judged to be a losing cause was overcome by a Roosevelt-inspired sense of duty.[38] So, as the Republicans entered the fall campaign, the Colonel appeared on the way to achieving his objectives of isolating the old guard, placing the New York party on a progressive footing, and yet shoring up the faltering Taft administration.

IV

Roosevelt's triumph at Saratoga proved to be a pyrrhic victory, however. In just a couple of months, the still badly divided GOP, already showing signs of weaknesses at the polls in recent elections, would suffer its first statewide defeat since the 1890s.[39] The Republican troubles of 1910 notwithstanding, the party had been a powerful and effective force over the past generation in the state's political life. The rich symbolism of its national program had captured the fancy of enterprising New Yorkers on the farm and in the city; and in response to new conditions and exigencies the GOP had brought to Albany the state's first major experiment in progressive government. But, of course, Governor Hughes's policies and outlook stretched Republicanism beyond its limits, given the conservative nature of the New York organization. Roosevelt's intervention in the summer of 1910 failed to smooth over existing differences; in fact, it worsened them. For the Colonel's vulnerabilities—his presumed presidential ambitions and his radical New Nationalism—made him an easy target for the resolute, frustrated county and state leaders who still controlled the party machinery and influenced Republican voters on Election Day.

2

Two Faces of a Party:
Charles F. Murphy,
Thomas Mott Osborne,
and the Politics of 1910

As elsewhere, the deep divisions in the Republican party in New York State, by 1910, gave the Democrats their greatest electoral opportunity in almost twenty years. But in New York the road to 1910 had been as hazardous for the Democrats as it was for the GOP. A minority party long out of power in state and nation, the Democracy had gained a reputation for negativism among the electorate. "There is no disguising the fact," lamented Thomas Mott Osborne in 1909, "that there is . . . a deepseated distrust of the Democratic party." This "distrust" extended not only to the party's leadership but also to its almost antiquated program and outlook. Moreover, defeat after defeat had left the Democratic state organization in a weakened condition; in some upstate communities it had no operational apparatus at all.[1] Where it did, petty rivalries among regulars or between regulars and independents often consumed much precious time and energy. Even in New York City, which traditionally supplied large Democratic majorities, the party was wracked by assaults from municipal reform clubs and fusion groups, by dissidence within the ranks, and by bitter crosstown rivalries. Keeping local organizations together at election time was a difficult job. Sustaining party unity statewide, often in the face of sure-fire defeat, was a mammoth task.

That the New York Democracy was a collection of dispirited, contentious factions there is no doubt. But the major division in the party was between Tammany and anti-Tammany elements. The anti-Tammanyites liked to reduce the struggle to that old Democratic conflict that pitted themselves as "reformers" against the "machines," linking the Hall with the regular organizations in Buffalo and other upstate cities. It was for them a rerun of Grover Cleveland's fight with the "bosses" one generation earlier for clean, honest, and efficient government. Certainly there was some truth in this view. Yet already by 1910 Tammany had begun what Robert Binkerd has called that "very subtle change"—a change toward respectability and reformism, or at least a willingness to accommodate persistent reform sentiment in this, the progressive era. The battle, then, can be more profitably seen in other terms. "It was," as Frances Perkins later commented, "an ancient conflict in American life between the old families, and the newcomers, really."² Such a "conflict," already outlined briefly in the broader context of the state's politics, was best represented by the leaders of the respective factions: Charles F. Murphy, boasting a Catholic, immigrant, big-city background and disciplined in the politics of regularity and the machine; and Thomas Mott Osborne, possessed of Yankee, Protestant, small-town (or city) origins and cherishing political independence. It was the struggle of these two men—and the organizations they led—that shaped the contours of Democratic politics in New York in 1910.

I

Since 1902 Charles F. Murphy had been the leader of Tammany Hall. In most ways his rise to power was little different from that of other successful machine men of his time. Born in 1858 on New York City's East Side of Irish-Catholic, immigrant parents, Murphy spent his youth on the streets of the Gas House District, so called because of the large storage tanks owned by the Consolidated Gas Company located at various places in the area. It was, indeed, a grim section of the city with its dingy tenements; dimly lighted saloons; and roaming gangs of unruly, mischievous boys. Most of the district's inhabitants in Murphy's early years were Irish and German newcomers who labored in the shipyards and the gasworks. Even for an ambitious youth like Murphy life was very hard. Ending his formal education at the age of fourteen in order to help support his family, he moved from odd job to odd job. Then, in 1875, he obtained a position as driver of a cross-town horse car, and within five years he had accumulated enough savings to open up a saloon at Avenue A and Nineteenth Street.[3]

Serving as a poor man's club, "Charlie's Place" promoted the kind of camaraderie and good fellowship from which a political following was organized in those days. Patiently and attentively the taciturn Murphy would listen to the problems and troubles of his clientele, which included mostly common laborers, a sprinkling of white-collar people, and even a few neighborhood politicians. An accomplished athlete in his own right, he also sponsored baseball and rowing teams of considerable achievement. Among Murphy's patrons was State Assemblyman Edward Hagan, Tammany leader of the Gas House District. Hagan encouraged Murphy's obvious interest in politics, and Murphy in turn did Hagan's bidding. So close did these two become and so fully identified was Murphy with Hagan's political supporters that, on the leader's death in 1892, Charlie could legitimately claim the vacant position. ("Boys, when I'm gone, see that nobody gets the leadership but Charlie," Hagan reputedly told his lieutenants.)[4] Already the owner of three other saloons, Murphy made one of them, better located and more spacious than his first establishment, the headquarters of the Anawanda Club, which was the name of his district organization.

By all counts Charles Murphy was a superb Tammany district leader. Standing each evening in front of the Anawanda Club, he met with constituents in search of jobs or other favors and directed them to equally accessible ward-heelers and precinct captains. He often drew money from his saloon profits to tide over needy families in times of unusual distress. His charity extended to the major religious groups of the area—the Lutherans, the Episcopalians, as well as the Catholics. Most important, Murphy ran a morally clean district as Tammany districts went. He later noted: "That part of the community which disobeys and flouts the laws always wants to maintain a friendly connection with the police, and for this connection its leaders are always willing to pay liberally."[5] Thus, he used his influence to end police protection of vice and thereby reduced the incidence of gambling and prostitution. These achievements, but especially his performance in rounding up votes on Election Day, won him the respect of Boss Richard Croker.

When, in 1897, Tammany Hall returned to power in New York City, Croker and Mayor Van Wyck rewarded Murphy with his first and only public office. The position was dock commissioner, one of the most lucrative jobs at the organization's disposal. During the next four years Murphy made the most of this opportunity. His aversion to vices of the flesh and blatant forms of corruption did not mean that he was opposed to making money, as his entrepreneurial success had already proved. Indeed, he used the commissionership to indulge widely in what George Washington Plunkitt has called "honest graft." Charlie and his brother John helped to organize the New York Contracting and Trucking Company, which leased docks from the city, then sublet them, and earned profits estimated at 5,000 percent. The concern also received a number of rich contracts from various public service corporations—all of which purportedly made Murphy a millionaire. Nor was the commissioner apologetic about activities that were so much a part of the "system." Testifying before the state legislature's Mazet committee in 1899, he said frankly: "When I can do it without violating the law, it is perfectly right to give out contracts to organization men. . . . I do not excuse myself for anything I have done."[6] Some of this wealth Murphy used to purchase a country estate at Good Ground, Long Island, where later as Tammany boss he would hold many a public outing for his political disciples. And in the city he changed his headquarters to "The Scarlet Room of Mystery" on the second floor of the fashionable Delmonico's Restaurant.

The big chance for Charlie Murphy came in 1902. Seth Low's fusion victory in the city the previous fall had retired Boss Croker to his Ireland hermitage (though at the time Croker did not view his "retirement" as permanent). Tammany Hall was ruled briefly by Lewis Nixon, then for six months by a triumverate of Daniel McMahon, Louis Haffen, and Murphy. One Tammanyite aptly described the trio: "McMahon is a two-spot, Haffen is a joke, but Murphy is a sport." In a brief power struggle that followed, the "sport" won out, and in September 1902 the Hall's executive committee made the appointment official with the following: "Resolved that the powers and duties heretofore exercised and performed by the Committee of Three be hereafter exercised and performed by Charles Francis Murphy."[7]

Much has been written about the character and political tactics of the man who would rule Tammany Hall for over two decades. The image of Murphy projected by his enemies among press and politicians was that of a crude and cunning Irish opportunist careless about the means by which he gained and wielded power, even a ruthless, double-dealing hack. Those people who knew him best, however, have given a very different view of the "boss." To the patrician James W. Gerard, one of the Hall's "high-brow" confidants, Murphy was a "real states-man" who "always kept his word" and who "with the hard-boiled eggs in Tammany . . . just knocked their heads together as leader." Jeremiah Mahoney, law partner of Robert F. Wagner, thought of him as "one of the most forward-looking leaders in the whole country." Ed Flynn, later to be boss of the Bronx, agreed thoroughly with this as-sessment. Speaking further about Murphy's best qualities, Mahoney added: "He was picking young men always, two or three years in advance, so that when the proper time came he slipped them in. These young men that he picked like Smith, Wagner and myself—we all re-ceived the endorsements of the most rabid reform organizations." Even the *New York World,* one of Tammany's harshest critics during the progressive era, conceded as much at the time of Murphy's death in 1924. Editorially the *World* eulogized the fallen leader as a man who could "grow from unpromising beginnings, as a typical boss over men strangely varied from the corrupt to the fanatically partisan, into a better sense of public responsibility."[8]

In truth Murphy presented a many-faceted, complex personality and character. A product of the brawling Gas House District, he often did exhibit in his actions and behavior the toughness and ruthlessness of the old Irish ward-heeler. He could exercise raw power with a vengeance as the Sulzer episode would show.[9] Doubtless, too, he was instinctively conservative; as a successful businessman himself he epitomized the second-generation American made good. But this very success mixed with a strain of puritan morality to impel Murphy to search for social and political respectability. Furthermore, he did embrace, as Lawson Purdy has argued, a far broader vision than his predecessor, Richard

Croker. That vision included some sense of civic responsibility rooted in the belief that the Democratic party was the best vehicle for change in city and state. And Murphy would play a key role in expanding Tammany's interests from the personal and parochial politics of the old system to the issue-oriented politics of the early twentieth century. Above all, the boss balanced ambition, ability, and perspicacity with a pragmatic turn of mind that permitted him at once to withdraw from a position, at another to move forward, and yet usually succeed in keeping his rivals off guard. A total politician ("Murphy thinks of . . . [no]thing but politics from one end of the year to another," observed a contemporary[10]), he was a ready and willing compromiser: in his quest for winning combinations, he sometimes moved to the left and other times to the right of the political spectrum. He was no ideologue, and his brand of leadership was that of a technician, one who specialized in conciliating differences among men, forging acceptable combinations, then delivering the vote on Election Day. These qualities, in particular his breadth and flexibility, made Charlie Murphy the most accomplished political boss of his time.

With greetings such as "Tammany remains as rotten as ever," Murphy faced tough sledding in his early years as leader of the Hall. The organization that he inherited in 1902 was far less secure and powerful than the anti-Tammany press made it out to be. Across the state it had little real clout—and, indeed, had wielded minimal influence since David B. Hill's fragile alliance of upstate-downstate interests fell apart in the wake of the party disaster of 1896. In New York City itself Tammany was in some trouble despite its large constituency in Manhattan. Almost a decade of continuous assaults by good government clubs, crusading independents, and the muckraking press had exposed the machine's weaknesses, ranging from police protection of vice and gambling in the mid-1890s to political corruption affecting high-ranking city officials at the turn of the century. It was this latter revelation that brought Low's fusion victory in 1901 and retired Croker to Ireland. Nor could the Hall easily dominate other political forces in the city, especially the unruly Kings organization under Hugh McLaughlin and his successor, Patrick McCarren. "I would rather be a serf in Russia than a satrap of Tammany," McCarren stated frankly when he became Brooklyn boss, then spent the next half-dozen years, until his death in 1909, resisting Murphy.[11] Even in his own bailiwick, New York County, Murphy faced serious challenges. These emanated from Republicans who usually spearheaded fusion and from Socialists and the forces of William Randolph Hearst, which threatened Tammany Hall in Manhattan districts of traditional Democratic supremacy.

Aware that there was "plenty of work to be done," Murphy began immediately after he was named boss to set his own house in order. Such symbols of the Hall's alliance with vice and gambling as "Big Bill" Devery he repudiated. He quickly reduced to a minimum the vicious infighting among district leaders and appointed solid, respectable officers and advisors. He chose as treasurer Frank O'Donnell, a City College graduate whom the *Tammany Times* labeled "an expert accountant," and James Gerard became chairman of the campaign committee. Murphy's closest confidant continued to be J. Sergeant Cram, a Harvard-educated member of the Social Register who, it is claimed, taught him how "to eat peas with a fork."[12] Though most of the Tammany board in these early days remained politically conservative, Murphy did begin to encourage younger men of talent in the organization. (By 1911 some of these—notably Alfred E. Smith and Robert F. Wagner—had cracked the inner circle of advisors.) Murphy's search for respectability extended to the first citywide election held during his regime. In 1903 he stole the reformers' thunder by nominating the Princeton "gentleman" George B. McClellan, Jr., for mayor and two members of Low's fusion administration for his running mates. "When reform came into power," remarked one cynic some years later, "Charlie Murphy tried to brush the dust off his wings."[13] McClellan went on to victory, and Tammany's stock rose considerably.

Then, in 1905, came the Hearst challenge, the first of many that the erratic publisher would hurl at Murphy and Tammany Hall over the years. By the politics of that day William Randolph Hearst and his newspapers—the *New York Journal* and the *New York American*—were radical, though Hearst always thought of himself as an "urban Jeffersonian." In blazing headlines he lambasted the machine and espoused good government; he blistered the trusts and private utility interests, calling for municipal ownership and operation of gas and electric companies; and he championed social and labor reforms that went beyond the limited program of the more respectable city reform-

27

ers. Hearst was, conceded the *Tammany Times,* "the only man of prominence who to-day has the courage to stand between the organized forces of plutocracy and the common people." Generally the publisher became the "knight-errant of the tenements" and the self-appointed protector of the working class and the immigrants. He even made special appeals to Catholics by widely publicizing the pope's gratitude for his relief work and to the Jews by angrily condemning Russian persecutions.[14]

Translating his "ideals" into action proved to be easy for the politically ambitious Hearst. In 1902 he struck a bargain with Murphy by which he was given Tammany's backing for a New York City congressional seat in return for newspaper support for the newly chosen boss. Midway through his second term in Congress, Hearst, dismayed by the slowness and drudgery of Washington, looked elsewhere for political gratification and found it in the Municipal Ownership League. This organization, established in 1904, was close to the publisher's heart. Its program assumed special relevance the next year when the state legislature's special investigating committee blamed New York's skyrocketing gas and electric rates on corporate mismanagement and politico-business shenanigans. By then Hearst had become its chairman and quickly steered the MOL into city politics. Repudiating Murphy (for Tammany, after all, was entangled in the utility scandal), he himself accepted the league's mayoralty nomination. He ran a spirited campaign on the third-party ticket with broad appeals to reformers of all stripes. In one of the closest elections in New York history, Hearst lost out to Tammany's Mayor McClellan.[15] The results, indeed, stunned Murphy and his lieutenants. Not only did Hearst win Brooklyn and Queens largely on the strength of his vote in working-class districts, but he also carried eleven of thirty-five assembly districts in Manhattan. Four of these were heavily Jewish areas on the Lower East Side that had already shown some vulnerability to Republican and Socialist penetration. Even more devastating—and foreboding—was the fact that in New York County Republican-Municipal Ownership League candidates or candidates running alone on the league label won seventeen assembly races and finished a close second to Democrats in three others. In the thirtieth district Robert Wagner lost his assembly seat to his MOL opponent. Thus, Hearst's "organized army of protest," if left unchecked, posed a real threat to Tammany Hall in a substantial number of Manhattan's working-class, heavily ethnic areas.[16]

Hearst's "army of protest" did march on. In the year following his mayoralty defeat, the Municipal Ownership League, now called the Independence League, advanced Hearst for the governorship on an expanded reformist platform. If ever in recent times the Democrats had a fighting chance for a statewide victory, it was in 1906, for the sensational insurance investigations had severely crippled the Republican party. But a third-party challenge in light of powerful support for Hearst in New York City and in the upstate cities of Buffalo and Rochester would spell Democratic defeat. Therefore, Murphy, bowing to political exigency, struck another deal with Hearst, this time through Buffalo's "redhot Hearst man," William J. ("Fingy") Conners, who subsequently became Democratic state chairman. Though he sustained unmerciful abuse from the antimachine press and from unhappy independent Democrats for this alliance of "bosses" and "radicals," Murphy had made a brilliant move. Hearst went on to lose the election to Hughes (because of Tammany knifing in New York City, it was widely believed), but the rest of the Democratic state ticket, consisting mainly of regulars friendly to the Hall, was elected. Not only would Tammany at long last receive some state patronage; its strength in Manhattan assembly districts was restored, since organization leaders had chosen most of the Democratic–Independence League fusion candidates who easily defeated their Republican opponents.[17]

Hearst's second electoral defeat in two years truly discouraged the publisher in his quest for public office. "I shall never again be a candidate," he announced dramatically after the 1906 elections. But Hearst would remain a menace to Murphy and Tammany down to 1910 (and long afterward). He continued to use his newspapers in New York City to heap abuse on his opponents and "advocate and support . . . principles of reform." The year 1909 brought another municipal election, and again Murphy was under pressure from the Hearst crowd, other reformers, and Republicans determined to run an anti-Tammany ticket on the fusion line. Murphy had already dumped McClellan, with whom he had fought over patronage, and searched for a viable candidate in what promised to be a tough race. He settled on an even less likely Tammany nominee than McClellan, Brooklyn Supreme Court

Judge William Jay Gaynor, an independent with views on the major issues not unlike Hearst's. In fact, the publisher had been an early Gaynor supporter (for Gaynor was one of his key backers in 1905 and 1906) and, along with the Committee of One Hundred, looked to the judge as the man to "tame the tiger." But Gaynor's desire for a major party nomination—and "Murphy's boys could deliver the goods"—settled the matter. Gaynor accepted Tammany's bid; Hearst fumed at both, then in desperation ran on his own ticket; and the fusionists were left with Republican Otto Bannard for their standard-bearer. In the three-cornered race Gaynor was elected in November with over 40 percent of the vote; the other two divided about equally the remaining ballots. While Charlie Murphy thus had outmaneuvered his foes once more, the 1909 election was at best a mixed blessing for the regular Democratic organization: the fusion forces, which included Hearst's Independence League, captured the rest of the major offices in New York City—four of five borough presidencies, the board of estimate and apportionment, and the board of aldermen.[18] And once in office Gaynor himself offered little to Tammany—except economy, good government, and reform.[19]

Still, as the year 1910 loomed, Murphy could look back with some satisfaction on his first half-dozen years as Tammany boss. His organization had been instrumental in winning three mayoralty elections for the Democratic party—in 1903, 1905, and 1909. In so doing he withstood serious political threats in the city. By now the Hall even commanded the grudging respect of some of its most vocal critics. "Tammany had been moved by public opinion," conceded the progressive *New York World* in 1909.[20] It was true. As a pragmatic opportunist, Murphy had successfully accommodated the myriad groups and forces that agitated for change in the city. In 1910 he would be faced with a similar challenge statewide, and his response to it would bespeak the astuteness of his leadership in the larger political arena.

II

Unlike many of his predecessors in Tammany Hall, Charlie Murphy was not content to limit his political activities to the capture of city hall and the spoils of municipal office. He was "the first Tammany chief who dared aspire above the Bronx," asserts one writer with only slight exaggeration.[21] Early in his tenure the boss ventured into the state and national affairs of his party. In 1906 and 1908 he played a leading role in the Democratic state conventions. In 1904 and 1908 he used his influence in the selection of delegates from New York to the national party conventions. But before Murphy could exercise a controlling interest in the state organization, he had to consolidate his authority in the city and forge alliances upstate. By 1910 he had achieved the first objective, and he was well on his way to attaining the second.

 While Murphy was busily engaged in outmaneuvering his New York City opponents in electoral politics from 1903 to 1909, he also labored quietly behind the scenes to bring under his wing the Bronx, Queens, and Richmond organizations. Brooklyn, of course, proved to be a more serious problem. However, Pat McCarren's death in 1909 and Murphy's long-standing cultivation of dissident elements within the Kings County Democratic Committee quickly drew the new leader, John McCooey, into the Tammany orbit. Indeed, the election of William Jay Gaynor as mayor that fall attested to the boss' "expanded forces" in Greater New York. Upstate the situation was somewhat more complex. But, generally, Democratic county leaders in the interior population centers, who, in any case, were ethnically and culturally compatible with the downstate machine, acted out of self-interest in developing ties with the strengthened Tammany Hall. As Buffalo's Norman Mack later explained the reason for his organization's drift to Murphy through Conners in 1906: "New York City is a State in itself, and just as long as Erie County wants a place on the State ticket, or consideration in State affairs . . . it will have to co-operate with New York to get it." Thus, Patrick ("Packy") McCabe of Albany also came to terms with Tammany in the days when Hearst first broke into state politics, and in 1911 William ("Will") Kelley steered the Onondaga Democratic party into the fold. It was this system of alliances—and particularly the accord with Buffalo's Irish-German machine—that would win for Murphy the dubious title of "Czar of the State Democracy" and, at the same time, generate the determined opposition of that group of independents, mainly from the upstate, who fancied themselves the saviors of New York's beleaguered Democracy.[22] These self-styled reformers or progressives, closely resembling the "mugwumps" of the previous century, would mount a sustained offensive against the "alliance of bosses" that tailed off only in 1910, when Republican misfortunes offered the Democrats a marvelous opportunity for statewide electoral success.

Chief among these reformers was Thomas Mott Osborne, whose aristocratic background and training formed a marked contrast to that of Tammany's Charlie Murphy. Osborne hailed from the small but picturesque city of Auburn in central New York, home of Abraham Lincoln's secretary of state, William H. Seward. His father, a manufacturer of farm machinery, traced his ancestry back to the early settlers of Massachusetts Bay. Young Osborne attended the best schools (Adams Academy and Harvard College), traveled widely, and prepared himself for a career in the family business. Dutifully, he settled down as president of the D. M. Osborne and Company on his father's death in 1885. Osborne was then only twenty-six years of age and could look forward to a quiet life as a businessman and a highly respected member of Auburn's "South Street Aristocracy."[23]

But Osborne was not only a practical man. He was also restless, sensitive, and romantic—qualities that he had inherited from his mother and his mother's family, which boasted a long line of visionaries and reformers. (His great-aunt was the feminist Lucretia Mott.) This side of his nature often impelled Osborne to find ways to escape the humdrum existence of the businessman. These ranged from organizing theatrical productions for the Auburn Amateur Dramatic Club to masquerading in town as a worker in his own factory, a derelict in local saloons, or a peddler in the streets. Such "fantasizing," in which he engaged more frequently after the death of his wife in 1896, may have proved embarrassing to Osborne and his family, but it also provided him with valuable firsthand information about the lives of the underprivileged. Far more important among Osborne's "romantic" indulgences were his activities in various philanthropic and humanitarian endeavors and his pursuit of a public career. In politics he would be guided most powerfully by the idealism of his mother's family. "He viewed life as a morality play with virtue and vice struggling for the soul of mankind," writes one historian.[24] To Osborne, the political boss personified evil, the corrupter of democracy, and the disinterested public servant the force of good that would liberate men from the tyranny of the machine. Eagerly accepting this latter "obligation," he went about the business of reform almost with a vengeance. Worthy as it was, Osborne's dedication also had its drawbacks. His self-confidence bordered on the self-righteous, and he often made enemies of friends and bitter antagonists of those only mildly opposed to him. Nor did it make compromise easy, for how could one cavort with the devil?

As a young man Osborne chose the Democratic party as the vehicle for his reformism. There may have been a tinge of rebelliousness in this decision, for his family and community were rock-ribbed Republican. More important, however, was his genuine attraction to the politics of Grover Cleveland, who in the mid- and late-1880s afforded youthful idealists an alternative to the party machines in New York State—the Democracy's Tammany Hall and the Republican organization only recently abandoned by Roscoe Conkling and now under the growing influence of Thomas Platt. Cleveland's stance on civil service reform and tariff moderation, whose virtues Osborne had learned at Harvard, impelled him to plunge headlong into the 1888 presidential campaign. Thereafter he remained a loyal supporter of the Cleveland cause in New York. In Auburn he declared war on the local Democratic leadership, partly because it owed less to Cleveland than to Hill, and partly because of his own deep-seated aversion to entrenched interests. "I am going to make an endeavor to start a new Democratic organization in this place, which I hope may lead to some good," he announced to a friend.[25] His rebuilding effort, however, had to await Grover Cleveland's return to the White House in 1893. Then Osborne used his contacts in Washington and New York to influence the patronage in Auburn. He seemed on the verge of obtaining the recognition he needed to "take over" the local party when, in 1896, the props were pulled out from under him by Bryan's capture of the national Democratic party. The subsequent free-silver campaign cut Osborne adrift from whatever regularity his devotion to Cleveland had given him.

Osborne's independence burned intensely during the next decade or so. In 1898 he led a group of upstaters that sought an alliance with the Citizens Union in New York City to nominate and elect an anti-machine candidate for governor. They approached Theodore Roosevelt before Platt got hold of him, felt betrayed when the Colonel accepted the Republican nod, and ran a ticket of their own. Soundly trounced in his own bid for the lieutenant governorship, Osborne settled down once again to local politics. Shortly after the turn of the century he served two terms as Auburn's mayor, during which he carried his independence to such extremes as to alienate totally the local Democratic leadership. Even his sympathetic biographer has judged Osborne "too disputatious," "too denunciatory," and consumed with a fervor that occasionally "led him to extremes and . . . to unfairness."[26] The height of Osborne's apostasy came in 1906 with Murphy's accord with Conners, giving Conners the party's state chairmanship and Hearst the gubernatorial nomination. Repulsed by Hearst's "ambitious effort to be President" as well as by his "rabble-rousing" qualities, disturbed by this "unholy and un-Democratic alliance," and worried lest his own ambitions be thwarted (he had hoped early in the year to win the state chairmanship himself), Osborne spearheaded a movement among independent Democrats against the publisher's election. For his role in Hughes's victory that fall, the Auburn insurgent, in 1907, received a post on the newly established public service commission for upstate New York. To "Hughes Democrats" Osborne may have been a hero. To party regulars he was at best a rebel, at worst a traitor.[27]

During the next few years, Osborne never forgot his major objective—to reconstruct the state Democratic party using as a nucleus old Cleveland supporters and independents from both New York City and the upstate. Convinced, however, that Governor Hughes represented "the fight against *boss-rule* better than anyone . . . in our time," and that such a fight would enhance "liberal Democracy" as well as "progressive Republicanism," he remained content until 1909 to keep up a lively correspondence with independent newspaper editors Louis Antisdale in Rochester and Oswald Garrison Villard in New York.[28] Occasionally he and his private secretary, Louis M. Howe, attempted little schemes to advance the reform cause, but these bore no fruit. Osborne's main thrust came after the Democratic defeat at the hands of William Howard Taft and Charles Evans Hughes in 1908. The next year, and again in 1910, he sponsored statewide conferences designed to mobilize the antimachine forces and create a formal structure that would challenge the Murphy-Conners alliance. The first conference was held in Saratoga in September 1909 and attracted representation from

all the counties in the state, though it was weighted heavily in favor of
the upstate. Here lively discussions were conducted, a "Democratic
Creed" was hammered out, and a permanent organization, the Democratic League of New York State, was formally established. The creed,
relating to both national and state issues, formed a curious mixture of
old Bourbon Democratic formulas like taxation for revenue only; economy in expenditures; and limited government with a mild progressive
program advocating a federal income tax, the direct election of U.S.
senators, and home rule for cities.[29] The second conference was held
in Albany in January 1910 and had for its main purpose the organization of a general committee with Osborne himself to serve as chairman and the forging of a program exclusively for New York State. The
program embraced the Massachusetts ballot and the direct primary—
two major issues on which Governor Hughes was then doing battle
with the recalcitrant state legislature. To devote full time to his duties
with the league, Osborne resigned his position on the public service
commission.[30] He was now ready for the elections of 1910.

The Democratic League would have amounted to little if it existed
solely to advance the ambitions of Thomas Mott Osborne. It was ob-
viously far more than that. In the 1909 elections the movement had
already yielded results, as the Democrats captured assembly seats in
the heavily Republican counties of Clinton, Warren, Genesee, Steuben,
Onondaga, and Sullivan. These victories, observers noted, were won
mostly at the expense of GOP opponents of Hughes's direct primary
reform—men who failed to receive the backing of the governor's bi-
partisan Direct Primary Association. "The league has already come to
be a power in the State and is making its influence felt in every section,"
conceded the *Tammany Times* in early 1910 with regard to Osborne's
group.[31] By then, it had attracted the support of a host of prominent
party figures—not mere dissidents or insurgents—but politicians who
had distinguished themselves on the local and national levels. There
were New York City men like Judge Alton B. Parker, Edward M. Shepard, Morgan J. O'Brien, and William Travers Jerome. The more dominant upstate contingent, in addition to Osborne, included John N.
Carlisle of Watertown, Louis Antisdale of Rochester, John Sague and
John Mack of Poughkeepsie, and John A. Dix of Washington County.
Most of these men shared with the Auburn independent the determi-

nation to reconstruct the state Democratic party by "cleansing" it of bossism and returning it to tried-and-true Democratic principles.

III

The deep party divisions notwithstanding, there was ample reason for the Democratic League to bury the hatchet with its machine opponents in 1910. To be sure, Osborne and his "silk-stocking" element, as they were sometimes called, would remain alien from the Tammany system—its "unprincipled politics"; its lower-class, ethnic constituencies; and its New York City base. But only through reasonable party harmony, they must have concluded, could the Democracy fully exploit Republican disarray in the fall elections. Under such circumstances, Osborne pushed for the minimum concession—that is, the removal of Conners as state chairman and the effacement of "bossism" from the upstate party. "The business of the Democratic League," he wrote, "is not with Murphy but with Conners." Thus, the league would be assured of a large piece of the political action—to be consulted, to be conciliated, and to be represented with a top spot on the state ticket in the fall. (All year long Osborne himself angled for the gubernatorial nomination.) Nor was the league's program really meant to ruffle the feathers of regular Democrats. The creed was cast in generally acceptable party doctrine, at least among New Yorkers, of the latter nineteenth century. It implicitly rejected Bryanism and lauded Cleveland's limited government and Bourbon formulas. Even the progressive program for the state upset few of the party faithful. The key item, the direct primary, was itself a moderate version of direct nominations and deliberately exempted New York City from its provisions—a gesture that Osborne felt constrained to make to Murphy and Tammany Hall.[32]

If Thomas Mott Osborne and his followers seemed amenable to accommodation, the essential work in striking party unity fell to the most powerful Democrat in the state—the pragmatic Charlie Murphy. It was Murphy who gave the league what it wanted in 1910. The first move came in early June when in a widely publicized meeting of the state committee William Conners stepped down as Democratic state chairman, thus removing for Osborne the last ugly remembrance of the Hearst aberration of 1906. Conners's successor was John A. Dix, charter member of the Democratic League and party harmonizer par excellence. "We have a chance now that we have not had for a generation," Osborne recorded exuberantly to a compatriot.[33] Dix soon launched a speaking tour of the state's senate districts to define the issues on which all segments of the Democratic party could agree— the high tariff policy of the Taft administration that was allegedly instrumental in the increased cost of living; the higher cost of government, both federal and state, under Republican rule; and an array of misdeeds perpetrated by the GOP in New York State. Using these issues as a common denominator, Dix capped his efforts with a harmony conference held in Albany in early August to which were invited representatives of the Democratic League, the Progressive Democrats (a second splinter group), and the state committee. This "love feast" adopted the Dix program with special emphasis on the tariff, "the pet solely of the predatory rich," as one friendly newspaper put it.[34]

The Democratic harmony movement reached its zenith in late September at the party's state convention in Rochester. Here again the major responsibility rested with Murphy, whose alliance with the upstate regulars, now principally William Fitzpatrick and Norman Mack of Buffalo, gave him a firm hold on at least half of the delegates. The boss remained conciliatory toward Osborne and his followers and exercised his vast power gently and judiciously. "If the up-State delegates unite on any one man, Mr. Murphy will support him," declared Tammany spokesman Daniel Cohalan in an obvious gesture to the minority. For two days and two nights delegation after delegation descended on Murphy and bombarded him with fourteen names for the gubernatorial nomination. "They put up one man and then the next one comes along and puts him down," Cohalan complained in bewilderment. But Murphy heard them all out. He then met with the other leaders and checked carefully each of the contenders, a task that proved so onerous as to prompt one observer to suggest that the convention was sinking into chaos and disorder. By the "process of elimination," the leaders finally settled on State Chairman John A. Dix, who at first resisted, then at the eleventh hour answered the call. Dix seemed the logical candidate at the time. He was an upstater and a member of the league, and he had done yeoman work for the party. A prominent businessman and banker, he represented for many the "successful citizenship of the Empire State," making him the perfect antidote for Roosevelt's New Nationalism.[35] Even Thomas Mott Osborne seemed content with the Dix nomination, though later he would bitterly assail the work of the convention. The activities in Rochester terminated with the selection of Dix's running mates, who were mainly regulars, and the adoption of a platform that reiterated the principles and issues on which the harmony campaign had been grounded.[36]

IV

The campaign of 1910 in New York State was a curious spectacle as Democrat John A. Dix waged an ambitious canvass against Theodore Roosevelt and the New Nationalism, even though Henry L. Stimson was his opponent. Stimson, for his part, stiffly lectured voters on his philosophy of government, labored to convince them that he was his own man, and ably defended the Hughes record. Try as he might, however, he could not extricate himself from the "ambitions" of the Colonel. "A vote for Stimson will be a vote for Roosevelt and his future possibilities as a national dictator," argued the *Springfield Republican* in a typical attack. Even a tour of the upstate, guided by party stalwarts Job Hedges and James W. Wadsworth, Jr., did Stimson little good in his effort to stir up the traditional Republican vote. Nor did President Taft's assurance that he and Roosevelt battled as one convince conservative GOP skeptics who would take no chances with the unorthodox former president. And while the Republicans tottered, the Democrats rolled right along. Grumblings from Osborne's league and William Lustgarten's Progressive Democrats over the lackluster party ticket from lieutenant governor down failed to disturb the harmony achieved in Rochester.[37] Reports that men of property were endorsing Dix and that Republican farmers threatened to stay home on Election Day further encouraged the Democracy. The result seemed to be a foregone conclusion.

In November the Empire State joined the rest of the Northeast in a Democratic party sweep. The Democrats not only won the governorship and elected their entire state ticket but also captured the two houses of the legislature and a large majority of the state's congressional delegation. Dix's plurality over Stimson was 67,401. He did precisely what Democrats had to do in order to achieve victory in New York: he came out of New York City with a plurality in excess of 100,000 votes, having reduced the Republican vote there to under 40 percent for the first time in the new century, and cut the GOP margin upstate, losing in traditional Republican territory by only 37,800 votes. (In both 1908 and 1906 the Democrats had been beaten by nearly four times that number.) Dix won seventeen upstate counties, eleven of which were Republican bastions. One source estimated that in rural and small-town precincts Stimson defeated Dix by less than 34,000 votes, whereas Hughes's plurality in these same areas in 1908 had been 108,000. In addition, practically all the upstate cities witnessed some Democratic gains. Among the larger ones Buffalo and Utica went for Dix. Albany, Syracuse, and Rochester remained Republican but by lower margins than two years earlier.[38]

For most observers the election results were more a repudiation of Roosevelt and the New Nationalism than an affirmation of the bland Democratic program. "Seized by the heels in its very cradle, the 'new Nationalism' has been pitched into its grave," declared the *New York Times*.[39] Others added, some ruefully many gleefully, that the Colonel's ambitions for 1912 were dashed on the rocks of the party defeat. There was, in fact, much substance to the negative evaluations of this election, especially in light of the overall GOP decline. The low voter turnout in 1910 (as compared with 1908 and even 1906), greater proportionately in the upstate than in New York City, meant that hosts of Republicans simply stayed home. Undoubtedly, some were discouraged from going to the polls because of the rain, snow, and sleet that fell across the state on Election Day. Some bridled at the intraparty squabbling and the scandals in Albany. Nor did the upstate Republican managers make much of an effort to "get out the vote." William Barnes, it was widely rumored, cut Stimson in Albany County in order to get back at Roosevelt. Men of property who had long been Republicans, so the reports went, left the party for fear of the adverse effect that the New Nationalism would have on business prosperity. The banner GOP ward in Rochester, for example, cast an unprecedented number of Democratic votes, and three "silk-stocking" districts in Manhattan went for Dix. (The latter was especially devastating since these areas represented the heart of Republican progressivism.) Nor was Republican money in plentiful supply in 1910. Some of it evidently found its way into Democratic coffers. "I was the only man in Wall Street who was openly supporting Stimson," confessed George W. Perkins over one year later, adding that "most of my partners and associates . . . [were] very much opposed to his candidacy."[40]

Whether any of the specific issues that the Democrats raised actually influenced voters is difficult to ascertain. Some commentators have argued that the "ordinary voter" was moved by the repeated charge against the Republicans for the rising cost of living. There may have been some truth in this proposition, but the issue apparently had greater effect on "middle-income" groups than on "low-income" groups.[41] A glance at a number of working-class, heavily ethnic districts in cities across the state suggests two facts. First, in practically all these areas, in New York as well as in the larger interior cities, there was a decline in voter turnout roughly comparable to the general decrease. Second, the preponderance of these districts showed no higher percentage of Democratic votes than in 1908 and, in most cases, a smaller one than Hearst garnered in 1906. Overall the voting habits of these people appeared to change little from the pattern of two or four years earlier. Irish wards in cities investigated went uniformly for Dix, whereas Germans tended to divide themselves between the two parties. In New York City, Utica, and Buffalo, Italian areas fell to the Democrats. Buffalo's growing Polish vote seemed to add greatly to Dix's plurality in the Queen City. Elsewhere—in Albany, Rochester, and Syracuse particularly—new-stock wards were usually Republican.[42]

Some New Yorkers—in larger numbers in 1910 than in many years—registered their dissatisfaction with both major parties by voting for neither. The major beneficiary of the "protest" vote was the Socialist party that, as left-wing organizations go, struck a truly moderate posture that year (as it would in New York throughout the progressive era). The party platform purposely deemphasized the socialist state and called on those who might hold public office to "support and work for every measure which will tend to better the material condition of the workers . . . as well as measures tending to secure to the people a fuller measure of true democracy in government and justice in social relations." In actuality the program was not much different from Hearst's four years earlier or the Progressives' two years hence. The Socialists in 1910 chose for their gubernatorial nominee the muckraker Charles E. Russell, who labeled himself a "side-line reformer."[43] Russell and his party waged a strong statewide campaign and on Election Day were greatly pleased by the result. The Socialists raised their vote approximately one quarter over that in 1908, and as the *Call* noted, the percentage increase in New York was exceeded in only two other states, California and Connecticut.[44] These gains permitted the Socialists to overtake Hearst's Independence League as the third party in the state. Most of the increase came in the cities of Buffalo, Rochester, Syracuse, and Schenectady. In New York City the vote for Russell reached nearly 40,000, or about 1,400 more than the 1908 ticket had polled in the entire state. And the biggest vote was cast in the same areas where Hearst had run strongly four years earlier—in German and eastern European Jewish districts. In the latter the combined Socialist and Independence League vote averaged almost 18 percent of the total, and in seven of thirteen principally Jewish districts Dix's margin fell below 50 percent.[45]

V

The major characteristics of the election of 1910 in New York State were negativism and indifference mixed with a dash of protest. The first was directed against Theodore Roosevelt, his ambitions and his New Nationalism. Some New Yorkers may have taken part in what *The Outlook* identified vaguely as "that wave of restless change which affected the whole country."[46] But for many Roosevelt himself offered too much of a change—one that threatened disruption of a system that had brought considerable prosperity to the state over the years. They had no choice but to turn to Dix and the Democrats, though they did so with little enthusiasm. Neither Dix nor his party, which in some quarters meant simply Tammany bossism, captured the imagination of the electorate in 1910. For the most part the Democrats fell back on the old Cleveland program of limited government updated with a mild version of political progressivism as an essential ingredient in unifying their badly divided party, and concentrated their attack on the Republican "system of centralization," as Buffalo's Norman Mack phrased it.[47] There was little or nothing on social and economic justice in the

Democracy's campaign that fall. To scores of disenchanted voters, therefore, the Democratic alternative could not have been a very promising one.

Overall, the party managers in New York State may well have cast an alarming glance at the 1910 election results. Surely the low voter turnout across the state combined with the rising protest vote pointed to a growing disenchantment among many citizens toward both major parties. For the Republicans a subpar performance in New York City and a disastrous showing upstate meant that party's first statewide defeat in the twentieth century. And while Democrats Murphy and Osborne could exult over their big victory, no one in the Democracy appeared sufficiently confident to view the "sweep" as a touchstone for a new permanent majority in the Empire State.

3

The Dix Years:
1911–1912

"The Democratic party is on trial," wrote Franklin D. Roosevelt on New Year's Day 1911. Roosevelt's remark, though prompted by a specific issue in his home state, could well have been directed at the general plight of the Democracy following the 1910 elections. For the Democrats had won control of the House of Representatives for the first time in nearly two decades. And in several states, usually considered Republican bastions, GOP schisms had resulted in Democratic victories. As press and politicians fastened their attention on such unfamiliar faces as Eugene Foss in Massachusetts and Woodrow Wilson in New Jersey, New Yorkers wondered about their new governor, John A. Dix. Indeed, speculation was rife about Democratic prospects in the Empire State. Republican standpatters dismissed the incoming administration as an "interregnum" that would pave the way for a quick GOP recovery purged of Rooseveltian radicalism. Reformers in both parties dreaded the anticipated revival of the infamous "bipartisan alliance" that had so often frustrated Governor Hughes's efforts. Others, only slightly more sanguine, focused on the greatest challenge facing the New York Democrats—that of pulling together and forging a program that Tammany and the upstate rebels could stand by.[1]

The herculean task in New York State fell to John Dix, who would soon prove that he was not up to it. Scion of an illustrious family and a Cornell University graduate, this upstater had carved out an impressive career in manufacturing and banking in Washington and Albany counties. He had been chosen to head the Democratic ticket in 1910,

43

in part to appease Osborne's league of which he was a member, and in part to offset Roosevelt's New Nationalism. Dix shared with other eastern Democrats, Woodrow Wilson included, an economic conservatism. Business "goes to the places and enjoys the conditions that give stability," he once told George Perkins; he intended as governor to help provide that stability in the Empire State. By instinct and inclination Dix was also a champion of good government, though his enemies would insist that he missed the mark here. His major deficiencies, however, were his indecisiveness, his narrow view of executive responsibility, and his tendency to shy away from political battle. These qualities set Dix apart from his contemporary in New Jersey (or even his predecessor in New York), with whom he was often compared. One critic, perhaps too harshly, condemned Dix as a "nice nonentity [with] no force of intellect and no force of character."[2]

If Governor Dix's leadership was fumbling, Democratic troubles in 1911–1912 were not entirely his fault. The party itself remained a sectional-cultural incongruity. Harmony had been achieved in 1910 only under the most extraordinary of circumstances and, in any case, would be threatened after the hoopla of the elections subsided. Upstate Democrats of Osborne's persuasion had made as their raison d'être an all-out assault on the bosses and the machines. Their constituencies, agitated by a vocal anti-Tammany press, demanded no less once the party seized the reins of government. The Democratic League's renewal of the crusade against bossism, in turn, invited counterattack and recrimination from the Hall's forces, now supreme in the legislature, and ugly internecine squabbling preoccupied the Democracy through much of 1911 and into 1912. These battles—waged over preferment, patronage, and program—obscured whatever progressive achievements the Democrats made and confirmed for skeptics their earlier judgment that the "party of Jefferson" was ill-suited to effective rule in New York State.

I

The Democrats got off to what appeared to be a good start in early 1911. Dix went out of his way to represent among his personal staff and in his "cabinet" such avowed independents as Thomas Mott Osborne, Charles E. Treman, and William Church Osborn. Though his inaugural address and his first message to the legislature were somewhat narrow in scope, they did capture the mild Democratic reformism of that day. Dix came out for home rule, the direct primary, the direct election of U.S. senators, the federal income tax amendment, and conservation. Retrenchment formed a major theme of his initial thrusts. He scored the high cost of government under the Republicans and promised the "rigid application of plain business methods to the public affairs of the state." Several days later he even announced his intention to establish Moreland commissions to systematize administration and check waste—a move that elicited the comment from one observer that he would "out-Hughes Governor Hughes." What received scant attention in these early declarations of public policy was Dix's candid admonition that his suggestions to the legislature were "merely suggestions"—a fair warning that he expected to step back and leave the initiative to others.³

In the meantime, the legislature had organized itself—and in a manner that was totally unexpected. Charlie Murphy's firm grip on the New York City delegation and his alliance with upstate regulars gave him the upper hand in naming the senate and assembly officers. When Dix made clear in December that he would not interfere in the process, critics anticipated the worst from Tammany. But the "boss," in almost typical fashion, stunned his detractors by turning to younger, more respected legislators for the major leadership positions. The move was less dramatic in the assembly where Daniel Frisbie, a Schoharie County Cleveland man, was given the speakership. (Two years earlier, Frisbie had replaced Tammany's "Paradise Park Jimmie" Oliver as Democratic spokesman.) His first lieutenant would be Al Smith, prominent member of Murphy's "kindergarten class" and already widely acclaimed for his excellent knowledge of the legislative process. Smith was also highly popular among his colleagues for his fairness and effectiveness as a lawmaker. In the senate, long the more conservative of the two houses, the change in Democratic leadership was nothing less than astonishing. By virtue of seniority and service to the party, Thomas F. Grady was the odds-on favorite for president pro tempore and majority leader. Symbolic of all that was venal in Tammany, Grady, it was commonly felt, would lead the spoilsmen of 1911. "It is dull, it is stupid, it is

45

inconceivably idiotic as a political move," fumed the *New York Times* about reports that Murphy would bow to tradition. Instead, the boss took the unusual step of bypassing Grady and handing the lofty position to Robert F. Wagner, the most promising—and the most independent—among the young Tammanyites in the senate. The full significance of the Smith and Wagner selections would not become apparent until later; for the time being they showed Murphy's willingness once again to accommodate the Osborne wing of the party. The youthful Franklin D. Roosevelt, himself just elected to the senate with league support, admitted precisely this in regard to the Wagner choice which, "on behalf of the new and of the up-State Senators," he even seconded in the party caucus.[4]

But Charlie Murphy's goodwill and Dix's early promise quickly melted in the caldron of party troubles. The issue that provoked a renewal of the conflict was the naming of a U.S. senator to replace the retiring incumbent, Republican Chauncey M. Depew. Since New York was one of those states that did not yet follow the direct method, the election would take place in the legislature. Long before this stage was reached, however, politicians were jockeying for position. A great deal was at stake. To Democratic stalwarts the prospect of a presidential victory in 1912 meant that *this* senator two years hence would be the dispenser of federal patronage in New York. For Osborne and the league the issue provided a test for their newfound strength in the continuing battle with Tammany: specifically, a vigorous effort in behalf of an independent would at once consolidate their tenuous hold in upstate districts that were usually Republican and cement the league's relations with dissident elements in New York City. Shortly after the 1910 elections, therefore, Osborne's group emerged with a candidate for Depew's seat and launched a sales campaign for him. He was Edward M. Shepard (personally chosen by Osborne, it was widely believed), a counsel for the Pennsylvania Railroad and longtime independent from Brooklyn. Shepard's career went back to the 1890s, when, as a Cleveland supporter, he waged war against the old Croker organization. Like that of most reformist Democrats, his progressivism revolved about honest government, the low tariff, and opposition to Roosevelt's New Nationalism. By the time the legislature met in early January, the league's ambitious canvass for Shepard had managed to win the backing of groups that were potentially threatening to Tammany. These included influential independents in New York City such as Francis Lynde Stetson and Montgomery Hare (who was really a "contact man" for Osborne in Manhattan), dissenters within the Hall itself, a substantial contingent of McCooey's Brooklyn organization, and disaffected party members in western New York led by "Fingy" Conners. There was even the rumor that the Morgan interests, with which Shepard had ties, were applying intense pressure on Murphy for a return on their heavy investments in the 1910 state campaign.[5]

"Mr. Murphy is distressingly vexed," announced a Tammany friend as the Shepard candidacy gained momentum.[6] To the boss the upstaters must have seemed unreasonable and headstrong. It was true that Osborne's league had been instrumental in helping the Democrats seize control of the legislature. Yet the upstaters constituted a small minority of the party's total representation in Albany. Now they were using what leverage they had to "dictate" the Democratic choice for senator. Even worse was the league's deliberate provocation of Tammany: with his characteristic fervor Osborne sought to transform the issue into a cause célèbre, insisting that there could be no compromise with "bossism" and tugging at the incoming Dix administration for support in the fight. And this at the very time that Murphy was making overtures to the league!

Meanwhile, Tammanyites were being pulled in another direction— to the candidacy of William F. ("Blue-Eyed Billy") Sheehan. Like Shepard, Sheehan's political career harked back to the nineteenth century. But unlike Shepard he was thoroughly partisan and regular. Indeed, Sheehan had emerged from Buffalo politics as an organization man allied with Croker and Hill. After serving in Albany as speaker of the assembly and lieutenant governor, Sheehan, in the mid-1890s, moved to New York City where he pursued his legal career. A law partner of Alton B. Parker, he was also affiliated with Thomas Fortune Ryan's Brooklyn Transit Company and gained the reputation as a traction and utilities magnate. So closely identified with the "interests" was Sheehan that even the *Tammany Times,* after the Roosevelt-Parker campaign of 1904, conceded his "one weakness—his pocketbook." In 1910 it seems that Blue-Eyed Billy, anticipating a Democratic victory, spread his money around for the state party, pouring large sums into key districts, particularly in Erie County and along the southern tier. For this "service" he evidently extracted a promise from Murphy that the Tammany organization would not block his efforts to obtain the nomination for U.S. senator.[7]

But Murphy's commitment to Sheehan was never as firm as the league's was to Shepard. In fact, there is ample evidence that the boss sought accommodation early in the impasse—long before the Democracy's ill-fated legislative caucus in mid-January. All during this period he let it be known that Shepard was unacceptable to Tammany but held off making a public announcement for Sheehan, thus paving the way for a third candidate. From Murphy's own lieutenants and from Governor Dix, who mistakenly remained aloof from the tussle, flowed the names of prospective nominees, including Alton B. Parker, D-Cady Herrick, and respectable Tammanyites like Daniel Cohalan and James Gerard. None won approval from the upstaters, however. Finally, on the eve of the party caucus, Sheehan offered to withdraw his candidacy if Shepard would do the same. When Shepard refused, the issue was drawn, and as Murphy saw it, Osborne's forces sought to "wreck the party and prevent it from holding control of the State and contributing its share to Democratic victory in 1912."[8]

On January 16 the long-awaited party caucus took place. In preparation for the event a group of legislators, mainly but not exclusively upstaters, had been meeting secretly for nearly two weeks. These men, "prone to rebel at any use of the party lash," were already feeling pressures from the organization: committee assignments were being delayed, and patronage was being withheld. In the face of Tammany's great strength their only chance was to bolt the Democratic conference (thus freeing themselves from the unit rule), scatter their votes in the legislature, and in this way deny Sheehan the requisite 101 ballots for the election. So it was that twenty-five legislators, mostly assemblymen, signed a "Declaration of Independence," informed Murphy of their intentions, and on the evening of the caucus adjourned to Albany's Hampton Hotel. The conference was paralyzed; and the insurgents, nervous over the possibility of desertions from their ranks, celebrated round one of the struggle. "All that I have to say is that we have taken the first trick," exulted Thomas Mott Osborne.[9] Even as Osborne spoke the leadership of the rebels was shifting from the controversial

Auburn independent to another—Senator Franklin D. Roosevelt of Dutchess County, who had just been elected chairman of the legislative insurgents.

Roosevelt's quick rise from obscurity to prominence in state politics stemmed from the peculiar conditions of the day. Hailing from Hyde Park, the Harvard-educated, youthful aristocrat had been nominated for the senate in 1910 as part of the league's massive effort to reorganize the Democratic party statewide. Neither of his sponsors, Osborne allies John Mack and John Sague, thought FDR had much of a chance in the solidly Republican district comprising Columbia, Dutchess, and Putnam counties. Most likely, they viewed him as a wealthy upstart who could afford a political drubbing in his initial foray. But Roosevelt worked hard, campaigned on a mild reform platform (lashing out especially at the "machines" and heaping praise on Governor Hughes), and was elected in that year of Republican division.[10] Once in Albany he acted like most other Democratic lawmakers who had come from essentially GOP districts. He kept his distance from Tammany and seized on every opportunity to trumpet his independence. Early in January he flirted with insurgency on the senate majority leadership question but backed off with Wagner's candidacy. One of only half-a-dozen senators to join the rebels, he played an important role in trying to obtain Governor Dix's endorsement of Shepard. This effort, together with his name's symbolic quality and his personal wealth (he could "afford" to resist organization pressures), made him the natural spokesman for the insurgents. "He was the shepard of the flock," confessed Edmund Terry, "and his house was indeed . . . a harbor of refuge every evening."[11]

A "Roosevelt" leading the insurgency assured the bolters the widespread publicity they needed and wanted. What followed, for over two and one half months, was a verbal tug-of-war. While the legislature again and again went through the motions of trying to elect a senator, the contending factions played out for an eager public the game of maneuver and manipulation. Here the rebels enjoyed a certain edge, for they were "David" fighting "Goliath," and their course was likened to that of Hughes earlier in New York and Woodrow Wilson in New Jersey as they flayed the "bosses," ostensibly holding principle above politics. Though himself inexperienced, Roosevelt did well in supplying reporters with information, adroitly answering their questions and generally supervising propaganda for the insurgents. He quickly became the "Galahad of the Insurgency,"[12] was sought out for special interviews, and was the subject of character sketches for many a newspaper.

Tammany and its supporters responded to the rebels in their own way. Much of the counterattack was directed at the Hyde Park Democrat who was made to look like a party renegade working in cahoots with his "distinguished" Republican cousin and an anti-Catholic, anti-Irish bigot. Such charges, leveled first by the *New York Sun* and then repeated later by others, stung Roosevelt to the point where he felt constrained to announce a list of Irish-Catholic candidates he could support for the senatorship. His colleagues, too, were lampooned as a little group of "willful men" determined to sabotage majority rule. Sheehan personally added the charge that through Francis Lynde Stetson, the attorney "for more of the 'big interests' than all the rest of the lawyers of the country combined," they were Wall Street-financed and living in plush Albany hotel suites.[13] To the tremendous verbal abuse heaped on the rebels came all those other pressures from county leaders, state committeemen, and Tammany's legislative high command. Insurgency was at least as hazardous as it was glamorous.

Even while the public battle raged, the two groups paced themselves behind the scenes for an amicable settlement of their differences. If Murphy and the Tammanyites were agreeable to compromise, so was Roosevelt—certainly after the insurgents drove home their point that they could veto a Tammany nominee they did not want and, in the process, win so much public acclaim. FDR himself was a realist. "Tammany should receive what belongs to it," he assured a constituent evidently critical of the Democratic spectacle perpetrated by the rebels.[14] At the end of January he met with Murphy, then with Sheehan, but to no avail. The reason was that though the boss wished to abandon Blue-Eyed Billy, Sheehan now showed no inclination to withdraw. (He was, after all, the choice of a large majority of his party.) Negotiations continued sporadically through February and into March. As Sheehan's hopes faded, Roosevelt's forces inched away from Shepard and began screening names "acceptable" to them. The first real break came on March 27, when another Democratic caucus was held. The insurgents had been invited to attend, but most refused because their leadership was unable to reach an agreement beforehand with Smith and Wagner on a compromise candidate. Still, at the conference Murphy released the Tammany lawmakers from their commitment to Sheehan, and the Democrats scattered their votes widely, giving no one a majority. In the meantime, Roosevelt and his colleagues, amid overtures from Republicans to join forces and elect a "conservative Democrat,"[15.] had completed their list and submitted it to Murphy. This last stage was hurried by a devastating fire that swept the capitol on the evening of March 28. Adjourning to Albany's city hall, weary legislators urged an immediate settlement of the long-standing dispute. The Tammany leadership seized advantage of the confusion and rejected the insurgent list without the addition of the name of Justice James O'Gorman, a former Grand Sachem of the Hall and now Murphy's personal choice. In the quick turn of events Roosevelt lost control of the insurgents. When Smith and Wagner promised no reprisals to the group if they would enter a party caucus, a majority of them went along and ratified the O'Gorman nomination. Although Roosevelt and nearly a dozen others stayed out (it seems more for show than for anything else), they joined their fellow Democrats in the subsequent legislative session that gave O'Gorman the senatorship. FDR even lauded the choice and claimed a triumph for insurgency.[16]

Following the O'Gorman election there occurred a lengthy debate in the press—and among the politicians—on whether or not Roosevelt and the insurgents had lost the battle with Tammany at the eleventh hour. For days afterward, FDR himself was preoccupied with a defense of his ultimate "capitulation." But if it was a capitulation, it made little difference to Roosevelt's political career: overnight he had been established as a spokesman for independent Democracy in the state and a coleader of Osborne's league. In addition, the party had named a progressive-minded Democrat, albeit a product of the machine. In fact, to all but the purists the new senator met every test. He had been a highly respected jurist earlier on the New York City Civil Court, and in the previous ten years on the state supreme court. He had displayed some political independence, having been a follower of Henry George's United Labor party in the 1890s and an enthusiastic supporter of the Bryan candidacy, in 1896, when the Croker organization remained cool to the "Silver-tongued Orator." In a public statement at the time of his election, he came out firmly for the income tax amendment, the direct election of U.S. senators (which to some seemed ironic in light of the way he was chosen), the parcel post, and a downward revision of the tariff. Like most other Democrats in New York and elsewhere, O'Gorman cringed at Theodore Roosevelt's New Nationalism and opposed what he labeled "the centralizing tendencies of the Republican party." Even William Randolph Hearst's *New York American,* usually critical of the Hall, conceded that "if all Tammany men were like O'Gorman, there would be no objection to Tammany."[17]

Yet the fight against Tammany all along meant much less than the party rebels and the vocal antiorganization press insisted. In terms of issues it was more a battle of symbols than of substance. For despite the insurgent claims to the contrary, no real "democratic" principles separated the two sides. Tammanyites never once defended the caucus system and, indeed, supported (and worked for) the direct election reform. Nor could the independents make a legitimate case for their candidate as a representative of the "people" against the "interests." In some quarters, at least, the Shepard-Sheehan conflict was dismissed as merely "cutthroat competition among the giants of Manhattan finance."[18] If anything, the senatorial contest was but another manifestation of the political struggle between the two wings of the New York State Democratic party separated by attitudes grounded on sectional and cultural differences. It is noteworthy on this score that a tinge of nativism entered the tussle. In the end, of course, the party rebels capitulated, and what evidently weighed heavily with them was O'Gorman's commitment, as Hare put it, "absolutely to the impartial and just treatment of all Democrats, irrespective of present and past divisions."[19] With such an assurance the insurgents could scamper back to the party leadership content that they had rebelled at what seemed to be less of a cost than they had originally anticipated.

II

The long battle over the U.S. senatorship, however, did raise serious questions among political observers about the effectiveness of the Democratic party as a governing force in New York State. Most of the independent press, especially in New York City, delighted in condemning Tammanyism and bossism. Resolution of the senatorial conflict neither stilled the voices of protest nor, for that matter, substantially reduced tensions within the Democracy. What kept these troubles alive—and, in fact, worsened them—was the scramble by party members for patronage and influence in the Dix administration. Before long the political in-fighting again settled down to a tug-of-war between the Osborne-Roosevelt forces, backed by a host of reform organizations, and the besmirched Tammany Hall. In the process the middle man, Governor Dix, was ruined politically, and his administration was dismissed as a consummate failure.

That John Dix was unable to rise above the role of mere arbiter of groups and individuals elbowing for advantage within the Democracy became evident in his handling of the patronage during the winter and spring of 1911. In response to demands by spoils-hungry Democrats, Dix loaded the state civil service commission with flunkies and fierce partisans. The end result (in a day when good government was equated with an expanding civil service) was the commission's removal, in 1911 alone, of over two hundred positions from the classified list. Included among them were eight new supervising factory inspectors recently created under a much-hailed reorganization of the labor department. This mistake, interpreted as a "grab" on the part of the regulars, was compounded by errors Dix committed in making several of his major appointments. Doubtless here the governor faced tremendous pressure from Tammany, which held the trump card in the legislature: the Hall was in a position to trade off program for patronage, or even job for job (if Dix or the league wished to reward supporters). And Dix's inclusion of Osborne, Osborn, and Treman in his "administration," together with his insistence that a prominent Albany Republican be made superintendent of banking, left him vulnerable to organization demands for preferment. Several key appointments then were made with a seeming vengeance. The governor was maneuvered into naming Dan Cohalan, Tammany Grand Sachem and brother-in-law to Murphy, as O'Gorman's successor on the state supreme court in Manhattan. This was followed by equally controversial appointments—J. Sergeant Cram, Murphy's "social mentor," and W. A. Huppuch, Dix's successor as Democratic state chairman and a Sheehan supporter, to the public service commissions.[20] Few, if any, of these men lacked the requisite qualifications for the respective positions, but their selection made Dix appear to be surrendering to "Tammanyism."

Indeed, the governor's handling of the patronage and his major appointments, far more than the Shepard-Sheehan contest, turned reformers and reform organizations against him. Villard, in May, dismissed Dix as "literally a disaster," while others accused him of specific misdeeds ranging from "putting the judiciary up for sale" to flagrant violations of the spirit (if not the letter) of the civil service law.[21] Dix may have had a good defense for his actions, but he and his supporters failed to articulate it effectively. When asked at one point if he considered the opinion on the merit system of those he named to the civil service commission, he answered cryptically: "No, not at all." The positions that he arranged to have declassified, chimed in his defenders rather obtusely, were done so because the "Republican Civil Service Commission" had placed them on the competitive list when a Democratic victory in 1910 seemed assured.[22] To reformers the governor appeared all the more callous when he continued in a similar vein through the rest of the year. By early 1912 the Civil Service Reform Association, in appraising the entire Dix record, condemned what it called "an administration of unredeemed pledges and violation of faith with the people." Already social progressives, speaking through organizations such as the Consumers' League, the New York Child Labor Committee, and the American Association for Labor Legislation, had slammed Dix and Tammany for "spoilsmanship." What bothered these reformers most of all was that their hard-fought victories in behalf of more effective labor regulations were being undermined by "political" personnel. The "stirring advance" in enforcement machinery in 1911, charged *The Survey* editorially, "was frittered into a vote-getting contraption."[23]

While reformers on the outside were becoming increasingly disenchanted with Dix, Thomas Mott Osborne underwent a similar transformation in Albany. Osborne's unhappiness began with the governor's passive role in the "sorry" episode that ended in O'Gorman's election (though he harbored no ill feelings toward the new senator). After that Dix could do little that satisfied Osborne's suspicious nature and delicate sensitivities. "I must tell you," he warned the governor about one appointment, "that it threatens political ruin to you." Already by late

February, Osborne, stung by Dix's failure to consult with him on anything, confessed to a confidant that he found it "quite abhorrent" to
be "part of a *Tammany* administration."[24] Matters went from bad to
worse in the spring with the governor's major appointments and his
increasing reliance on the Hall's senate and assembly leadership to
hammer out a legislative program implementing the party's 1910 Rochester platform. It was not so much differences on specific issues that
widened the chasm; rather, it was what Osborne perceived as Dix's
total capitulation to Murphy and Tammany. The crowning blow came
with the governor's refusal to support Osborne for a better post in the
administration. Osborne's official position in Albany was chairman of
the forest, fish, and game commission, which he evidently had accepted
until something more suitable opened up. ("Osborne detested both
hunting and fishing," notes his biographer.[25]) In fact, he had the clear
understanding that he would be offered the superintendency of prisons
when the vacancy occurred. However, doubt that Osborne could be
confirmed by "Tammany's senate" turned Dix elsewhere. There was
yet another opportunity for the Auburn independent—that of head of
the newly formed conservation department in whose creation he himself had played a major role. But again the governor disappointed Osborne and named someone else to the position. Osborne now had little
choice. A serious illness gave him the excuse to leave a situation that
had become untenable. "I was in a false position," he lamented to
Villard, "and I couldn't open my mouth without making it harder for
Dix along the line that he has chosen to follow."[26]

Osborne's departure from Albany symbolized the reformers' abandonment of Governor Dix. To them the governor had proved himself
beyond doubt a mere puppet of Tammany, and the first order of business was the "absolute elimination of Murphy as a State leader." This
thought, contained in an "open letter" to a prominent league member
in June, represented for Osborne a return to his earlier pursuit.[27] He
now envisioned a twofold assault on the machine. The first called for
the maintenance of an insurgent bloc in the legislature, headed by
Franklin Roosevelt, which would generally advance the progressive
cause in that arena. (It would oppose further efforts to enhance the
organization's patronage, and it would stand for reform legislation,
with special emphasis on the direct primary.) The second involved the

Democratic League, whose base was to be broadened in Manhattan so that independents could hurl a direct challenge at Murphy in his own bailiwick. Osborne himself would play a major role in this task.

Osborne's plan sounded fine on paper but ran into serious trouble when put into operation. It assumed a greater degree of like-mindedness among the independents than actually existed. In fact, Osborne and Roosevelt discovered that their compatriots were divided in countless ways on both overall objectives and tactics. Sometimes they were even co-opted by the very forces they were presumably opposing. (Nor would FDR, the pragmatic politician, usually go as far as Osborne in pressing the cause.) Roosevelt's part of the plan was set into motion in mid-April while Osborne was still brooding over his resignation. Neither on patronage nor on specific legislation could he count on consistent backing from those who aided him in the senatorial imbroglio. "Their insurgency was not one of principle," scowled the *Tribune* cynically, after one abortive attempt to block a Dix-Tammany appointment.[28] (In this case Roosevelt himself joined the majority when it became clear that his efforts were in vain.) Osborne had equally tough sledding in his work outside Albany. Well before his departure his "allies" in the Shepard-Sheehan contest had incorporated a league chapter in New York County. Its objective was cast in broad terms— "to foster, disseminate, and give effect to Democratic principles." To Osborne such language was plain; it meant all-out warfare against Murphy and Tammany. But the local leaders believed otherwise: one of them exercised his prerogative to support Sheehan, and the chapter only cautiously backed fusion candidates against Tammany in selected assembly districts in the 1911 elections. Far worse, some thirty members of the league, including several prominent figures, reportedly bolted fusion and worked for the regular party ticket in the city! It was much less than Osborne had hoped for, but he had to bow to the "Democratic principle" of home rule. "If you want him [Murphy] in the city as your leader you are welcome to him," he muttered unhappily after a league executive committee meeting in New York. All Osborne could do was to issue a feeble statement slamming at "dictation or control of any individual" and memorializing the state legislature to fulfill the promises made in the 1910 Rochester platform.[29]

III

By the time the 1911 legislature got down to serious business in the late spring, few expected much constructive work from the already battered Democracy. The Rochester platform had charted a moderate reform program for the party, but the issue of "bossism" and "Tammany" seemed to sweep everything else aside. Preoccupied with Dix's "capitulation" to Murphy, Osborne and the reform forces tended to reject or belittle practically everything that was done in the legislature. And whatever achievements were made—in light of the governor's earlier statement that his role would be minimal in the lawmaking process—came from the labor of the senate and assembly leaders, principally Robert F. Wagner and Alfred E. Smith. Dedicated to Democratic success as much as Osborne and Roosevelt, these "Tammany twins" rendered a creditable, if less than brilliant, performance under difficult conditions. In large part because they were organization men they were given little credit for Democratic legislative successes.

Wagner and Smith had made their debut on the state scene shortly after Charlie Murphy became leader of Tammany Hall. Like Murphy, they grew up in New York City's immigrant quarters—Smith on the Lower East Side, and Wagner in the "little Germany" of the Upper East Side. Smith's parentage was of Irish, German, and Italian extraction. The Wagners had emigrated to America when Robert was a boy of nine. Neither family was poverty-stricken, but each fell far short of attaining the comforts of the middle class: Al was forced to quit school at the age of thirteen and go to work because of the premature death of his father; Wagner struggled through his early years holding various part-time jobs ("My boyhood was a pretty rough passage," he later recalled)[30] and, with the help of his older brother, made his way through City College and the New York Law School. The two entered politics in a strikingly similar fashion, this less a coincidence and more an indication of the way things were done in those days in the organization. Smith's lingering about the local Tammany club and neighborhood saloon won him the patronage of Tom Foley, jovial Democratic boss of the Fourth Ward. After several years of faithful service to Foley and Foley's capture of the second district leadership, Smith, in 1903, was handed the assembly nomination. He easily won the election. Wagner's way to Albany was paved by his friend and law partner, Jeremiah Mahoney, and a Yorkville Tammany leader, Mike Cosgrove. In 1904, one year after Smith went to the assembly, Wagner followed along. They did not yet know one another, but each represented that new trend in Tammany, launched by Murphy and his supporters, of giving "young men a chance."[31] Smith was then thirty-one years old, and Wagner was twenty-seven.

Their early years in the legislature had been nightmarish for both Wagner and Smith, who became fast friends and close confidants shortly after Wagner's arrival in Albany. As junior lawmakers among a dispirited minority, they obtained few favors and little recognition from the leadership. Nor could they identify fully with their "own kind," senior Democrats such as Grady, McCarren, and Oliver. For these carryovers from the Croker days often worked hand in glove with Republican standpatters to beat back reform legislation and eagerly joined in the sponsorship of "strike" bills designed to bilk utility interests and fiduciary institutions. The worst of it was that Wagner, Smith, and other young Democrats were often tarred with the same brush by the muckraking press and the reform organizations as the older, much-maligned Tammany leadership. So discouraged was Smith with the lot of the beginning assemblyman that he very nearly retired from Albany politics after his second year in the legislature. Wagner's career was almost cut short when, in 1905, he lost his bid for reelection to his Municipal Ownership League opponent. The next year he returned somewhat less loyal to the entrenched leaders and more aware of the growing reform spirit in the city and state. Wagner remained in the assembly until 1908, then moved over to the senate. Soon he won the reputation as an independent among Tammanyites.[32]

Wagner and Smith served a major portion of their apprenticeship in Albany during the progressive administration of Charles Evans Hughes. It was a good time for young lawmakers to obtain valuable experience. The old order—Republican and Democratic—came under increasing attack, and the governor's program raised considerably the level of political debate in the legislature. Possessed of few ties to the past, Wagner, Smith, and other young Tammanyites made easy adjustments to the changing conditions. In these years they emerged out of the legislative shadows: they held better committee assignments (thanks partly to James Wadsworth's reform of the assembly beginning in 1906); they became more outspoken on the issues; and they wielded greater influence in party councils and caucuses. One result was that the Democratic minority made a respectable record for itself. There were still the occasional bipartisan deals by which Hughes measures were relegated to the legislative scrap heap. But the essential problem that the reform governor faced was not an obstructionist minority; it was, rather, as Smith himself noted, "the hostility of the reactionary leaders of his own party." (Smith fondly records the continuity between Hughes's governorship and his own administrations some years later.)[33]

On specific issues in the Hughes years the Democrats acquitted themselves very well indeed. In 1907 they sought to amend the governor's key measure, the public service commissions bill, so that the proposed commission for New York City would be chosen in accordance with the principle of home rule. When that failed, they voted almost unanimously for the measure in its original form.[34] In that same session they supported the Moreland Act designed to increase the authority of the governor's office in the investigation of state boards, bureaus, departments, and commissions. Subsequently the Democrats backed most of the administration's bills calling for tighter state regulation of banking and trust institutions as well as those dealing with social and labor reforms, particularly the workmen's compensation measure of 1910. Only on the issues of the direct primary and the Massachusetts ballot— which regulars from both parties feared—did the Democrats offer stiff opposition. Even here, however, the resistance was not total, as a large number of minority assemblymen supported Hughes; moreover, in the complicated legislative wrangling of 1910, Democrats introduced and fought for a primary bill of their own.[35]

By the end of Hughes's governorship there were clear signs that the Democratic "machine" under Murphy was responding in Albany (as it had been responding in New York City) to the reformism of the day. Occasionally Democrats even reached beyond Republican progressivism. Such was usually the case with the "bread-and-butter" issues that came before the legislature—measures that affected directly the welfare of the urban masses, Tammany's natural constituency. The best example was the proposed amendment to the U.S. Constitution on the federal income tax. Hughes himself objected to the amendment on the narrow ground that the clause "from whatever sources derived" granted the federal government the authority to tax state and municipal bonds. "For all practical purposes he might as well have declared himself against an income tax in any form," complained the disappointed *New York World*.[36] What disturbed the *World* and other critics was that Hughes's declaration provided a mask for many a wealthy conservative in New York—men like John D. Rockefeller, Joseph Hodges Choate, and George Baker—who objected to shifting the tax burden from the poor to the rich. Wagner and Smith led the forces in favor of the reform. To Wagner, simply stated, the tax principle would be "a tax on plenty instead of on necessity, [which] will lighten the burdens of the poor."[37] The culmination of several stormy debates on the proposition was senate passage and assembly rejection on roll calls showing a divided Republican party, on the one hand, and a nearly unified Democracy for the reform, on the other.[38]

When Wagner and Smith took over their leadership positions in 1911, they had their first real opportunity to show what the "new" Tammany could do. But to reformers the shadow of the "boss," Charlie Murphy, hung over the legislature like a curse. Few believed Wagner's insistence that "Mr. Murphy has not attempted to influence the legislature in any way."[39] And as the session developed, the critics, peering closely at the nature of that influence, saw only the "ripper" bills, the "jokers," and the private measures that seemed especially bountiful. Even worse, the inept majority of the Shepard-Sheehan fiasco appeared transformed into a group of stumbling, bumbling incompetents as lawmakers: legislation was shoddily written; committee hearings were often desultory; and there was needless wrangling over procedures and priorities. "In comparison with the present lawmakers," suggested the *New York Times* cynically, "Raines, Allds, and McCarren must be remembered with some respect."[40] When it was all over—and the 1911 session was one of the longest in the state's history—few except the most rabid Democratic partisans would disagree with so harsh a judgment.

The Wagner-Smith leadership, however, did show flashes of brilliance and signs of excellent potential in 1911. Each brought superb qualities to the partnership—Wagner, the serious lawyer and master legislator;

Smith, the jovial but shrewd politician and wire-puller. Neither possessed a well-thought-out political or social philosophy when they assumed their new positions, but both were highly ambitious, acutely sensitive to present-day reform currents, and bent on making a good party record. Like Murphy they were pragmatic, and as "Murphy's boys" they carried forth one of the boss' principal objectives: to reconcile the needs of the organization with Democratic progressivism as outlined in the Rochester platform of 1910. On a few issues they met with success. On others the internal party conflict resulted in legislation that satisfied neither side. And on still others, where independent Democrats could unite with Republicans, they failed miserably.

In the first category were the proposed amendments to the Constitution—the one on the federal income tax and the other on the direct election of U.S. senators. To Franklin Roosevelt these were "two of the most important propositions confronting [the senate]." Wagner and Smith led the fight for the income tax just as they had done one year earlier and, on an almost strict party vote, won the legislature's ratification of the reform. "I don't think Congress will ever unjustly tax us," Smith replied confidently to Republican opponents who sought to resurrect Hughes's argument against the measure.[41] Democrats were equally enthusiastic about the direct election amendment. To Roosevelt, who sponsored the resolution urging New York's congressmen to support the proposal, the reform penetrated to the core of the movement for popular democracy. To the more pragmatic Wagner and Smith its adoption could not help but benefit the party: Democrats would have a better chance to win U.S. Senate seats in statewide elections than in the usually Republican legislature. Again the principal opposition came from the GOP, some condemning the amendment "as a popular passion come upon us from the West," others insisting simply that the legislature had no business "instructing" the state's congressional delegation what to do. In the end, the Roosevelt resolution passed both houses handily with Democrats almost unanimous for it and Republicans badly divided.[42]

Nor did the Democratic party have trouble with another issue, conservation, which was high on Governor Dix's own list of priorities in his 1911 message. Since it was of special concern to the upstaters, Thomas Mott Osborne, self-proclaimed heir to Hughes's policies and currently forest, fish, and game commissioner, took the lead and drafted appropriate legislation. The major bill called for the creation of a unified department of conservation out of several agencies responsible for specific tasks in regard to the state's natural resources. As such it fulfilled one of Dix's major objectives—economy and efficiency in government—and with two other significant provisions also advanced conservation policy and resource development.[43] "It is the most far-reaching measure of its kind ever presented to the Legislature," remarked the *Times,* fearful that it could not be passed. But the Tammany leadership provided support among the regulars for the bill: Wagner took personal interest in modifying and amending it to assure its success in the senate (and it would emerge as the "Wagner bill"). "I am suspicious of constructive legislation offered us by Tammany Hall," cautioned Republican senate leader Edgar T. Brackett, "but I can safely vote for this measure." Similar sentiments prevailed in the assembly, where the GOP found the legislation "fairly sensible." It received almost unanimous approval in both houses.[44]

Party unity could not be as easily sustained for political reform, and the best that the Democracy could get was badly flawed legislation through tortuous compromise. On two major items in 1911—personal registration of voters and the direct primary—Democrats divided along the usual lines. The Tammany leadership sponsored the Levy bill that, in establishing a system of uniform voter registration in the state, would, it was argued, minimize fraudulent voting. But independents quickly discovered that the measure really "discriminated" against rural folk who would find it hard to make personal appearances to register and, even more devastating, discouraged fusion movements by rendering it unlawful for candidates to appear twice or more on the same ballot. "The Levy bill is in most respects utterly bad," charged Roosevelt, who echoed the sentiments of both his rural constituency and New York City reform organizations. Yet when the final vote was taken Roosevelt's upstate colleagues (much to his dismay) helped to pass the measure in a purported bargain with Tammany.[45]

Far more divisive was the direct primary that Wagner and Smith would have liked to sweep under the rug—and they tried to do so. Even Roosevelt, who after the Sheehan fight made the primary a key reform for the independents, recognized that it "must be delicately handled at first." As usual, a host of bills were introduced in the legislature. One of them, the Ferris-Blauvelt bill, a mild form of direct nominations and one which the organization could accept, passed the assembly in July but failed in the senate, where it met with stiff opposition from Republicans and Roosevelt-type Democrats. Under constant agitation from reform groups, Governor Dix, sensitive to charges that the party was ducking its 1910 pledge, prodded lawmakers to come forward with a meaningful piece of legislation in the special session in the fall. The Ferris-Blauvelt bill was then resurrected. At a critical moment in the legislative process, however, the Democratic leadership lost control of the situation, and a somewhat more comprehensive measure got by the senate, where again several Democrats joined almost the entire Republican minority (doubtless hopeful of winning whatever credit could be claimed for the reform). Smith now faced enormous pressure in the assembly and, unsure of what to do, got directly in touch with Murphy. Murphy agreed that some form of the primary had to be enacted. "Don't give them more than you have to," the boss reportedly told Smith. The upshot was legislative approval of an amended version of the Ferris-Blauvelt bill that brought it closer to the senate-passed Republican measure. "I have become converted to direct primaries during the last four hours," Smith asserted half-humorously on the day that the legislation passed the assembly.[46] Roosevelt and his friends were less than joyous over what amounted to a compromise twice removed but contented themselves that it, as the *Tribune* lamented, "is at least an advance over the present system."[47]

Finally, there were those items on which Democratic divisions were so pronounced that no compromise could be attained. Such was the case with home rule—and particularly home rule for New York City. For years reform organizations in the city had bombarded the legislature with requests to remove defects in the existent charter, clarify certain vague and indefinite regulations, and lift crippling restraints on the municipal government. These efforts had much in common with the home rule movement elsewhere, whose main thrust was to free the urban center from the shackles of rural-oriented legislatures. Until 1910 the battle in New York had pitted progressive Republicans and independent Democrats (with Tammanyites playing a minor role) against the dominant upstate wing of the GOP. And though two Hughes-appointed commissions had proffered various recommendations, nothing substantial was accomplished. Then, in 1911, the Democratic leadership in the legislature came forward with the so-called Gaynor charter, a comprehensive attempt to streamline and reorganize various aspects of the city government. Tendered by a New York City mayor whose own reputation was that of an independent, the charter bill, nonetheless, generated immediate opposition. Gaynor, after all, had made his peace with Tammany, and there were "jokers" in the measure that reform organizations, independent Democrats, and Republicans concluded benefited the machine.[48]

The battle over the Gaynor charter raged all during the regular session until finally in July, Wagner and Smith, on special request from Governor Dix, sent the measure back to committee. Over the summer thousands of amendments were considered; many were incorporated; and the matter was again brought before the legislature in the special session. Almost from the outset the Gaynor charter faced the same opposition as earlier, for hardly any of the critics could be convinced that the changes improved the legislation. Indeed, organizations such as the Citizens Union, the City Club, and the Bureau of Municipal Research mounted a powerful lobby campaign against the bill. When the Republicans opposed it as a party measure, the Tammany leadership resorted to desperate tactics. Smith twisted arms to obtain passage in the assembly. "That is the dirtiest day's work I have ever done," he admitted candidly after the vote.[49] In the senate Thomas Grady, who had taken over for the ailing Robert Wagner, succeeded in tying the charter issue to a reapportionment scheme that threatened Roosevelt and his colleagues in their upstate districts. In a series of complex deals involving Tammany and the Roosevelt people the worst of the redistricting was quashed, and the Gaynor charter was on the verge of obtaining full Democratic support. Then, however, a group of reformers visited Roosevelt and threatened to destroy him politically if he did not stick with them. He (with several of his colleagues) relented at the eleventh hour and remained out of the party caucus. Faced with almost surefire defeat, Grady had no alternative but to allow the bill to die in committee.[50] The proposed charter was dead, and home rule "Tammany-style" had failed.

All told, the 1911 legislature was not so bad as the critics protested nor so good as the leadership maintained. Wagner himself, ignoring Governor Hughes's achievements in 1907, was excessive in his praise of the results. "The Democratic party," he asserted, "has given to the people more broad, constructive legislation and more laws of a genuinely reform character than any other session within the last decade." As an official spokesman for the Democracy, Wagner could be forgiven his exaggeration. What is significant is that he, like Smith, measured success by the enactment of bills that advanced policies and programs that sought to accommodate the party (and the organization) to progressivism. Most of these efforts, however, could not satisfy the reformers and their vocal press. To them Murphy's agents were little more than slick politicians who failed the acid test of sincerity and commitment. They twisted legitimate reform ideas—voter registration, the direct primary, and home rule—to narrow partisan or sectional ends.[51] Public attention, therefore, remained riveted, not on Democratic achievement, but on the party split and the negative side of "machine" rule.

IV

Unabated intraparty wrangling, an already discredited state administration, and what to critics had been an unproductive legislature boded ill for the Democrats in the 1911 elections. The party went down to a devastating defeat across the state. In the assembly races (which were then held annually) the Republicans won overwhelmingly. Most GOP districts that had swung Democratic in 1910 returned to normalcy: only five of well over twenty insurgents involved in the senatorial contest survived the election; some had been dumped by the regular organizations earlier, and others fell to Republicans in November. One of the defeated assemblymen explained the rebels' plight: "Half of our Democrats up-State won't stand for any opposition to Tammany, and the other half and the independent vote . . . won't stand for having anything to do with Tammany."[52] The regulars themselves took a terrible pounding in the more populous sections of the upstate. Albany and Syracuse as usual went Republican. In Utica, Rochester, and Buffalo the Democrats were beaten in the citywide as well as in most of the assembly contests. The Buffalo loss was especially telling because much of the campaign had focused on the "heinous" Murphy-Fitzpatrick alliance (that the Democratic *Courier* had dismissed as "the gang of rippers and political spoilsmen"). In New York City the party also lost ground. It is true that Tammany did elect a sheriff and a surrogate in New York County but, in each case, by unimpressive margins. Moreover, the Hall lost the board of aldermen to fusion and suffered a real setback in the assembly races: Manhattan and the Bronx elected twice the number of Republicans as one year earlier, and Brooklyn quadrupled its GOP representation in Albany.[53]

"The results in every part of the State," gloated William Barnes, "indicate new confidence in the Republican party." A fierce partisan, Barnes might be expected to read the returns in so favorable a light. Closer to the mark, however, was the *Buffalo Courier*'s insistence that the election was more an "uprising of an outraged electorate" than a GOP triumph.[54] That "outrage" was again expressed in the large protest vote recorded that year. In much of the upstate, particularly in the rural areas, voters doubtless returned to their traditional voting habits. But elsewhere it was often Socialist gains that upset the Democratic applecart. In Auburn, Thomas Mott Osborne made the run again for mayor and lost out to a Republican; his campaign manager conceded that the unusually large Socialist vote defeated his bid. At the same time, the Socialists won an aldermanic seat for the first time in that city's history. Disgust over corruption and mismanagement in both major parties led Schenectadians to elect a Socialist city ticket headed by George R. Lunn, a Protestant clergyman only recently converted to the cause. "The one important Eastern city won for the Socialists" in the movement's national upswing in 1911, Schenectady also sent a Socialist assemblyman to Albany.[55] The voice of protest was heard in New York City, too, where the party showed itself much stronger than in the previous year: in three of eight assembly districts in Manhattan and the Bronx that switched from Democrat to Republican, the Socialist vote made the difference; four of fifteen races in Brooklyn went to the GOP because of the Socialists; and in one of two Queens districts that swung against the Democrats the Socialist vote accounted for the upset. Virtually all these areas had heavy concentrations of German, German-Jewish, or east European Jewish voters.[56]

V

After the 1911 elections the Democrats seemed to slide further down-hill. Each faction of the party blamed the other for the November debacle. While the Tammany Tiger retreated quietly to its Manhattan haunts to lick its wounds, the Osborne-Roosevelt group sought to take advantage of what they sensed was a vulnerable Charlie Murphy. (In December, Murphy's ally, Joseph Cassidy of Queens, was dislodged from his chairmanship, and another ally, John McCooey of Brooklyn, very nearly lost his to a band of rebels.) For his part Roosevelt publicly blasted the "bosses" as "noxious weeds" and predicted that the in-surgents, whose ranks had actually been decimated, would wield the balance of power in the 1912 legislature. Osborne, meanwhile, moved to revitalize the league in New York City with the call that "the voters . . . have no confidence whatever in the present control of the Demo-cratic organization." They were both unsuccessful. The new legislature was a divided body, and the Republicans gave neither Roosevelt's little coterie nor the senate's Tammany leadership much maneuvering room. "It will be impossible to enact any laws that will be a radical departure from the present statutes," declared the new Republican assembly speaker in January.[57] And when the legislature adjourned less than three months later, little had been accomplished. As for Osborne's work, a falling away of supporters and dwindling finances, doubtless due to his organization's own failures in the 1911 elections, weakened the league to the point where, by early 1912, it could barely limp along, let alone spur another campaign against Tammany Hall.

Thus, the New York Democrats were in trouble as they faced the crucial elections of 1912. A creditable legislative record in Albany had not helped at all. So many of the electoral gains they had made two years earlier were lost in the wake of intraparty quarrels and voter disenchantment; in New York City they failed to strengthen their po-sition. Whether the Democracy could recoup its 1911 losses depended on the extent to which the forces of political disintegration, now an essential ingredient in the New York scene, sapped Republican vitality in the Empire State.

4

1912:
The Politics of Turmoil

"Here in New York," wrote Theodore Roosevelt in late 1911, "I am in the midst of what is politically really a very backward community."[1] The Colonel's principal complaints were that there were few progressives in his home state; that judges were reactionary on industrial, economic, and social questions; and that, therefore, many a sensitive citizen was being driven into the Socialist party for relief. Beneath it all for him—as well as for other reformers of his ilk—was an inflexible, unresponsive political system in which the two major parties were dominated by monolithic, overpowering machines—the Republicans led by Albany stalwart William Barnes, Jr., and the Democrats by the indomitable Tammany chieftain, Charlie Murphy. "Men of enlightenment," as Roosevelt-type progressives liked to think of themselves, seemed frozen out of the process.

Roosevelt's gloomy appraisal of conditions in New York was only partially accurate, however. Various signs did point to the electorate's growing disillusionment with what many thought was the politics-as-usual attitude of major party spokesmen, and both Democrats and Republicans boasted strong, entrenched organizations. Yet, at the same time, there was no dearth of progressives or progressivism in the state during the Colonel's most trying days—from his shattering defeat in 1910 through the elections of 1912. There were large numbers of political reformers who championed the direct primary, the Massachusetts ballot, and a host of other devices to enhance voter participation and "open up" the party system. Likewise, critics of economic concentration abounded here as elsewhere. And social progressives, working in the settlements or through their many societies, agitated long and hard for the alleviation of poverty, the improvement of working conditions, and a variety of social insurance schemes. Prophets of change, then, were not lacking in New York State. What did appear to be missing was a common, unifying principle, or set of principles, and a dynamic, inspiring leader that could bring together these often disparate groups into an enduring political coalition.

Theodore Roosevelt would spend the first part of 1912 trying to make himself that necessary cohesive force in both state and nation for his beloved Republican party. (Taft proved utterly hopeless in this regard, even though his administration had promoted more reform measures than his renowned predecessor's.)[2] Failing that, he struggled the remainder of the year to forge a new political combination on behalf of his New Nationalism. But for several reasons Roosevelt's efforts did not meet with resounding success among the reform-minded in the Empire State. Many New York reformers simply shunned partisan politics of any kind and continued on their own or through their clubs and organizations to effect change. Others saw too much Rooseveltian ambition in the Bull Moose, and for them substituting one "boss" for another, a Roosevelt for a Barnes or a Murphy, could hardly be deemed "progressive." Still others dismissed the doctrines of the New Nationalism as excessive in an environment where representative government and established economic institutions had perhaps faltered but certainly had not failed. New York's plutocracy was by no means as harmful to the commonweal as Wisconsin's before La Follette or California's before Johnson. Finally, a substantial group of self-styled progressives with Democratic or Republican affiliations concluded that the major parties, unresponsive as they were commonly viewed, yet in the long run afforded more realistic opportunities for the implementation of reform objectives and the gratification of personal ambitions than the risky alternative proffered by Roosevelt's Progressives. At bottom was the fact that the Democratic and Republican parties were deeply rooted in the political soil of the state—each possessed of a solid enough geographic and ethnocultural foundation to withstand the Roosevelt challenge. While, therefore, the Bull Moose remained incapable of overwhelming the New York polity, it could and would play an influential role in the state's political life during its brief existence. In 1912, and again in 1913, the new party served as a rallying cry for some of New York's disgruntled politicians and reformers as well as for much of its disenchanted electorate. Also, the Progressives' positive program and strong candidates for office put the Democratic and Republican organizations squarely on notice that neglect of reform aspirations was, indeed, a risky business.

I

An analysis of the politics of 1912 in the Empire State begins with a review of two conditions: first, certain economic and social stresses that the reigning Democrats would exploit in their persistent efforts to accommodate reformism; and second, the simultaneous drift rightward of the state GOP, rendering that party highly vulnerable to attacks like those voiced by Theodore Roosevelt in 1911. Although seemingly unrelated, these occurrences probably had some bearing on the relative perceptions of the voting public toward the major parties in this year of political turmoil *and* surely influenced long-term political developments in New York.

Doubtless, New Yorkers had benefited greatly from the impressive business-industrial expansion in the past decade or so. However, the rising cost of living in recent years swallowed up much of the economic gain they had won. The middle class was hard hit. Suffering even more—beginning especially in 1910—were laboring men and women. This issue had surfaced in the elections that November. Far more serious was the rash of strikes it helped to generate across the state between 1910 and 1913. On the average 100,000 workers were involved in job actions each year. A bitter textile strike in Little Falls in 1912 and several ugly work stoppages in Buffalo in early 1913 highlighted the struggle in the upstate.[3] But, as already noted, the major labor-industrial disturbances took place in New York City. Here immigrant garment workers on the East Side, mainly Jews and Italians who suffered from rapidly rising food prices and skyrocketing rent increases, struck for higher wages, better working conditions, and union recognition. To one Socialist reflecting on a walkout of 150,000 in the winter of 1912–1913, it was "the time of revolution in the economic field."[4]

While the powerful drive for unionization by the new immigrants, particularly the Jews, may have injected an ominous note of class conflict into the social fabric, it was actually applauded by "public spirited reformers" and "citizens' groups" in New York City. Indeed, reformers contributed in the broadest sense to a community environment that encouraged the "amelioration of immediate circumstances" and the growth of political consciousness among these peoples.[5] One event amid all the turbulence on the East Side stands out in this development of an environment conducive to change. That was the Triangle Shirtwaist Factory Fire in 1911—an industrial disaster that spurred an investigation of working conditions all across the state and left an indelible mark on the history of reform in New York.

The Triangle Company was housed in the top three stories of the relatively new Asch Building in Washington Place. On March 25, 1911, shortly before quitting time, a fire broke out on the eighth floor and swept upward to the last two levels. Within thirty minutes the fire department had the blaze under control, and the employees on the top and bottom floors had been able to abandon the building without loss of life or limb. However, inadequate escape facilities entrapped laborers on the middle level. Nearly 150 workers, mostly young Jewish and Italian women, met their deaths—some by trying to jump to safety and crashing to the sidewalk below; others by jamming the small elevators and being engulfed in flames; and the large majority by attempting to open locked doors to an escape stairway or by crowding together in the narrow aisles of the factory itself, then being burned to ashes. It was truly "the most murderous fire that New York has seen in many years," commented the *New York Times* on the day after the conflagration.[6] Although some responsibility for the tragedy could be placed squarely at the hands of the factory owners, critics quickly condemned the "system" at large for its careless disregard of the poor and the innocent.

The terrible loss of life in Washington Place immediately stirred the consciences of New Yorkers of all persuasions and affiliations. Even the *Times,* conservative on labor-industrial disputes in that day, referred to "the great excitement all about the city over the unpardonable sacrifice" of humanity.[7] There followed a bevy of activity. The Women's Trade Union League (WTUL), which had failed recently in efforts to obtain union recognition for the shirtwaist workers, took the lead by collecting and distributing relief funds to the families of victims and by organizing a funeral procession of over 100,000 laborers in silent tribute to their deceased brethren. League members also met with officers of philanthropic clubs, labor organizations, settlement house groups, and the Socialist party, and arranged a protest gathering at the Metropolitan Opera House for April 2. Filled to capacity, the Opera House meeting heard reformers lash out at public indifference and plead for social justice. Then a committee of safety was established to formulate a plan of action that included the creation of public sentiment for stiffer fire prevention laws, the sponsorship of an examination "of the hazardous conditions to which the City is now exposed," and the enlistment of support from other organizations interested in such social problems. In May representatives of this group, in cooperation with the Fifth Avenue Association, transmitted to Albany a request for a legislative investigation of working conditions in the entire state of New York. They received a warm welcome from Al Smith and Robert Wagner, who subsequently steered the resolution, setting up the Factory Investigating Commission (FIC), through the assembly and the senate, respectively.[8] Almost three months later the inquiry got under way.

The FIC investigation was, as Wagner's biographer has stated, "the most intensive study of industrialism yet undertaken, not only in the Empire State but in the nation."[9] Its success was due largely to the quality of the commission's leadership and the dedication of its membership. Wagner served as chairman, Smith as vice-chairman, and its remaining members were carefully chosen to represent the legislature, the public, and organized labor. (Samuel Gompers stayed for the life of the commission, and Mary Drier, president of the WTUL, provided an excellent link to the social progressives.) The FIC also drew heavily on experts in key specialties, like Dr. George Price in industrial medicine and sanitation, H. F. J. Porter in fire prevention, and Frances Perkins in wages. These consultants—Perkins called herself an "investigator"—often took the lead. She writes:

We used to make it our business to take Al Smith . . . to see the women, thousands of them, coming off the ten-hour nightshift on the rope walks in Auburn. We made sure that Robert Wagner personally crawled through the tiny hole in the wall that gave egress to a steep iron ladder covered with ice and ending twelve feet from the ground, which was euphemistically labeled "Fire Escape" in many factories. We saw to it that the austere legislative members of the Commission got up at dawn and drove with us for an unannounced visit to a Cattaraugus County cannery and that they saw with their own eyes the little children, not adolescents, but five-, six-, and seven-year-olds, snipping beans and shelling peas. We made sure that they saw the machinery that would scalp a girl or cut off a man's arm. Hours so long that both men and women were depleted and exhausted became realities to them through seeing for themselves the dirty little factories.[10]

The year 1912 witnessed the commission's most grueling schedule. In addition to thousands of miles of travel, the FIC, with able counsel from Abram Elkus and Bernard Shientag, conducted 37 public hearings and published over 3,000 pages of testimony from 250 witnesses. Out of this massive effort came approximately 50 pieces of corrective legislation and a large-scale reorganization of the state labor department. Some bills were passed in 1912 (though few major ones), and others later, but the most productive legislature was that in 1913, which, as one student of the commission has observed, "enacted a virtually new labor code" for New York.[11]

While the FIC and its legislative champions were rewriting the state code, the commission developed a life of its own. Given limited scope and modest funds at its creation (Smith and Wagner queried Henry Morgenthau in jest if he might not personally supplement their initial $10,000 appropriation!), it tackled the vital task of building a constituency. This it did effectively. Counsel Elkus, Smith, and Wagner, aware of the rocky shoals of partisanship, took steps to keep petty politics out of the inquiry. Seldom in commission deliberations or in the legislature did the Democratic leadership make FIC recommendations *theirs* exclusively. On the positive side the commission courted its natural allies—organized labor and the social progressives—with care and thoroughness. Gompers was successful in winning AF of L endorsement of the probe, though some unions would give only lukewarm support (and the Socialists would remain indifferent). More important, the FIC turned to the major progressive societies in the state— the New York Child Labor Committee, the Consumers' League, and the New York branch of the American Association for Labor Legislation. Long involved in the fight for social justice, these organizations had perfected the wherewithal to achieve results. So the commission invited countless social reformers to testify in its extensive public hearings, embraced specific measures that the societies themselves had been pushing, and even tapped the services in the legislature of the skilled lobbyists they had groomed over the years. In turn, the FIC gained the plaudits of the reformers. It "has valued our cooperation," declared Maude Nathan of the commission's work in 1913, "proving that the Consumers' League has won for itself a dignified position in the field of social activities."[12] Organization reports and bulletins and, more significantly, the influential social welfare journal, *The Survey,* gave the commission excellent publicity all during its existence.

The FIC investigation, spanning a period of nearly four years, formed a bench mark in the evolution of the Democratic party as the principal champion of ethnic minorities, organized labor, and the urban masses in the state of New York. Playing a key role as agents in this transformation were Al Smith and Robert Wagner, themselves deeply moved by their commission experiences and in turn backed by the pragmatic Charlie Murphy. ("Caring . . . was also good politics," Murphy's biographer reminds us.)[13] For it was they who, from 1912 onward, carried the ball in the state legislature for social and economic reforms. Chiefly through the FIC it was they who first built bridges between Tammany Hall, on the one hand, and the reform societies and labor leaders, on the other, in the heyday of progressivism. Yet in these early years such an association hardly amounted to a working political coalition; indeed, it remained halting and uncertain while the Democracy waged war against itself and while "Tammanyism" persisted as a dominant issue in the state's politics. Its full development somewhat later depended on a host of factors, not least of which was Republican abandonment of reform, a process that was very much in evidence in the days following Governor Hughes's departure from Albany. In 1912, however, the work of the FIC and the conditions that spawned its creation did help pave the way for the Democratic party in New York to strike a more positive reform posture on social and economic issues than it had two years earlier.

While the Democracy was moving in new legislative directions in

1911–1912, Empire State Republicanism was being pushed more and more toward conservatism. Brutally beaten at the polls in 1910, the progressive wing of the GOP fell into sad disarray—and was leaderless: Stimson would go to Washington as Taft's secretary of war, and Roosevelt announced his "retirement" to Oyster Bay. Only a smattering of old Hughes supporters—in New York City and in some of the interior urban centers—had survived the debacle. What remained almost intact were the old upstate county machines whose leaders were ready and determined to pick up the pieces. With no one else "possessing the requisite qualifications . . . willing to make the requisite sacrifice," noted Elihu Root, William Barnes of Albany claimed the mantle of party leadership, the state chairmanship, in 1911.[14] For the next year and one half this former Platt lieutenant and nemesis of Governor Hughes worked indefatigably to steer the Republican state organization as far away from Theodore Roosevelt and reform as possible.

William Barnes, Jr., was a tough, seasoned politician and a brilliant spokesman for conservative values all during the progressive era. By dint of shrewd maneuvering, organizational talent, and his own newspaper (the *Albany Evening Journal*), this Harvard-educated grandson of Thurlow Weed had built for himself in the 1890s a county machine second to none in efficiency and strength in the upstate. From that time onward he used his organization—and his position—to check the "radical" tendencies of the day. Ideologically, Barnes was close to such contemporaries as Joseph G. Cannon, Nelson W. Aldrich, Murray Crane, and James S. Sherman, whom he considered his allies. Like them, he justified activism in government only in the distributive sense. The state, Barnes argued, should encourage business investment and expansion via the protective tariff and a program of subsidies. For him, as for other upstate conservatives of the Platt mold, this was "the old line," traditional Republican doctrine that "had to be protected." Protected from what? Specifically, Barnes worried about a two-pronged development in America, each the inevitable extension of reformism: one was the change in the nature of government from republicanism, by which he meant representative government, to democracy; the other was the gradual transformation of the economic system from capitalism to socialism. Barnes's greater worry, at least in 1911–1912, was the former perhaps because the latter was less imminent, or perhaps because the first was a necessary condition for the second. Democratizing government—and thus pandering to the masses—constituted the heart of the appeal of America's most dangerous "demagogue," Theodore Roosevelt. More than his trust program or even his stance on social justice, Roosevelt's endorsement of the direct primary; the direct election of U.S. senators; and the initiative, the referendum, and the recall for Barnes made the former president the leader of those forces that threatened "to cast off the Constitution like a worn-out garment."[15]

Barnes's old-line Republicanism, in addition to thwarting Roosevelt, had for its major objective the construction of a truly conservative party in New York State, one that could influence the national organization to fight the upcoming presidential election on "principle." "The issue of next year," he wrote to Elihu Root with regard to 1912, "should be sharply and definitely drawn." To achieve his goal Barnes made several moves following his assumption of the state chairmanship: he used his contacts with "sympathetic" members of the Taft administration, particularly Vice-President Sherman, to enhance the federal patronage at his disposal and thus strengthen his position; he maneuvered to neutralize the progressive wing of the state party, centered in New York City, so that it could not effectively challenge him; and he laid plans to seize control of the 1912 state Republican convention in the spring in order to drive through a traditional platform and send "acceptable" delegates at large to the national convention in Chicago. All through 1911 and into 1912 Barnes and his allies outside New York— Crane, Aldrich, and Cannon—even kept their options open on the GOP presidential nomination. During this period none of them was especially enamored of William Howard Taft, for Taft was pursuing policies in Washington that hardly won their approval. The reciprocity treaty with Canada, announced in early 1911, violated the cherished principle of the protective tariff, and, in particular, Barnes maintained, it threatened competition to New York farmers and lumbermen. And renewal of the antitrust program, later in the year, flew in the face of standpat efforts to generate business support for the Republican ticket in 1912. There were, indeed, rumors that Barnes and his cohorts intended to boom "Sunny Jim" Sherman for the GOP nomination in place of President Taft.[16]

Barnes's dump Taft movement, if it ever was serious, became idle talk with the reemergence of Theodore Roosevelt on the national scene in February 1912. Roosevelt's declaration of his candidacy, which had been hinted for nearly three months, coupled with his controversial speech in Columbus advocating the recall of state judicial decisions rocked the Republican press and politicians alike. Taft suddenly became more palatable to the standpatters, and whatever differences existed within party ranks in New York now diminished considerably. The progressives, who all along had been moderate in national politics, joined the Barnes crowd in condemning the Colonel's attack on "orderly and constitutional government" and his blatant third-term ambitions. The first real indication of the relative strength of the chief Republican contenders came in the state's March primaries, where eighty-three of ninety delegates elected to the Chicago convention were Taftites. Roosevelt's loss was as devastating in "progressive" New York City as it was in the upstate; only in the city's immigrant quarters did the former president make anything resembling a respectable showing. "Not a crumb of comfort was left for the Colonel," declared the *New York Times* jubilantly.[17]

After the March primaries, Republican ranks closed even more. The Rochester state convention, held the next month, turned into a veritable party love feast. Barnes-chosen speakers blasted Roosevelt to the delight of the crowd; a pro-Taft platform was adopted with little dissent except for an occasional angry harangue from disgruntled Roosevelt backers; and the Chicago-bound delegates, though not pledged directly to Taft, received the "recommendation" that they support the president. This last was a concession to Barnes, who insisted that for strategic reasons New York hold back on a full commitment to the White House. However, a string of Roosevelt victories in the late spring primaries dispelled any doubt that the state chairman may still have harbored toward Taft. "No tariff, reciprocity, trust or other problem," Barnes confessed to the president in May, "is of the slightest importance in comparison with the assault upon our government."[18] On the same day the White House announced that William Barnes would serve as Taft's floor manager at the national convention. Thus, three weeks later, the once hesitant Albany stalwart joined Elihu Root, the convention's temporary chairman, in leading the Taft forces in Chicago—and in preventing their fellow New Yorker from obtaining the Republican presidential nomination.

Barnes's critical role in helping Taft defeat Roosevelt in the national convention further tightened his grip on the New York organization. Most regulars, believing as they had earlier, rallied to the administration and the state chairman. Roosevelt's bolt, his formation of the Progressive party in August, and his continued drift leftward, in turn, kept many a Hughes-type reformer in line. State Senator Jonathan M. Wainwright, for example, sympathized with some of "the Roosevelt propaganda" but could not bring himself "to part from the Republican party." Stimson, Parsons, and other New York City progressives, uncomfortable with Barnes's "Bourbonism," nonetheless consoled themselves in the thought that their regularity would prevent the New York party from veering too far to standpattism. Moreover, they believed that, once defeated in November, the GOP would reorganize under their benevolent tutelage. Few Republicans, in fact, felt the party had much of a chance in 1912.[19] Barnes himself remained content to stand on "principle" and even cared little who obtained the gubernatorial nomination so long as the candidate was not a progressive. A gloomy and listless Republican convention, meeting in Saratoga, then, chose a slate of candidates headed by a jocular party wheelhorse named Job Hedges on a platform described by one Democratic newspaper as "a bundle of plausible platitudes and an aggregation of elocutionary evasions." Its only real concessions to the reformers, aside from the usual GOP condemnation of Tammany misrule, were a promise to sponsor a referendum on woman suffrage and a plank favoring workmen's compensation legislation.[20]

Barnes's impressive work in "purifying" New York Republicanism and the reluctance of many a reformer to abandon the "old party" left the Roosevelt rebellion in the Empire State with a mere corporal's guard. As the Progressives' organizational drive gathered momentum in the summer, Bull Moose leader William H. Hotchkiss did boast that the "movement is sweeping the State" and that local committees were being formed all over—in fifty counties, at least.[21] Yet only in New York City and in Buffalo were these organizations more than shadow groups. Here some former Hughes followers disgusted with the "old school politicians" joined a noisy contingent of social reformers and certain ethnic leaders, mostly Germans and Jews, to rally behind the Roosevelt banner.[22] Progressive rhetoric notwithstanding, the New York party also attracted its share of conservatives, including several older Republican leaders disenchanted for one reason or another with the GOP hierarchy, a smattering of businessmen impressed with Roosevelt's views on consolidation, and farmers and other traditionalists convinced that the Colonel was safer on protectionism than President Taft. Not unlike the national movement, the Bull Moose in the Empire State was "a politician's Gothic horror."[23] It enlisted few Democrats, only an occasional labor spokesman, and virtually no newspaper support outside New York City.

Still, the reformers were firmly in the saddle. In September the Progressive state convention in Syracuse—described variously as a "family affair," an "assemblage," and a "spectacular scene"—attested this fact.[24] The platform committee was dominated by settlement workers; students of labor, social, and economic conditions; and experts on public health and education. This group advanced a document embracing the main features of Roosevelt's Chicago platform and adding planks on state issues that New York reformers of every stripe had advocated for years. The keynoter, ex-Hughes champion Frederick M. Davenport, exclaimed that progressivism afforded the only real alternative to socialism. And competition for the gubernatorial nomination pitted two like-minded reformers against one another—William Hotchkiss and William Prendergast—whose only difference was that the one hailed from the upstate and the other from New York City. Resolution of this spirited contest came with the surprise selection of Oscar Straus, well known as a philanthropist, humanitarian, and former cabinet official, to head a strongly reformist slate. ("I think that your nomination," TR wrote to Straus, "stands second only to that of Hiram Johnson as Vice-President.")[25] Most critics of Roosevelt believed, as one observer noted, that the Syracuse convention put the Progressives "in a position of undeniable strength."[26]

In sum, Roosevelt's band of rebels in New York remained just that— able, vocal, but small. At the same time, the Bull Moose embraced enough diversity and yet was sufficiently reformist to make a dent in the state's politics. It could and did play the part of spoiler, and many

Republicans would deeply regret what their own leaders—men such as Barnes and Root—had helped to bring about. "I am nearer a bull moose myself . . . than ever before," complained Stimson amid a campaign that witnessed Barnes's continued antiprogressivism.[27] It was, of course, too late for 1912. A demoralized GOP, retreating to a narrow traditionalism in the Empire State, left the way open for the Democracy, which again showed remarkable resiliency in the face of a fractured opposition.

II

In the meantime, however, the Democrats, too, behaved in their usually factious manner. The party divisions remained what they had been—principally along sectional and cultural lines, with the upstate independents pitted mainly against the dominant New York City machine. But, owing in large part to their own failures the preceding year, the dissidents operated from a weaker position than heretofore. Privately, Thomas Mott Osborne lamented his organization's financial problems, his own vulnerability as a leader, and Governor Dix's mediocre performance in Albany. The league's manifest weaknesses together with the regulars' surprising capacity to adapt to the new expressions of progressivism—Roosevelt's formation of the Bull Moose party and Woodrow Wilson's capture of the national Democratic party in June—would jolt further the independents and scatter them about as a political force by the end of the year. "Even Mr. Murphy is something of a progressive," conceded the anti-Tammany *New York Times* in the wake of the state party's nomination of a reform ticket and the adoption of a progressive platform for the fall elections.[28]

The first signs of what Murphy and Tammany Hall would do came early in the year. In February the boss displayed once again his firm control of the Democratic state organization by naming without serious opposition a new state chairman. But, in selecting George Palmer of Schoharie, Murphy gave some hope to his upstate detractors. Palmer "will remember Hill's struggles to keep the Tammany Tiger caged within the bounds of Manhattan," suggested Conners's *Buffalo Courier* optimistically. Two months later Palmer promised that the Democratic state platform prepared for the party's stance in the upcoming national convention would be "progressive, yet sane." Then in the spring convention in New York City the promise was fulfilled. Major responsibility for writing the document fell to Robert Wagner, who cleared his draft directly with Murphy. As finally approved, the platform pledged "the unfaltering support of the united, militant and progressive Democracy of the State of New York" to "a platform and candidates . . . at Baltimore which will appeal strongly to the enlightened and progressive spirit of the age."²⁹ The convention also selected delegates to the national convention—including Murphy as a delegate at large—and adopted the "unit rule" for voting on all issues at Baltimore. Only this last move caused a stir as some insisted on the right to vote their own consciences in the upcoming convention.

The adoption of the unit rule, in fact, gave Osborne and his followers the excuse to dismiss the New York City proceedings as a "dreadful apathy and debasement of the State Convention." What the Auburn independent feared most was that this device would be used by Tammany to keep New Yorkers from supporting a truly progressive candidate at Baltimore. And for the Democratic rebels the "only really available *Progressive* candidate," by the spring of 1912, was Governor Woodrow Wilson of New Jersey. It was the Wilson presidential movement, observes one historian accurately, that provided the league "its one last hope."³⁰ Everything about the governor appealed to Osborne and Roosevelt. Wilson was no toady to the bosses. True, he had been elected to the state house in Trenton on the strength of New Jersey's Smith machine, but once in office he swiftly repudiated the organization and pursued a moderate reform program. Even Wilson's presidential boom had an air of independence about it—led first by New York City publisher George Harvey, then in the later stages by those "transplanted southerners," Page, McCombs, and McAdoo, also headquartered in Manhattan. (Among prominent organization Democrats in the state only Senator James O'Gorman seemed sympathetic to Wilson.) The movement had garnered the support of antiorganization journals like the *Times,* the *World,* and the *Evening Post.* And although the Wilson campaign was heavily financed by wealthy New Yorkers, Wilson had shrewdly disavowed "Wall Street" interests—Ryan, Belmont, and Morgan—anathema to Bryan's western Democracy and reputed backers of the Tammany machine.³¹

Osborne had actually gotten matters rolling even before the "disappointing" state convention in April. "I am keeping the League headquarters at Albany open," he confessed to McAdoo, so that "the very valuable campaign materials there may later be of use in electing Wilson." Shortly he came up with the idea of a "Wilson Conference," an organization again mainly of upstaters, that would replace the controversial and shattered league. The "call" for the conference would go out under the names of others, including Roosevelt's, as Osborne elected to drift into the background and work behind the scenes. The call condemned the machine-dominated delegation to the Baltimore convention and insisted that Wilson's nomination was "indispensable for Democratic success in New York State." On April 29 the conference opened headquarters in Manhattan with a meeting that drew representatives from every county in the state. There was little about this gathering, however, that differed from so many other get-togethers in the past sponsored by Osborne's old organization. Some of the participants were league members, and typically, the resolutions advanced blasted "Boss" Murphy and the "big business" interests supporting Tammany Hall.[32]

For the next two months the Wilson Conference conducted an ambitious campaign for the governor all through New York State. The chief coordinators were Louis Dunham in Manhattan and Franklin Roosevelt in the upstate. By the end of May, Osborne reported to McAdoo, who kept in close touch with the rebels, that their "survey" had covered half the counties of the state and found Wilson sentiment strong. "We are trying to work without 'disharmonizing' the organization," Osborne added, "but we are not foolish enough to expect we shall get any help from them." Others were less sanguine, however. Franklin Roosevelt, appreciating the enormous task before them, averred cautiously that "we may do some good and can certainly do no harm." One of the conference's advance men, Louis M. Howe, whose main task was to gather petitions to be used in Baltimore to discredit the official delegation, resorted to shrewd and sometimes unsavory tactics for the Wilson cause—but in the end made little headway. To cap the conference work Roosevelt and Osborne planned a big rally on June 24 at Cooper Union. After the meeting a group of 150 "delegates" would travel to Baltimore intending to lobby for Wilson in every way possible. But even this endeavor went awry: no truly influential politicians attended the rally; Wilson personally chastised the independents for "dramatic and dangerous tactics"; and once in Baltimore they were virtually ignored at the expense of the Tammany-led official delegation.[33]

While the independent Democrats were engaged in their quixotic crusade, Charlie Murphy and his Tammany satraps maintained a stony silence, despite conference efforts to draw them into a public row. Rumor had it that the pragmatic boss could support any of several presidential contenders—moderate Ohio Governor Judson Harmon; Congressman Oscar Underwood of Alabama; or Missouri's Champ Clark, Speaker of the House of Representatives. But few doubted that the Osborne people were correct: Murphy could not champion Woodrow Wilson. For, overall, Wilson's friends were his enemies. McCombs had already conceded that to the eastern leaders of the party the New Jersey governor was "austere," "dictatorial," and "unreliable," the kind of politician who, as the bosses saw it, betrayed his friends (as he had in the Garden State). Nor had the Wilson boom managed by Osborne's group been a smashing success in New York. If the conference found it hard to drum up enthusiasm in the upstate, the candidate himself faced a bitter enemy, William Randolph Hearst, in New York City. Surely Hearst's motives were mixed: he had been snubbed by Wilson; he was deeply offended by the former professor's liking for the British parliamentary system; and he had already endorsed the candidacy of Champ Clark. But most of all Hearst doubted Wilson's liberalism. In early 1912 the "knight-errant of the tenements" put his newspapers nationwide to work attacking Wilson's nativistic tendencies, drawing heavily on disparaging comments in *History of the American People* on southern and eastern European immigrant groups. In New York City Polish-, Italian-, and Hungarian-American societies responded by vigorously protesting both Wilson's written word and his possible presidential nomination.[34] For Murphy such negative publicity must have telegraphed Wilson's weaknesses in areas of the city—the Lower East Side, for example—where, as in the recent past, Tammany Hall could least afford defections.

Yet the Wilson movement was not really Charlie Murphy's major concern in the upcoming Baltimore convention. His big worry was

William Jennings Bryan, thrice the Democratic party's standard-bearer and, many felt, a good bet to emerge from a deadlocked convention with the presidential nomination. Such a possibility loomed large after the spring primaries and state conventions: Clark had won a clear majority of the elected delegates; Wilson was second; but neither was in a position to stampede the Baltimore convention. Murphy's fear of—and objection to—Bryan was grounded on sound politics. Not only had "the Commoner" taken the Democracy down to defeat in each of his tries, but, in particular, he had been a disaster in the Northeast, especially in the Empire State. In both 1896 and 1908 he had even lost New York City to the Republicans! "Bryan would be a dead weight on the New York State ticket," explained one Tammanyite with reference to 1912, "and any candidate bearing his endorsement would lose the State." Bryan's earlier views on inflating the currency and later his western-style progressivism simply left eastern voters cold. Murphy's people were "eager to pick the ablest candidate . . . and place him on a progressive platform," argued the pro-Tammany *Buffalo Evening Times*.[35] But that candidate could not be Bryan.

Thoughts like these must have weighed heavily with Murphy when, on convention eve, he launched a stop-Bryan movement. At a national committee meeting chaired by his ally Norman Mack of Buffalo, Murphy joined forces with other organization leaders—Thomas Taggart of Indiana and Roger Sullivan of Illinois—to name Alton B. Parker as temporary chairman of the Baltimore convention. The Democratic presidential nominee in 1904 and symbol par excellence of the eastern wing of the party, Parker was Bryan's deadly enemy. He was also popularly identified with Wall Street interests, and to some New York regulars Murphy's tactics were questionable. Mack's own newspaper strained to describe Parker as "among the foremost progressive Democrats of the day." But if any doubted Murphy's resolve, such doubts were dispelled by a follow-up move: on June 24 the New York delegation voted overwhelmingly in caucus to have Bryan eliminated as a contender at any cost.[36]

The Baltimore convention opened officially on June 25, and there followed several days of unusual excitement and intense drama. "Mr. Murphy," observed one commentator, "is a bigger factor here . . . than any Tammany leader has ever been in a National Convention."[37] It was true and in the early proceedings Bryan made good use of this fact by pitting himself against all that the boss had come to represent—"Tammany," "Wall Street," and the party "reactionaries." Indeed, Bryan remained obsessed throughout with the symbols of politics. He held firm to the position that the present-day national Democracy was little different from the party of the 1890s: it embraced a struggle between his progressive western wing and the conservative eastern establishment directed by the New York "Bourbons." Anything Murphy did, alone or in concert with others, Bryan dismissed as the work of Morgan, Belmont, and Ryan—and in these charges he was usually supported by the anti-Tammany press both within and outside New York State.

On the first day the Commoner marshaled his forces on the convention floor to block Parker for the temporary chairmanship, but he was soundly beaten by a combination of Clark, Harmon, and Underwood men, backed by Murphy, Taggart, and Sullivan. For McCombs this defeat permitted Bryan to don the garb once again of the "Gladiator against Wall Street." It also moved him closer to Wilson, whose allies had shrewdly supported him on the Parker vote. "I know what has happened," Bryan remarked to a Wilson manager. "I am with you."[38] Next day the Bryanites rebounded and won several skirmishes, though not all of them neatly divided the "progressives" and the "conservatives," as Bryan interpreted the struggle. On the platform, for example, the eastern leaders, including Murphy, announced that they would support a "reasonably progressive" document, and they did. But Bryan refused to let up, and on June 27 he dropped his "bombshell." This was a two-part resolution lambasting Morgan, Ryan, and Belmont, "or any other members of the privilege-hunting and favor-seeking class," and demanding the withdrawal of delegates "representing the above-named interests." It was a thinly veiled assault on Murphy and Tammany. Amid jeers, catcalls, and shouts that no one could oust properly elected delegates, Bryan scrapped the second part. The emasculated resolution then passed easily, with Murphy refusing the bait and casting New York's votes in favor of it. "Now Augie," he remarked slyly to Belmont sitting next to him, "listen to yourself vote yourself out of the convention."[39] The boss seemed aware that Bryan's moves were chimerical.

The presidential balloting began on June 29 and dragged on inconclusively for two full days. Several early ballots divided the convention as expected: Clark held the lead; Wilson was second; and Harmon and Underwood remained far behind. Bryan as a Nebraska delegate was pledged to Clark, and New York's 90 votes went to Harmon. That Murphy's support of the Ohio governor was a ruse was known by many, including the Wilson managers. (McAdoo had said as much to Bryan in mid-June.) All signs pointed to a Tammany shift to Clark at the opportune moment. Why Clark? There were perhaps two reasons. First, the Missourian had a long progressive record and yet worked well with the regulars. "His popular strength and his organization favor," volunteered Mack's newspaper, "properly give Clark first call in convention."⁴⁰ Doubtless, Murphy wanted a "reliable" progressive. Second, Hearst was solidly behind Clark. Although some contemporaries suggested that this fact gave Murphy pause, it is more likely that the boss, evidently anxious for party unity in New York City for the 1913 municipal elections, wished to placate the dangerous publisher. Word circulated that Murphy had met earlier with Hearst and representatives of Clark "in a secret Clark conclave." The following day Murphy and Hearst reputedly agreed to stop Wilson. Hard on the heels of these conferences had come the national committee vote for Parker, with Clark's supporters joining Murphy, Taggart, and Sullivan. At the very least, there was a deal between the Clark men and Murphy (that probably also involved Hearst); this was later corroborated by Mack. It was, then, on the tenth ballot that Charlie Murphy "electrified the convention" with his shift to Clark. "Put over Clark quick," he had told Clark's manager that morning. The transfer of New York had been planned in such a way as to give the Missourian a majority of the delegates for the first time. In nearly seventy years no Democratic contender in this position had been denied the required two-thirds vote for the presidential nomination.⁴¹

Murphy's abandonment of Harmon for Clark did not achieve the expected break to the Missourian, as other delegations, particularly Underwood's, stood firm. But it did bring Bryan back into the fray with a vengeance. Infuriated at the boss and the "financiers of Wall Street," Bryan resolved "to prevent not Mr. Clark's nomination only but the nomination of any person by the New York delegation." Three ballots later he joined most of his Nebraska colleagues in betraying

Clark for Wilson. Bryan accompanied his switch with yet another indictment of the Empire State, insisting that the party's nominee, "when
elected, be absolutely free to carry out the anti-Morgan-Ryan-Belmont
resolution" of a few days earlier. Several New Yorkers were beside
themselves with rage over Bryan's most recent tirade. It was left to
John B. Stanchfield, a prominent New York City attorney and erstwhile
Bryan supporter, to answer the Commoner. Pointing to the critical role
that the Empire State traditionally played in electing Democratic pres-
idents, Stanchfield argued that "no one can go forth from this Convention stigmatized and branded with Bryanism, and come within half
a million votes of carrying the State of New York." He concluded
bitterly with the charge that Bryan was a "selfish, money-grabbing,
office-seeking, favor-hunting, publicity-loving marplot," whose real objective was to deadlock the convention and bring the nomination to
himself. Many agreed (Wilson's people included), for it was patently
obvious to observers that Bryan's shift to the New Jersey governor had
less to do with Wilson's merits than that Clark was being championed
by the party "reactionaries."[42]

On June 30 a series of conferences and strategy sessions took place,
with each contender searching for deals and combinations. For his part,
Murphy tried but failed to win delegates away from Wilson in favor of
a compromise candidate; Wilson was now too close to Bryan for the
boss' comfort. These efforts, in turn, brought the full wrath of the anti-
Tammany press upon Murphy. "Ryan and Murphy," proclaimed the
New York World, "have made Wilson's nomination the crucial test of
the Democratic party's fitness to live." The balloting resumed on July 1
and spilled over to the next day. Gradually the convention drifted to
Woodrow Wilson. The most dramatic shifts from Clark were those of
Indiana and Illinois, bossed by Murphy allies Taggart and Sullivan,
respectively. Taggart's switch brought Thomas Marshall the vice-pres-
idential nomination, but Sullivan's has never been adequately explained.
There is some evidence, too, that Murphy himself was prepared to go
over to Wilson in an apparent gesture of conciliation. "You are doing
the right thing, Roger," he allegedly told Sullivan at the moment Illinois'
votes were cast for Wilson. "New York would go to Wilson," Murphy
went on to explain, "if our support on account of the attitude of Bryan
might not hurt him more than it would help him." On the forty-sixth

87

ballot Underwood withdrew, Clark's delegates were released, and Wilson captured two thirds of the convention. "Make your speech as conciliatory as you possibly can," Murphy instructed Congressman John J. Fitzgerald, as New York State's 90 votes were finally thrown to the New Jersey governor.[43]

Charlie Murphy had gambled at Baltimore and lost: Woodrow Wilson was the Democratic presidential nominee, and William Jennings Bryan appeared to be his major domo. That Wilson had depended for his victory as much on the bosses—Taggart and Sullivan—as on the reformers, and that Murphy had only been searching for an acceptable progressive escaped the antiorganization press and politicians in the Empire State. Murphy's image was further blackened and the postmortem on Baltimore was bitter. Typically, the *Auburn Citizen* charged that Tammany wanted "to nominate either a reactionary candidate or a weak candidate." Murphy harbored "stupid and foolish ends," added Antisdale's *Rochester Herald*. Most critical—and most persistent of all—was Pulitzer's *World*. "Get rid of Murphy now," urged that journal in one of a barrage of editorials that would pillory Tammany Hall in the summer and fall of 1912.[44] The boss was even robbed of what little satisfaction he might have enjoyed for helping to knock off Bryan, anathema to scores of progressives as well as conservatives in New York State.[45]

Not surprisingly, Wilson's nomination and the press attacks on Murphy stirred the state's independent Democrats into action once again. On the chance that Tammany would do next to nothing for the national ticket, or might even "cut" Wilson and Marshall, the Osborne people redoubled their efforts in the summer. They quickly converted the Wilson Conference into the Empire State Democracy, "a younger and healthier body," Osborne believed. In several meetings and in an ensuing propaganda campaign, the new organization merely tailored the rhetoric of the old league to present-day exigencies. It assailed Murphy as an "Eminent Reactionary Republican" supported by "Thomas Fortune Ryan and the men of that class" (taking a leaf from Bryan's book), called for the election of delegates to the state party convention who were not "men of wax" (again using a Bryan phrase), and demanded that Dix be dumped as governor in favor of a truly progressive candidate on a legitimate reformist platform. Should the regulars remain

88

unmoved by the state Democracy's thrust, Osborne threatened that he would seek fusion with the newly forming Progressive party on a state-wide basis.[46]

But the noisy Osborne-Roosevelt contingent achieved little more success after the Baltimore convention than beforehand. Many a Democrat to whom their organization appealed questioned the wisdom of such a movement once an independent headed the national ticket. Nor did the Empire State Democracy, like its predecessor, catch on in New York City, where Murphy reigned supreme. Even in the upstate Osborne's forces faced competition from at least four other splinter groups, some carryovers from 1910, others newly organized that year. One of them, the Progressive Democrats of New York, was infested with supporters of East Side Congressman William Sulzer, an independent Tammanyite and a leading contender for the party's gubernatorial nomination. Another, the Rochester Conference, boasted a strong contingent of regulars led by anti-Murphy members of the state committee. In an obvious slight to Osborne this group resolved that it would not bolt the party. Attempts to unite these several organizations failed, and each went its own way—thus further weakening the battle against Tammany Hall. "The Democratic situation throughout the State [is] deplorable," Osborne admitted in September. Osborne and Roosevelt then salvaged what they could. After the Auburn rebel was named a delegate to the Syracuse state convention and the Empire State Democracy defiantly chose a ticket of its own, he resigned from the organization. "I [must] keep 'regular' as long as I can," he told a compatriot. Himself renominated for the senate and now challenged by two opponents in his Columbia-Dutchess-Putnam district, Roosevelt, too, came to appreciate "regularity" and also abandoned independence.[47] The Empire State Democracy, having lost its principal leaders, limped along the remainder of the year.

In any case, the independents' course, from the outset, had been guided by certain illusions: that Murphy and the regulars at best would pay lip service to the national ticket and that they enjoyed a special relationship with the Wilson managers. Both were farfetched. "No matter what injustices it may suffer at the hands of foes within the party," the *Tammany Times* assured skeptics after the Baltimore convention, "Tammany never forgets the great cause of the Democracy."[48]

Other public statements from organization spokesmen were followed during the summer by private assurances given to various Wilson people and to the candidate directly. Little doubt remained that the Hall would not cut the national ticket in November. William Randolph Hearst, too, pledged his support, though when the time came, Hearst contributed little to the Wilson-Marshall cause. For their part the Wilsonites, while listening sympathetically to the rebels' complaints, made gestures—even concessions—to the regulars, just as they had done in Baltimore. Wilson named Senator O'Gorman, one of his few Tammany friends, to his "verandah cabinet." In a more substantial vein, Wilson personally issued a statement, in early August, making clear that: "We are not intervening in the local situation in any State."[49] This disavowal, with apparent reference to New York, meant that Wilson and Tammany were working toward a quid pro quo.

The "delicate balance" was nearly ruptured, however, as the Democratic state convention approached in the fall. The Progressives' nomination of Straus, the new party's seriousness about reform, and Theodore Roosevelt's slashing attacks against bossism put the Democracy on its "mettle." Wilson was now constrained to edge away, at least publicly, from Murphy and Tammany Hall. At the state fair in Syracuse in early September the candidate snubbed the boss, who was also in attendance, and later the same month called for an "open convention" in that city. (The press, as usual, applauded Wilson's "courageous" stand.) In the context of New York politics the term meant simply the dumping of Governor Dix, the reformers' symbol of "Tammanyized" government. Amid this intensified campaign against him, Murphy, characteristically, said and did little. While listening to complaints from both regulars and independents concerning the governor's vulnerability across the state, the Tammany leader made infrequent statements affirming his personal "support" of Dix—doubtless, some ventured to guess, out of a deep sense of obligation.[50] Yet behind the scenes Murphy was cautiously pursuing another course. His lieutenants had already informed the Democratic National Committee that Tammany would go along with anyone acceptable to Wilson. A boom quickly developed for McAdoo, but McAdoo's duties as Wilson's campaign manager compelled him to remove his name from consideration. Two weeks after McAdoo's withdrawal, Colonel House recorded in his diary that he was hoping to find "some unobjectionable Tammany man for Governor." That "unobjectionable" person turned out to be William Sulzer—and there is some evidence that the Wilson forces played a role in the congressman's nomination.[51]

The Syracuse Democratic state convention, meeting in early October, was a charade, albeit a necessary one in light of the exigencies of 1912. Murphy's course of action in the opening stages became the subject of repeated speculation, and the anti-Tammany press joined the independents in applying pressure against Dix's renomination. But, by this time, the matter of the governor's future was for Murphy a smokescreen. The boss still spoke kindly of John Dix, yet confessed "an open mind" on other candidates. Actually, Murphy was now paving the way for William Sulzer, who seemed to satisfy everyone's needs—most independents, the Wilson crowd, and even some Tammanyites who saw the East Side congressman as a convenient vehicle for neutralizing Straus among eastern European voters. The boss, so the reports went, had told Sulzer's friends on convention eve that he could expect the gubernatorial nomination. Conference after conference he had with state and local leaders in Syracuse left the impression of Wilson's "open convention." Indeed, Murphy played the game right to the end with a long list of names of men who were "very much" in the running. "When I have this list complete," the Tammany leader said at one point with respect to the contenders, "I will be able to tell . . . whether it would be better to place some other man [than Dix] in the field."[52] Four ballots were needed to express the "will" of the convention. On the first roll call Dix appeared to be a serious candidate, but his vote total on the next two roll calls declined and Sulzer edged ahead. To clinch the convention's "openness," Murphy himself refrained from casting a ballot and ordered his New York County delegation to spread votes among several contenders. On the fourth ballot Tammany ally "Packy" McCabe of Albany signaled the convention by throwing his support to Sulzer. Fitzpatrick of Erie followed suit, and the gubernatorial nomination was decided. The rest of the ticket was named, and a platform, "more progressive than the Republican or the Bull Moose one" (declared the *Times* with only slight overstatement), was easily adopted. Hitting all the major issues—political, economic, and social— the 1912 Democratic platform, in fact, was the most advanced reform document that the party had offered in recent times in the Empire State.[53]

The vast majority of Democrats both in and out of New York were pleased with the results of the Syracuse convention. Even the anti-Tammany press, some of which surely must have known better, complimented Charlie Murphy on the "unbossed" proceedings. "It is simple elemental justice to commend and to heartily congratulate Mr. Murphy upon the fine spirit manifested in withdrawing his heavy hand," commented Hearst's *New York American*. Hearst dispatched a personal message of support to Martin H. Glynn, Sulzer's lieutenant-gubernatorial running mate. The Sulzer nomination, especially, generated warm responses. "He is fearless, independent, and honest," chirped a prominent member of the Empire State Democracy. Osborne's former group quickly withdrew its own slate, believing that Sulzer "was the clear choice of the majority." The other independent organizations added their endorsements. Organized labor praised the Democrats for their ticket and their platform; and the Wilsonites, through McAdoo, noted that Sulzer "in every way measures up to the standards which the Progressive Democracy demands of its candidates."[54]

A few disagreed with the encomiums showered on the Democratic party managers in Syracuse. Thomas Mott Osborne was a case in point. Having fought bitterly with Robert Wagner in the convention on the issue of Tammany's "progressivism," Osborne charged that "the freedom of the delegates was mere stage-play"; the Wilson people had betrayed their real friends; and Sulzer was "a poseur, a constant player to the galleries—in short, a demagogue." It would be easy to dismiss out of hand such complaints as reflecting nothing more than the frustrations of a longtime Tammany critic who had been totally outmaneuvered and whose independence had come to naught in the wake of Charlie Murphy's brilliant pragmatism. (Wagner even insisted that Osborne was "sore" because his own political ambitions had been thwarted.) But some of what Osborne said was true, and his harsh characterization of Sulzer was hardly inaccurate as one looks ahead to the next year. Even some Tammanyites were unhappy with Murphy's accommodation on the governorship. "He doesn't amount to anything. I'm surprised at you," remarked Tim Sullivan to Murphy about

Sulzer.[55] But Murphy, of course, had bowed to the needs of 1912. He had thus satisfied most of the upstate independents as well as the Wilsonites—a remarkable feat after the bitterness of the Baltimore convention.

III

In a year filled with political turmoil and confusion, the 1912 campaign in New York State was anticlimactic. From beginning to end, the Republicans behaved as if they could not win, and the Progressives viewed it as more an educational endeavor than a political contest. "The issues were greater than the parties," declared one Bull Mooser years later. Taft stayed in the White House, and Roosevelt left much of the work to Straus. Among the presidential contenders Wilson was the most energetic, for, as his biographer tells us, he was determined to put New York in the Democratic electoral column. He thus made several appearances in the state, opening the national campaign in Buffalo on Labor Day and closing it in New York City with the traditional Democratic rally in Madison Square Garden. Wilson's speeches attacked Roosevelt for the Colonel's concept of legalized monopoly and blamed "unregulated capitalism" for the trust problem; blasted the Progressive platform for its "paternalism" but conceded that the Bull Moose interest in social justice and the common man was laudable; and on at least one occasion in New York City appealed to ethnic Americans. Here he called for a standard of immigration that would admit "every voluntary immigrant" but would exclude those who "have been induced by steamship companies or others to come in order to get passage money." Designed to meet the charge that Wilson favored restriction, this overture was but one part of the governor's campaign to improve relations with ethnic voters, especially new-stock groups, and to offset obvious weaknesses with foreign-born Americans.[56]

The gubernatorial contest was livelier than the presidential campaign, albeit Republican Job Hedges was less serious than Oscar Straus and William Sulzer. Hedges toured the state politely criticizing Roosevelt and Wilson in a joking, folksy manner, and even occasionally assailed Sulzer's "Tammanyism." He explained that he intended "to spend no time on the bosses as I will be busy being Governor." On the issues the main battle was waged between Straus and Sulzer. Straus fashioned himself after Hughes as a "nonprofessional politician" free from the shackles of party machines. He hit "bossism" hard and condemned the "bossed" nature of both major parties. Yet he also appealed passionately for social justice—the key to the Progressive platform, he felt. Popular control of government, Straus told a supporter, meant that "the people will use the instrument of their government to realize the demands of social and industrial justice." The candidate's special emphasis on this issue was clinched with the appointment of Henry Moskowitz, a leading settlement house spokesman, as his campaign manager. For his part, Sulzer ably defended the charge that he was a tool of the machine. "I am my own master," he declared proudly to newspaper reporters. "If I am elected Governor," added Sulzer, "I pledge the people that I will be the Governor." All across the Empire State he promised an honest, efficient, businesslike administration, and like Straus stressed his party's specific proposals on social reform.[57]

On Election Day, November 5, over 1.5 million New Yorkers went to the polls, this being a larger turnout than two years earlier, below that in 1908, and several percentage points under the relatively high average of the combined presidential and gubernatorial contests in 1896, 1900, and 1904. As expected, the Republican-Progressive split put the state firmly in the Democratic column in the national, statewide, congressional, and legislative races for the first time in twenty years. Woodrow Wilson and William Sulzer swept New York City with big pluralities over William Howard Taft and Job Hedges, and smaller ones over Theodore Roosevelt and Oscar Straus. Perhaps surprisingly, in light of Wilson's anticipated weakness in the cities, the two Democrats ran about equally well against the opposition in Greater New York, with the New Jersey governor doing slightly better against Roosevelt than Sulzer did against Straus. Typically, the Republicans made their best showing in the less populous regions of the upstate—strong enough, in fact, to finish second in the presidential and gubernatorial contests. But proportionately low voter participation together with defections to the Bull Moose gave the Democrats two dozen counties outside New York City. And the Republican tally in the upstate was only 35.6 percent, a drop of 20 points from Taft's totals in 1908 and 13.6 percent worse than Stimson's disastrous performance in 1910.[58]

The Republican decline was particularly critical in the state's larger cities, where reform sentiment was acknowledged to be powerful. In New York City and Buffalo the GOP actually wound up a distant third. Rochester, Syracuse, and Utica all went Democratic, with the Progressive vote ranging from approximately 30 percent to 23 percent. It should be remembered that in none of the interior urban centers, except Buffalo, did Roosevelt's party boast an effective organization or more than a modicum of newspaper support. Bull Moose successes in the four major upstate cities came in numerous districts having a high percentage of native-born voters usually of GOP persuasion. But there was also a solid Progressive vote in working-class, heavily ethnic wards, some of which had been Republican, others Democratic, in the recent past. (The exceptions were areas of Irish concentration, which remained steadfastly Democratic across the state.) Thus, Buffalo's German wards recorded an impressive Roosevelt-Straus vote. Also in Buffalo two recently created Italian wards, both falling to Wilson and Sulzer, gave the Progressives much support, as did the Queen City's Polish districts. Rochester's Jewish and German areas, too, yielded a sizable Bull Moose vote.[59] What losses the Democrats sustained generally in the upstate cities in no sense matched those suffered by the Republicans where comparisons can be made with the 1908 and 1910 elections.

By far the most dramatic feature of the 1912 elections in New York State took place in New York City, where the three-way contest seemed to spark considerable voter interest. While the level of participation in traditional Republican country rose only slightly above that two years earlier, the turnout in the city jumped some 13 percent over 1910. Both the Democrats and the Progressives waged vigorous campaigns here, while the demoralized Republicans expended only token efforts. "Frankly, the enrolled voters wanted Roosevelt," confessed Samuel Koenig, chairman of the New York County Republican Committee. Election statistics confirmed this judgment, as the Taft-Hedges team averaged only 119,106 votes, or just about 18 percent of all the ballots cast in the city. Four years earlier Taft had defeated Bryan in New York City by piling up over 300,000 votes. The Republicans experienced huge losses everywhere in Greater New York—in the native American "silk-stocking" districts of Manhattan, where they were beaten in three assembly races; in twenty-three of twenty-four congressional districts, winning only one, in Kings; and in all the remaining state legislative districts, both senate and assembly. In a nutshell, the GOP lost everything it had regained in 1911 and for the moment was relegated to the status of a minor party in New York City. "This is a crisis in the affairs of the party," remarked a saddened Hedges worker shortly after the Republican debacle in Greater New York.[60]

Best symbolizing the political upheaval of 1912 were the results in New York City's predominantly foreign districts. The Democrats, as usual, carried the Irish and Italian areas, but there was some slippage here, especially on Wilson's part, to the fledgling Roosevelt party. In almost all instances, the combined Progressive-Socialist vote exceeded Republican totals. In one Italian district the Progressives-Socialists averaged 40 percent of the aggregate. The Democrats also made a characteristically good showing in the German districts, again with Sulzer usually outpolling Wilson. However, the Bull Moose and the Socialist vote was high in these sections as well, while the Republican count seldom surpassed the GOP mean for the entire city. It was in the Jewish quarters—those in the Lower East Side that had long been giving Murphy trouble, in the Bronx, and in Brooklyn—that the Democrats and Progressives really squared off against each other and left the Republicans cold in their tracks. Of special note is that these districts were the only heavily foreign ones that witnessed a substantial increase in voter turnout in 1912. The principal reasons for this upsurge may have been the Jews' identification with Straus together with the popularity of Sulzer, the presence of social reform as a major theme in the politics of the day, and the growing disenchantment of these peoples with the higher cost of living. While, to be sure, the Democrats outdistanced the Bull Moosers in seven of thirteen Jewish districts in the gubernatorial race and nine in the presidential contest, the drop in Democratic totals highlighted that party's persistent weakness in these areas. In fact, Roosevelt and Straus enjoyed remarkable success throughout Jewish New York. Furthermore, the Progressives won three assembly seats and one senate seat in Jewish districts evidently by attracting their share of new voters and by cutting into Democratic, Republican, and Socialist margins.[61]

Indeed, much of the Bull Moose penetration in Greater New York came at the expense of the Socialists who, with their total performance in the city slumping from the level of 1910, bitterly denounced Roosevelt as "a thief" and a "political highwayman" for stealing their thunder.[62] The party suffered losses on the Lower East Side in all four assembly districts in the gubernatorial contest and three of four in the presidential election. Straus's pull was equally strong in other sections of Jewish concentration in Manhattan and in Brooklyn. Finally, the two Bronx districts that, by virtue of the Socialist vote, had fallen to the Republicans one year earlier, went Democratic in 1912: in each case the Progressives finished a respectable second, and the Socialist aggregate declined sizably in the gubernatorial race. Only in the twelfth congressional district, comprising the four assembly districts on the Lower East Side, did the Socialists fulfill their expectations in 1912. Here the popular Meyer London nearly defeated Henry Goldfogle, the Tammany Democratic incumbent, and outpolled Bull Mooser Henry Moskowitz in a spirited campaign that saw London bid strongly for the support of Jewish garment workers. (The *Call* charged that London was beaten by Tammany "fraud, theft, intimidation and browbeating.") One Socialist report summed up the party's troubles by concluding that the "comrades" were defeated by a "radical Progressive Party."[63]

IV

The "radical Progressive Party" represented the logical culmination of the politics of alienation and disillusionment that had gripped the Empire State over the past few years. Although the Bull Moose had quickly burst on the scene in the summer of 1912 and drew the support of only a coterie of New York's prominent politicos, in just a few short months it emerged as an effective tool of protest in the state, far more potent than either William Randolph Hearst's Independence League earlier or the Socialists now or later. One measure of the depth of voter disenchantment across the state, in addition to the fact that large numbers of eligible citizens, in 1912, decided not to vote at all, is that approximately three of ten New Yorkers who went to the polls cast ballots for Progressives or Socialists, that is, against the two major parties, or, put more positively, in favor of some alternative to an almost antiquated Republicanism, on the one hand, and a somewhat rejuvenated but still tainted Democracy, on the other. Of course, the Republicans were the big losers in New York State in this year of turmoil. For the once mighty GOP, the election of 1912 was 1910 writ large: continued Republican slippage in the upstate, especially in the critically important cities, as well as in Greater New York, that gave the Democrats electoral pluralities in both regions for the first time in many years. Momentarily, at least, interparty sectional divisions that traditionally characterized the state's politics were disrupted.

But the triumphant Democrats, too, had to be wary about the politics of 1912. While the party victory was impressive in terms of the number of offices won and the rich patronage flowing from them, the leadership could hardly escape the fact that the win had come largely by default. What would happen if and when the Republicans healed over their wounds and reunified? While, moreover, it was probably true that Democratic progressivism, as manifested in Wilson's capture of the national party and Tammany's continued pragmatism in the state, helped stem the Bull Moose tide in the cities, the Democrats also lost supporters here to Roosevelt's forces. What had to be especially troublesome was the Progressive penetration of new-stock ethnic areas. Where would these voters go if politics were normalized? There was virtually nothing in the pattern of recent elections pointing to consistent Democratic gains that foreshadowed permanent changes in the way New Yorkers voted. And all the efforts of Charlie Murphy and the other leaders notwithstanding, the Democrats, in the fall of 1912, ironically faced political conditions not unlike those prevailing at the time of John Dix's election two years earlier: a tenuous and fragile party harmony that could easily be disrupted (even though the independents had taken another drubbing); a leader of unknown quantity in Albany's executive mansion; and a lingering anti-Tammanyism throughout the state. "The net result of the grand efforts of the Bull Moose party," editorialized one newspaper just after the election, "is to fasten on the state the worst political organization that is known to civilized man."[64] Such a harsh judgment was a haunting reminder that beneath the surface excitement of a presidential-gubernatorial election, where "Tammanyism" had been subordinated to the larger reform issues, lurked the same sentiment that in the Dix years made governing a monumental task for the Democracy in New York.

5

William Sulzer and
the Politics of Excess

Whatever the reasons for their sweeping victory in 1912 in New York State, many Democrats interpreted the election as a triumph for the middle way: in program and outlook Woodrow Wilson as president-elect and William Sulzer, the state's new governor, fell somewhere between Theodore Roosevelt's "radical" New Nationalism and William Barnes's conservatism. "The result," commented Tammany boss Charlie Murphy, "demonstrates most clearly that the reforms and changes which the people demand must be made without endangering the fundamental institutions of the country."[1] Nor apparently were most Democrats, regulars and independents alike, disappointed with Wilson's New Freedom of the next few years—embracing a lower tariff, banking legislation, trust regulation, and social and labor reform (even though, observe some historians, the Washington administration moved leftward and captured the New Nationalism).[2] Indeed, Wilson's successes spread hope among Democrats in New York, as elsewhere, that a new political coalition of farmers, laborers, small businessmen, and social reformers would spell future election victories for the party. On the state level, too, reform was advanced in several particulars, as regular Democrats, bowing even more to the spirit of the day, now commonly referred to themselves as "progressives" and behaved accordingly on most questions. And fulfillment of the major promises of the 1912 Syracuse platform gave the New York Democracy a legitimate claim to the reform heritage left by the near-defunct Bull Moose.

Nonetheless, the main theme of the state's politics in the Sulzer-

Glynn era would not be the realization of the progressive program or the remarkable way that Democratic regulars adapted machine rule to reform ends. Rather, it revolved about the narrow issue of antibossism, directed particularly at Murphy's Tammany Hall, and the hopeful New York Democrats would suffer in defeat, not revel in victory. The root cause of the trouble was the eruption once again of a bitter struggle in the Democracy played out against the party's long-standing divisions and the intensity with which the reform press agitated those differences. This time the two principals involved were: first, Charlie Murphy himself, who doubtless failed to do enough to alter Tammany's reputation as a spoils-grabbing, unresponsive machine, and more importantly, whose followers wielded naked power inimical to the very image that the organization was seeking to convey to a skeptical public; and second, the new governor, William Sulzer. A product of the peculiar conditions of 1912, yet not quite trusted by either the independents or Tammany, the erratic Sulzer conducted his office in such a fashion as to shake the state Democracy to its foundations and help perpetrate one of the most bizarre episodes in New York's history—his own impeachment and removal from office. Sulzer's downfall is a fascinating tale of misguided political leadership, unrestrained opportunism, and gross miscalculation.

The ensuing Democratic fiasco in the Empire State was not without certain ironies. Two of Tammany's most dedicated antagonists—Thomas Mott Osborne and Franklin D. Roosevelt—benefited little from the party rupture and the reinvigorated opposition to Murphy's domination of state government. Lacking the "physical and mental vitality" to keep up the good fight, Osborne in early 1913 bowed out of politics and fell to pleading for patronage for his close friends and allies. He would then reactivate himself briefly to defend the embattled Sulzer, whom he never liked, and finally plunge into a career of penal reform. Osborne's erstwhile organization, the Empire State Democracy, foundered in a sea of financial troubles and lapsed into a "purely local" club. Roosevelt, to be sure, was rewarded by the Wilson administration with an appointment as assistant secretary of the navy for his stellar work on behalf of the Wilson Conference in 1912 and went to Washington hoping to play a key role in "reconstructing" the New York Democracy free of bossism.[3] But the task proved to be no easy one, and his efforts were stymied by those of other, more prominent Wilsonians equally determined to cleanse the state of machine rule. These anti-Tammanyites, only lukewarmly supporting Sulzer and often working at cross-purposes with each other, yet managed some successes, most notably in the elections of 1913. In the end, however, no cohesive group emerged on the state scene to supplant the Osborne-Roosevelt organization and thus exploit fully the spirit of independence and protest that appeared to sweep through the electorate now as never before in the progressive era. The Democrats, then, limped along, far more vulnerable than they had been in the days of the unfortunate John Dix.

I

William Sulzer liked to be called "Plain Bill," a "man of the people." Born in Elizabeth, New Jersey, in 1863, of German and Scotch-Irish parents, Sulzer moved with his family to New York City's Lower East Side while still a boy. He early developed into a brilliant speaker and debater, studied law, and entered politics as a young man. Known as "Reilly's boy spellbinder"—an appelation given to him as a protégé of John Reilly, Tammany boss of the old fourteenth district—Sulzer was elected to the state assembly in 1889 in what was then a predominantly German and Irish district. An impressive performance in Albany won for him the lofty position of speaker four years later, the youngest man ever to lead that body. In 1894 he was moved up to Congress from the city's tenth district, whose ethnic base was rapidly becoming eastern European. For nine consecutive terms, Sulzer served well his lower-class constituency, identifying himself repeatedly with progressive legislation—the measures creating the bureau of corporations and an independent department of labor; the proposed amendments on the direct election of U.S. senators and the income tax; conservation bills; and bills to establish the parcel post, the eight-hour day for federal employees, and methods by which campaign contributions were to be publicized. In 1910 he became chairman of the House Foreign Relations Committee, where he further ingratiated himself with his Jewish constituency by championing the abrogation of the 1832 treaty with Russia for that nation's refusal to honor American passports held by

Jews. "He's regarded as a great man," admitted Charlie Murphy. "He's just done this for the Jews."⁴ Sulzer remained in Congress until his election to the governorship in 1912.

Sulzer's career was a blend of "regularity" and "independence"—a fact that was recognized by his peers and in the press. Ambition and preferment seemed to dictate which quality predominated. Not surprisingly, however, his later years saw him less subservient to the Tammany organization than his early years. Once possessed of a secure hold on his East Side district, Sulzer pressed the Tammany leadership harder and harder for higher office. In almost every state convention from the mid-1890s onward, he made a bid for the Democratic gubernatorial nomination. Repeatedly he was rebuffed, first by Croker, then by Murphy. In 1906 and thereafter the hallmark of Sulzer's candidacy was his appeal as a regular to the independent movement upstate, in part because of his disenchantment with Tammany, and in part because of the movement's gathering strength. (He also commanded much support within the ranks of organized labor, whose programs he championed in Congress.) By 1910 his upstate coordinator, *Batavia Times* publisher Chester C. Platt, almost won for him the backing of Lustgarten's Progressive Democrats, a rival group to Osborne's league. And when in the Rochester convention of that summer he was again turned down, he and his followers were bitter. Yet subsequently Sulzer rejected an overture from Hearst's Independence League, then in search of a gubernatorial candidate of its own. "Of course, I am a Democrat," he protested to Platt, "and my place is in the ranks fighting for reform and progressive legislation." During the period 1906–1912, Sulzer, in fact, kept up his contacts with Tammany, not so much directly with Charlie Murphy, but mainly with mutual friends who acted as intermediaries. He received the warm endorsement of the *Tammany Times* in each of his bids for the governorship from 1906 to 1910.⁵

Sulzer might be forgiven his "opportunism"—and many politicians did so in 1912—but certain of his qualities made him continually suspect and untrusting. A lack of substance was his most glaring weakness, for it made him vain and boastful. Sulzer "has lived all his life in a struggle for appearances," complained one critic, while another, less charitably, dismissed him as "just a singularly stupid man." (Thomas Mott Osborne, as already noted, called "Plain Bill" a "fake.") Sulzer's inflated rhetoric, which he often employed to defend republican institutions or to rail against his opponents, lent credence to these charges. He "was practically all wind," commented the reformer Robert Binkerd, who added: "He had almost no knowledge or ability and little character." Sulzer's physical demeanor and dress only heightened the ridicule heaped on him, and some newspapermen questioned his seriousness as a public figure. Looking very much like Henry Clay, he cultivated this resemblance by carefully grooming a forelock that hung over his eyes; and he dressed always in attire properly chosen to enhance his image as a tribune of the people. "Would either Hughes or Tilden or Wright walk to the executive chamber with a cigar in his mouth, a slouch hat, gray clothes and with a joking rabble?" queried the progressive *New York Evening Mail*. Sulzer's affectations so camouflaged his being that he remained a mystery to many. "William Sulzer, the man," recorded one writer, "is hard to reach. To get at the real Sulzer you have to wade through, not a man of red tape or ceremony or a retinue of lackeys, but an exasperating bag of bombast and 'hifalutin' oratory, best summed up in the effective slang word 'bunk.' "[6]

Amid such disquietude, Sulzer launched his reform administration in early 1913. From the beginning the governor mixed the histrionic with the serious. He renamed the executive mansion the "People's House" as a symbol of the openness of the new regime. In Jeffersonian simplicity he made his way to the capitol in Albany on a cold New Year's Day and delivered his inaugural address. "No influence controls me but the dictates of my conscience and the determination to do my duty," Sulzer assured a noisy, boisterous throng. Promising "progressive reforms along constructive and constitutional lines" in the same speech, he went on the next day to spell out the details in his first message to the legislature. He enthusiastically proposed ratification of the amendment calling for the direct election of U.S. senators; urged direct primaries, woman suffrage, extension of the civil service, and conservation legislation; and appealed for a program of social and labor reform, including the recommendations of the FIC, workmen's compensation, and the minimum wage. Capturing most attention, however, was Sulzer's strongly worded statement accompanying his request for an inquiry into all departments of the executive branch. "I am the democratic leader of the State of New York," he told reporters loftily. "If any democrat wants to challenge that leadership, let him come out in the open and the people will decide," he added in what was widely regarded as an affront to Charlie Murphy. President-elect Woodrow Wilson was sufficiently impressed to dispatch a congratulatory message to Sulzer. But when the rumor spread that Murphy was angered by the statement, Sulzer was quick to point out that he was not "mixing up in factional politics" and that "Mr. Murphy, the leader of Tammany Hall, and Mr. Osborne, representing the hostile faction, will both be welcome to see me."[7]

In truth Sulzer, the theatrics aside, did seem inclined at first to "get along" with all Democrats. His initial appointments were hardly unsatisfactory to Tammany, and he treated "the hostile factions" cordially. "I would be glad to see Brother Osborne at any time," he told the Auburn independent through his secretary in January.[8] Not always, however, was the new governor successful on his own in walking the tightrope. On one occasion he leaned on a personal friend, a Tammany contact, who helped him handle a "critical situation in such a way that will leave you in good position with the Organization and with all your other friends." Even Sulzer's much-hailed scheme to investigate the executive branch began on an essentially partisan note. During the campaign he had called for clean, efficient, and honest government—a theme that was interpreted by some as an attack on the Tammany-dominated Dix regime. But the Democratic leadership in the 1913 legislature faithfully endorsed his plan to "clean house." Majority leader Robert Wagner, indeed, assumed responsibility for steering the graft resolution through the senate, threatening protesting GOP legislators that the inquiry would go "many years back into the Republican administrations to see if there are not useless offices, created by the Republicans."[9] Any lingering doubt among Tammanyites that Sulzer was launching a carefully veiled attack on them was dispelled when the commission of three contained two of Murphy's allies and only one independent, John N. Carlisle of Watertown.

As one would expect, in its early days the graft inquiry unearthed little evidence of significant wrongdoing and corruption. In scrutinizing the executive departments the commissioners were cautious with officeholders commanding Tammany support, and in cutting away patronage they concentrated on Republicans. Some irregularities were discovered in the office of adjutant general, a Democrat, and steps were taken immediately to correct the situation. Hard on the heels of this action the commission, now strengthened by the vigorous John A. Hennessy as executive auditor, began looking into charges of excess profits made by contractors in the reconstruction of the state capitol following the devastating fire of 1911. Sulzer fueled speculation that at last the probe was hitting pay dirt. "If people knew what I know about some of the things that have been going on for years, they would stand aghast," he exclaimed as the inquiry was getting under way. The investigation did show a number of irregularities in the state architect's office and charged the architect, Herman Hoefer, with incompetence. Subsequently Hoefer, an organization Democrat, resigned his office under threat of gubernatorial removal.[10] But even here little fanfare accompanied the "revelations" of the commission.

As the graft inquiry continued, Sulzer displayed signs of growing irritation and impatience with the slowness of the proceedings. A case in point was his handling of the commission's investigation of the highway department, which had long been suspected of certain "irregularities." Based only on the charge that the department was guilty of waste, corruption, and political preference in the construction and repair of roads, the governor summarily dismissed its Democratic superintendent, C. Gordon Reel. Lacking a report from the commission, he insisted that the removal was made "in the interest of the public service." Reel tried valiantly to defend himself but to no avail. Sulzer would later concede that the firing had been based on incompetency, not on participation in graft and corruption.[11]

Even more questionable was the way that Sulzer used the graft commission to deal with the state prison department, especially its superintendent, Joseph F. Scott, a noted penologist and also a Democratic carryover from the Dix years. The trouble began in January when the governor asked Scott to name Charles F. Rattigan warden of Auburn Prison. Scott refused on the ground that the incumbent, a Republican, was an able man and that the push for Rattigan, one of Osborne's cronies, was politically motivated. (Presumably this appointment was Osborne's payoff for having supported Sulzer's candidacy in the 1912 campaign.) For a time the governor backed off, then returned to the matter amid growing speculation that his administration was being "Tammanyized." Osborne himself made the issue personal, pleading with Sulzer that he could not withdraw Rattigan's name lest he admit to being "a mere beggar for patronage." Scott's intransigence, he went on to argue, would leave the impression "that Charles F. Murphy is still Governor of the State." Though Scott was hardly a Tammany hack, Sulzer deemed Osborne's logic "conclusive" and found "other means of getting rid of Scott," as Franklin Roosevelt had put it earlier.[12] He ordered the commission of inquiry to investigate the prison department.

For nearly one month the graft hunters probed the superintendent and his department and emerged with a report charging "petty things already known," as Scott described it. The commission did not recommend Scott's removal. Nonetheless, Sulzer, still apparently impressed by Osborne's logic, resolved to force Scott's resignation. When Scott refused and appealed to the governor's "sense of fair play," Sulzer dismissed him for being "inefficient, incompetent, derelict and neglectful of duty." Members of the legislature quickly jumped into the fray with severe criticisms of the governor's injection of politics into the state's prison system. Led by John F. Murtaugh, a respected upstate Democrat, the senate passed a resolution condemning the Scott removal and calling for a hearing for the superintendent before an objective tribunal. Sulzer's response was to dispatch to the senate the nomination of another for the position and, at the same time, appoint a special investigator to scrutinize all the activities of the penal institutions in the state.[13] He was being willfully defiant.

The Scott firing—even the Reel removal—symbolized Sulzer's way of doing things. He was capricious, arbitrary, and tyrannical. He had wanted not to be factional, yet he wound up being worse than factional: in trying to placate the demanding Osborne, he antagonized not only Tammany Democrats who could hardly be expected to rejoice at giving anything to the Auburn independent but also independent Democrats and Republicans in the senate. Sulzer's behavior told even more than that. It told of a groping and grasping for support in the wake of declining public confidence in his administration. From the moment of Sulzer's inaugural exhortations, the anti-Tammany press had measured his deeds by his inflated rhetoric. "The Governor will be tested rather by what he accomplishes for the good of the State than by any triumphant declaration of independence and all that," warned one journal not untypically. He was soon found wanting. There were complaints that he failed to challenge Tammany in the organization of the legislature, something about which he could actually do very little. These were followed by more vocal criticisms—indeed, scathing denunciations—of his appointment of two "machine" men, one representing Tammany and the other Fitzpatrick's organization in Erie County, to the public service commissions. "His bark is worse than his bite," lamented the *New York Evening Mail* over these selections.[14] Such attacks were supplemented by letters from friends chastising him for his "sham battle" with Murphy and urging him to "throw down the gauntlet." They pointed out that Sulzer was forgoing his claim to independence, that "Wilson took his chance in Jersey," and that a "great Progressive element in this State . . . is itching for a great leader." What the governor should do, suggested one friend, was to revive the Sulzer clubs used in the election campaign and "establish an organization, such as Hearst did several years ago."[15]

This incessant prodding had a noticeable impact on the egocentric Sulzer, who seemed to want to take seriously the importunity that he become the reformers' "great leader." At about the time that Scott and Reel were being fired, the governor assumed generally a more anti-Tammany stance. He wrote directly to progressive newspapers like the *New York World* asking for support of bills and appointments that he believed, usually wrongly, the legislative leaders were bottling up. He refused to spike rumors that Murphy had applied pressure on the administration to have nominated a business associate as the new highway superintendent, considered to be one of the most lucrative of state executive posts. He charged that the legislature had launched a vendetta against him, though only one of his nominees—Milton E. Gibbs of Rochester for state hospital commissioner—had been turned down by the senate. (Gibbs's rejection had been unanimous after a senate committee deemed him unsuited for office.) And after publicly attacking "invisible government," he announced dramatically his new "county autonomy" plan for making appointments. Sulzer reserved to himself the exclusive right to name statewide officers. Nominations for other offices would come on the recommendation of county chairmen and duly elected county committees. In an obvious warning to Murphy, the governor declared: "I want to see each county in our state politically free and independent of political interference from any other county, and have the right to settle its own political affairs in its own political way." Sulzer's county autonomy scheme was hailed as an attempt to restrict Tammany's control over patronage to New York County; commit the Bronx, Kings, and upstate organizations to the governor; and thus shake loose Murphy's grip on the legislature.[16]

But, like Sulzer's earlier declarations, these were given the closest scrutiny by the press. Rumor persisted that his main objective was to engage in "a lifelike imitation" of a fight with Murphy and Tammany Hall, and his fitful behavior seemed to bear out the charge. Only a few days after the governor's much-publicized denunciation of "invisible government," Sulzer and Murphy reportedly reached a compromise, evidently through Senator O'Gorman, on appointments. For his part, Sulzer agreed to name organization men to two supreme court positions in New York County and to a vacancy on the upstate public service commission; in return, he would have a free hand in making appointments to several state offices. "If he is willing to do the right thing by the Governor," commented one of Sulzer's friends in reference to Murphy, "the Governor is willing to do the right thing by him." However, Sulzer, who remained suspicious of the senate leadership, subsequently withheld the judicial nominations and submitted the names of his other nominees, one by one, in turn. Still smarting from the Scott fiasco, and now under fire from the governor on another matter, the senate balked and refused outright to consider any names until all nominations were in. After considerable delay, Sulzer came forward with a long list of appointments, including two organization men for the supreme court and a Murphy confidant for the newly created commissioner of efficiency and economy. Among the many names submitted, the senate, on a strict party vote, rejected two—labor leader John Mitchell, a Republican, for commissioner of labor; and John Riley, who was declared unqualified for superintendent of prisons. There followed a protracted struggle, with the governor and the senate jockeying for advantage. Neither post was filled by the time Sulzer left office.[17]

Sulzer's "battle" over the patronage and his use of the graft inquiry satisfied almost no one. Legislators in both parties were annoyed at his high-handed tactics in the unfortunate Scott episode and at his behavior in the later appointments. Tammany spokesmen remained disgruntled by the governor's "play to the galleries," though Murphy himself seldom showed more than mild irritation. Only once did the boss issue a lengthy public statement—this, on March 11, to deny the rumor that he had insisted on the appointment of his business associate as highway superintendent. Nor did the independent politicians or the reformist press become terribly excited by the wrangling over the "spoils," even if Sulzer were involved in more than a "lifelike imitation" of a fight, which many thought he was not. Osborne, it is true, encouraged the governor once or twice, for he reveled in Tammany's continued bad press. "The country is watching you with interest and sympathy," he volunteered to Sulzer in mid-March.[18] But Osborne, too, would require something of greater substance to overcome his mistrust of the governor. That "something" would be another battle with the legislature, and the issue would be the direct primary.

II

In the early days of the 1913 session, Sulzer enjoyed a reasonably good working relationship with the legislature on matters other than patronage. Tammany leaders Robert Wagner, again majority leader in the senate, and Al Smith, now speaker of the assembly, left no stone unturned in fulfilling the major planks of the 1912 Democratic platform and in implementing the governor's own legislative priorities. Skeptics who at first had dreaded another "boss-ridden" legislature reached for explanations, some intimating cynically that Charlie Murphy was temporarily capitulating to reform sentiment in the face of a tough mayoralty fight in New York City that fall. Only five weeks after his inauguration, Sulzer himself expressed delight in the passage of several key proposals, including the amendment on the direct election of U.S. senators and the bill appropriating money for the graft commission. Even as tensions developed between the Tammany leadership and the administration over the graft inquiry and the gubernatorial appointments, the legislature remained cooperative. "We decided . . . that all the constructive legislation recommended by Governor Sulzer was to be enacted," declared Lieutenant Governor Glynn amid the Scott imbroglio. "If the Governor is looking for a fight," Glynn added half-jokingly, "I am afraid he will have to manufacture it himself." All through March the leadership spiked rumors of an impending rupture between Sulzer and the legislature. "Evidence of harmony," Speaker Smith assured reporters later that month, "will be found in the wonderful record the legislature is making."[19]

The spirit of harmony about which Smith spoke was perhaps best illustrated by the legislature's reception of the reports of Sulzer's commission of inquiry. The commission found little that Governor Hughes, in his concern for administrative efficiency, had not discovered and often articulated. "The business and financial affairs of the State," one of its reports asserted, "are conducted without system, extravagantly and with adverse and divided responsibility, which would bring ruin to any business not having the resources of the State." To correct these deficiencies, the commission recommended a series of measures, including the creation of three new agencies—one on efficiency and economy, a second on estimate, and a third on contract and supply. Another set of proposals was designed to enhance the authority of the state comptroller to audit departmental and agency expenditures. The major items passed the legislature with relative ease. To these administrative reforms were added others in the 1913 session, some recommended directly by the governor, and one the result of the work of the Factory Investigating Commission. Thus, the highway, health, and labor departments were reorganized. In all the Democratic program of administrative streamlining carried forward Governor Hughes's efforts to bring efficiency and accountability to the state executive departments.[20]

The Democrats also advanced the cause of economic regulation in 1913. In the wake of public furor over the revelations concerning the "money trust" by Congress' Pujo committee, Governor Sulzer addressed himself to needed reforms of the New York Stock Exchange. An earlier investigation, conducted in the Hughes years, had resulted in some internal reforms in the exchange, but none of those requiring passage by the legislature had been effected. "How flagrantly Stock Exchange reform was flouted," complained the *World* editorially in December 1912. Sulzer's recommendations came in steps, some in a special message the next month; others, the more "radical" measures, a little later in the legislative session. "All I am trying to do is to

WILLIAM SULZER AND THE POLITICS OF EXCESS

accomplish results along the lines of reform demanded by the people,"
he stated at the time he dispatched the second group to the legislature.
The first measures, called the Seven Half-Sisters because they were
modeled after seven antitrust bills proposed earlier by Governor Wilson
to the New Jersey legislature, elicited little negative reaction. They were
even dubbed safe, sane, and necessary by members of the New York
Stock Exchange.[21]

The second batch, however, contained one measure, in particular,
that caused a real stir. This was an incorporation bill, requiring the
exchange to incorporate under the banking laws of the state, bringing
it within the supervisory authority of the banking department. Exchange spokesmen, who had already implemented additional internal
reforms, labeled this proposal "radical" and freely expressed their opposition in legislative committee hearings. The governor again turned
to publicity for his chief weapon. But before the legislative session
concluded, he became so deeply involved in publicizing other, more
dramatic issues, that he paid scant attention to the Wall Street bills.
Still, a substantial part of the total package was enacted, including bills
prohibiting various broker practices and tightening regulations on certain types of sales. The incorporation bill, the most controversial of
all, passed the assembly but was killed by an adverse report of the
senate judiciary committee—with Robert Wagner strongly supporting
the bill.[22]

The Tammany legislature cooperated with Sulzer on various other
reform measures. Economic regulation was further advanced by extension of the powers of the much-hailed public service commissions.
Home rule was extended with the passage of several bills—one, supported by the Municipal Government Association and the Citizens
Union, which granted cities more authority to regulate and control
exclusively local affairs; the others, flowing from a special committee
investigation headed by Wagner, freeing the police administration of
New York City from unnecessary legislative management. Most important was enactment of that vast array of legislation having to do
with social reform and the public welfare. The first state scholarships
were established—five of them for each of the 150 assembly districts—
with William Sulzer hailing this measure as "the greatest permanent
contribution to higher education in this State that has been made in

all our history." Truly impressive was the enactment of some twenty bills recommended by the Factory Investigating Commission. The *New York Times,* hardly sympathetic to Tammany Democrats, concluded that this legislature "eclipsed the records of all its predecessors" in passing "more legislation for the benefit of labor than any Legislature in twenty years."[23]

Good as the record was, the Democratic performance in 1913 could not satisfy the critics, especially the independent, reformist press. Much of their attack was leveled at the legislature itself—with its "low standard of intelligence and public morals"—simply because it was "boss-controlled." But a good part of it was also directed at Governor Sulzer. His "hopeful deeds," claimed the *New York World* as the regular session was winding down, "are now recognized as the mere idle and empty boasting of a politician whose vanity hourly drives him to court a publicity his official acts and his personal qualifications cannot bear." This assault was a stinging rebuke from a powerful voice of progressivism. It was followed the next day by a private letter from Frank Cobb, a *World* editor, to Sulzer. "We are . . . warning you of certain dangers that you must deal with, a certain state of public opinion that you cannot afford to ignore," Cobb wrote candidly.[24] For these critics and others, the governor, in "shadowboxing" with the Tammany politicians, had pussyfooted what for them was the vital mandate of progressivism in New York State: to expunge from politics and public life the sinister influence of "bossism" and "machine rule." A key weapon in this battle was the direct primary, which to many represented the one issue that separated the independents from the regulars, the "progressives" from the "reactionaries." Thus, after three stormy months in office, the frustrated Sulzer turned suddenly to this reform. By making direct nominations the test of progressivism, he could at once placate his critics and rally the reformers in the state to his banner. He had decided finally to cast his lot with the enemies of Tammany Hall.

III

The direct primary had long been a divisive issue in New York politics. Governor Charles Evans Hughes had spent practically his entire second administration trying to get the leaders of his own party to accept the reform. Even a much-watered-down version of his original proposal, itself a compromise measure, was defeated by the legislature in 1910, and the issue became a cause célèbre among Hughes supporters, though, in fact, many moderate Republicans refused to champion the primary. When the Democrats came to power in 1911, they handled direct nominations gingerly. Compromise that year resulted in passage of the Ferris-Blauvelt bill providing for the primary in all nominations except for members of the state ticket. Independents like Franklin D. Roosevelt had not insisted on the ultimate—extension of the reform to all state offices and elimination of the party nominating convention—because they knew that Murphy's organizatiaon would reject it just as the Republicans had earlier. It is true that the Democrats in the 1912 Syracuse convention promised a statewide direct nominations plan. But few paid much attention to this plank, and those who did could not agree on what it meant.[25]

In early 1913 the Tammany legislative leadership sponsored a mild primary measure, introduced again by George Blauvelt, that was designed merely to streamline the present machinery and to make independent nominations somewhat easier. At this time, Sulzer gave no sign that the proposed changes were inadequate, though he had intimated in January that he favored a statewide primary. It was not until after the press attacks in April that the governor dispatched a crisp special message to the legislature urging the more sweeping version of direct nominations. This reform, he stated bluntly, was aimed at restoring "to the people rights and privileges which have been usurped by the few, for the benefit of invisible interests which aim to control governmental officials, to pass laws, to prevent the passage of other laws, and to violate laws with impunity."[26] Sulzer's rhetoric was again inflated, but, more important, his concept of primary reform went well beyond that which was acceptable to Smith, Wagner, and most of the regulars in the Democratic party. Indeed, the bill embracing his ideas grew out of a meeting of independents and anti-Tammanyites held in his office on April 5 and contained provisions that would abolish committee designations as well as the state nominating convention and that would prohibit party emblems on primary ballots and the use of party funds in nominations contests. "It is practically the Massachusetts and the Australian ballot combined," crowed William Lustgarten, head of the

Progressive Democrats.[27] This sweeping measure, the most advanced primary scheme offered by any governor, formed the real basis of the rupture between Sulzer and Tammany Hall.

The debate that followed was long and bitter. Much of it revolved about what the Democrats had actually promised and how effective would be a plan that some thought would fundamentally alter the existing party structure. On these matters there were honest differences of opinion just as there had been in the Hughes years. Not all reform Democrats supported the statewide primary, and they ably rehearsed the arguments against the Sulzer bill. But of greater significance than the debate itself were what many concluded to be the realities behind it. Few doubted that the governor harbored clear-cut political objectives. "He hopes that by using it [the primary] he will be able to gain control of the Democratic Party in the State of New York," claimed one reformer unabashedly.[28] With Charlie Murphy's downfall, some conjectured, Sulzer would easily win reelection in 1914 (which was not at all assured otherwise), and perhaps emerge a presidential contender two years later. The example of Wilson in New Jersey was again dangled before him by friends and supporters. Further, the governor's appeal to Roosevelt Bull Moosers, moderate Republicans of the Hughes stripe, as well as to dissident Democrats might serve as a foundation for an "alignment of parties in the near future . . . in a Progressive and Conservative division." There was the rumor, almost as if the process were already under way, that Sulzer had made a pact with Tammany nemesis and rebel Democrat, William Randolph Hearst, involving a dual leadership in the state, with Hearst to be elected to the U.S. Senate the next year. Hearst, in fact, became one of the most active battlers for the direct primary and put his influential newspapers to work for the cause in 1913.[29] Some of this talk, to be sure, was farfetched, but in the heady days of progressivism speculation was rife that the old political institutions were rapidly disintegrating.

Superficially, Sulzer's campaign for the direct primary resembled that of Governor Hughes three years earlier. Sulzer himself often resurrected the former chief executive's fight with the "bosses." "They beat Governor Hughes," he charged on one occasion, "but I am determined that they shall not beat Governor Sulzer." In the months that followed he resorted to various tactics. He arranged special conferences in the executive chamber to which he invited progressives of all parties and pleaded for their support. He made clear that he would brook no compromise on this critical reform. "My bill or nothing. That is the slogan," he told reporters bluntly. When the legislature refused to bow to his demands, Sulzer convoked the body in special session and tried to muster public opinion to pressure recalcitrant lawmakers into submission. Chief among his tactics was a well-organized bipartisan canvass directed by his energetic secretary, Chester C. Platt, that sought to penetrate every assembly district in the state. Even Theodore Roosevelt was brought into the "war" between the "machine" and the "people" (as the Colonel put it) to do battle as he had done in 1910 for Hughes. "The bi-partisan combine of bosses," the agitated Roosevelt charged in Rochester in June, "beat the demand for State-wide direct primaries when the Republicans were in power, and now that same bi-partisan combine is beating the same demand under Democratic rule at Albany."[30] Sulzer personally took to the hustings and toured the entire state from mid-May through mid-June in behalf of "his" primary plan. His audiences were large—for he was truly colorful on the stump— and he received the kind of widespread publicity that only such attacks against bossism could command in that era. "The eyes of the country are turned toward New York," summed up *The Literary Digest,* not for the local question of the direct primary, but for the larger issue of whether Murphy's "usefulness as a boss [is] at an end."[31]

But the tone and quality of Sulzer's primary campaign was far different from that waged earlier by another progressive governor. His rhetoric was excessive and highly abusive; his methods were questionable, at times outrageous. Overall, he substituted coercion for persuasion. After carefully examining the governor's efforts in 1913, the Citizens Union, supporter of direct nominations, concluded tersely that Sulzer's techniques were "of questionable character."[32]

The main object of Sulzer's scorn was the legislature and its operations, though he insisted always that the real battle was with Boss Murphy. One of his first actions came in the form of a blistering veto message directed at the Blauvelt bill, which passed the legislature in late April. He blasted this measure as a "fraud," "a miserable makeshift," "mere patchwork," and "a glaring breach of the pledged faith of every member." He charged that the senate, in particular, was "not

a free agency" and insulted Republican leader Elon Brown as "a sur-
vivor of the Black Horse Cavalry of unsavory memory" and "a fossil
of the paleozoic age in our State politics."³³ While the words of abuse
flowed, Sulzer tried to exert various kinds of pressure, direct and in-
direct, on "uncooperative" legislators. This included the threat of the
veto. In one instance he rejected several local bills—a drastic action in
those days—because one senator and three assemblymen refused to
back his primary in the special session. In others he turned aside major
legislation for the same reason, or so it was believed.³⁴ More telling
were his assaults on the men behind the lawmakers. "Get right on
direct primaries," he admonished Norman Mack of Buffalo. He demanded that county chairmen, whom he ordered to meet with him in
Albany, toe the mark or suffer the consequences. "If any Democrat in
this State is against the Democratic State platform," he warned party
leaders, "I shall do everything in my power to drive that recreant Democrat out of the Democratic party." In some cases, as in Albany
County, he refused to recognize the duly elected chairman, Tammany
ally "Packy" McCabe, and tried to substitute his own crony. In Erie
he launched a frontal attack against William Fitzpatrick, the key Murphy man upstate. "Not another job will go to Erie County from the
Executive Chamber until the Legislators from Erie County see fit to
vote for my direct nominations bill," Sulzer fumed publicly. Even his
secretary penned an occasional threat to county leaders whose senators
or assemblymen remained stubbornly opposed to the Sulzer plan.
Sulzer himself hinted at a complete party purge when he ordered all
executive officers not under civil service to remove "disloyal" employ-
ees.³⁵

Not surprisingly, the governor's slashing attacks and coercive methods brought strong reactions from the legislature. At first the Tammany
leadership, completing work on the other administration reforms, went
easy on Sulzer. "The tone of this message is decidedly offensive," complained Robert Wagner with reference to the veto of the Blauvelt bill.
Several days later, Wagner expressed regret that Sulzer had been so
critical "merely because we disagreed with the details, and not with
the principles of one of those reforms." As the battle wore on, he
became more outspoken. "I would not sell my soul or my conscience

for mere party patronage and I think little of an official who attempts
to threaten or tempts with patronage," Wagner maintained when the
Sulzer bill was defeated in the senate. Then at the close of the regular
session the majority leader defended the legislature for its progressive
record and lamented Sulzer's insistence that on the primary "it no
longer . . . perform its Constitutional function of making the law."
When the special session took place, Wagner threw caution to the wind
and challenged Sulzer's "insinuations" and "direct charges" against his
colleagues. "The people will know," he exclaimed, "what promises and
corrupt bargains have been made to get votes for a bill the governor is
so anxious to pass."[36]

Wagner's growing impatience mirrored that of the state legislature
as a whole. Independent Democrats joined Republicans and Tammanyites in the wake of the governor's "reign of terror." Both the senate
and the assembly overwhelmingly turned down his primary bill. In the
senate it received only 8 votes, including 2 Republican. Elon Brown
had led the attack for the GOP. Rebel Democrat John Murtaugh took
the occasion to accuse Sulzer of "blazing a crimson trail all the way
from the Capitol steps to the placid waters of Chautauqua Lake."
Anthony Griffin, outspoken critic from the Bronx, added bitterly: "Until we destroy the Constitution, I will not take the dictation of any one
man as to what I shall do as a legislator." Later Griffin would charge
that the governor was attempting "to usurp legislative functions" and
denounced him as "Sulzer the First" plunging headlong into a "policy
of rule or ruin."[37]

In the special session the story was the same except that individual
legislators appealed privately to Sulzer for a compromise measure—
one that would extend direct nominations statewide but retain the state
convention. "I believe, if he does not justify his seeming obstinacy in
his refusal to accept this modification of his bill and if we fail to get
primary legislation this year," wrote one assemblyman to Platt, "the
blame must rest with [the] governor." Some reports had it that Sulzer
would relent; he did not, however. And again the Sulzer bill was beaten
back quite handily—this time with 54 votes in its favor in the assembly
and only 10 in the senate. Lawmakers, who claimed they found no
sentiment back home for the measure, blasted the governor as a "trai-

tor," a "hypocrite," "the Judas of the Democratic Party."[38] No one came to his defense. To add insult to injury, the legislature adopted an amended version of the Blauvelt bill and adjourned.[39]

The price that William Sulzer paid for his win-or-lose campaign in behalf of the direct primary was abject defeat at the hands of an embittered state legislature. Many a well-wisher had already testified that the battle would not have been worth it if he had won. He had badly overextended himself. They were right and excess bred excess. The enmity generated by Sulzer's outrageous methods ran deep. In the war of words that followed, the governor's enemies—of whom he now had many—launched a sustained counteroffensive, in which ultimately they accused him of all sorts of indiscretions and illegalities. Leading this movement against Sulzer, of course, was the legislature's Tammany leadership, but behind Smith, Wagner, and the others was probably Charlie Murphy himself. At some point late in the spring, the boss and his confidants must have concluded that Sulzer's primary campaign and methods were sufficiently dangerous to justify "getting something" on him.[40] A series of earlier private conferences between the governor and the leaders had failed to solve whatever their differences were on patronage and the graft investigations. Sulzer's "real" war on Tammany and its allies, threatening disruption of Murphy's state organization, dictated a more effective strategy. While the boss would continue to stay in the background and only occasionally break his silence, his followers would labor in various ways to discredit the governor in the eyes of a skeptical public. Exactly when Murphy ordered Sulzer's removal from office, if he ever did so directly, cannot be ascertained.[41]

The mainspring of the counteroffensive against Sulzer was a special committee of the legislature set up by joint resolution near the end of the regular session. Composed mainly of organization men and headed by Tammanyite James Frawley, the committee's ostensible purpose was to investigate the administration of state government, that is, "to take up the investigations where the Sulzer [graft] commission left off and complete the work." From the beginning critics were aware that the Frawley committee was "retaliatory." During Sulzer's stepped-up attacks in the legislature's special session, the committee asked for specific authority to probe such "irregularities" as the governor's unusual use of the veto, the relationship between local legislation and support for the direct primary, and Sulzer's alleged failure to report fully his receipts and expenditures of monies in the 1912 campaign. This request was approved by the legislature without debate or dissent.[42]

Begun as a means of showing Sulzer "in his true light to the voters," the Frawley inquiry accomplished far more than anyone could have planned—or imagined. First in private investigations, then in public hearings in July and August, the legislative snoopers unraveled a web of wrongdoing and chicanery that made a mockery of the governor's charges against the "crooks" and "grafters" of Tammany Hall. They discovered that his widely publicized scrutiny of the prison department was a farce and a fraud. They heard testimony that he indirectly bargained with legislators for their support of his primary bill.[43] They found that after the campaign of 1912 Sulzer had failed to report thousands of dollars as political contributions in violation of state law. Where had the money gone? The investigators learned that some of it went into Sulzer's personal account with the Farmers' Loan and Trust Company. Some of it also made its way into a secret investment account held by the New York brokerage firm of Fuller and Gray. Known as "number 500" on the company books, this account was used to purchase nearly $12,000 of stocks in a midwestern railroad. The stocks were delivered to Sulzer by a "bagman." The committee then heard testimony about the existence of a second investment account, this one with Harris and Fuller, and designated "number 63." Sulzer had utilized this account, kept open until July 15, 1913, to speculate in the market at the very time that he was sponsoring the Wall Street reform legislation. Even committee members who thought the worst of Sulzer were shocked by these disclosures. "When our committee began work," Frawley confessed later, "we had a hunch that the full account of the Governor's campaign expenditures had not been published, as the law requires, but it was a surprise to all of us to find that he had used some of the money contributed for his political expenses to try a flyer in Wall Street."[44]

The Frawley committee hearings ended on August 8. "I think we've got about enough," declared the chairman, implying that additional evidence would only serve to corroborate what they already had on Sulzer's 1912 violation of the New York Corrupt Practices Act. One day earlier an unidentified committee member had hinted at the prospect of the governor's removal. And within a week the state assembly, exhausted by hours of debate, adopted a resolution of impeachment citing Sulzer for "willful and corrupt conduct in office and for high crimes and misdemeanors." The trial was scheduled to begin on September 18.[45]

Sulzer must have been stunned by the rapid turn of events; at least he acted so. During the early stages of the hearings, he said and did little. Occasionally he punctured his silence with a diatribe against Murphy. Not once did he seek to explain the charges against him. In his private correspondence he coupled his customary attack on bossism with protestations of innocence. To John Purroy Mitchel he complained:

> When the political bosses found out they could not control me, and make me a rubber stamp, they threatened to destroy me politically, and they have been doing everything in their power, ever since, to that end.
>
> However, I have no fear of the ultimate result. The people will win. The truth will prevail, and right makes might. In the future as in the past, you and all your friends, can rely on me to do my duty to all the people, as I see the right—and God gives me the light—regardless of political or personal consequences.
>
> Of course the grafters are hounding me. Mr. Murphy and his hirelings necessarily are traducing me. They have had detectives following me around, and searching high and low to find out everything I have ever done since my birth. Why? Just to get some mud if possible to throw at me.
>
> However, I can assure you there is little, or nothing, in any of the charges they make against me. Most of the stuff they get in the newspapers is baseless, and pure fabrication. They know this, and they know it will not in the last analysis hurt me; but they also know that it worries my mother and annoys Mrs. Sulzer.
>
> When Boss Murphy told me he would destroy me if I did not do his bidding, I defied him to do his worst, and declared I would continue to do my best. The fight for good government will go on. The bridges are burned. With the aid of the decent God-fearing people of our State I shall go forward—come what may.[46]

As the evidence against him mounted, Sulzer tried on a technicality to have the Frawley committee dissolved. The effort failed in early August. Influential elements of the anti-Tammany press in New York City—the *Times*, the *World*, the *Evening Post*, even Hearst's *American*—became increasingly impatient with the governor. "The shame and disgrace that William Sulzer has brought upon the State of New York," insisted the *Times* editorially, "will end his career and put him out and keep him out of public life." In the face of impeachment, the *World* posed a challenging question: "Will he resign and thereby win, perhaps, the charitable forbearance of a people whose . . . faith he has exhausted and shattered?"[47] Such prodding brought from the beleaguered Sulzer only categorical denials of wrongdoing with no particulars. By this time he was suffering from nervous exhaustion, and his wife was gravely ill. In desperation Sulzer finally appealed to Frawley, confessing that he had been taken down the anti-Tammany path by foolish advisors. "Jim" he pleaded, "this has gone too far. I didn't expect anything like this and I know you didn't."[48] It was too late, however. As Sulzer had said earlier, "the bridges are burned." Last-minute telegrams and telephone calls to state and county leaders, as well as to Franklin Roosevelt and John Purroy Mitchel in the Wilson administration, could not stem the tide. Sulzer would go on trial.

In the ensuing weeks the course charted by the Frawley committee was followed relentlessly to its inevitable conclusion. Politicians could not help but detect that public support for Sulzer was waning rapidly, though upstate anti-Tammany sentiment remained powerful. Independent Democrats mixed concern with hope and encouragement. "Sulzer, in spite of his crudeness, his vanity, his lack of many desirable and admirable qualities," wrote Osborne, "has been fighting . . . the fight of every man who wants honest government." Republicans and Progressives seemed sympathetic, but Republicans, in particular, fell into the background, evidently eager to have the Democrats tear themselves apart. Occasionally they would break their silence, expressing thoughts like those uttered by one prominent GOP assemblyman at the time formal impeachment charges were made: "We have our own dignity to maintain."[49] So, on September 18, the High Court of Impeachment, consisting of the state senate and the ten justices of the court of appeals, gathered to hear the assembly's case against the governor.

The trial itself produced more drama than revelation. Much of the evidence used in the indictment was reintroduced. What new facts there were only corroborated those things already known. The prosecution concentrated on the most obvious and easily proved of the charges: Sulzer's failure to report a considerable portion of his campaign money, estimated at $60,000 in cash and checks; his alleged perjury in swearing to the accuracy of his statement on financial contributions and disbursements; and his diversion of funds to stock speculation, amounting to over $40,000. Testimony did show that Sulzer had actually demanded some of these monies and, during the Frawley hearings or the impeachment proceedings, urged donors to conceal their contributions. The governor's defense was embarrassingly feeble. Headed by the eminent Louis Marshall, it tried first to have the charges dismissed on the ground that the impeachment came in a special session of the legislature, when only items recommended by the governor could be considered. This rejected, it turned to a defense against the counts of indictment. Marshall and his colleagues argued that the acts for which most of the evidence had been adduced occurred before Sulzer was in office, and the state constitution allowed for impeachment only for acts committed by a sitting official. "Was the proceeding instituted because of a desire to accomplish a public good," queried one of the attorneys, "or was it for the purpose of getting rid of a public official who was performing his duty?"[50] Witnesses then were called to answer the specific accusations, but they were unconvincing. Strong testimony by Sulzer himself might have saved the day, and the governor gave heart to his backers with the repeated promise of "amazing revelations" with regard to Murphy and Tammany and complete vindication of his record. (For days the press was filled with rumors about Sulzer's plans to tell all.) When the time came, however, he did not appear and offered excuse upon excuse for his silence. The real reason apparently was that his lawyers urged him not to testify for fear that merciless cross-examination by the prosecution would further weaken his case. As one opposing attorney had said: "If Sulzer doesn't go on the stand, his failure will be interpreted as a confession; if he does go on, it will be suicide."[51] Sulzer chose confession by absence.

By mid-October the drama of Sulzer's trial was over. Much to the surprise of everyone, it had been conducted with dignity and fairness. "The great New York impeachment trial of 1913," declared the *New York Times,* "will be cited for its precedents and for the calm, learned, wise, and just rulings of Presiding Judge [Edgar T.] Cullen." Nor was there much question about the nature of the verdict. Following the lead of a majority of the judges, senators voted overwhelmingly—and across party lines—for conviction of the governor on three of the eight counts. Skeptics found it hard to exonerate Sulzer of anything but political heresy when all of the judges except one declared Sulzer guilty of at least one offense. And when the final question, "Shall the respondent be removed from office?" was put to the jury, the vote was affirmative, 43–12–2, with nine of ten justices going along. Only Judge Cullen held out, but Cullen seized the occasion to remonstrate with Sulzer, whom he accused of committing acts showing "such moral turpitude and delinquency that if they had been committed during the respondent's incumbency of office I think they would require his removal."[52]

Cullen's abstention—he did not actually vote against removal—was hardly consoling to the beaten Governor Sulzer. Nor did press reaction provide him with much solace. It is true that many upstate newspapers, which were mostly Republican or independent Democratic in persuasion, stuck by him. "The removal of Governor Sulzer," insisted the *Rochester Herald*, "will be greeted with unconcealed joy by every crooked politician, every grafter in or out of office, and every criminal in or out of office."[53] But the New York City press, which had been so helpful to Governor Hughes and on which Sulzer apparently counted so heavily, had almost totally deserted him. All he could do now was to make one last ringing address to the "people"—labeling the impeachment court "Murphy's High Court of Infamy" and whimper as Lieutenant Governor Martin Glynn moved into the executive mansion. Sulzer then turned to the comeback trail: that fall he ran for and was elected assemblyman from his Lower East Side district as a Progressive; the next year, he would try again for the governorship, this time as the nominee of the nativist American party. His attempt at vindication failed; few respectable politicians would have anything more to do with him; and he soon slipped into oblivion, a figure of the past.

The Sulzer lesson was clear. As one student has said: "No man can afford to pit himself against a powerful political organization unless his own record is above reproach."[54] But the impeachment story also affords an excellent commentary on the politics of excess—in an era when politicians often substituted hyperbole for rational discourse and willy-nilly seized on popular nostrums. William Sulzer was such a politician. He was disingenuous, opportunistic, reckless, and rash— qualities that made him less than endearing to his contemporaries. In large part to answer the call of mistrusting independents and a vocal reform press not content with the Democrats' progressive record, and surely to advance his own career, Sulzer issued demands that were unacceptable to the legislature and to the hierarchy of his own party. And he did so with a vengeance. He thus invited recriminations—with Charlie Murphy's Tammany Hall, often depicted as the sole villain in the impeachment drama, becoming the chief agent for retribution.[55] The boss and his followers, then, were at once successful in removing from power a badly tarnished chief executive and in sparing the Democratic state organization a dangerous, unpredictable antagonist.

IV

The Sulzer impeachment, however, was a costly indulgence for Charlie Murphy and his allies, and they themselves soon paid the price for the politics of excess. Indeed, it is astonishing that the otherwise shrewd Tammanyites did not weigh more heavily the electoral consequences of their actions in Albany, given the persistent sentiment against "boss-ism" and machine rule in the state. Even as the impeachment trial was getting under way, the September primaries boded ill for the Democratic organization. "The primaries . . . showed a strong anti-Tammany feeling up the state," exulted Progressive leader George W. Perkins. In county after county "regular" assemblymen were defeated by pro-Sulzer candidates standing against "Tammanyism" and in favor of direct nominations. In Albany, "Packy" McCabe nearly lost his county chairmanship to party rebels. In Rochester, Louis Antisdale's friends, who in 1912 had ousted the local Tammany satrap as Monroe County leader, consolidated their hold on the county committee.[56]

But it was in Buffalo that Tammany Hall suffered its worst setback in the upstate, thus placing in serious jeopardy Murphy's iron grip on the New York Democracy. "Old campaigners," gloated Conners's *Courier,* "said there was never such a notable overturning . . . in the history of Democratic politics in Buffalo." Here the Mack-Fitzpatrick candidate for the party's mayoralty nomination was soundly trounced by the incumbent, Louis Fuhrmann, backed by Conners, Henry Burgard, and other dissidents. In reality, the split in Erie County was a fight among regulars, with both sides making claims to progressivism.

But the Conners forces were successful in transforming their campaign into a crusade against bossism and in favor of the direct primary. They cleverly exploited an ill-advised statement issued by Mack that justified Erie's subordination to New York County in Democratic party affairs. "The larger unit will always control the smaller," concluded Mack's unfortunate comment. In addition to their citywide loss, the Fitzpatrick group saw four of their assemblymen go down to defeat at the hands of pro-Sulzer candidates. One week later, Fitzpatrick resigned as Erie County chairman and was replaced by Conners's friend, Henry Burgard.[57]

Even more devastating than the reverses in upstate New York was the great challenge to Charlie Murphy in Tammany's own bailiwick, New York City. Although, to be sure, the reform press in the city had abandoned Sulzer in the heat of the impeachment battle, antimachine journals were filled with "outrage" over Democratic mismanagement of the state's business. Villard's *Evening Post* put it well: "Sulzer may have been as crooked as his assailants declare, but . . . he is an angel of light compared to Murphy." This powerful anti-Tammanyism tended to consolidate those forces already joined together against the Hall as the municipal elections approached in November. Each of the constituent groups had its own special reasons for cooperation. The Progressives, rejecting a natural inclination to run a separate ticket, sought to advance their 1912 platform and, in particular, destroy "the old political system of machine control." Republicans, especially reformers like Parsons and Stimson, hoped to use fusion as a means of rebuilding the New York City GOP organization, thence to challenge Barnes's reactionary leadership in the state.[58] And independent Democrats, characteristically, looked to snatch the city government from the clutches of Tammany and to starve the Tiger out of existence.

The origins of the 1913 fusion movement actually dated back to the early part of the year, even before Governor Sulzer's "real" declaration of war against Murphy's state organization. Two separate but not wholly unrelated groups assumed the initiative in what would develop into an effective anti-Tammany coalition. The first was that loose collection of Progressives, Republicans, and dissident Democrats (including Hearstites), noted above, that gathered together in the spring to form the so-called Committee of 107. "The campaign to be launched," explained one prominent fusion organizer, "is anti-Tammany because Tammany has symbolized the 'shame of our cities.' "⁵⁹ The second was a coterie of Wilsonians operating out of Washington, D.C.—men whose dabbling in New York politics unwittingly touched off a chain of events that brought to the fore John Purroy Mitchel, around whom ultimately the fusionists would rally.

The most prominent of the Wilsonians interested generally in the tangled New York situation were presidential confidant Colonel Edward M. House and Treasury Secretary William G. McAdoo. Like others among the Wilson people similarly disposed, these two evidently concluded in the spring that the Sulzer they were observing provided little hope for a reconstructed Democratic party in the Empire State. In March they concocted a plan that House recorded in his diary at the time:

We both have a keen desire to revamp New York City and State, and to give them efficient government. We will try to nominate a proper man for Governor two years from now, and in the meantime get a Mayor of New York City who will cleanse it. Our first move will be to get a proper man for Collector of the Port. He should have ability of a high order and a great deal of courage. He should not be affiliated with Tammany, but should be an independent Democrat.

This rather far-reaching venture was, of course, directed principally against Murphy's organization, but, in part, it was also designed to gratify the political ambitions of McAdoo, who, a noted scholar has written, sought control of the New York party as a "springboard to the presidency."⁶⁰

The success of the House-McAdoo plan hinged on two factors: one, that President Wilson himself would lend it his maximum support; and two, that other Democrats involved in New York politics would go along. Neither condition could be met fully. Wilson was constrained to approach the Empire State with extreme caution as he had in 1912. Sympathetic to the anti-Tammany cause, he was yet dependent on O'Gorman in the Senate and key Tammany congressmen for his New Freedom. This was basic, for when it came time to dole out the patronage, the administration tried to satisfy both the regulars and the independents. Neither side was happy, but the unhappiest of all was McAdoo, who later complained to Joseph Tumulty that "the real friends of the President are not being appointed to positions in New York State." The only major post that the old Osborne group received was that of assistant secretary of the navy, given to Franklin Roosevelt.[61]

The House-McAdoo scheme also conflicted with the aims and ambitions of other New Yorkers in Washington elbowing for advantage. This was best illustrated in the complex struggle over the appointment of collector of the port, traditionally the "royal prize" of the federal patronage in the state and the base from which House and McAdoo hoped to seize control of the city, then the state. McAdoo had his own candidate, former Democratic Leaguer Frank L. Polk, whose credentials he impressed on Wilson. In the meantime, Franklin Roosevelt, himself maneuvering to reorganize the New York Democracy, pushed for his friend, Poughkeepsie mayor John Sague. (For Roosevelt, Polk was simply not the man to battle Tammany.) Word that Polk was about to be appointed brought O'Gorman, reputed spokesman for Tammany, into the picture. Angry at Wilson because he was not consulted and at McAdoo for the secretary's brashness, O'Gorman invoked senatorial courtesy, threatening to block Polk on the Senate floor if necessary. What really antagonized O'Gorman was that he had submitted a list of five possible appointees to the president, any one of whom was acceptable to him and only one of whom could be considered close to Tammany. The controversy dragged on for several weeks, during which Roosevelt dropped out, McAdoo toyed with resignation from the cabinet, and O'Gorman remained adamant against Polk. Finally, the reluctant President Wilson edged toward a solution of his own. Concluding that neither McAdoo nor Tammany "should have any political control over the custom-house," he named John Purroy Mitchel to the post.[62] Mitchel was then president of the board of aldermen and was often mentioned as a possible fusion candidate for mayor. That he was an anti-Tammany Democrat was clear. But Mitchel had never been affiliated with Osborne's league or with any other groups that over the years had waged war against the Hall. Furthermore, he was an Irish Catholic, a fact, commented Wilson's friend, James Kerney, "which would bar the organization crowd from repeating their silly charges of religious bigotry." Both McAdoo and O'Gorman assented to the appointment, and Tammany looked upon it as a mixed blessing.[63]

Mitchel's advancement created the distinct impression, evidently intended by the president, that the new collector of the port was the national administration's "favorite" Democrat in New York City and thus enhanced his claim to the mayoralty. By the summer, indeed, Mitchel had emerged as one of the three leading fusion candidates. His bid for the nomination—he announced his candidacy on July 17—now commanded powerful support among influential groups within the coalition, including several young Wilsonians in New York City who quietly followed the president's lead, Bull Moosers intent on outflanking the Republicans, and representatives of William Randolph Hearst's Independence League. Mitchel became especially attractive to Theodore Roosevelt as "the most liberal candidate," and he, in turn, courted the Progressives by endorsing the main features of their proposed platform for fusion.[64] His chief rivals were New York County District Attorney Charles S. Whitman, a Republican, who had the backing of GOP regulars, and City Club President George McAneny, popular with some of the anti-Tammany Democrats, a number of social reformers, and newspapers like the *Times*. On July 31 the Committee of 107 took nine ballots to give Mitchel the mayoralty nomination. The committee then named his rivals to the fusion ticket—Whitman for reelection as district attorney and McAneny as candidate for president of the board of aldermen. Rounding out the slate was Progressive William Prendergast for the position of comptroller. Adopting a truly "positive" platform, the fusionists of 1913 succeeded admirably in creating what seemed to be a broad-based appeal in the city.[65]

Such a powerful union of anti-Tammany forces against the backdrop of the Sulzer-Murphy battle would ultimately prove decisive in the New York City elections. But fusion was not without its rough spots in the beginning—very serious ones, in fact. Some harbored grave doubts about Mitchel's vote-getting ability and his "radicalism" for embracing the Bull Moosers. "Fusion Gone Astray," snapped an August 2 *Times* editorial, capturing the feeling of a considerable portion of the city press, which blasted Hearstian, Socialist, and Progressive influences at work in this, "a conservative city." Neither McAneny nor Whitman rushed to accept their nominations. McAneny agreed to make the run after Mitchel issued a personal appeal to him. Whitman delayed longer, for Republicans had been deeply disappointed that he had not received the top spot on the ticket. Lengthy discussions with GOP officials finally brought Whitman's acceptance. Still, Mitchel and the fusionists were not out of the dark. Only two days after Whitman made his decision, Hearst's Independence League, taking its orders directly from the publisher, repudiated both McAneny and Prendergast, who, Hearst charged, had surrendered "themselves and the public interest to the privilege-seeking and franchise-stealing corporations."[66] The Hearst attack stemmed from the fact that McAneny and Prendergast, in 1911 and 1912, had approved the so-called dual subway contracts, by which new subway lines were to be built jointly by the city and private companies. Mitchel, as president of the board of aldermen, had been a fervent champion of municipal construction and operation of the new lines and thereby had received warm support from the Hearst press. He was now on the spot. Already under great pressure for his "radical tendencies," Mitchel took the only political course open to him: he withdrew his acceptance of the Independence League nomination on a slate that "denies nomination to my two associates," then added plaintively: "The issue is, and must remain, the defeat of Tammany Hall, and the establishment in the City Hall of honest and efficient government."[67] Mitchel's act was generally hailed as courageous, though hardly exculpatory to his critics.

But even now the anti-Tammanyites were not out of the wilderness, for they had to reckon with an immensely popular, Tammany-elected mayor, William Jay Gaynor. In 1909 Gaynor had walked into office largely because the then fusion forces split on the mayoralty nomination and Hearst ran on a third-party ticket. (The fusion nominee for all other major offices, running only against Tammanyites, were elected.) Gaynor had made a solid record for himself. "The recent Democratic administration," conceded one Progressive in early 1913, "has surely been better than average." Many a Bull Mooser, indeed, favored the mayor's renomination. The Committee of 107 had approached him, but his refusal to reject a Tammany bid if offered to him ended such talk. Yet there were still two possibilities for Gaynor: he might run as an independent, or he might again receive the Hall's backing. Doubtless, the pragmatic Murphy, if left to his own designs, would have renominated Gaynor in spite of the mayor's independence on patronage matters. But enormous pressures from McCooey's Brooklyn organization as well as from some of his own hard-boiled district leaders persuaded the boss to back down. Murphy, it was rumored, finally bowed to those around him because he reckoned that Gaynor would run independently, divide the opposition, and once again pave the way for a Tammany victory. So on August 23 the Hall nominated one of its own, Edward E. McCall, chairman of the downstate public service commission, for the mayoralty.[68]

Murphy's scenario, hardly fathomed by his critics, almost came to pass. One week after McCall's nomination Gaynor declared his candidacy, following which his supporters, adopting a shovel as their emblem, declared him officially in the running. The mayor quickly took to the hustings, combining furious attacks on Murphy and Tammany Hall with well-timed appeals to independents and businessmen still fearful of Mitchel's radicalism. Amid press reports that some Progressives and large numbers of Republicans disappointed with Mitchel were bolting the fusion ticket, Mitchel rushed back from his vacation to counter "the Tammany twins," McCall and Gaynor. Fate then altered the course of events in New York City. On September 12 Gaynor, while at sea on a precampaign holiday, suddenly took ill and died. Some of the mayor's friends hoped to keep the independent movement alive but to no avail. "I suppose it is now a closed chapter," declared one of them on hearing of Gaynor's passing.[69] Thus, virtually all the anti-Tammanyites rallied to the fusion banner, and Murphy's strategy backfired.

"It is Mitchel or Tammany," declared one New York City newspaper hard on the heels of Gaynor's death. From this point on the fusionists had no trouble in keeping the McCall forces on the defensive. Sulzer's own nomination by the Progressives for assemblyman in his old East Side district joined the city campaign with efforts in the upstate to vindicate the deposed governor. After his removal from office, Sulzer, indeed, returned home "like a conqueror." On October 20 he gave a lengthy interview to James Creelman of the *Evening Mail* in which he detailed his long-developing feud with Murphy. The interview was particularly damaging to Tammany interests because Sulzer accused Judge McCall of serving as an errand boy in Murphy's repeated attempts to reach an understanding with the governor early in the year. "Sulzer Exposes Murphy and McCall; Judge was 'Chief's' Messenger; Accused

Named for Assembly"—blazed the *New York American* headline next day.[70] Not long after the well-publicized Sulzer interview, John Hennessy, one of the former governor's investigators, stormed the city with specific charges of graft and corruption against the battered New York County Democratic organization. He reiterated Sulzer's points but with even more venom. "He was so full of his subject," the *Tribune* reported, "that he seldom needed the few notes at his side." Nor did McCall escape Hennessy's blast; he accused the judge of having shelled out $35,000 to George W. Plunkitt for Plunkitt's support of McCall's nomination for the state supreme court ten years earlier. These assaults seemed to bewilder McCall, who spent most of his time in the last days of the campaign flailing newspapers like the *World* for their support of fusion. Whatever reservations the New York City press had harbored concerning Sulzer earlier and Mitchel later melted in the excitement of the powerful anti-Tammany canvass.[71]

The magnitude of the Democratic loss on Election Day was astounding. "Tammany Hall was never before so thoroughly defeated," conceded the *Tammany Times*. Fusion marched triumphant in New York City, as all members of the ticket won easily. In running up a plurality of 121,000, Mitchel carried every borough, and the Democrats lost New York County for the first time since 1901. Fusionists also won control of the board of estimate and the board of aldermen as well as most of the county and judicial offices. It was estimated that the Hall thus gave up patronage worth more than $1 million per year. What was left? "We've still got air here—good, pure, fresh air," remarked one Tammanyite dejectedly. Compounding the disaster was the fact that the Democrats in Greater New York did just as badly in the state assembly contests. Murphy's forces in Manhattan and McCooey's organization in Brooklyn together were beaten in thirty-three of the sixty-two races; in 1912 the party had won all but three of these districts. Such results, claimed the *Tribune* accurately, represented "rock-bottom Tammany strength here" not unlike that sustained in 1896 or 1901. Even the most "reliable" Democratic areas in New York County—those with heavy Irish concentration— suffered an average decline of slightly under 6 percent from the vote cast in 1912. Normally Democratic German districts in Manhattan, Brooklyn, and Queens fell to Mitchel and sent Republican or Progressive assemblymen to Albany.

One heavily Italian area, Manhattan's twenty-eighth assembly district, went fusion, while eastern European Jewish districts, in electing a dozen fusion or Progressive assemblymen, slid further away from the Democracy than in 1912. Charlie Murphy's only comment about the party debacle in New York City was: "There'll be another day."[72]

Upstate "friends" of Murphy's Tammany were also badly beaten in the fall elections. Many regulars, of course, had already gone down to defeat in the September primaries. Now all thirty-seven anti-Sulzer assemblymen who had been renominated lost their seats, and the next assembly would have even fewer organization Democrats than that following the disastrous 1911 elections. In most rural areas Republicans running alone or with Progressive support recaptured the districts they had surrendered one year earlier as a result of the Bull Moose defections. Democratic assembly victories in the less populous counties—in Cattaraugus, Columbia, Orleans, and Schoharie—took place because of cooperation with Progressives or local fusion movements. In the larger upstate cities the story was about the same, though with few exceptions the GOP gain was minimal. Rochester reelected its popular Republican mayor, but the pro-Sulzer Democratic organization, joining with Bull Moosers and other citizens' groups, made a respectable showing; in fact, they were victorious in three of five assembly districts in Monroe County. The Democrats were successful in the city races in Buffalo and Utica, but in Erie County the party had already undergone its "reorganization," and Oneida Democrats were not under "the Tammany shadow." In addition, Democrats in Erie suffered a net loss of six assemblymen, in most cases to Republican-fusion candidates and in one instance to a Progressive. (All assemblymen elected in Buffalo were advocates of the direct primary.) And the Syracuse electorate, searching "for a political change in the local administration," rejected both major parties and chose a Progressive mayor in what one newspaper described as "the most remarkable municipal campaign ever waged in this city."[73] Johnstown, Amsterdam, and Auburn also went Bull Moose, the last two in fusion movements involving principally the Republicans.

V

In their simplest terms, the elections of 1913 in New York dealt a more severe blow to the Democratic state organization and specifically to

Charlie Murphy's leadership than those rebuking John Dix's "Tam-manyized" regime two years earlier. By the same token, the Democratic defeat could hardly be considered a Republican triumph; rather, the elections served as another warning to both major parties of what one journal described as an "increasing independence of mind" of the average voter.[74] Such independence was well documented by the "respectable" gains made by the Socialists together with the Progressive successes, already noted, across the state. In his mayoralty contest with Mitchel and McCall, Charles E. Russell picked up 20 percent more votes in 1913 than he had won in Greater New York the previous year when he ran for the governorship. (Most of this increase came in German and Jewish districts, many of which had been strong for Straus.)[75] As for the Progressives, Bull Moose candidates, joining with Democrats here and Republicans there (as well as citizens' groups in some cases), actually captured many more offices in the state than they had in 1912. Even where Progressive-backed candidates lost, as for example in the Buffalo mayoralty race, they often finished a strong second. And though the 1914 New York assembly would be organized by the Republicans, some three dozen legislators, elected with Bull Moose support, could wield the balance of power in that body. "The next assembly," proclaimed the Progressive state chairman, "will not be controlled by Mr. Barnes and Mr. Murphy."[76] Whether true or not, this statement underscored the enhanced optimism of those politicians and citizens in the state who, in the wake of a heightened antipathy toward bossism and the "machines," concluded that neither major party deserved an expression of confidence.

6

Martin Glynn and
the Politics of Reform

"Viewed broadly," editorialized the *New York World,* "the election results . . . go to show that the Progressive party is disintegrating."[1] Meant to apply to the eastern states of New Jersey and Massachusetts, this judgment hardly seemed to embrace the New York experience in 1913, for here Bull Moose gains actually surpassed the new party's performance the year before. Indeed, as the politicians saw it, various signs pointed to a dangerously leftward trend in the state's politics, while, at the same time, the electorate drifted more toward independence. Accordingly, both Democratic and Republican party leaders searched for ways to accommodate "enlightened public opinion" and sought either to contain Bull Moose influence, in particular, or, at least, appeal more effectively to those segments of the electorate on which the Progressives depended for support.

Republican moves were less dramatic than those of the Democrats but nonetheless bore some significance given that party's archconservative stance in 1912. All during the course of 1913, the New York City progressives loyal to the GOP had fenced with reactionary State Chairman William Barnes, attempting at several junctures to force his resignation in favor of a less intransigent leader with a more liberal outlook. Successful only in persuading Barnes to go along with fusion in Greater New York, they redoubled their efforts after the fall elections. To Parsons, Stimson, and their upstate reform colleagues, Republican unity along progressive lines still provided the best opportunity for attracting Bull Moosers back into the fold—a necessary condition, they believed, for future party victories. This agitation culminated in a well-publicized state GOP conference held on December 5 in New York City. Chaired by Elihu Root, now a spearhead of the harmony movement, the Republican gathering adopted a moderately progressive program that included workmen's compensation legislation, the short ballot, and a direct primary bill that would do away with the party emblem and party column but retain the state convention. Even Barnes consented to this "liberal" platform, though it was his opposition that resulted in a watering down of the primary plank.[2] Deemed "remarkable" in some quarters, the Republican conference seemed to give the party a proper focus for the 1914 elections—and the struggle once again for control of the state.

Meanwhile, Tammany Hall, sustaining most of the Democracy's November losses, came under blistering attacks for that party's alleged abuse of office and violation of the public trust. The cry for Murphy's ouster—and retirement from politics—was louder now than in the heyday of Osborne's league four years earlier. "Politicians are of the opinion that Charles F. Murphy cannot recover from the staggering blow to his leadership," conceded the *Tammany Times* in a post-election editorial.[3] The pot was really brewing in New York City, where independent critics outside the Hall, some urging an alliance with Murphy's enemies upstate, were joined by dissident splinter groups within several Tammany district organizations in Manhattan. Such furor momentarily threw Murphy on the defensive, but, in characteristic fashion, the boss quickly rebounded with a plan of action. Concentrating on the troubles from within, he made necessary concessions in the districts of greatest weakness, sponsoring in some instances reform counterorganizations and granting assurances in others that legitimate demands for changes in leadership would be met. By the end of November the worst of Murphy's troubles were over, as twenty-eight of thirty-one members of Tammany's executive committee stood pat for his retention—and the boss was saved.[4]

Murphy's adroit maneuvering, as usual, showed that there was probably more smoke than fire in the anti-Tammany assaults. Once again the outsiders had been unsuccessful in finding a leader around whom they could rally. There had been talk of Dudley Field Malone, recently appointed collector of the port of New York to replace Mitchel, National Democratic Chairman McCombs, and even newly elected Mayor Mitchel—but none proved ready or willing. Nor was there anyone inside Tammany, concluded the district leaders, better equipped to guide the party in the city than Murphy himself. "Under the rule of Charles F. Murphy," remarked one satrap, "it [Tammany] has been a straightforward, outspoken organization." Others lauded the boss' personal qualities and his "marvelous" achievements since his takeover in 1902, including the election of two New York City mayors together with the winning of state offices going back to Hughes's governorship. "Croker never had a record like that," commented a Tammany spokesman quite accurately. But several of these same leaders, sensitive to the shrill cry of the anti-Tammany journals, did prevail upon Murphy to restrict his activities to New York City, at least for the time being, where the Democratic party desperately needed his attention. The boss in December thus left his lieutenants in Albany completely on their own with the sage advice: "Give the people everything they want."⁵ With the major obstacle to reform (or so the critics thought) having drifted into the background, the task of working out a specific strategy to accommodate enlightened public opinion and thereby strengthen the battered Democracy fell principally to the new governor, Martin H. Glynn.

Measured by the record and performance of his Democratic predecessors Dix and Sulzer, Glynn in the months ahead would achieve solid success in program development and party leadership. Such accomplishments, however, could not overcome the sagging fortunes of the New York Democracy. The heightened and persistent anti-Tammany-ism in the wake of the Sulzer impeachment, a combination of rapid Progressive decline and Republican reemergence, and a deepened sectional-cultural cleavage fueled by a resurgent anti-Catholicism foredoomed Glynn and his Democratic colleagues to the worst statewide party disaster in years. In fact, in 1914 the Democracy would fall to its lowest point electorally in New York State during the entire progressive era.

I

Martin Glynn entered the governorship under the most inauspicious of circumstances—William Sulzer's removal from office. Yet, by this time, he was well prepared for the difficult road that lay ahead. Born in 1871 of poor Irish-Catholic parents in the small Hudson Valley community of Kinderhook, Glynn attended the public schools and worked part-time to supplement his family's meager income. Through the generosity of a prosperous local banker, he was able to matriculate in Fordham University, where he graduated first in his class in 1894. Thereafter Glynn divided his time between a newspaper job with the *Albany Times-Union* and the study of law. In 1897 he passed the state bar examination but subsequently never practiced law. Instead, he remained in the newspaper business, working his way up the ladder to managing editor and finally editor and owner of the *Times-Union*. Like William Barnes, his Republican counterpart in Albany, Glynn used his journalistic training—and his newspaper—as a springboard into politics. He served one term in Congress—he was the youngest man in the House of Representatives in 1899–1900—and became a winning member of the New York State Democratic ticket in 1906, when he was elected comptroller. Six years later, he was handed the lieutenant governor's nomination to run with William Sulzer.[6]

Glynn's political career, not unlike Sulzer's, was a mixture of organizational politics and independence. His critics accused him of being a protégé of Albany Democratic boss "Packy" McCabe, and indeed he was. Yet Glynn also considered himself a reformer and thus served as another example of the regular Democrat who could pursue progressive policies. In fact, both he and McCabe formed the vanguard of supporters for William Randolph Hearst's gubernatorial movement upstate in 1906. After Hearst's nomination that fall by a reluctant Charlie Murphy, Glynn daily wrote editorials in the *Times-Union* acclaiming the publisher's "radicalism" and "socialism," hailing especially the Independence League stance against corporations and in favor of the public ownership of utilities. His own nomination for comptroller helped establish a bridge between Hearst insurgents and Democratic party regulars. In turn, Glynn's two years as New York's comptroller, paralleling Hughes's first gubernatorial term, were characterized by independence and reform. He used his office to reconstruct the stock transfer tax bureau, investigate and expose irregularities in financing among several county officials, tighten up the collection of corporation and inheritance taxes, and protect state money during the panic of

1907. How much of this constructive work grew out of a close relationship between Democrat Glynn and Republican Hughes remains unknown. But Glynn did develop a healthy respect and great admiration for the GOP chief executive. "He was a pretty good Governor. Even if I am a Democrat, I say it," Glynn later spoke of Hughes.[7]

The Glynn-Sulzer relationship was another matter. In appearance, personality, and temperament, the two were worlds apart. Glynn was short and stockily built, almost always bearing a conservative demeanor. He was no poseur and harbored none of the Sulzer-type bravado or flamboyance. Robert Binkerd described him as "an intellectually-inclined Irishman," and Glynn saw himself in somewhat the same vein. "Like Wouter Van Twiller," he once said, "I am for reflection before action, for consultation before agitation."[8] Glynn's reflectiveness was anchored in a deep-seated honesty and punctured by a good sense of humor. These differences aside, Glynn and Sulzer at first seemed to get along rather well. As lieutenant governor Glynn cooperated with Robert Wagner and Al Smith in drumming up support for the governor's progressive program in the legislature and used his influence to keep the party together. But when the torrents of abuse poured from Sulzer's office onto his critics, Glynn grew distant. Like so many others, he also harbored serious misgivings about the governor's sincerity on the direct primary. (Later he would charge Sulzer with faking the whole issue.) But for Glynn the straw that broke the camel's back was Sulzer's veto of the Murtaugh hydroelectric bill that would have appropriated funds for the construction of a state-owned plant on the Mohawk River to generate and sell electricity to the capital district. Glynn believed that he had received Sulzer's assurances of support for the measure, and he found the veto "indefensible." "When he vetoed this bill," Glynn charged angrily, "he was an enemy of the people and a friend of the corporations." Colleagues thought it was Sulzer's way of retaliating against those who abandoned him in the direct nominations fight. And Glynn fell even more to the defensive when the governor launched his summer campaign against Murphy and his upstate allies. At the time, he indignantly likened Sulzer to the "great" liars of history, who, he insisted, were "tyros in the name of falsehood compared to William Sulzer."[9]

The chance for a real confrontation between the two came with

Sulzer's impeachment in August. For some five weeks—until the trial got under way—they fenced with one another over the exercise of gubernatorial authority. Despite the attorney general's ruling that Glynn was acting governor, Sulzer refused to turn over the state's privy seal and ordered that all executive department records be placed under lock and key. The situation was almost as bizarre as the impeachment episode itself, for no one doing business with the state knew where to turn. Finally, when the vote came on Sulzer's removal, Glynn assumed the full power of the office. He accompanied his acceptance of the position with a statement of conciliation. Dismissing factionalism and promising to minimize partisan politics, the new governor thus assured "the people of the State an honest, peaceful, progressive and wise conduct of their public affairs."[10]

Glynn moved quickly to develop a party strategy that implemented his deeply felt ideas on good government and progressivism. He sponsored a legislative program that well-nigh completed the main agenda of reforms for New York State during that era. Convinced that Sulzer had perpetrated the rupture in the Democratic party by his excessive rhetoric, his hyperbole, and his constant play to the independent press (Glynn called it "first pagetta"), he sought to reunify the warring elements: he refused himself to participate in factional politics; he made overtures to those upstate independents still active—Havens, Treman, and Antisdale, for example—without antagonizing Tammany Hall; and, as 1914 dawned, he attempted party reorganization with the help of key Wilsonians. For Glynn the reward may have been, as he put it, the satisfaction of being "the real Governor the year I have."[11] It was, in addition, the party's gubernatorial nomination in the fall.

Glynn first addressed himself to the legislative side of his program. Facing a divided legislature after January 1, he shrewdly convoked the senate and assembly in special session in December and delivered a rousing reform message. He called for various political reforms, including the direct primary, the Massachusetts ballot, and a measure adjusting the state's election machinery to prepare for the direct election of U.S. senators beginning the next fall. "I am satisfied that the enlightened public opinion of this day demands a change in our election laws," Glynn declared flatly. The "change" he wanted most was the very thing that the major party organizations, Republican and Democratic, had long battled and that had formed the basis of the Sulzer-Murphy imbroglio—that is, a scheme abolishing the state party convention and effecting nominations for statewide offices by petitions and primaries. Finally, he demanded the passage of a workmen's compensation bill "appropriately recognizing the right to compulsory compensation to injured employees"—one that, indeed, resembled closely the measure championed by the social progressive societies and the New York State Federation of Labor.[12]

The Glynn program, much to the astonishment of Democratic critics, had smooth sailing through the "irresponsible," Tammany-dominated state legislature. In the interim between the November elections and the opening of the special session, the governor had been served notice that the senate and assembly leadership would accord him a free hand. Murphy himself, of course, had paved the way with his well-publicized "retirement" to New York City. "It was the 122,000 majority given to Mitchel," admitted one politician in explaining the regulars' unexpected cooperativeness on political reforms. At first Al Smith seemed to balk on the direct primary plan. "Show me the bill," he exclaimed, "and I'll tell you whether the boys will come back here to pass it." A series of conferences between Glynn and the legislative leaders dispelled any remaining doubts. Wagner, himself, drafted the primary measure, worked closely with Edward Jackson of Buffalo on the workmen's compensation bill, and was the chief sponsor of the proposed Massachusetts ballot. When the senate and assembly received the package, little opposition was voiced from either side of the aisle—and the Progressives expressed sheer delight. Doubtless, many a lawmaker agreed with one "dazed" old-time Tammanyite, who remarked largely in reference to the political reforms:

It is the bitterest dose of medicine anybody has ever made me swallow. But what's the use? We know that some of the bills are crazy. . . . The mob Upstate seems to want it. I have done my share, and I have done it out of a conscientious belief that these new-fangled ideas are going to work havoc in this State. But I'm tired of trying to stem the tide: I am tired of being a target for the people to heave bricks at. I am a reformer, indeed.[13]

Efforts were made to amend the primary bill, but when these failed it sailed through easily. The Massachusetts ballot resolution divided the senate along party lines, the Democrats in favor and the Republicans opposed, but passed the assembly with only 4 dissenting votes. And though the Republican leadership preferred delay on the advanced workmen's compensation scheme, only employers' groups lobbied against the measure. It received almost unanimous support in both bodies.[14]

Needless to say, the Glynn program, driven through a "chastened" legislature, won the accolades of political and social reformers as well as labor leaders only recently converted to the ideal of compulsory workmen's compensation. And the otherwise skeptical *New York Times* epitomized independent opinion by hailing the special session as having adopted "more constructive legislation in a week than other Legislatures have enacted in an entire session."[15] Yet Governor Glynn did not stop here. With the reform agenda completed, he turned, in January 1914, to economy and retrenchment and impressed even the new Republican leadership in the assembly with his annual message charging that "the most serious problem now confronting us is the question of State finances." He subsequently vetoed special appropriation bills amounting to $6 million, "the greatest amount vetoed by any Governor," and proposed scores of ways in which executive departments might be streamlined. Glynn established a Moreland commission to investigate graft and corruption in the notorious highway department, though the inquiry would unearth little that was new and nothing of consequence in either his or Sulzer's administration. In all, Glynn's efforts resulted in a state budget that anticipated a surplus of $1.5 million for the fiscal year, prompting some Tammany spokesmen to gloat about so "remarkable" a feat.[16]

Glynn's final contribution to Democratic "revival" concerned party reorganization on the state level. "I recognized that party confidence must be restored," he stated flatly, "or all the splendid work of the Wilson administration and everything that the Democratic legislature might do would not avert disaster in the fall." Murphy's withdrawal to New York City in November had been the first step. Yet this move had served only to encourage another conspiracy on the part of those two high-ranking members of the Wilson administration, House and McAdoo, who had earlier laid plans for reconstructing the New York party. Called the New Democracy, the latest House-McAdoo scheme was hatched in December apparently with the president's sympathy; it envisioned a coalition of upstate independents, Mitchel followers in Manhattan, and dissident Brooklyn leaders that would endeavor to seize control of the Democratic state organization. Like the 1913 plot, however, this one stood little chance of success. Franklin Roosevelt was involved in his own "conspiracy"; Mitchel continued to display no interest in state politics; and President Wilson, still in need of Tammany support in Congress and once again suspicious of the House-McAdoo motives, backed off and then pulled the rug out from under the plan. But the scheme's existence may have been the principal factor in galvanizing Glynn into action. By the end of January the governor had consulted with Democrats across the state and had come forward with his own proposal to reorganize the state committee by naming a new chairman, William C. Osborn.[17]

Before Glynn dared to implement his plan, he sought the blessing of President Wilson himself, lest the governor be sabotaged by plotters in the federal administration. Making contact through National Democratic Chairman William McCombs, a rival of House and McAdoo, he arranged several conferences in Washington on February 9. The key meeting was held in the White House and involved Glynn, McCombs, and Wilson. Here McCombs advised the president that Glynn was giving New York State "progressive government." Glynn and McCombs then outlined "their" reorganization scheme, which called for Osborn's election as state chairman and Glynn's resolve to bypass Tammany in the rest of his state appointments. Wilson, in return, would not only recognize the Glynn-McCombs leadership in New York, but also promised to give serious consideration to backing the governor in his reelection bid. "I believe that from that conference," Glynn crowed on his return to Albany, "there has resulted a perfect mutual understanding, which will mean co-operation in the reorganization of the party."[18]

The Glynn-McCombs reorganization plan was less sweeping than at first it appeared and was far more attuned to the political realities in New York than the governor himself would publicly admit. It was, of course, not really a declaration of war against Murphy and Tammany Hall. Murphy's disavowal of state leadership meant that the naming of a state chairman not totally loyal to him was hardly a blow to his "prestige." Osborn's own qualifications for the position shed further light on the nature of Glynn's program. A wealthy upstate attorney with an "aristocratic make up," he had a reputation for being a "sterling independent," yet he was also known to get on well with the organization element. He had served as Governor Dix's legal advisor and thus had been properly tutored in the politics of the state capital. If any doubt remained about the plan, it must have been dispelled by Glynn's affirmation of the principle of county autonomy, which presumably Sulzer had been prepared to use against Murphy. "Any appointment I should make in New York County," declared the governor after his return from conferences in the city, "would be an appointment that I thought met the approval of the Democratic sentiment of New York County." In effect, that sentiment would be determined by the duly established organization, Tammany Hall, for McCombs had made clear to Wilson that he would not interfere in the local New York City situation if Murphy accepted "reorganization." Quickly, and some suggested cynically, the pragmatic boss embraced the Glynn-McCombs scheme with the pronouncement: "I shall . . . aid in any way in the uplift—if 'uplift' is the word—of the Democratic party." The arrangements were completed three weeks later when, in early March, Osborn was unanimously chosen Democratic state chairman by the state committee.[19]

To many of the independents—and to the reformist press—in New York the Glynn-McCombs reorganization was little more than a "sham." "A scheme of Democratic reform that does not contemplate the complete separation of the Democratic organization from Tammany will never get far," charged the uncompromising *New York World*. The Sulzerites were also bitter. Equally disenchanted were upstaters such as Louis Antisdale. "Roses and skunk cabbage smell the same as before to rural noses, tho' they be decorated with new names with every change of gardeners," he complained.[20] What enthusiasm Glynn's progressive legislative program had generated among these anti-Tammanyites quickly evaporated, and a number of the old dissidents were spurred into action once again in the spring and summer of 1914. Alas, however, the movement was now a shadow of its former self, and the reasons were obvious. For one thing, the independents no longer had Thomas Mott Osborne, who, with all his idiosyncrasies, had supplied spirit, organization, and finances to aid the anti-Tammany cause. For another, the regulars had taken away from them, then implemented, most of the political reforms the independents had championed. Finally, President Wilson's approval of the Glynn-McCombs reorganization plan not only lent respectability to the new state administration but also robbed the independents of natural leadership in Washington. It severely hampered the outspoken Dudley Field Malone, Mitchel's successor as collector of the port of New York, and William G. McAdoo, the man Franklin Roosevelt dubbed "the only one who could 'lead.' " In the months ahead McAdoo was constrained to work behind the scenes as Wilson clamped a lid of silence on members of his administration engaged in politicking on the state level: he quietly influenced the patronage and supported in various ways the machinations of others, like Roosevelt, in the Empire State. In disgust, McAdoo decried a more active role. "New York situation! What a *mess* it is! I am not going to be drawn into that situation," he exclaimed to Colonel House as if he had a choice.[21]

The upshot was that the ineffectual independents in the state were left floundering in a sea of confusion. Abandoned by Wilson essentially for Tammany's support in Congress yet given just enough encouragement by McAdoo and House to carry on the fight, they challenged the Glynn-Osborn forces in the fall primaries. Here they believed they stood some chance for the new direct nominations law would be going into effect. Since Osborn had paved the way for an open primary by rejecting an informal party convention (except to hammer out a platform), they could make their pitch in both the gubernatorial and the senatorial contests. The figures around whom they eventually rallied were Franklin Roosevelt and John Hennessy, Sulzer's private investigator. But the course they pursued in making these selections was tortuous, once again the consequence of their lack of central direction and coordination.

Roosevelt, to be sure, had long been a leading figure among the upstate Wilsonians. Since the latter part of 1913, especially after Tammany's defeat in the fall elections, the Hyde Park Democrat exhibited an interest in running for either senator or governor. Increasingly, FDR's name was associated with the governorship, and through the middle part of 1914 he publicly disclaimed such ambitions but privately canvassed his strength. His caution was dictated by the Wilson administration's attempts to harmonize party differences in New York. Even after the president cast his lot with Glynn and McCombs, Roosevelt and his supporters sought White House backing apparently because they did not know the extent of the president's commitments. "We are completely at sea as to what the national administration have in their minds," confessed Frank Polk to FDR in mid-March. When four months later Wilson made crystal-clear his "capitulation" to the regulars in New York, Roosevelt, the realist, bowed out of the gubernatorial race. Antisdale and his upstate friends quickly "drafted" Hennessy, some thought to head off a Sulzer boom as much as to name a confirmed anti-Tammanyite. They now approached Roosevelt to accept their support for the senatorial nomination. In a New York City conference held on August 12, FDR acceded to their offer, apparently more out of a sense of duty than a compelling desire to make the run. (The regulars as yet had not identified their candidate for the senatorship.) Maintaining that he was taking this step without consulting administration officials, Roosevelt formally announced his candidacy and the theme of the primary campaign: "I do so with the belief that the coming campaign will determine whether the State of New York is to be found on the side of intelligent progress and honest administration of government."[22]

Thus, through Hennessy and Roosevelt the pesky independents hoped to use the ensuing primary contest to step up their assault on the Democratic organization for its "reactionary" policies and to insist once again that they were the true representatives of Wilsonian progressivism in New York State. Their efforts were ineffective, even ludicrous at times, because they were constantly outmaneuvered by the regulars. Shortly after the Hennessy announcement, Glynn threw himself into the gubernatorial race, emphasizing his own reform program. "It is natural that having instituted these reforms," he proclaimed, "I should desire to watch over their first operations." Later the same month the Democratic state conference, meeting in Saratoga to forge a state platform, was "extraordinary for the complete harmony that prevailed." Few of the older leaders were present, and Osborn and McCombs dominated the proceedings. Following Charlie Murphy's own advice, "We are in favor of standing by the primary law and against the endorsement of any candidate," the conference issued as its most positive statement a ringing endorsement of the Wilson administration. The platform also called for structural reforms in the executive and administrative departments of state government as well as the short ballot. "The Democratic leaders talked as gravely as the Colonel himself now does about confiding in the wisdom of the people," remarked one progressive newspaper cynically.[23]

The final blow to the Hennessy-Roosevelt team came in early September, when petitions circulated around the state for the candidacy of James W. Gerard, then ambassador to Germany, for the senatorial nomination. Since his own commitment to run, Roosevelt had been preoccupied with the identity of his primary opponent. He registered delight at the early rumors that Murphy and the regulars would again turn to Hearst. But the Hearst "movement" quickly fizzled, and Roosevelt and Louis Howe returned to speculating about Tammany's strategy. "The truth is," suggested Howe almost wistfully, "[they] haven't anything to say against you and no one is very anxious to bell the cat." Such backslapping ceased with talk of a prospective Gerard candidacy supported by the Hearst press. Gerard's name, now that war had broken out in Europe, was daily in the headlines of American newspapers. No one, including FDR, was more closely identified with the Wilson administration. At once respected and regular, Gerard was one of those gentlemanly types affiliated with Tammany Hall. Roosevelt responded initially to the rumors with expressions of disbelief. Disbelief became despair when Gerard finally declared his willingness to accept the nomination and Wilson again refused to intervene in the New York situation.[24]

Roosevelt suffered through the primary campaign knowing that his was a lost cause. He tried hard. He used the patronage at his disposal to twist arms in the upstate regions, where his efforts were concentrated. For over two weeks, in September, FDR toured the state four times hitting hard the anti-Tammany theme and attacking Gerard as a "tool" of Murphy. He extracted commitments from John Purroy Mitchel and Dudley Field Malone in an obvious attempt to link himself as closely as possible to the Wilson administration. Yet because of poor preparation and lack of finances, among other factors, the Roosevelt canvass failed to catch on. Nor was Hennessy, his running mate, terribly effective. His slashing assaults on the corruption of machine politics, something he claimed he knew at first hand, did raise eyebrows, but the Irishman's heavy brogue and flashy mannerisms made him seem clownish to upstate audiences. "He ruined us," Howe declared later, "and he will sink any ship on which he is a passenger." More than that, however, the Glynn-Gerard ticket, though Glynn did little campaigning and Gerard did none, was solid and unbeatable. With scores of county chairmen and even independents, now impressed with the Wilson-Glynn alliance, falling into line, Hennessy and Roosevelt, on September 28, were beaten by landslide proportions. They lost New York City by an almost four-to-one margin and the upstate by over two to one.[25]

The Hennessy-Roosevelt drubbing essentially marked the end of the independent Democratic movement begun nearly one decade earlier by Osborne and his upstate allies. There were, indeed, ironies about the 1914 debacle: it came, not in a boss-dominated convention, but by means of the independents' favorite reform, the direct primary; and it was abetted by the progressive Woodrow Wilson, hero of Osborne and Roosevelt. Wilson subsequently tendered his personal endorsement of Glynn's candidacy "as embodying the cause of progressive legislation and advancement . . . of the interests of the people." Also, administration officials, including McAdoo, were pressured to support—and in some cases campaign for—Glynn and Gerard in the fall elections. Mayor Mitchel, too, openly declared for the state ticket. Hennessy bolted to the Republicans, but Roosevelt salved his wounds, then delivered speeches for the regular candidates, and thereafter gave up the anti-Tammany cause.[26] With a reiteration of Murphy's earlier pledge to withdraw to New York City, Glynn reveled in the party unity that his reorganization program had manifestly created.

II

Although Martin Glynn's ventures in progressive government helped still the voices of independence among Democrats, other reformers, mostly of Bull Moose persuasion, continued their forays against "Barnesism" and "Murphyism" in New York. "I doubt whether there is a State in the Union," charged Theodore Roosevelt in familiar tones, "that shows more conclusively than this State the dreadful evil of the two boss system in political life."[27] Surely the Bull Moose emphasis on this theme, at the virtual exclusion of all others in 1914, represented at once an implicit recognition that the "discredited" Democrats in Albany had stolen much of the reform program that the Progressives themselves had championed two years earlier and yet was a reflection of the heightened antibossism in the public mind following the Sulzer impeachment. In fact, many a Bull Mooser could not help but equate the recent success of fusion in New York City (as well as in various upstate communities) with the immense popularity of the good government appeal, and some viewed the loose coalition of independents and party renegades forged in 1913 as a likely nucleus for a statewide union of the disenchanted. Such a Progressive vision, however, remained just that, for by mid-1914 the fledgling Roosevelt party was itself engulfed in serious problems—problems that soon would render it an ineffectual political force in state and nation. Mainly Bull Moose troubles transcended the New York experience and penetrated to the very core of the third-party movement.

Formed quickly in the wake of the Republican cataclysm of 1912, the Progressive party raced through its early days in the exuberance of its stirring reformism. But in that year and again in 1913, it failed to win enough offices across the nation to sustain its followers or its organization. Nor was the party graced by many philanthropists who could shore up its sagging fortunes. The greater part of the Progressives' 1912 campaign chest had been supplied by National Chairman George W. Perkins and publisher Frank Munsey. But Munsey's early return to the Republicans left Perkins alone as Roosevelt's "sugar daddy." And Perkins, a partner in the J. P. Morgan and Company, was vulnerable to the charge of coddling "big business" leveled by the Bull Moose's radical left. Disputes between Perkins and the Pinchot brothers, Amos and Gifford, erupted in 1912 then again in 1914, just as the Bull Moosers were preparing for the fall elections. Even as Roosevelt was adroitly smoothing over these differences the second time around—together with others that divided his organization—the Colonel himself harbored greater and greater misgivings about the Progressives' future. A faltering, bickering party was, after all, symptomatic of a deeper malady—uselessness. With Woodrow Wilson pursuing his New Freedom and exercising bold, aggressive presidential leadership, what chances would a third party have in 1916? Roosevelt's answer to this question seemed to be to keep the Bull Moose together as best he could on the chance that, as George Mowry has argued, "some sudden whirl of the political wheel might make it the nucleus of . . . a [1916] victory," or that, at least, it might command a trading value of several million votes presumably with the GOP. For fear of antagonizing his most loyal supporters, Roosevelt publicly denied the likelihood of union with the Republicans but privately weighed its probable success, as he put it in 1913, "a year or two hence."[28]

Most of the problems facing the national Progressive party were present in the New York organization in 1914. While, to be sure, the Bull Moose had done well enough electorally the previous year to scare the major party leaders, their victories in the Empire State had been principally in local contests and were mainly attained through fusion with others. Day-by-day Progressive membership lists dwindled, as both upstaters and downstaters returned to their traditional Republican home, the more so, it appeared, as the state GOP moved in a liberal direction. "Wo is dot barty now?" queried the ever critical *Tammany Times* half-humorously in February. Despite Perkins's presence in New York City, the financial picture was bleak. With over 30 percent of the state's national committeemen failing to pay their annual dues of ten dollars, one member was prompted to ask: "How can we raise money when our own committeemen won't pay up?"[29] Such realities impelled New York Progressives to search for formulas to keep the party alive. After giving some thought to "drafting" Roosevelt himself for governor, the Colonel and the state leaders—some of them quite reluctantly—formulated a plan embracing a fusion "arrangement" with the Republicans. Harvey D. Hinman, an upstate Hughes progressive who had remained loyal to the GOP, would be offered the gubernatorial nomination. In return the Republicans were asked to accept a Progressive for the U.S. Senate vacancy, with Oscar Straus "as the standard of the nominee," together with Bull Moosers for other offices, including a congressman or two from New York City and a few upstate legislators.[30]

The GOP leadership, however, would have no part of the Bull Moose scheme. To Perkins the Republicans were thus behaving cockily, but the reason for their recalcitrance must have been obvious to anyone:

neither progressives nor conservatives wanted to "save" the Roosevelt party. New York City Republicans did welcome support from Bull Moosers in their ongoing fight with Barnes, but they were getting it anyway from the returning renegades. "We want the Progressives back," confided Herbert Parsons in early 1914, "but . . . we don't want Roosevelt as a nominee." As the days wore on, it became clear that Parsons's concern about Roosevelt as a "nominee" was not limited to that year but, in fact, extended to the presidency in 1916. On this point Barnes and the conservatives could hardly disagree. Ideologically at odds with the former president, the state chairman still pressed for guarantees that the more liberal Republican contingent would not cement a deal with the Progressives. He therefore announced early his backing of New York City's Charles S. Whitman for the GOP gubernatorial nomination, a move that really delighted the New York City Republicans. And in a much-heralded state committee meeting held shortly after Roosevelt's appeal for fusion, Republican harmony was attained to a most unusual degree. "The Colonel has made two discoveries," gloated stalwart Job Hedges afterward. "One discovery is a river—of doubt [in reference to Roosevelt's recent exploration of a hitherto uncharted river in South America]. The other is a fearless militant Republican Party."[31] Ironically, those Republicans who held out longest for an easy path for the Progressives' return were conservatives George Aldridge of Rochester and Francis Hendricks of Syracuse, men whose constituencies had returned a substantial Bull Moose vote in 1913.

The Republican-Progressive scenario was played out in the months that followed. Whitman was unacceptable to the Bull Moosers because they claimed that he was "duplicitous" and even persuaded some Republican regulars that this was the case. A number of Roosevelt loyalists in desperation reopened the issue of the Colonel's gubernatorial candidacy, but TR quickly reiterated his earlier decision and announced his intention to tour the nation to work for "those principles embodied in the Progressive Platform of 1912."[32] Resolved to force "the Hinman candidacy on the Republican Party," the Bull Moosers next extracted what they thought was a firm commitment from Hinman, then through Roosevelt denounced Bosses Barnes and Murphy for pursuing "identical" interests (a statement that prompted Barnes to launch a libel suit against Roosevelt). With much of the press agreeing that the Colonel was "going back into the Republican Party . . . if he can capture and dominate it," GOP lines hardened further. On the eve of the unofficial Republican convention in Saratoga Hinman, evidently under intense pressure from Barnes, reversed himself on entering the Progressive primary and asserted that he would accept no other nomination if he lost the GOP bid. Two days later the Republicans met and hammered out a platform described as "conservative but not reactionary."[33] The new primary law precluded official designation of candidates, but delegate support for Whitman for governor and James W. Wadsworth, Jr., for U.S. senator was evident.

The rest of the way was downhill for the Progressives. Terribly embittered by the Hinman fiasco, Roosevelt withdrew his support from the upstater and searched for a ticket of his own in New York. There was some talk of Sulzer, who, since early in the year, had been striking out in several directions in his stepped-up effort at self-redemption. But the Bull Moose state committee, following a Sulzer-Roosevelt conference, overwhelmingly turned down the former governor's bid in a stormy session punctured with epithets like "crook" and "faker." Instead, the state committee endorsed a ticket of Frederick M. Davenport for governor and Bainbridge Colby for senator on an almost exclusively antibossism platform. In the ensuing primary Sulzer and Davenport thus slugged it out for what Roosevelt now believed was a worthless nomination. Progressive affiliation in the state had plummeted to about 120,000 and was declining by the day. "All the Democrats have either withdrawn from the organization or been forced out of it," lamented one disgruntled Bull Mooser amid the primary campaign. The result was a Davenport victory, but a narrow one, indeed, as Sulzer came within 3,000 votes of winning in an unusually low voter turnout.[34] The end was near for the Progressive party in New York State.

Meanwhile, the Republicans made the most of Progressive travails. On the eve of the primary campaign, Barnes announced his retirement as state chairman, a decision that GOP progressives truly welcomed. No longer could the Albany conservative serve as the symbol of Republican bossism in the state, and this proved to be a real blow to the Bull Moose strategy. Though Whitman lost the backing of key New York City Republicans like Stimson and Ogden Mills, he carried into the primaries the blessing of Frederick Tanner's New York County organization as well as the more conservative upstate organizations still under Barnes's influence. Whitman, therefore, easily won the gubernatorial nomination over Hinman and assured party unity in the fall elections by turning the state chairmanship over to Tanner. Possessed of a "certain political kinship" with Barnes, Tanner had earlier encouraged the Albany boss to sponsor Wadsworth's candidacy while he concentrated on Whitman's.[35] Accommodation had worked beautifully for the GOP; the Progressives had been badly outmaneuvered; and the Republicans once again looked "fighting trim" for the fall elections.

III

Much of the 1914 campaign in New York was predictable as Martin Glynn's opponents harped on the familiar theme of "antibossism." For the Progressives, Roosevelt toured the state with Davenport attacking both "Murphyism" and "Barnesism." Bull Moosers actually concentrated on the latter, for, though Barnes played a minimal role in the Republican canvass, they apparently preferred a Democratic victory to show the GOP how badly they were needed in 1916. Nonetheless, gloom and doom permeated the Roosevelt camp, as neither major candidate, Glynn nor Whitman, put much stock in the Progressives' charges. Glynn repeatedly professed his independence from Tammany Hall; emphasized his reform record (especially the enactment of workmen's compensation, which won him the support of organized labor); but also boasted of the efficiency and retrenchment he brought to Albany. This last achievement, a "rigid policy of saving the taxpayers' money," proclaimed one newspaper, would give the governor an upstate following.[36] All the while, Whitman's campaign, "reactionary" to some, emphasized corruption in state government and "Tammanyism." A fourth contender, William Sulzer, already repudiated by the Bull Moose, entered the race as the gubernatorial nominee of two parties, the Prohibitionists and the American party, the latter a hastily prepared creation of his close friends and former Albany associates. Sulzer's major objective was to defeat Glynn, and his calumny was reserved for the incumbent governor. Short of money, and fully aware that the electorate would choose principally between Glynn and Whitman, Sulzer's managers, indeed, resorted to the most unsavory tactics against their erstwhile colleagues—the exploitation of a growing anti-Catholicism in state and nation in this, the later progressive era.[37]

From time to time earlier in the year and during the primary campaign, driblets of religious bigotry were evidenced in the upstate. As the primary gave way to the general election campaign, rumors flew that a secret organization headquartered in western New York, subsequently identified as the Guardians of Liberty (GOL), was busily distributing anti-Catholic propaganda directed mainly against Martin Glynn, the state's first Roman Catholic governor. Much of the literature came in the form of questioning Glynn on whether his religious beliefs would influence his performance as chief executive. Though Glynn forthrightly assured his detractors that he opposed using public funds for the support of parochial schools, the attacks persisted, even intensified in certain areas. "The State of New York is being flooded with the most venomous documents," protested the (Syracuse) *Catholic Sun* near the end of the campaign.[38] At least one GOL circular offered voters a preferred list of candidates, representing a mix of Republicans, Progressives, and Prohibitionists. All, of course, were Protestants, including Whitman for governor and Wadsworth for U.S. senator.[39]

Spokesmen for the Progressives and the Democrats quickly repudiated the obvious bigotry, and Bull Moosers rejected the GOL's endorsement of their candidates. Republicans were less courageous and kept silent, for, in fact, they were the movement's chief beneficiaries. But it was Sulzer's new political organ that made the most blatant use of this vicious anti-Catholicism. The American party, founded early in 1914 on the likelihood that the former governor could not win the Democratic or Progressive nomination, was steeped in nativism from the beginning. Sulzer's upstate aide, Chester C. Platt, had labeled it "the new No-Nothings" only two weeks after its birth.[40] As the summer wore on, the party attracted to its banner a host of racist and evangelical Protestant organizations. There was, for example, the National Democratic Fair Play Association, one of whose main objectives was the passage of tougher naturalization laws. Another was the Reverend O. R. Miller's Civic League, an Albany-based group concerned with moral reform. Miller confessed to Frederick Davenport that after his talks with Protestant ministers all over the state, "three-fourths of them will vote for Sulzer . . . and they will carry thousands of votes with them for Sulzer." Miller pledged his personal support to the former governor, and he insisted that his publication, *The Reform Bulletin,* would "have a large influence on the elections this Fall." More important, Sulzer's close associates pulled out all the stops once the campaign was under way. The American party secretary forwarded to Whitman a copy of a recently published pro-Sulzer tract, *The Boss or the Governor,* with the assurance: "It is my duty to bring all pressure possible against the Tammany candidate, whether it comes from your side or mine." In mid-October, Sulzer's good friend and cofounder of the American party, Samuel Bell Thomas, accepted sample copies of *The Protestant Magazine,* whose motto was "Advocate of Primitive Christianity," and agreed to "distribute them in places where they will do the most good."[41]

Sulzer himself carefully avoided the religious issue in his public speeches but privately made the same association between "bossism" and Catholicism that much of the hate literature advanced. To Democratic State Chairman Osborn he wrote acidly:

You know, and so does every decent Democrat in the State, that if I had not been a 32nd degree Mason; that if I had not been a Protestant; that if my name had not been Sulzer; that if I had connived at corruption; that if I had taken orders from the Bosses; that if I had not prosecuted the Grafters; the Bosses, and the forces of Invisible Government would never have removed me.[42]

To be an honest, independent, hard-hitting Protestant for Sulzer had been a serious disadvantage in the boss system of New York politics, and the former governor struck back with all of his venom right up through Election Day.[43]

IV

The scurrilous anti-Catholic campaign was but one aspect of a general reaction against the Democratic party in New York in 1914, as the Republicans virtually swept the state in the November elections. Whitman smothered Glynn by a plurality of nearly 122,000, the largest enjoyed by any Republican gubernatorial candidate since the 1890s.

Sulzer finished third and Davenport ran a poor fourth. In the U.S. senatorial election Wadsworth defeated Gerard by a lesser margin, and the Republicans won a substantial majority of both houses of the legislature as well as a small majority of the state's congressional delegation. "The story of the election in a nutshell," summarized Mack's *Buffalo Evening Times*, "is that the Republicans pulled a surprisingly large upstate vote and the Democrats fell below expectations in Greater New York." Whitman, for example, piled up a plurality of about 179,000 votes outside New York City and lost the city by only 54,000 votes; and he took every upstate county but one. (Wadsworth ran almost as well in the upstate but was beaten badly in New York City by the Tammany-affiliated Gerard.) For the first time since 1908, therefore, the Republicans reached their traditional strength of well over one half of the upstate vote and approximately 40 percent in Greater New York.[44]

Both urban and rural communities across the state recorded a nominal Progressive vote and usually a much lower Democratic total than in the tumultuous year of 1912. "The up-state districts have returned to the fold," exclaimed one Republican newspaper quite accurately. Democratic losses were especially critical in the major interior cities: Rochester, Syracuse, and Albany went overwhelmingly Republican, with the Democracy failing to win a single ward in the Flower City; even Buffalo and Utica fell to the GOP. Heavily ethnic and working-class areas in these cities followed suit as thousands of voters, many of whom had supported the Bull Moose in 1912, seemingly went Republican in disproportionate numbers. The Democrats remained secure only in Irish wards, where in Buffalo, Syracuse, Troy, and Yonkers Glynn's percentages were among the highest garnered by the party in several elections; in Buffalo's and Utica's Polish districts the Democracy also did reasonably well.[45] Finally, the Republicans swept the legislative races in the upstate, capturing seventeen of twenty-four senate seats, fifty-one of sixty-three in the assembly, and nineteen of twenty-two in the new U.S. Congress.

If the upstate returned with a vengeance to its old-line Republicanism, Greater New York went back to the Democracy, albeit far less conclusively—that is, unless measured against the party disaster in 1913. Indeed, the Democratic vote total in New York City in 1914 was the lowest in a gubernatorial election in the twentieth century and almost plummeted to Bryan's level in 1908. Undoubtedly, much of this decline was due to an unusually low voter turnout. Another factor was the content and direction of the former Bull Moose vote. The "second" party in New York City two years earlier, the Progressives did as badly here in 1914 as in the upstate: Bull Moose totals dropped from an average of 31 percent to slightly under 4 percent in just two years. And the decline occurred throughout Greater New York. In the more heavily native American districts, most of which had been Republican before 1910, the GOP naturally was the chief beneficiary, though some with smaller pluralities than expected. It is true that in the predominantly ethnic districts—and particularly those that had usually been under Tammany's thumb—the return to two-party politics spelled Democratic victory in the gubernatorial, U.S. senatorial, and state legislative races. In the assembly contests, in fact, the Democrats did unexpectedly well, recovering over one dozen seats they had lost in 1913 but falling short of the fifty they had won in the banner year of 1910. Irish strongholds, as in the upstate cities, recorded the largest Democratic vote in several elections probably because an Irish Catholic headed the ticket. Italian districts and all but one German district also went Democratic, yet the vote totals here were lower than two years earlier. And the city's Jewish areas did witness a modest Democratic comeback: eight were more strongly Democratic than in 1912; three were about the same; and two were less strong. Only Manhattan's sixth and twenty-sixth and Brooklyn's twenty-second districts, none of which had been securely Democratic since 1906, fell to the Republicans in 1914; in these districts the combined Sulzer-Socialist vote averaged 20 percent, and in the first two Sulzer himself made the difference for the GOP.[46]

Generally, however, Democrats could take little solace even in those ethnic districts, except the Irish ones, where the party won handily or apparently experienced a revival. Not only did they fail to reach the vote aggregate of 1912 in Italian and German areas, but the results in the eastern European Jewish community were truly mixed. Two years earlier Tammany's Henry Goldfogle had barely squeezed out a victory over Socialist Meyer London in the Lower East Side congressional race. In the 1914 London-Goldfogle rematch, London waged a vigorous campaign that combined anti-Tammanyism with appeals to the working class, especially the Jewish needle trades unions. Successful also in garnering the support of independents and Bull Moosers like Henry Moskowitz, he won the election by a plurality of nearly 1,000 votes, thus becoming New York's first (and only) Socialist congressman. "We have done to Czar Murphy what we would like to do to Czar Nicholas," crowed Abraham Cahan, editor of the *Daily Forward*. Yet in 1914 the Socialists themselves had little to celebrate. While the party eclipsed the Progressives statewide, Socialist totals were smaller than in 1912,[47] and in New York City only half-a-dozen districts where the Socialists had done well in 1910 witnessed as large or larger a vote than that year (except in assembly contests where generally the vote aggregate was higher). These were principally German-Jewish areas.[48]

Overall, the Democrats' reversal in New York State, as commentators noted, stemmed from a convergence of national patterns and local conditions. In the larger arena, the Democracy suffered a loss of fifty-eight seats in Congress, and the Republicans scored significant victories in Pennsylvania, Ohio, Illinois, Wisconsin, and Kansas. The factors behind this "revulsion" against the Wilson party were considered numerous, but, in essence, they boiled down to two: a decline in the reform spirit and the war recession turned near depression by the summer of 1914. The latter certainly seemed applicable in New York, where industrial dislocation, unemployment, and rising food prices were evident. This might, for example, help explain the unusual Democratic weaknesses in a number of ethnic, working-class districts across the state. "The depression . . . was seized by the Republicans with eagerness," asserted the *Utica Daily Observer,* "and in every congressional district . . . it was 'worked' to the extreme limit."[49] Republican newspapers in several of the most populous counties agreed with this judgment and often reminded their readers that it was the GOP that had returned the nation to prosperity after the "Cleveland depression" of the 1890s. Such critics blamed Wilson's peculiar version of reform, the New Freedom—with its "lowering the tariff," its "war taxes," its "harassment of business," and its southern orientation "at the expense of the rich state of New York"—rather than the European war for the current economic dislocation. Progressives, too, deemed this factor to be vitally important in the Republican resurgence.[50]

But surely state and local conditions contributed powerfully to the

Democracy's heavy losses in New York State. Some cited the obvious connection with national trends. "The Republican landslide," argued the *New York Tribune* not untypically, represents "a desire to rebuke a reform President who, for the sake of his administration, cast his lot with 'grab and graft' Tammany." Most observers simply dwelt on the aftermath of the Sulzer impeachment of 1913, particularly evident in the upstate where antibossism, in any case, commanded great appeal; Glynn's failure to dissociate himself fully from Tammany, making it appear that he was neither here nor there; and the campaign of religious bigotry that swept through the old "burned-over" districts of the state.[51]

It is difficult to pinpoint the role of Glynn's religion in the exceptionally poor Democratic showing in New York's interior regions. Party Chairman Osborn insisted that "the religious question was much exaggerated." And Sulzer's statement on the day after the election—"I have elected Whitman, beaten Glynn, and made Roosevelt look like 30 cents"—addressed itself to his general anti-Tammany appeal, then was widely discredited on the narrow ground that his total vote, if added to Glynn's, would have made no difference. But the former governor may also have had in mind the very thing that some of his close advisors were doing just before the election—that is, abetting Whitman's candidacy by flaying Murphyism and quietly exploiting the religious issue.[52] Separation of the two seems almost impossible. Various comparisons and surveys were made even at the time to gauge the reasons for the heavy upstate vote against Glynn. The *New York Times,* for example, maintained that the big differential between the Whitman-Glynn and Wadsworth-Gerard pluralities, totaling 60,000 votes, stemmed from the fact that Glynn was Catholic and Gerard was not. What made the Wadsworth-Gerard contest the more striking was that Gerard remained as ambassador to Germany all during the campaign. Then, too, in Erie County, "the home of the propaganda of bigotry," Whitman's plurality over Glynn reached 20,000. Another journal volunteered that in Rochester the disparity between Davenport's and Hamlin's vote for governor and lieutenant governor on the Progressive ticket arose from the fact that Hamlin was a preferred candidate of the Guardians of Liberty and Davenport was not. Yet it is also true that Hamlin was the Bull Moose chairman of nearby Erie County and an unusually effective campaigner.[53] Finally, a few days after the election the *New York Times* dispatched correspondents into ten counties to discover the reasons for the strong Sulzer vote in them. The results were mixed and complex. In only one county, Tioga, did they encounter concrete evidence of a religious vote. Here a nonpartisan, secret anti-Catholic organization mounted an ambitious campaign on behalf of Sulzer and Wadsworth. Elsewhere most of Sulzer's support came in the form of a sympathy vote directed against the "political gang" that impeached him. But it is noteworthy that so much of the "sympathy" was registered in heavily Protestant farm communities that gave the Prohibition ticket substantial backing. Railroadmen, it was reported, also went for Sulzer because of the full crew bill in 1913.[54]

V

The elections of 1914 brought to an abrupt halt Democratic control of New York State's government in the progressive era. Always precarious, even tenuous, that control yet had produced an impressive array of reform legislation and initiatives—with the Glynn program, in effect, completing the main agenda of reforms begun several years earlier by Republican Governor Charles Evans Hughes and carried forward in the Dix and Sulzer administrations. In addition, the Democrats had shifted the locus of reform into the area of social welfare progressivism with the brilliant work of the Factory Investigating Commission that spanned Glynn's brief tenure in the governorship. However, the party was given little credit for its achievements, shrouded as they were in what critics dismissed as the politics of expediency whose main design was the gratification of venal men and the corrupt machines. Specifically, in 1914 the renewed popular outcry against "Tammanyism" and "bossism" blended with a host of other factors and conditions to produce a Republican triumph that resembled GOP victories in the period from the mid-1890s through 1908—that is, a virtual sweep of the upstate, including the major cities as well as the rural areas, and a respectable performance in the Democratic bastion of New York City. Even heavily ethnic districts in the interior urban centers seemed, for the most part, to return to their old ways. Things looked so "normal" that it was almost as if the Bull Moose rebellion had never taken place. Yet while the older patterns reasserted themselves, other vital characteristics of politics associated with progressivism persisted in 1914; one, low voter participation, indeed, the lowest turnout in New York State in the twentieth century; and two, a large vote— approximately 15 percent—cast against the major parties. Taken together, these factors suggest that the electorate's alienation from major party politics still persisted as the state entered the period of World War I.

7

The Republican Ascendancy:
1915–1916

"It is now extinct," declared the Socialist *New York Call* quite accurately with reference to Theodore Roosevelt's Progressive party immediately following the elections of 1914.[1] This prescient observation, confirmed by events in the next two years, unwittingly anticipated a more traditional brand of politics in the days ahead than the nation had experienced since the first visible indications of the Republican disruption in 1910. Such was not exactly the case, however, as the GOP would have to await another presidential election for a genuine return to "normalcy." Yet in New York State the signs of political traditionalism seemed very much in evidence in the years 1915–1918. For one thing, the Republicans reigned supreme, just as they had from the time of their dramatic ascendancy in the 1890s down to the early stages of what developed into the Roosevelt rebellion. For another, the long-standing interparty sectional divisions, which had been mitigated during the Bull Moose years only to reappear in 1914, persisted in aggravated form through the period of World War I. But there were also important differences, not least of which was the almost total reversal of the roles of the major parties toward reform. Specifically, New York Republicans would hasten their retreat from progressivism in the war era, while the Democrats would continue to champion their version of reform or, as often as not, defend the party's recent legislative record against conservative encroachments—yet, at the same time, deflecting attacks on "bossism" and "Murphyism" directed at their leadership. Indeed, as GOP orthodoxy deepened, Democrats found themselves in a position to expand their social welfare progressivism to embrace a broader guardianship of the interests of ethnic minorities and, generally speaking, the urban masses.[2] These stellar efforts, combined with a shrewd party strategy and a faltering Republican administration in Albany, would enable the Democracy, in 1918, to wage an unexpected political comeback.

Several of the trends suggested above can be discerned in key developments in the state in 1915 and 1916: the direction and performance of government and administration in Albany; the proceedings and results of the much-written-about 1915 constitutional convention; and the general elections of 1916. Consideration of these events requires that the focus of our analysis shift somewhat away from the Democrats to the Republicans, though Democratic behavior remains a vital part of the story. And while the events themselves may seem disparate and disconnected, they, in fact, compose thematic patterns that, in turn, helped shape the contours of New York politics in 1918—and for many years into the future.

I

The signs pointed to a long and thoroughgoing Republican ascendancy in New York State. Charles Whitman's smashing election to the governorship in 1914, as already noted, was accompanied by an equally impressive GOP victory in the senate and assembly races. In the next year the party once again triumphed in the annual assembly contests, and in 1916 the Republicans swept the state in the presidential, gubernatorial, and legislative elections. These repeated successes were attributed, in part at least, to an unusual degree of GOP unity in the post–Bull Moose days. For, at last, the Republicans had harmonized the traditional differences that divided their more progressive downstate wing, now headed by Whitman himself, from the conservative upstate group, best represented by the new legislative leadership—Assembly Speaker Thaddeus Sweet of Oswego and senate majority leader Elon Brown of Watertown. But on policy and program development harmony would mean a veritable capitulation by the liberal element to the standpatters, though, ironically, the chief practitioner of the "oldline" values, William Barnes, would bow out of state politics in 1917.

This pronounced conservatism (some critics called it reactionaryism), tenaciously pursued in the days that Barnes held the party reins and then modified to meet the exigencies in 1913 and 1914, would reach high tide in 1915 and thereafter.

The Republican pursuit of a Barnesian-style conservatism in the Empire State stemmed from several factors—one of them being Governor Whitman himself. Whitman was not much of a reformer and never had been. His only real claim to reformism had come in his service as the crime-busting New York County district attorney and his spirited anti-Tammany campaign of 1914. The future governor's acceptability to Barnes and other upstaters had been grounded largely on the fact that, as Manhattan Republicans went, his attitudes on most public questions seemed sufficiently "moderate" and flexible so that he could easily cooperate with the conservatives. Equally important, Whitman, not unlike John Dix a few years earlier, believed in what he referred to as a "constitutional governor"—one who observed scrupulously the principle of the separation of powers and only on rare occasions exercised vigorous leadership over the legislature. The result was a lawyerlike handling of the executive office that, together with his failure to deal effectively with the various political pressures on him, made the governor's performance appear all the more faltering and clumsy. Not bad enough to be turned out of office, remarked Henry L. Stimson in 1915, Whitman would easily win renomination to the governorship but, at the same time, possessed "no personal strength or following to carry him further."[3] That he, nonetheless, harbored strong ambitions for higher office, and that these ambitions were widely publicized only further weakened Whitman's position. Even conservatives who on a majority of issues supported him came to dismiss his "achievements" as the work of a rank opportunist determined to build his own personal machine at any cost.

Whitman's personal weaknesses, his narrow vision of executive-legislative relationships, and his flexible political outlook paved the way for the more orthodox Republicans in the senate and the assembly to grab the initiative in policymaking. Traditionally a refuge of localism and conservatism in New York State by virtue of upstate rural and small-town overrepresentation, the legislature was especially so in these years when the GOP commanded a near two-thirds majority in both houses. The most articulate spokesman of this powerful Republican bloc was senate leader Brown who, midway through the 1915 session, managed to get himself named head of the combined legislative party caucus. "Czar of the Senate" and master legislator, Brown mixed a deeply rooted orthodoxy with a callous disregard for the men who had borne the standards of progressivism. "Look at Chicago; we can get away with anything," declaimed Brown speaking of the treatment accorded Theodore Roosevelt and his followers in the 1912 Republican national convention. Like other standpatters, Brown was terribly disturbed by what conservatives labeled the "class legislation" recently enacted in Albany. As he expressed it:

> We are at the end of an era—an era of vain and costly effort to substitute new forms of government for old. . . . The state and its people must be relieved of the vast and incalculable waste of capital and energy resulting from laws passed in the name of the public welfare, but really for the benefit of classes at the expense of the whole people.

Singling out the New York workmen's compensation law as the most "burdensome" of all, Brown went on to insist that the incumbent administration had a "mandate" in Albany. (Nor did Governor Whitman disagree in principle with this judgment.) "There was never so much to do," concluded the Watertown senator, "unsound legislation to amend or repeal, extravagance to curtail, favoritism of law to abate, shackles and burdens on equal opportunities to remove."[4]

At bottom, of course, were the general conditions prevalent in the post–Bull Moose era that encouraged and abetted Republican standpattism in the state. If conservatives could seize upon the commonly accepted notion that progressivism as a movement had fallen upon hard times, they could with equal fervor exploit the "Democratic" recession affecting the nation that carried into 1915. Some even argued a simplistic causal relationship between the two reminiscent of that used against Theodore Roosevelt by his political opponents during the financial panic of 1907: the economic downturn resulted from, or was exacerbated by, administration programs—in this instance, Woodrow Wilson's New Freedom in Washington and the "socialistic" Democratic reforms in Albany. The onset of World War I and the interposition of war-related issues only intensified GOP traditionalism as

Republicans in New York, as elsewhere, scrambled to outdo Democrats in protestations of loyalty and patriotism. In 1916, amid the growing debate over preparedness, Frederick Davenport, who had followed Roosevelt back into the Republican party, urged his cohorts not to "allow the Democrats to speak more firmly, more wisely, more patriotically then they." At the same time, the intensifying war spirit, followed by the whipped-up patriotism of the war itself, bred intolerance toward anything different or foreign. So it was that Republican politicians in New York, pandering to their fellow native-born, willy-nilly trumpeted "Americanistic" sentiments by railing against "hyphenated" groups, by attacking "un-American" New York City, and by rejecting "Prussian" bills like a health insurance measure or a minimum wage proposal introduced by Democrats in the state legislature.[5]

It is hardly surprising, then, that the Republican legislative record in Albany during Charles Whitman's tenure in office was replete with reaction, narrow partisanship, sectionalism, and jingoism. Perhaps the most partisan and reactionary—certainly the most sectionally oriented—legislature of all was the one that sat in 1915, for here Brown and the upstate leadership, flushed by the party triumph in the previous November, went about their business with a vengeance. While they left unscathed the political reforms only recently enacted, they moved in several other directions against their Democratic rivals. They succeeded in clamping a stiff direct tax on Greater New York, so that by the next fiscal year New York City would pay nearly three quarters of the revenues collected by the state and receive far less in return. Much of the money, in fact, found its way into the construction and repair of roads in the Republican upstate, as highway department appropriations were increased substantially. To rub salt in the wound, Brown threatened to trim the budget of the state health department, whose major operations were in the urban centers, including New York City. Only an ambitious campaign mounted by Homer Folks and other public welfare advocates restored the funds and, in addition, beat back several bills that would have undermined the Public Health Act of 1913. The Republicans reorganized the state conservation commission with a view to increasing the party spoils and made an abortive attempt to snatch supervision of New York City building codes from the reform-minded tenement house department. Most outrageous of all from the reformers' perspective was the powerful assault on labor and social legislation. The GOP grabbed control of the newly established workmen's compensation commission and the progressively oriented labor department by creating, in the name of "efficiency," a three-man, gubernatorially appointed industrial commission that would oversee the work of both bodies. Specific legislation, too, was introduced to modify the FIC laws, including measures to weaken restrictions on mercantile establishments, to permit private compensation settlements, and to remove regulations over upstate canneries. All this "mischief" prompted Florence Kelley to throw up her hands in despair. "This is such a dreadful Legislature," she protested, "that it is no use asking anything of them; but that they stop sinning a little."[6]

Kelley's outrage epitomized the response of progressive politicians, reform organizations, and the New York City press. Almost totally forgotten were the "sins" of Tammany in the wake of what the *Nation* described as proceedings in Albany "of the most unedifying character." In the legislative chambers the bulwark of the reform defense was manned by the Tammany leadership—cooperating more closely than ever with progressive societies such as the Consumers' League, the American Association for Labor Legislation, the New York State Federation of Labor, and others seeking to stem the tide of reaction. "There never was a Legislature so completely owned by the private interests," charged the indignant Robert Wagner to "Czar" Brown in one of their many heated exchanges. "And you—you blind fools," he added bitterly. Al Smith was equally caustic. "Tammany Hall," he asserted, "is a bed of roses compared to the Barren Island [a city garbage dump] of the Republican Party of New York." Away from Albany, especially in New York City, protest meetings were sponsored by the reform organizations to stir up public opinion against the GOP. The metropolitan press chimed in, accusing the Republicans of "legislative barbarism"; "Hannaism"; "Bourbonism"; and, as Villard's *Evening Post* put it, with returning the state "to those ideas of the function of parties which were dominant when Platt and Quay held the same kind of sway in . . . government." These accumulated pressures sufficiently weakened the Republican resolve, particularly in the assembly, so that the worst bills designed to subvert the FIC legislation were scuttled; others were modified; but some few were passed and signed into law by Governor Whitman.[7]

II

New York State held a constitutional convention in 1915, hard on the heels of the conservative record of the Republican legislature and the anguished cries of the defenders of reform. It is no doubt true, as one historian has stated, that the proceedings of this convention "are a remarkable source of information about the final reflection of a whole generation about their political experience and the philosophy developed out of that experience." Also, constitution-making did provide fertile ground for progressive societies and citizens' clubs agitating through study groups and lobbying activities for their chosen reforms. Finally, reformers across the nation looked with eager anticipation to the New York conclave for the implementation of their advanced concepts of governmental reorganization.[8] But the 1915 Albany convention—its background, its organization, and its work as well as the subsequent campaign for and against the proposed constitutional changes—speaks even more eloquently to the mix of deepening sectionalism and partisanship that enveloped New York politics at that time together with the shifting locus of reformism in the state. And certainly the Republican drift toward conservatism was no better evidenced than in this episode of constitution-making in 1915.

The calling of the constitutional convention itself had been an act of partisanship. New York's constitution requires that at least once every twenty years the question of a convention must be submitted to the electorate in the form of a referendum. Such a referendum was due in 1916. However, the Democrats, beginning in the spring of 1913, pushed for an earlier date—first for the summer of that year apparently to forestall Republican-Progressive fusion in the upcoming elections in Greater New York, then, failing that, again in the fall to help prevent a statewide union of the opposition forces the following November. For the same reason that the Democrats favored an early referendum the Republicans and the Progressives opposed it, though a number of Bull Moosers went along with the idea in the hope of incorporating their 1912 party platform into the New York constitution. The Democratic resolution finally passed the legislature in late 1913, and the referendum was held in April of the next year. In an unusually low voter turnout—a total of only 305,000 or approximately 13 percent of the eligible electorate across the state—the question carried by a razor-thin margin. If, generally, the 1914 referendum showed New Yorkers' indifference to the proposed convention, the geographic breakdown of the vote gives some clue as to the support for, and opposition to, constitution-making. Most of the affirmative vote came from New York City, where the Democratic regular organizations, led by Tammany Hall, had conducted a formidable campaign. The main opposition, on the other hand, was recorded in the Republican upstate. The referendum lost in all but four upstate counties, two of which were Erie and Onondaga where heavy pluralities in Buffalo and Syracuse, respectively, carried the day for the proposition.[9] In each of these counties the regular Democratic organization was relatively strong.

During the course of 1914, both major parties made preparations for the convention. The Democrats were in basic agreement on a reform package, and their state platform embraced a number of recommended constitutional revisions. As politics turned more sharply sectional, however, Tammany regulars placed greater emphasis than their upstate brethren on the issues of home rule and equitable representation for Greater New York in the state legislature.[10] Meanwhile, Republican planning fell largely to that group of New York City progressives—Herbert Parsons, Henry L. Stimson, and Seth Low—who had remained loyal to the GOP in 1912 but who, since then, had been fighting doggedly to modify William Barnes's conservative state leadership. In one sense their program for the convention was a spin-off of that battle. In the broader vein, it reflected a determination to modernize public administration and policymaking in New York State. For Stimson, himself versed in government on all levels, the major progressive goal was to replace "invisible government" plagued by "bossism" and "localism" with "responsible government" distinguished by humanitarian social service, a strong executive, and efficient financial management. This objective, reasoned Stimson, might be attained by means of three new devices: the short ballot, empowering the governor to select most of his subordinate officers in cabinetlike fahion; the executive budget, granting the governor the principal responsibility for making the state budget; and the seating of executive officers in the legislature, giving them the opportunity to advocate and defend their policies. To these proposals Elihu Root would add greater home rule for cities and non-partisan election of municipal officers. Stimson and his colleagues were successful in getting their ideas accepted by the conservatives at the August Republican state conference but only with the proviso that delegates to the constitutional convention be guided, not bound, by these principles.[11]

Democratic hopes of controlling the 1915 conclave were shattered by the devastating party defeat in the 1914 elections. In the upstate campaign for delegates Republican conservatives made much of what one newspaper insisted was Tammany's intention to modify the "fundamental law" so "that the powers to govern the state shall lodge for all time in the metropolis."[12] But if the Democrats fell victim to GOP sectional appeals, neither could the progressive Republicans take heart in their party's victory that fall. For, in fact, most of the convention delegates, chosen on the basis of three for each senate district, were members of the very faction with which the reformers had been jousting. To be sure, Stimson, Low, Parsons, and several other New York City Republicans were themselves elected as delegates at large, but the task they had resolved to achieve—that of imposing their will on constitutional revision—would now be extremely difficult. To do so, they devised the strategy of engineering the election of Elihu Root as convention president. This move was a good one—and easily accomplished—for Root, by virtue of his superior service to party and country, had emerged as the elder statesman of New York Republicanism. Moreover, Root had spent much of his long career successfully bridging the gap between the contending wings of the GOP. (The events leading to 1912 were an exception.) With the independents and progressives he shared a disdain for bossism and localism, and he was easily won over by Stimson to the principles of efficiency in government and the strong executive. Indeed, Root held a special fondness for Stimson, Parsons, and Wickersham, who as a group would be known as the "federal crowd" at the convention. At the same time, he was trusted implicitly by the conservatives; to William Barnes, who had fought at his side in Chicago, Root remained a patron saint of Taft

Republicanism.[13] What the reformers hoped Root could do in Albany was to use his influence and prestige on behalf of a modern, progressive state constitution and yet keep in line the party's large standpat faction.

When the 1915 constitutional convention opened in April, Republican control, and with it Elihu Root's election to the presidency, was assured. The GOP held 116 seats, most of which were filled by upstaters. "I find the most noteworthy feature of it," remarked William Barnes gleefully in regard to the assemblage, "is the intense conservatism of the Republican members." The progressive Republicans numbered no more than a couple of dozen. A large majority of this group hailed from New York City, though John Lord O'Brian of Buffalo headed a handful of upstate reformers. Since the Bull Moosers had elected no one, the remaining 52 delegates were Democrats, and these were divided between an "older" and a "younger" contingent. The former included conservative independents such as Morgan J. O'Brien and DeLancey Nicoll. (Nicoll held the distinction of having served with Elihu Root in the 1894 constitutional convention.) The younger Democrats, "men of comparative strength," were led by Al Smith and Robert Wagner, who, observed the *New Republic,* "can and will do much to keep the Tammany men out of mischief." As it turned out, Murphy's "boys" dominated the minority, for only a handful of Democrats came from the upstate. And Smith especially won accolades for being what one Republican said was "the best informed man in the crowd on the state."[14]

During the next five months New Yorkers were treated to an unusual spectacle in Albany's legislative chambers. The Republican federal crowd exercised a disproportionate amount of influence and power, for through Root they controlled the convention machinery and assumed the major responsibility for initiating proposals to revise the constitution. As a small faction, however, they would have a tough time winning the support of delegates, mainly from their own party, whose attitudes toward change ranged from indifference to hostility. Thus, in their speechmaking, their distribution of committee assignments, and the presentation of their ideas, the reformers struck the note of nonpartisanship and balance—a balance, Root stressed in his opening address to the convention, that was grounded on the need "to preserve as well as to improve."[15] Yet, in the final analysis, that delicate equilibrium between "change" and "continuity," as Root described it, would be difficult to attain, for each of the other contingents in the assemblage—the upstate Republicans and the Democrats—had their own ideas and priorities on constitution-making.

The upstate conservatives boasted as their leaders the indomitable William Barnes of Albany and the mellifluent Edgar T. Brackett of Saratoga who, in essence, agreed with one delegate's insistence "that there is a general disposition not to do anything." They remained champions of the status quo, for the status quo meant preservation of the Republicanism of 1894. They resisted the short ballot, balked at the executive budget, and opposed an appointive judiciary all because gubernatorial authority would be enhanced at the expense of the local leaders or the legislature, through which the local leaders traditionally wielded great power. Their feelings about New York City—Brackett once called it "the iniquity"—were best illustrated in their reluctance to extend home rule and their opposition to any change in the 1894 apportionment formula that practically guaranteed Republican control of the legislature, especially the senate. The only substantial constitutional revision that any of the upstaters advanced was a Barnes-sponsored amendment curtailing the legislature's right to pass "class legislation," Barnes's own term for the social and labor reforms enacted since 1906. For the Albany stalwart, indeed, the choice still lay between "Democracy and Socialism," and he had no trouble identifying "Prussian inspired" laws like workmen's compensation or a proposed minimum wage amendment that Smith and Wagner introduced in the convention.[16] In sum, the posture of these upstate conservatives on constitutional reform most closely resembled that of Brown and his cohorts in the 1915 legislature.

The extreme conservatism of the upstate Republicans placed the Democrats in a critical position in the convention. Often the progressive Republicans were forced to depend upon the support of Tammanyites Smith and Wagner as well as independents Nicoll and O'Brien to ward off Barnes, Brackett, and others in their own party. It was mainly for this reason that Root found it desirable to sustain an air of nonpartisanship throughout the proceedings. Nor were the federal crowd and the Democrats in serious disagreement on the need to achieve greater efficiency and responsibility in state government, though they might differ on details. After all, Smith and Wagner as legislative leaders had witnessed at first hand the follies in the performance of both the executive and legislative branches over the past dozen years, and Smith, in particular, had digested most of the writings and documents on governmental streamlining that so influenced Root, Stimson, and their group. Yet the Democrats had priorities of their own, which, together with their support of the progressive Republican changes, made them the most consistently liberal force in the convention. As the self-styled champions of the urban masses, Smith and Wagner pushed hard for constitutional provisions permitting an extension of labor and social reforms. Drawing freely on their FIC experiences, they agitated for a minimum wage amendment, a proposal granting the legislature additional authority to regulate tenement house manufacturing, and a measure making it possible to bring occupational diseases within the scope of the workmen's compensation law.[17] At the same time, the Democrats—not the progressive Republicans—seized the initiative in battling Barnes's reactionary proposal on "class legislation" and beating back a literacy amendment that would have discriminated against newly naturalized citizens in exercising their privilege to vote. Such strains of nativism that ran through the Albany proceedings were resisted inexorably by the Tammanyites. Also, the Democrats were far more outspoken than the New York City Republicans on the vital issue of home rule for the cities. Finally, as champions of the interests of Greater New York, they argued passionately that equal representation—the "one-man-one-vote" principle of a later day—should be accorded all areas of the state.

It was this last issue—the explosively political one of legislative representation and apportionment—that threatened to tear the convention apart and dash the hopes and aspirations of the progressive Republicans. The apportionment wrangle was provoked not by the Democrats but, and many thought deliberately, by the upstate Republicans and, in particular, Brackett of Saratoga, whom Root had named chairman of the committee on legislative organization. Brackett must have driven his committee hard, for it was the first to make a report to the convention. Issued on June 8, this brief document simply urged the retention of the bicameral system and the election of senators and assemblymen on the present district lines. While the Brackett initiative seemed harmless enough, it was to keen observers "an aggressive move" designed to curb other proposals then in committee that would modify upstate domination of the legislature. It was evident, too, that if Brackett could settle the basic issue early, his committee might proceed to reapportion the legislature then and there, a task that he and his allies relished. And three weeks later the committee requested, but was denied, authorization from the convention to do just that. Nor did Brackett hide his personal feelings on apportionment. "No matter how you try to avoid it," he once stated flatly, the question was "between what the interest is which the city of New York has and the interest which the country has." At another time he expressed even more bluntly the upstate point of view: "The ability to cram human beings into crowded tenements should not be the final test of representation in the city or in the country."[18] William Barnes and Lemuel Quigg added their voices of support to Brackett and the committee on legislative organization.

Democrats Smith and Wagner unhesitatingly rose to the challenge hurled by the upstate "moss-backs." Conceding that twenty years earlier there had been little real worry over the matter of apportionment, Smith charged that the current interest was sparked by recent Republican behavior. "Every time we danced together the New York chickens have been stepped on by the upstate donkey," he declared half-facetiously. Smith then recounted the performance of the 1913 Democratic legislature to show its regard for the upstate. The Democrats, he argued, gladly supported the health department bill, the construction and maintenance of highways and bridges outside New York City, and in numerous ways the agricultural interests of rural New York. This record, Smith contended, contrasted sharply with the Republican attitude toward New York City as expressed in the 1915 legislature. Wagner was even more pointed in meeting the Brackett challenge. Citing population trends in the state since the 1890s, he put the issue bluntly: "If representation in the Legislature were based upon population, New York City would have 28 of 51 Senators and 83 out of 150 Assemblymen." Wagner also defended against critics the "foreignness" of the city and the threat of "alien" control of the state, lashing out at one juncture: "I say . . . that the days of the Know-Nothing Party have gone forever from the land."[19]

The upstate GOP challenge and New York City's Democratic response cast gloom into the forces of liberal Republicanism. The progressives were caught between the interests of Greater New York and loyalty to their party. "Today the question of the discrimination of New York City comes up," lamented Stimson on June 20, "[with us] Republicans from New York City being rather caught between the two forces." Keenly aware of the larger danger to the very integrity of the convention, these progressives tried to work closely with independent Democrats, first to delay consideration of the issue, then to soften as much as possible the harsh partisanship it interjected into the proceedings. Yet in the end they were forced to choose, and they went with their Republican compatriots. Parsons maintained that the actual vote cast in the last presidential election should be the determining factor in representation and apportionment; in this case, he explained, New York City had precisely the representation in the legislature it should have. Louis Marshall added that the so-called crime of 1894 was a provision "ingrained in the Constitution of this and other States" so that no one section prevailed over another. Even Stimson wrote privately that "we have for twenty years been committed to a system which . . . has thus far not created any substantial injustice." When, therefore, the final vote was taken on the Brackett amendment to retain the status quo on representation, the convention divided almost strictly on party lines—with the Republicans in favor and the Democrats opposed in what Wagner concluded was much less a "territorial restriction" than a restriction on a "Democratic community."[20]

On the major proposed changes in the constitution other than apportionment, divisions in the convention were less sharp. In fact, several upstate Republican attempts to drive a wedge between Democrats and the federal crowd proved abortive at least in the debates and the committee deliberations. Tammanyites Smith and Wagner effected changes in Stimson's executive budget amendment, then carried a unanimous vote in its favor. As passed, the measure, commented Stimson happily, "is far more complete and radical than I dreamed was possible."[21] Again rejecting overtures from the upstaters, Smith labored to improve the short ballot proposal and finally led a substantial contingent of his own party in winning its adoption. But on the issue of home rule there was a bitterness—and division—reminiscent of the apportionment wrangle. Here in the long, involved debates over precisely how independent the cities should be from state control the convention split mainly, though not exclusively, between Democratic New York City and the Republican upstate with the federal crowd caught in the middle. Joining Smith and Wagner in their efforts to obtain more for the city than what Smith maintained was "home rule *a la* Filipino" were fusion mayor John Purroy Mitchel and the Citizens Union. (Smith even twitted the reformers: "I don't mind annexing them when they are right.") The task of compromise subsequently fell to Seth Low, chairman of the cities committee, and he came forth with a proposal that, according to Root, would give "to the most extreme advocates of home rule three fourths of all they have demanded." But the Tammanyites disagreed, Smith tried and failed to amend the measure, and the compromise won approval without their support.[22]

When, in early September, the 1915 constitutional convention adjourned with a "package" of over thirty proposed changes, Elihu Root and the progressive Republicans exulted over their triumph. "This convention has risen above the plane of partisan politics," Root declared jubilantly. In support of his contention he could point to the fact that two dozen amendments had been adopted by majorities of at least ten to one and the rest by decreasing majorities but none less than two to one. Also, the final vote on the document was overwhelmingly in favor of its submission to the electorate in November. Yet such "facts" masked certain realities about the convention that the progressives seemed to ignore, the most important of which was their own minority position in the proceedings. A large number of their fellow Republicans—probably most of them—backed the document essentially out of party loyalty. Some "country" delegates like Barnes and Quigg continued to grumble. Barnes dismissed the new constitution as setting "the course of State Socialism" and as "Herbert Parsons' pro-socialistic proposals," while Quigg complained of the massive power handed over to the governor on appointments (because of the short ballot) and expenditures (because of the executive budget). In addition, the Tammany Democrats, who had played so critical a role in "perfecting" several of the reforms, refused at the eleventh hour to support the revision. The federal crowd found it hard to explain this anomaly except to pass the rumor that Smith, Wagner, and the boys "got their orders" from the "Wigwam in Fourteenth Street."[23] Whether or not such "orders" were issued, the Tammanyites had repeatedly articulated their deep resentment and bitterness over what they firmly believed was the "betrayal" of one section of the state by another—a betrayal that had commenced early in the year with the invidious anti–New York City legislature and ended with a constitutional convention that reenacted the old Republican apportionment scheme together with an inadequate home rule article. "We have a right, after twenty years, to expect something better," Smith insisted at the time he recorded his negative vote on the final draft. No amount of liberal Republican pleading—even to the point of separating the apportionment section from the rest of the document for the November referendum—could change that judgment. To the Tammanyites the 1915 constitution was, in the final analysis, an instrument of Republicanism. And Smith frankly told Root that it would not be ratified at the polls.[24]

Smith's prediction in September rang true in November as the 1915 proposed revisions fell victim to the very conditions that surrounded the convention—lack of a firm mandate, public apathy, partisanship, and intraparty wrangling. The burden of sparking the electorate and selling the constitution to the politicians naturally rested with the New York City Republicans, and Root and Stimson, in particular, launched an "aggressive campaign." They established a Committee of Thirty that flooded the state with literature and sponsored public meetings devoted to "educating" the citizenry on the benefits of the constitution. Stimson made a personal tour of the upstate delivering speeches along the way and prodding "our timid or halting Republicans" to rally to the cause. Privately he admonished some that party failure would bring a Democratic convention in 1917.[25] But the progressives got the same cool reception from the upstate county machines that they had elicited earlier from Barnes, Brackett, and Quigg in Albany. Enough of the local leaders fell into line to win the endorsement of the Republican state committee, but the committee did so without enthusiasm. (State Chairman Frederick Tanner was himself "unexcited" about the campaign.) Brackett, Quigg, and Elon Brown actually spoke out against the "novel government," as Quigg described it. Others like Hendricks of Onondaga, Aldridge of Monroe, and Betts of Wayne remained indifferent, ultimately tendering lukewarm support or ignoring the constitution altogether. For many of these upstaters the basic issue was that of power, "the question," explained one of them, "of whether the Republican organization in this State is to be controlled by the Republican leaders of New York City, where the Republican party is in a minority, or by the leaders up-state, where Republican majorities come from." Some even speculated that the campaign marked the first step of a Root presidential bid and another run by Stimson for the governorship in 1916.[26]

While the liberal Republicans were drumming up party backing for the constitution, they tried simultaneously to cultivate a public image of nonpartisanship, as they had in the convention. The purpose, of course, was to mobilize support outside the GOP. Many citizens' groups did favor the revisions, and several independent Democrats came to the aid of Stimson and Root. But generally the strategy worked no better in the fall than it had in the summer, especially after formal endorsement by the state Republican party. "Any way one looks at it," grumbled a Democratic critic, "the Republican committee has certainly gummed up the situation." Root himself made a mockery of nonpartisanship when, late in the campaign, he issued a joint statement with Senator James W. Wadsworth linking the constitution's defeat in November with "Republican failure." Most Democrats, including Wilsonians, were thus inclined to agree with the *New York World,* hardly a mouthpiece for party regulars, that the constitution was a "rotten-borough," "Republican" document, and acted accordingly.[27] Smith and Wagner seized the occasion of a Tammany Hall meeting in New York City to lambast the revisions and flay GOP conservatism. Ten days later, on October 31, Tammany's executive committee, in pursuance of an earlier resolution, sent letters through the district leaders to some 150,000 enrolled Democrats in New York City urging them to "protect your city by voting against the Constitution."[28] The Hall committed its full resources to the campaign in its last days.

Caught between contending factions of the Republican party and condemned by the Democracy's most powerful organization, the 1915 constitution also invited attacks from a score of special-interest groups unhappy about this or that provision. Most important among them was organized labor, whose battle against adoption closely paralleled the Democratic campaign. Samuel Gompers, the State Federation of Labor, and local unions across the state had gotten up their dander for two reasons: first, the convention leadership had ignored a list of twenty-four demands—"Labor's Bill of Rights"—that Gompers and others placed before the committee on industrial relations; second, the proposed constitution embraced several items that labor leaders considered inimical to the interests of the workingman. Following hard on the heels of the 1915 legislature, the convention became for the labor leadership what it had become for the Democracy—another illustration of Republican reaction: its product was an "aristocratic document" foisted on the "people" by Elihu Root in all his "legalism" and "abstractionism" and by Barnes and Wickersham, servants for "the cause of vested interests."[29] On October 4 the executive council of the State Federation met with delegates from local unions and central councils representing about 2 million workers and declared war on the constitution. In New York City the Central Federated Union with Socialist affiliates canvassed on a district-by-district basis. In the upstate, particularly in the larger cities, local councils and unions carried the burden of distributing pamphlets provided by the State Federation, sponsored mass meetings with speakers brought in from outside the localities, and even manned the polls as watchers on Election Day. "The result," commented the Federation president with some justification, "demonstrated labor's solidarity as it never was demonstrated before."[30]

Not unexpectedly, then, the beleaguered and embattled 1915 constitution was smashed at the polls on November 2. Over 900,000 votes were piled up against the document in what the *New York Times* claimed was "the biggest majority . . . in any State against any man or measure in the history of the country."[31] Not a single county supported the proposed revisions. The largest negative vote was recorded in Democratic New York City, but some of the more heavily Republican upstate areas were just as decisive: William Barnes's Albany County, for example, rejected the constitution by a margin of over two to one. While Democrats openly celebrated their "victory," most GOP leaders, evading the substantive reasons behind the defeat, either remained discreetly silent or proffered the safe, if innocuous, explanation that the electorate rebelled against the convention for refusing "to present its propositions separately, so that a discriminating vote could not be cast." (Students over the years have accepted this explanation as the principal reason for the revisions' defeat.) In this way, Republicans avoided the charge that *their* party, no less than the Democrats, bore responsibility for the result. Furthermore, Republicans masked their role in the referendum's failure by emphasizing the party victories that fall. The state "is safely Republican again," exclaimed Fred Tanner with reference to a solid GOP triumph in the annual assembly contests and a strong showing in most of the upstate cities.[32]

Indeed, the elections of 1915 in New York State repeated the patterns of the previous year. While the Republicans nearly swept the interior regions, the Democrats were reasonably successful in New York City. Some even argued that Murphy and Tammany Hall thereby scored "their first real victory since 1903," as the regular organization grabbed control of the board of aldermen from fusion, and elected Al Smith as sheriff together with a district attorney in New York County. One New York City GOP newspaper had no trouble understanding the reason for this Republican misfortune. "New York City has gone back to Tammany," lamented the *Tribune*, "to escape the present evils of excessive taxation and unfair discrimination." Of course, the big losers in 1915 (aside from the suffragists whose referendum also went down to defeat) were the Republican federal crowd, those progressives who had staked their reputation and prestige on constitution-making during a time of "feeble mandate." As a noted historian has concluded, this heroic attempt represented "the last and highest tide" reached by "the constructive spirit that had been evolving in the Republican party since 1901."[33] But surely it was also an abject failure for which fellow Republicans, determined to purge the state organization of what reform influences remained, were as much to blame as the Democrats or any of the special-interest groups that opposed the revisions. Perhaps demoralized, certainly humiliated, the New York City progressives returned home to lick their wounds and then quickly immersed themselves in matters of graver importance to the society at large—World War I and war-related issues. Republican reform in New York State, at least for the time being, was buried with the constitution of 1915.

III

Even as the constitutional revisions were being debated by New Yorkers in the summer and fall of 1915, events abroad captured more and more public attention. The sinking of the British liner *Lusitania* in May, followed by the long controversy over submarine warfare between Imperial Germany and the Wilson government in Washington, drove home to Americans the immediacy of the European conflict and sparked a great debate in the nation over preparedness. The movement to make the country stronger militarily was powerful in the Empire State, as it was generally in the financial-industrial Northeast. In fact, New York boasted the headquarters of the chauvinistic National Security League, supplied the Navy League with a large membership, and introduced to the rest of the nation the "Plattsburg" plan for summer military camps. As early as the spring of 1916, the state had adopted legislation mandating military training.[34] That, in sum, New York proved to be fertile ground for jingoist politicians—and even interventionists—there is no doubt.

While patriotism, strictly speaking, was hardly a partisan matter, chiefly politicians of the Republican persuasion succumbed to—and in turn exploited—the "martial spirit." President Wilson's cautious neutrality and his slow pursuit of preparedness stirred anew the Grand Old Party's traditional nationalism. In New York State the war-related questions propelled a unity and cohesiveness that Republicans had not enjoyed in many years. Downstate progressives and upstate conservatives who were sparring with each other on the proposed changes to the state constitution simultaneously were being drawn together by the more "vital," national concerns. Also, the few diehard Bull Moosers, still clinging to their 1912 reform platform, yet began to doubt the wisdom of their stubborn course. "Party strife and party advantage," declared Progressive leaders from the state's sixty-two counties in early 1916, "should be subordinated to the nation's present needs." And while George W. Perkins remained convinced that William Barnes continued to exercise too much power in GOP councils, he mused that rank-and-file Republicans were more and more impressed with Theodore Roosevelt's "Americanism."[35] Presidential politics would drive the most stubborn New York dissenters back into the Grand Old Party.

Amalgamation between the Bull Moosers and the Republicans, in the final analysis, rested principally on the shoulders of Colonel Theodore Roosevelt. Since the disappointing Progressive showing in 1914, the former president had pursued the twin themes of preparedness and conservatism—both, he felt, reflecting the dominant national mood. That TR was himself edging back to the GOP was obvious to careful observers of the political scene. But when fellow Bull Moosers—Fred Davenport, Theodore D. Robinson, and Chauncey Hamlin in New York, for example—reaffirmed their 1912 loyalties, Roosevelt was obliged to announce that he, too, "shall enroll as a Progressive." The pronouncement, of course, had more to do with strategy than with obligation, for the Bull Moose had to be kept alive as trading bait with the GOP in 1916. The Colonel's price was his own renomination to the presidency *or* the nomination of a Republican acceptable to him and the rest of the Progressive high command. Events would prove the first impossible, for the scars of apostasy remained. The second was more feasible, particularly as Roosevelt stepped up his attacks on Wilson and rehearsed his old partisanship. All that was needed was the right man, and the right man would be Charles Evans Hughes, since 1910 an associate justice of the Supreme Court. As one Roosevelt biographer has written, Hughes was "tinged with enough progressivism to be acceptable to the Bull Moosers, orthodox enough on the tariff to keep contributions from manufacturers rolling in, and mild enough on the war to appease the German-Americans."[36]

With patriotism and conservatism the prevailing mood among Republicans in the Empire State as elsewhere, presidential politics for them in 1916 was far less painful than for many a year. At no time was Roosevelt's candidacy taken seriously in New York: the Colonel's name was anathema to the state's GOP hierarchy. An early boom developed for Governor Charles Whitman, but this soon fizzled, and Whitman immediately jumped on the Hughes bandwagon. In February 1916 the New York Republicans met in Carnegie Hall where they heard Elihu Root deliver a stirring speech on "Americanism" and "preparedness," following which they elected delegates to the upcoming national convention. Loyalties among those assembled were divided about equally between Hughes and Root, but there was no discernible split along progressive-conservative lines. Indeed, little of the old bitterness and acrimony could be found at this gathering.[37] Hughes's subsequent nomination victory in Chicago followed by Barnes's retirement from the Republican National Committee satisfied all except a few extremists in New York. A quick Roosevelt endorsement of the GOP presidential ticket paved the way for the final rapprochement between Bull Moosers and the Republicans in the state. The finishing touch came in August when the Progressives invited Whitman to enter their gubernatorial primary. The governor gladly accepted, and George Perkins appealed personally to his compatriots to support the man they had bitterly assailed only two years earlier. "The national situation transcends everything else at the moment," Perkins claimed sheepishly. Whitman went on to win both the Progressive and Republican primaries by landslide proportions and carried for himself and Hughes a thoroughly patriotic and conservative state platform into the fall campaign.[38]

National Republican unity in 1916 put the Democrats squarely on their mettle, for a harmonious opposition seriously threatened Woodrow Wilson's reelection chances. Accordingly, the president geared his own campaign to the twin issues of "peace" and "progressivism." But in the Empire State, where chauvinist sentiments ran deep and where Wilson's "natural" allies were weaker than ever, such a campaign was perilous. Here the administration's only hope of success—and curiously Wilson's advisors were optimistic about carrying the state—lay in placating Tammany and its allies without simultaneously destroying what was left of the independent movement. For a time after 1914, Washington's collective efforts seemed to reach some balance in the dispensing of favors and patronage between the pro-Tammany and the scattered anti-Tammany organizations across the state. (Even so, however, Louis Antisdale's Rochester Democrats complained bitterly about all that went to the "machine.") But in late 1915 and early 1916, the Wilson administration began to tilt noticeably toward Tammany Hall and its upstate friends in a vigorous attempt to assure their loyalty in the face of the GOP harmony drive: several Wilson people helped in the campaign to defeat the "Republican" constitution; some worked openly for Al Smith in the New York County sheriff's contest; and, most importantly, Postmaster General Albert Burleson funneled a number of federal appointments to the regular organizations.[39]

The Wilson administration's decision to court the regulars in New York was certainly not a new departure. Rather, it marked a renewal of the strategy the president had followed two years earlier. It was grounded on Tammany Hall's sustained influence and power, which, to be sure, had faltered badly after the Sulzer debacle and Murphy's announced "retirement" from state politics. By the spring of 1916, however, the boss and his followers had bounced back: the election victories in 1915 in Greater New York had strengthened Murphy's downstate power base, and upstate the key alliance with the Erie organization was revived when William Fitzpatrick returned to the driver's seat among Buffalo Democrats by defeating his rivals, Conners and Burgard, in another local power struggle. In fact, this series of events formed the backdrop of a many-faceted bargain in 1916 between Tammany Hall and the Wilsonians in Washington. Hints of a "deal" came in January with Murphy's warm support of a resolution before the state committee praising the virtues of the Wilson administration and on March 1 with what one newspaper described as "the most peaceful and harmonious of Democratic conventions, in which the president's foreign policy was heartily approved." (Republican "jingoism," on the other hand, was denounced as meaning "a sheer plunge of the country into the European struggle.") The major agreement called for Murphy's public endorsement of Wilson's renomination in return for the elimination of "federal" influence in the organization of the New York party together with the naming of a state chairman more friendly than William C. Osborn to Tammany Hall. The deal was consummated on April 15, when the state committee elected Edwin Harris as chairman and unanimously approved an endorsement resolution.[40] Following these actions came two additional moves: former Governor Martin Glynn was chosen temporary chairman of the pending national Democratic convention in St. Louis; and Robert Wagner was given a bid, which he subsequently rejected, for the postmastership of New York City. Two months later in St. Louis, Charlie Murphy and his satraps thus could be found in the vanguard of the cheering section for Woodrow Wilson's renomination—in marked contrast to Tammany's posture four years earlier.[41]

Naturally, the final "peace settlement" between the Wilsonians and Tammany Hall was a bitter pill for the few active independent Democrats in the Empire State. By early 1916, this group had shrunk to a cadre of Sulzerites and fellow travelers who still trumpeted the anti-Murphy cause. Led by the former governor's secretary, Chester Platt, these diehards tried but failed to generate support at the March state convention for the election of "their" delegates to the party's national gathering in St. Louis. (On the day before the conference met in Syracuse they had even sponsored a "get-together" of independents, to which almost no one of stature had come.) "The administration is apparently with the Organization," concluded one Platt confidant gloomily, who then queried: "Why do anything more?"[42] But the stubborn Platt and his friends refused to give up their impossible dream of scoring a stunning upset over Murphy, or, failing that, at least carving out for themselves some niche in the New York party. During the winter and spring they had championed the candidacy of Judge Samuel Seabury for the Democratic gubernatorial nomination, and they now redoubled their efforts. The Seabury cause seemed tailor-made for the dissidents, since the judge had always been a party maverick: he was once an active member of Hearst's Municipal Ownership League in New York City; in 1913 he ran (but lost) on the Progressive ticket for a seat on the court of appeals; then the next year, when Whitman and the Republicans swept the state, he won the court of appeals race as a Progressive Democrat.[43] From the bench Seabury looked like a good antidote to the Wilson-Tammany compromise that was so deplorable to the Platt group.

In actuality, Seabury's credentials as a reformer went well beyond the essential quality—independence from Tammany Hall—that made him so attractive to the anti-Murphy people. He was widely known for his powerful attacks on special interests, his forthright commitment to social and economic justice, and his deep sympathy for organized labor. Thus, by the summer of 1916, the Seabury candidacy had enlisted the backing not only of the insurgent Democrats in the state but also the New York County and Erie County Progressive committees as well as the state labor conference comprising New York City's Central Federated Union (CFU) and unions in the upstate with an estimated membership of 600,000 workers. So broad-based was Seabury's appeal that he had developed into the leading contender for the gubernatorial nod as the Democrats gathered for their "unofficial" state conference in August. According to one politico, he "was at least 75,000 votes stronger than his party."[44]

Such facts as these about Seabury did not escape Wilson's advisors, then in search of candidates in key states to strengthen the president's progressivism theme, or, for that matter, Tammany regulars in New

York, whose recent protestations of loyalty to Wilson were being put to the test and who were themselves looking for an "appropriate" reformer. At first, however, Charlie Murphy demurred on Seabury, and in the party's Saratoga conference trotted out the candidacy of one of "his" boys, Robert F. Wagner: Wagner himself boasted an enviable progressive record; he could help Wilson with the large German vote in New York City and Buffalo; and in any case upstaters McCabe of Albany, Kelley of Syracuse, and Fitzpatrick of Buffalo believed the time was ripe to run "an out and out organization man." But in the informal negotiations that followed, the pragmatic boss backed down, evidently because of the importunities for Seabury by Wilsonians Stuart Gibboney, representing McAdoo, and Franklin D. Roosevelt. "I helped to put Seabury across," FDR later boasted.[45] On the convention floor Al Smith confirmed the Hall's agreement "to give our hearty support to Judge Samuel Seabury," then cast all New York County's votes for him. The only "slap" at the Wilson administration in the entire conference was the nomination of William McCombs for U.S. senator; earlier the president had removed McCombs as chairman of the Democratic National Committee. Finally, the Democrats adopted a platform applauding Woodrow Wilson's achievements, attacking Whitman's conservatism, and advocating a reasonable reform program for the state.[46] If there was any doubt that the New York Democracy, in 1916, was pursuing its "progressive" image as the Wilsonians hoped it would, these events certainly dispelled it.

Notwithstanding Democratic harmony, the task for Wilson and Seabury in the Empire State was herculean. The Republicans had the candidates and the issues that touched the minds and hearts of New Yorkers that year. In the ensuing campaign, GOP orators, including both Hughes and Wadsworth, and local party rallies stressed Wilson's "weak" foreign policy, declared protectionism to be the key to prosperity and the Underwood tariff the cause of "Democratic" hard times, and dismissed the Democracy as "no friend of labor and industry of the North." The vocal Republican press in the central and western sections of the state, for its part, chimed in with standard party doctrine, but also emphasized Americanism à la 1916. "The Republican party stands for America First and American efficient," bellowed a Syracuse newspaper not untypically.[47] To these themes was added just a dash of progressivism: Hughes was remembered "as a governor . . . whose one guiding principle . . . was to do right with equal consideration and equal justice for all citizens."[48] And Whitman put the icing on the cake with his usual anti-Tammanyism and antibossism.

Meanwhile, the Democratic campaign limped along. On the surface, the Wilson-Seabury ticket nicely blended the issues that the national administration wished to highlight. Seabury bore the standard of progressivism, applauding the New Freedom and further detailing his own reform program for New York. He defended the workmen's compensation law that the Republicans had attacked, championed prison reform, called for necessary changes in the judiciary, and advocated adoption of the executive budget. "Whitman," he charged, "stands for the application of reactionary principles to the government of this state." Seabury also dutifully praised Wilson's "statesmanship" in international affairs that, he argued, kept "this . . . nation at peace with the world."[49] Yet the combination of Seabury's judicial style, the final rapprochement of the Republicans and Bull Moosers behind Whitman, and the surprising attacks of the Hearst press (which originally supported the judge) all undermined his effectiveness. Stripped of his "side endorsements"—except for organized labor, which stuck with him— Seabury lost whatever advantage he had enjoyed in past campaigns as a "man above his party."[50]

But as much as anything else one aspect of Woodrow Wilson's own campaign strategy proved nettlesome for the Democrats, especially in areas of New York State where the party had to maximize its vote: the cities. This was the president's powerful reply in late September to the "O'Leary Telegram" in which he verbally attacked "disloyal Americans" who refused to support him because of ties to their motherland. Such assaults on "foreignness," as already noted, were not new to Wilson; his earlier nativistic writings and his well-known views on immigrants had gotten him into difficulties four years earlier with the Hearst people. Doubtless, Wilson's September 1916 statement—to be followed by others—was meant as a defense of his peace policy, since Irish- and German-American societies particularly in Greater New York were accusing him of being pro-British. In addition, he may have felt compelled to reassert his own Americanism in light of Theodore Roosevelt's excessively patriotic campaign on behalf of Hughes.[51] Roosevelt, indeed, had almost scored a big victory in the statewide primaries on September 20, when "his" candidate, Robert Bacon, came close as an "avowed unneutral" to upsetting the less bellicose William Calder for the Republican U.S. Senate nomination.[52] Whatever the connection between these events, if any, one Democratic official asserted that the party would "make the hyphen issue the big talking point of this campaign." And segments of the Democratic press in New York City, most notably the *World* and the *Evening Post,* picked up the theme and turned it on the Republicans, maintaining that Hughes had held secret conferences with pro-German organizations to obtain their backing. With vicious insults hurled at both Hughes and German-Americans by these champions of the Democracy, and with what seemed to be mounting evidence of the administration's "anti-Catholicism," it is hardly surprising that complaints filtered into Wilson headquarters from Tammany officials that the campaign in New York was "all shot to pieces." At one critical moment, several of Murphy's lieutenants, heavily dependent on their Irish and German constituencies, claimed that they were going to vote for Hughes.[53]

In the end, Wilson and the national committee moderated their attacks on hyphenism with the obvious hope of minimizing Democratic losses among German-Americans, and especially Irish-Americans who formed the backbone of the party in several of the nation's large cities. At the same time, Irish-American spokesmen in New York City tempered their enthusiasm for Hughes as the Republican campaign stalled; and in the upstate city of Syracuse, Wilson was again touted as the peace candidate. Words of encouragement now flowed from Colonel House to the president. "Tammany seems to be getting in full swing," House wrote jubilantly on October 23, and armed with forecasts that the Democrats still had a chance in New York, he urged Wilson to tour the Empire State for a couple of days before the climactic Democratic rally in Madison Square Garden on November 2. The president did so, but he remained skeptical—as he had been all along—that he could garner New York's big electoral vote. In fact, Wilson was disgusted enough at one juncture to chide House and Vance McCormick for their "New Yorkitis." As if to answer the president's skepticism

Charlie Murphy on election eve made the rosy prediction that the Democrats would carry Greater New York with pluralities so large as to defeat Hughes statewide.[54]

Murphy was wrong, however. "It was the same old story of New York State politics," averred the *New York Times* on the day after the election, as Hughes and Whitman won on the strength of a large upstate plurality and a respectable vote in New York City. The GOP carried two thirds of both houses of the legislature, a majority of the state's congressional delegation, and the U.S. Senate race. While the overall turnout in 1916 was slightly smaller than in 1912, the vote aggregate outside the city jumped about 77,000 over the 1912 level and 161,450 over the total in 1914. The Republicans, therefore, captured practically all of the interior counties as well as the major cities of Buffalo, Rochester, Syracuse, Utica, and Albany. Yet not all the news from the upstate was bad for the Democracy: Democrats actually did better proportionately than the GOP with the increased vote in the cities. "The industrial centers voted strongly for President Wilson," declared one newspaper with only slight exaggeration.[55] In all of them the president ran ahead of Glynn two years earlier, improved on his own 1912 performance, and generally outpolled Bryan in 1908. (Seabury did not do quite so well, but the pattern was about the same.) Certainly a key factor here was that Wilson's losses in German wards were minimized, and Irish strongholds in Buffalo, Syracuse, and Troy held firm for him. At the same time, Polish areas in Buffalo and Utica went heavily Democratic, and although Wilson lost most of the major Italian districts in the interior urban centers, the Democratic vote swung upward in a majority of them from its low point in 1914. This was also the case in the upstate Jewish wards.[56]

To many, however, it was New York City that proved to be the big disappointment for the Democracy in 1916. Here Wilson's plurality, expected in some quarters to be in the neighborhood of 75,000, instead was just about 40,000, while Seabury's was much less. And in New York County, Tammany's stronghold, not only did the vote turnout decline considerably from the level of four years earlier, but the aggregate vote fell markedly in proportion to the rest of the city total in 1916. These results gave rise to the charge—"the old familiar cry," noted an independent Democratic newspaper—that Murphy and Tammany Hall betrayed promises made to the Wilsonians earlier in the year and confirmed during the campaign. The *Tribune,* for example, attributed the president's loss statewide to the use of "th' harpoon" in Greater New York. But Murphy's defenders were quick to point out that voters could not be led where they refused to go—and Wilson was not so popular among hyphenate Americans. "The hyphen issue should never have been emphasized," proclaimed one Tammany leader in utter candor.[57]

Actually, however, the Democrats did not fare so poorly in New York County—or generally in New York City—as Murphy's detractors maintained. For one thing, Wilson ran better in the city as a whole than any Democratic presidential candidate since 1900; and in Manhattan his plurality was second best to Alton B. Parker's in 1904. Even Seabury garnered the largest vote total of any Democratic gubernatorial contender in Greater New York in a decade. For another, the Democracy exhibited respectability in the strongly ethnic areas. It is true that Wilson lost ground in Manhattan's Yorkville district, and he was defeated in two German districts in Brooklyn and one in Queens, the last having gone Democratic in the past several elections. But he did retrieve much of the Irish vote in Greater New York as he had in the upstate cities. Indeed, Wilson's percentages in most of the Irish areas were higher than his own four years earlier or, for that matter, Bryan's in 1908, though a tailing off of the aggregate vote in these districts suggests that some citizens may have registered their protest by staying away from the polls. Italian districts tended to combine aspects of these patterns: in two of four in Manhattan and Brooklyn Wilson garnered a lower percentage of a small vote yet captured them.[58] Such "losses" were made up essentially by the Democracy's decent showing in Jewish strongholds throughout the city where, it had been anticipated, President Wilson would divide the "peace" vote with the weak Socialist candidate, Allan Benson. Here the party's revival, a trend noted in the 1914 elections, proceeded apace: eleven districts returned a higher percentage Democratic vote than two years earlier, and all but one more so than 1912. In Manhattan only the sixth district, as usual, slipped to the Republicans, while the Bronx thirty-third and Brooklyn's twenty-second, both with large numbers of Germans, were lost to Wilson. (The pattern for Seabury was not substantially different except that he won the Bronx thirty-third and lost Brooklyn's twenty-third.) Also noteworthy about the Jewish areas was that they displayed a significantly increased voter turnout over 1912—and this increase went in large proportions to the Democracy.[59]

Yet, as had been the case two years earlier, Democratic success in New York City's Jewish districts was not undiluted. In two congressional districts in Manhattan and in a half-dozen or so assembly contests in Manhattan and Brooklyn, Socialist candidates mounted a fierce campaign of protest on several counts: the "militarism" of Wilson on the national scene and Whitman in the state; the "poor" labor record of both major parties together with their "friendly" attitude toward big business; and the "class warfare" in the metropolis stemming from the bitter transit workers' strike. "The Socialist party is the only progressive party," insisted the *New York Call* amid the heated canvass.[60] In those parts of the Lower East Side comprising the twelfth congressional district, Socialist spokesmen made a concerted effort to transfer the CFU's endorsement of the popular Meyer London, now running for reelection, to their assembly candidates. Anticipating "trouble," Murphy's Tammany had turned to a more appealing congressional candidate than the old wheelhorse, Henry Goldfogle, to oppose London, and selected carefully their nominees in the assembly races. When the votes were in, however, London captured a second term by defeating his Democratic challenger in every assembly district but the fourth; a preelection survey showed that he would win three quarters of the Progressive party vote that was apparently earmarked for the Republican candidate who withdrew from the race at the eleventh hour. Also, Socialist vote totals in the city's assembly contests jumped 47 percent over 1914 and 21 percent over 1915. Only two Socialist assemblymen were elected—in Brooklyn's twenty-first and twenty-third districts— but several others came close. And Morris Hillquit barely lost his bid for a House seat in East Harlem's twentieth congressional district after an intense battle in which Socialist leaders charged both Democrats and Republicans with fraud.[61]

On the whole, the Democrats, in 1916, lost the Empire State to a reunited Republican party that successfully combined its traditional appeals with a call for "peace with honor." Wilson and Seabury certainly had their assets, but these were not compelling to a majority of

New York's citizenry. The president's own version of progressivism offered less to the state as a whole—and overall to the financial-industrial Northeast—than elsewhere in the nation. "It has been the radical West that he has sought to satisfy," complained one upstate newspaper disillusioned with the New Freedom's tariff and taxation policies. To many New Yorkers, Wilson's foreign policy was weak, vacillating, and inadequate. Nor did Seabury's candidacy for the governorship, contrary to expectations, lend strength to the ticket: the regular organizations in New York City hardly worked vigorously for him, and upstate, argued the *Tribune*, he had to face voters "with only the Tammany hallmark on him."[62]

IV

Still, however, the Democrats in New York could not help but discern several bright spots as they surveyed the wreckage of their defeat in the 1916 elections. First, they had forged and sustained a degree of party unity that might be used as a building block for the future. The Wilson-Tammany accord ended a four-year period of intermittent sparring and peacemaking between the president's men and Charlie Murphy's forces in the state. In effect, Tammany Hall and its upstate allies would henceforth go virtually unchallenged, for the few remaining insurgent Democrats had nowhere to turn for support and sustenance. Second, the politics of 1916 had afforded the Democratic regulars the opportunity to reaffirm their commitment to progressive values—a commitment that had carried them through the legislative battles in 1915–1916 and the constitutional convention of 1915. This reaffirmation strengthened the Democracy's positive, forward-looking image as the rival Republicans slipped into a complacent conservatism and a narrow patriotism. Finally, the elections of 1916 showed the Democrats to be on the upswing in the state's larger interior cities, stemming in part from their improved performance among most ethnic groups who may have been moved by a combination of that party's ability to get across its peace-progressivism themes and Republican negativism. If this trend continued, the politics of 1918 would be shaped differently from the patterns down to 1910 and since 1914. And although the Socialists in Greater New York persisted in giving the Democracy fits, the declining percentage overall of the anti–major party vote in 1916 together with Tammany's proven ability to handle left-wing dissent offered some promise that radicalism could be contained as a political force in the days ahead.[63]

8

The Democratic Rebound:
1917–1918

Within five months after the 1916 elections, President Woodrow Wilson took America into the foreign conflict his administration had resolved to avoid. The nation's war machine was quickly geared up. America's systems of production, distribution, and transportation were regimented for war needs. Selective service supplied the necessary U.S. fighting force. Protection and defense against the enemy at home became the special province of the federal government in the form of the Espionage Act of 1917 and the Sedition Act of the next year. Citizen support of the "crusade to make the world safe for democracy" fell to the committee on public information, that truly effective propaganda organization headed by the journalist George Creel. In these ways the war was brought close to all Americans whether as fighting men abroad or disciplined citizen-soldiers at home.

New Yorkers shared in the enthusiasm, the hoopla, and the patriotism of the Great War. The state supplied its quota of doughboys and even more than its share of Liberty bond subscriptions—indeed, well over one third of the total amount of the entire nation. Charles Whitman's Republican administration in Albany, earlier in the vanguard of the preparedness movement, spent much of its energy in 1917–1918 making New York "fighting trim." Agencies paralleling federal commissions on food and fuel were established to conserve these commodities. A 1918 conscription law in effect "drafted" labor into useful employment for the duration. The state police was organized as a defense force and was supplemented by the Home Defense Corps, cadres of local policemen for use in the upstate counties. Even Creel committee efforts were duplicated on the state level: a New York committee on public safety distributed propaganda pamphlets on the war in both English and foreign tongues; sponsored speakers and parades across the state; and encouraged schools, churches, and clubs to put on patriotic programs. For those who dissented there was not only federal proscription but state legislation as well that authorized the attorney general to undertake investigations of disloyalty.[1]

And there was a good deal of dissent in the Empire State. Not surprisingly, most of it emanated from the politicial left—Socialists, civil libertarians, and an occasional Wobbly (though the Industrial Workers of the World [IWW] was never powerful in New York). The main trouble occurred in Greater New York, where the Socialists commanded a respectable following in the Lower East Side and among needle trades unionists. Their clarion call was the St. Louis Proclamation importuning "workers of all countries to refuse support to their government in their [capitalist] wars." Radicals thus responded to the patriots' campaign of words and deeds with pamphlets, flyers, and a vigorous press; conducted antidraft rallies; and sponsored street demonstrations. Recriminations followed fast and furious as police broke up meetings for fear of violence and, in some instances, denied the right of public assemblage. Outspoken radicals like Emma Goldman, Scott Nearing, John Reed, and Max Eastman were rounded up; prosecuted; and, in many cases, jailed. Similar incidents, though far fewer, took place in Yonkers, Albany, Rochester, Niagara Falls, and Buffalo. The radical press was subsequently muzzled: both the New York Call and the (Buffalo) New Age lost their second-class mailing privilege, while the Jewish Daily Forward and the Advocate adopted self-censorship to avoid being closed down.[2]

Such wartime conditions tended to sustain—even exacerbate—the sharp divisions and conflicts of 1914–1916 in the state. It is true that tensions heightened generally between country and city, but far more critical was the widened chasm between the more highly Yankee Protestant upstate and New York City, denizen of "foreignness" and "radicalism." These attitudes had the effect of further intensifying interparty differences. The Republicans unabashedly pursued their "100 percent Americanism," became increasingly nativistic and conservative, and in the process virtually abandoned Greater New York to the rival Democrats. As they did so, the Democracy, certainly no less patriotic, moved in an almost opposite direction. In 1917 the Democrats in New York City orchestrated a clever left-of-center campaign that was designed to appeal to the city's polyglot masses and thus complete the task they initiated two years earlier—that is, win back from Mitchel's fusion forces full control of government in the downstate metropolis. In that year and in the next, they postured themselves in such a fashion as to reap maximum advantage over the stumbling Republicans on the twin issues of woman suffrage and prohibition. This strategy, in turn, placed the Democrats in a strong position for the crucial statewide elections in November 1918.

I

The Democrats' initial opportunity came in Greater New York, where in 1917 municipal elections were to be held. John Purroy Mitchel, chosen as a Wilsonian fusion mayor in the wake of the Sulzer fiasco four years earlier, had decided to make a bid for a second term. While Mitchel was—and remained—the darling of certain reform types, his administration had come under fire for several reasons. Mitchel himself was a high-brow, independent Democrat who, in pursuit of efficient, businesslike government, had conveyed the unfortunate image of aloofness and unconcern toward the lot of common, ordinary citizens. His was the usual malady that plagued fusion government in New York City, though conditions in Mitchel's day only worsened the mayor's troubles. Rising unemployment in 1913–1914 and skyrocketing food prices particularly in 1917 spurred modest city relief programs that were, alas, doomed to failure. Furthermore, the administration was charged with anti-Catholicism in its investigation of irregularities in the Catholic Charities (albeit Mitchel was personally a Catholic) and with turning the city over to the "Rockefeller interests" in its adoption of the controversial Gary plan for the public schools. Finally, Mitchel's heartfelt patriotism, which made him an advanced agent of preparedness even to the chagrin of President Wilson, deeply antagonized the powerful antiwar forces in the metropolis. The administration had become especially unpopular in the city's immigrant, working-class districts where all these issues and concerns came into focus.[3]

Under the circumstances, efforts to reestablish anti-Tammany fusion collapsed. Although most Republicans preferred to go the way of 1913, one among them, William M. Bennett, challenged Mitchel in the GOP citywide primary and won that party's mayoralty nomination in a disputed contest. Meanwhile, Democratic dissident groups, convinced that Mitchel had been too cozy with the Republicans, returned to the party fold and joined up with Tammany Hall and its allies. With assurances that the Wilson government in Washington would abide by the 1916 agreements and not interfere in municipal politics, Murphy Democrats in New York County bowed to the wishes of McCooey's strong Kings organization as well as the "demands" of William Randolph Hearst in naming Brooklyn Judge John F. Hylan, "an Irishman without a sense of humor," as the party's mayoralty candidate. Completing the field was Socialist Morris Hillquit, whose outspoken antiwar stance nettled the others. Mitchel remained isolated as an independent, with his chances for victory dwindling as the fall campaign moved toward a conclusion.[4]

Mainly Democratic strategy in Greater New York, in 1917, evolved in response to the themes that Mitchel chose for his reelection canvass. The mayor resolved to make patriotism the "Supreme Issue," and his battle cry became: "Hearst, Hylan, and the Hohenzollerns." The reference was to William Randolph Hearst's allegedly pro-German sentiments, his endorsement of the Democratic ticket, and Hylan's guilt by association. Mitchel also tarred Hillquit with the same brush of disloyalty. Prominent Republicans like Theodore Roosevelt and Charles Evans Hughes, together with most of the New York City press, joined in the attack against the Socialist ticket principally over Hillquit's refusal to back the Liberty loan drives, largely ignored Bennett, and urged the mayor's reelection. Nor did Mitchel, with GOP supporters at his side, spare certain ethnic groups, especially the Irish and the Germans, for their less than "100 percent Americanism." Democratic orators reacted by skirting the loyalty question except to insist in the beginning that no man "has a monopoly of patriotism" and to reiterate the point occasionally during the campaign. All along Hylan emphasized what he maintained was the real issue to the voters: "the moneyed interests versus the people." And the Democrats hit hard the major planks of their municipal platform. Constructed in July by Robert Wagner, this "model" of progressivism, forged in part to appease Hearst, championed home rule, public ownership of all utilities, slum clearance and housing construction, expansion of educational facilities, and the entire "program of progressive development which has enabled so many cities to outstrip New York in every condition." (The *New York Times* angrily dismissed the platform as a collection of "ancient Populist rhetoric and the vain nostrums of a dishonest socialism.") Democratic exploitation of such themes had the effect at once of dealing Mitchel a mortal blow in the ethnic, lower-class districts where his "tactless" campaign had further weakened him and yet neutralizing the Socialists by stealing their thunder. "Star municipal ownership and the high cost of living" went the orders of Tammany leaders determined to "save the city" from Hillquit and his followers. Thus, many a moderate, persuaded that neither Bennett nor Mitchel stood much of a chance, drifted to Hylan and Tammany.[5]

The Democratic strategy worked beautifully as John Hylan triumphed easily in November, defeating his nearest opponent Mitchel by a two-to-one margin with Hillquit running a close third. Bennett was not even in the race for he garnered less than 10 percent of the aggregate vote. Along with the mayoralty Tammany and its friends captured the boards of alderman and estimate and a large majority of New York City's assembly delegation. "The victory for the Democratic organization," commented one journal, "was the most emphatic and most complete given to any party in the history of Greater New York." Hylan himself actually swept two thirds of the city's assembly districts and piled up huge pluralities in most of the ethnic areas, including those dominated by Irish-, German-, and Italian-Americans. Mitchel's vote was only 42 percent of what it had been four years earlier, and he carried just nine districts, all of which but one contained a high proportion of middle- and upper-class native Americans. But to most observers the truly distinctive feature of the New York City elections, aside from Tammany Hall's "vindication," was the dazzling performance of Morris Hillquit and the Socialists. Hillquit's candidacy was especially appealing to Jewish voters all through the metropolis: In New York County he won East Harlem and the four districts of the Lower

East Side, where the aggregate vote jumped 20 percent on the average over 1916 while the city vote actually declined; he carried the predominantly Jewish areas in the Bronx and in Kings; and he finished a strong second in several other districts inhabited by large numbers of Jews. In addition, the Socialists elected several members of the board of aldermen and ten state assemblymen, all representing mainly Jewish districts. "The election," proclaimed Hillquit, "has established the Socialist party as an important and permanent factor in the politics of the city."[6]

Morris Hillquit's unbounded optimism was hardly grounded in reality, however. For, in 1917, socialism was essentially a vehicle of protest, as it had been traditionally: in this instance a protest voiced largely against the war but also, to a degree, against deteriorating social and economic conditions, and probably against ethnic intolerance. (Surely east European Jews had no trouble identifying with Hillquit.) Indeed, the results in Greater New York were somewhat duplicated in the state's larger interior cities, particularly in Buffalo, Rochester, and Syracuse, where a sizable radical vote was generally recorded in German, German-Jewish, and east European Jewish wards primarily, it appears, on the war issue. What was unique about New York City was that two thirds of the electorate succumbed to Socialist pacifism *or* Democratic "class" appeals in angry rejection of John Purroy Mitchel's version of Americanism and his "high-brow" regime. In the upstate urban centers, by contrast, the more competitive Republicans were successful in marshaling their forces against "disloyalty" and "radicalism" and, for the most part, swept to victory. So it was that New York City, in 1917, was roundly dismissed in many quarters for being out of touch with the rest of the Empire State—and with America generally. In what was widely regarded that year as a drift to conservatism across the nation, the city seemed all the more "un-American" and "foreign." On the other hand, Tammany's Charlie Murphy interpreted the 1917 municipal elections in quite a different light. The Democrats, he announced, had won in Greater New York because their candidates and platform "are progressive and in accordance with the world-wide progressive tendencies of the day."[7]

II

In the meantime, both Democrats and Republicans were constrained to grapple with two other important issues—woman suffrage and prohibition—that reached their zenith in New York during the war years. In much of the nation these "reforms" had been closely intertwined with a general movement for the moral and political purification of man and society. Its major objective was the preservation of a socio-cultural ethos dominated by the Protestant middle class against the "threat" of newcomers, the machines, and the "interests." Many of the suffragists themselves had drifted into women's rights through their participation in the temperance crusade, and several states adopted one, then the other, reform in quick succession.[8] In the state of New York, and generally in the Northeast, however, the two issues—enfranchise-ment and prohibition—became somewhat distinct from one another and took different paths. Woman suffrage was both expansive and opportunistic and consistently reflected its democratic, progressive roots. Prohibition, on the other hand, retained a nativism and provin-cialism befitting its ethnocultural origins and geographic base and, therefore, persisted as an expression of illiberalism. While neither movement could capture a major party organization in the state, suf-frage, in the end, would be more closely identified with the Democrats and temperance with the Republicans.

It is no doubt the case that most of the suffrage leaders in New York as elsewhere hailed from the middle or upper stratum of society, and a goodly portion of them participated in the dry crusade. Yet these resolute women and their male supporters almost from the beginning realized that achieving their goal in so diverse and polyglot an envi-ronment dictated an enlarged constituency and an expanded image. Accordingly, they scrupulously avoided any outward display of sym-pathy for prohibition. Moreover, organizations like Harriet Stanton Blatch's Women's Political Union and Carrie Chapman Catt's New York City Woman Suffrage party appealed boldly to labor unions; social progressives; and, in numerous ways, ethnic Americans for back-ing. Catt's organizational apparatus was even modeled after the district system of Tammany Hall. As the movement gathered momentum, it became "a tool for social regeneration," that is, a means by which women would use their newly won political power to ameliorate eco-nomic and industrial ills.[9] Thus, the suffrage cause in New York State coincided with the thrust of reform championed by the Democratic party under Tammany's leadership.

In the early stages of the suffrage movement neither the Democrats nor the Republicans paid much attention to the women reformers. Before 1912 only the Socialists did anything to help them. In 1911 the Socialist central committee urged all locals in New York to launch "an effective campaign" to collect signatures for an enfranchisement petition. At that time, records Harriet Blatch, "Tammany was our arch enemy." Matters changed dramatically in 1912 when, under the pressure from Roosevelt Progressives, each of the major parties included a plank in its platform calling for a referendum on a state constitutional amendment extending the vote to women. For the Democrats the pragmatic Charlie Murphy personally received the platform statement written by the suffragists. The next year Robert Wagner, admitting that he still harbored certain reservations about the reform, nonetheless introduced and steered to passage in the senate a measure "obedient to that platform." Al Smith did likewise in the assembly. The Wagner resolution was approved again in the 1914 legislature, a step necessitated by the amendment process in New York. In each instance the margin of victory was wide, attesting not so much to the popularity of suffrage among the politicians at the time but rather to the comforting feeling that the issue would be decided—and probably beaten—at the polls in 1915.[10]

"Let us wake up the old State if we can!" became the battle cry of the women as Catt sought to rally the reformers in the 1915 suffrage campaign. But that fall, as the politicians had anticipated, New York went the way of other eastern states—Massachusetts, New Jersey, and Pennsylvania. The referendum lost out everywhere in the state: in New York City, where Blatch believed Tammany "swamped us"; in the rural upstate and the small towns; and in the interior urban centers.[11] While the suffragists had conducted a thorough canvass, they faced tough obstacles. In the first place, the question was subordinated to local issues where municipal contests were held and was confused all over with the propositions containing the unpopular revisions of the state constitution forged that summer in the Albany convention. Second, traditional attitudes toward the role of women embraced by males of German, Italian, and Irish extraction apparently turned away large numbers of those ethnic groups whom the suffragists had been trying to court. (Eastern European Jews in New York City seemed to be the exception to this pattern.) Third, both local Democratic *and* Republican leaders across the state professed indifference or outright hostility to the issue. Most surprising to the suffrage champions was the discovery late in the campaign of unexpected weaknesses in certain rural areas. "I guess the people have become gospel hardened," complained one woman with reference to farmer indifference in Wyoming, Allegany, and Cattaraugus counties. At bottom, however, was the fact, argues a historian of the movement, that "the referendum had simply taken place too soon."[12] The suffragists needed more time to make the issue irresistible to the politicians and to the electorate.

Armed with the motto, "Victory in 1917," the women redoubled their efforts in New York to conquer what to them was "the key to the Federal Suffrage Amendment." In 1916, and again in 1917, they had trouble with the Republican state legislature but nevertheless won the right to a second referendum. Few of the politicians apparently believed that the reform had any greater chance of success this time than the last. However, America's entry in World War I gave the suffragists unexpected opportunities that they were quick to exploit. Delaying the main thrust of their campaign till they "became alarmed at the disintegration of their organization," they "plunged into war work" by knitting for the Red Cross, by canvassing for fuel conservation, by conducting the state's military census, and by participating in Liberty bond drives. When at last the fall 1917 campaign got rolling, the women made the most of their "patriotic" contributions in public meetings, parades, and press releases.[13] They also pleaded for fairness and justice while at the same time intensifying their work in heavily ethnic neighborhoods in the cities. "If we are to play our part in the world struggle for democracy," exclaimed a friendly newspaper echoing suffragist rhetoric, "we must not deny the spirit of democracy within our borders." It was widely reported that President Wilson was so moved by these appeals that he staged a well-publicized interview in the White House with a prominent New York champion of the vote for women, then urged the men of the Empire State to approve the November referendum.[14]

Wilson's declaration in favor of the suffrage cause in 1917 was but one of several steps in his own gradual accommodation to the growing women's movement. The year before he had been cautious in his support of a plank in the national Democratic platform recommending to the states that they adopt suffrage amendments. But in the ensuing presidential contest Wilson garnered the electoral vote of almost all the western states where women cast the ballot, perhaps fulfilling an earlier prophecy made by Harriet Blatch that "with women enfranchised the Democratic party is destined to benefit." Shortly after the presidential importunity, organization Democrats in New York jumped on the suffrage bandwagon. Near campaign's end Charlie Murphy and his Tammany minions signaled their capitulation to the reform by announcing the appointment of three dozen women to membership in the Hall, and on Election Day Tammany district captains were observed hard at work for the referendum.[15] Such a transformation from two years earlier was grounded on certain realities that Tammany faced in 1917: first, the ambitious canvass on the issue waged by the Socialists in New York City's Lower East Side where, as already noted, the Murphy people labored to limit defections in the municipal and assembly races; and second, the realization among Democratic leaders that suffrage would soon be adopted nationally in any case.

The result on November 6 was a dramatic reversal of the vote in 1915. "Suffrage Fight Won in the Cities," emblazoned a *New York Times* headline with regard to the referendum, as several of the large upstate cities—Buffalo, Syracuse, Utica, Schenectady, and Troy—joined Greater New York in approving the question (while much of the rest of the upstate went against it). In New York City alone the plurality for suffrage exceeded 102,000, this representing a turnover of nearly 116,000 votes from the total in support of the reform in 1915. A substantial portion of this vote increase came in the heavily ethnic districts where the Democrats and/or the Socialists were strong. In the interior urban centers where the referendum had lost two years earlier, the 1917 patterns were less clear, although in Buffalo, for example, most of the predominantly foreign wards cast a larger prosuffrage vote than in 1915.[16]

Suffrage opponents and social conservatives dismissed the franchise victory in the Empire State as yet another illustration of the workings of "radicalism" and "pacificism" in the cities, especially in Greater New York. But at least some of the suffragists and their backers, in citing the host of factors behind the triumph, paid special tribute to the Democrats. "We owe a great debt to Tammany Hall," declared one of them. Later Charlie Murphy was even given credit for "turning" the "National tide" in favor of the Nineteenth Amendment to the U.S. Constitution.[17] This lavish praise heaped on Democratic politicians who really threw their support to the referendum at the eleventh hour can only be understood in relative terms: the posture of New York's Republicans. It is true that some—like Governor Whitman and former Congressman Herbert Parsons—were favorable to suffrage. At the same time, however, the most implacable foes of the reform, characteristically, were the upstate conservatives, most notably William Barnes, George Aldridge, and James W. Wadsworth (kingpin of the antisuffrage movement in the U.S. Senate). To Ida Harper these men constituted a "machine," which, she argued, "did everything possible to defeat the amendment." In short, Republican extremism, not untypically in the war era, drove the reformers, themselves masters of pragmatism, into the arms of an adaptable, flexible Democracy.[18]

True to form, the Democrats also moved quickly after the suffrage victory to involve women in the political process. In early 1918 Tammany sponsored the creation of the Women's Regular Democratic Organization of Greater New York. Known as the "Feminine Tammany Hall," this group resolved to concentrate, not on partisan politics, but rather on an "uplift programme." One month later, the Hall's executive committee was opened to women, and in May thirty-two members of the committee were installed. "Women, after all, are the real leaders," remarked Charlie Murphy half-jokingly at the initiation ceremony. The Kings County Democratic Committee followed suit, and the party's state committee, in April, added the names of twenty-one women to its rolls. These moves were capped by an ambitious voter registration drive spearheaded by Tammany beginning late in the spring. Flushed with early successes in this effort, the independent Democratic *New York World* mused over the likelihood "of electing a strong New York City man in the next Gubernatorial election." Though enrollment figures in the city never reached the dizzying heights Democrats anticipated, party leaders did everything they could, by the September primaries, to maximize Democratic gains, or at least to offset Republican registration increases in the upstate.[19]

Perhaps by its very nature, prohibition was incapable of developing the kind of expansiveness in New York State that characterized the woman suffrage crusade. Far more than suffrage the temperance agitation of that day tapped the wellsprings of nativism: the movement in large measure was directed against the city and the immigrant as well as the "privileged" beer and liquor interests. It was in some sense a device for Americanization and social control. In the Empire State, therefore, the most profound dry sentiment could be found—and remained—in the interior regions among farmers, small townsfolk, and others of Yankee Protestant origins. Yet these groups had declined in numbers as the state's first- and second-class cities, peopled more and more by foreigners and their children, mushroomed in population through the first two decades of the twentieth century. At the very time that the prohibition fever was sweeping the nation, then, its natural domain in New York had shrunken considerably from what it had been forty years earlier. "It seems to have no conception of what is going on in the Middle West," lamented temperance leader William Anderson speaking of the state as a whole in 1914.[20]

What successes the temperance movement achieved in New York up to the adoption of the Eighteenth Amendment rested chiefly with the Anti-Saloon League (ASL) and Anderson, its able state superintendent. The league followed the usual formula—utilize varied and piecemeal methods to drive "the saloon from a large section of New York State." Anderson, known as the "Arch Foe of Demon Rum," launched an early campaign for the enforcement of the Sunday closing law in New York City but, aware that "Tammany was wholly and hopelessly pro-liquor" and that the city itself would never "respond to the moral sentiment," abandoned the effort and concentrated on the friendlier and safer upstate.[21] During the next few years, the ASL took advantage of a 1902 local option law to add scores of townships to the no-license column. By 1915, reported one Rochester newspaper, the most exciting issue in western New York was prohibition. But the league's major thrust in 1916 and 1917 was the passage of a bill in the state legislature extending local option to the interior cities. No doubt wishing to give upstate urban dwellers the same choice on the liquor question that their rural brethren enjoyed, Anderson also hoped, he once admitted, "to keep the New York liquor men so busy at home with local fights that they have no time nor money to contribute energy and funds to the national fight." In any case, the complicated bill was enacted with the support of Governor Charles Whitman.[22] For the next ten months the ASL waged a spirited battle in nearly forty communities, earmarking Syracuse, the largest city in which the referendum was to take place, as the prime target. The results in April 1918 were mixed: while half of the cities went wet and half voted dry, the larger ones generally remained wet, and the "forces of evil" won two thirds of the total number of licenses at stake. Syracuse was lost to the wets as heavily ethnic wards recorded about eight to one in favor of "demon rum" and the newly enfranchised women, a boon to the prohibition crusade elsewhere, evidently voted about the way the men did. The temperance agitators were spared surefire losses in New York City, Buffalo, and Rochester, their 1919 targets, with the ratification of the federal prohibition amendment.[23]

Essentially New York's politicos at first approached the prohibition issue about as gingerly as they had woman suffrage, for, as one newspaper observed in 1916, "nobody can tell just who will be injured when the big blow-up comes." It was no secret, however, that the Democrats, representing urban, wet constituencies, were mostly hostile to the dry crusade. Their major goal was to develop a strategy that would at once delay or defeat the prohibitionists and yet embarrass the Republicans. During and after the local option fight, Democratic leaders settled on a safe, sensible formula: bring the main question before the voters of the state in a fall referendum, which, explained Robert Wagner, would inform "us" whether the people "want or do not want to surrender their personal rights." The politicians would then know what to do with amendments proposed to the New York and the U.S. constitutions.[24] Throughout late 1917 and 1918 the Democrats held consistently to this position.

If Anderson and the Anti-Saloon League laid claim to the support of any political organization in the Empire State, it was the Republican party, whose greatest strength, after all, lay in the territory where prohibition sentiment was most pronounced. But the GOP was itself divided on the liquor issue just as it had been in the late nineteenth century. With Republican politicians from interior population centers often as wet as the Democrats—and with others from "country districts" who simply liked to drink—dodging the question, or at least delaying action on specific legislation, seemed the only safe ploy for that party's lawmakers in Albany. But in practice this tack brought down upon the Republican leadership the wrath of the ASL, Women's Christian Temperance Union, and other prohibition groups. At various times, Assembly Speaker Thaddeus Sweet and Senate Majority Leader Elon Brown became the targets of nasty barbs unleashed by ASL spokesman Anderson. And it was only after Governor Whitman "properly laid out" recalcitrant GOP senators in 1917 that the dry forces were able to win enactment of the cities' local option bill. Ten days earlier this group had joined the Democrats in "weakening" the measure.[25]

Among the high-ranking Republicans in New York State, it was Charles Whitman himself who emerged as the chief proponent of the temperance cause. In early 1918 Whitman's fired-up patriotism, his obvious need to shore up his administration with disaffected farm groups, his mistaken belief that dry sentiment was engulfing the state as it was the nation, and his own presidential ambitions (the Republican party was fast becoming the dry party nationally) all pushed him one step further—pressure the legislature into immediate ratification of the federal amendment. "I am for prohibition in State and nation," he declared unequivocally. But most Republicans wanted to await the results of the local option referendum in April, and neither the senate nor the assembly would take up the amendment. Well before the spring vote Whitman's colleagues were already warning that the governor "got himself too deep" on the liquor question. Many actually favored the Democratic solution of providing for a statewide referendum, then perhaps of dealing with prohibition more decisively in the 1919 legislature.[26]

Whitman's extreme stance on prohibition continued unabated into his campaign for renomination and reelection as governor later in the year. Such reckless abandon was possible largely because he held an iron grip on the Republican state organization. Nonetheless, vigorous protests were voiced and signs of deepening divisions in the GOP were manifest by the summer. These centered on a primary challenge hurled at Whitman by State Attorney General Merton Lewis. Lewis attacked the governor on several counts, not least of which was his decision to sacrifice the governorship of New York for the presidency of the United

States. Lewis, however, concentrated on the prohibition issue and called for the statewide referendum. Reflecting on the results of the local option elections in April, he commented prophetically that Whitman's renomination would elect a Democrat who would "receive in the cities enough votes to overcome the prohibition vote in the country districts." Lewis also charged Whitman with having Anti-Saloon League leader William Anderson as his "campaign manager and campaign fund collector." Indeed, by this time, the two were working closely together, and the rumor circulated—later to be confirmed—that they had reached an accord involving ASL support for a Whitman presidential bid in 1920.[27] Anderson, for his part, accused Lewis of obtaining the "backing" of the brewery interests. The challenger was joined by Barnes of Albany who dismissed prohibition, as he had social legislation, "as thoroughly Prussian in its will to power" and by Senator Wadsworth, whose own wetness was a matter of common knowledge. Barnes then collaborated with several others in an abortive attempt to inveigle his erstwhile enemy, Theodore Roosevelt, into running for the governorship. But in the September primaries these dissenters were crushed as Whitman's henchmen cracked the party whip and won for him an easy renomination. To cap his reelection drive the governor also walked off with the nomination of the Prohibition party, defeating the Prohibitionists' designated candidate in a write-in vote.[28] Thus it was that Charles Whitman attained his goal of arrogating the cause of temperance to himself and to a reluctant Grand Old Party.

It may be that under different circumstances the Republicans in the Empire State could have afforded to stumble on the temperance issue or permit the Democrats to grab the initiative on the question of woman suffrage and yet escape damaging consequences. Not so in 1918, however. For as the already narrowly based GOP showed signs of internal squabbling, the Democracy swept toward harmony. That harmony was borne of several ingredients, one negative—the Sulzer fiasco and the troubles it triggered had receded into the background— and several positive: the 1917 triumph in New York City, which fully reestablished Tammany Hall's power base and allowed the Murphy people to venture into statewide politics once again; the party's continually improving image as a forward-looking, progressive entity in contrast to Republican provincialism and conservatism; and the truly positive attributes of the man, Alfred E. Smith, who would move to center stage in the fall of 1918.

III

The Democrats hardly started out in 1918 on the note of unity. Early in the year the citizens of New York State were treated to another boom for newspaper publisher William Randolph Hearst, nemesis of Charlie Murphy and the regular party organizations. Typically, Hearst employed his popular dailies and a few of his political friends to advance his "renewed" ambitions—that is, first, in 1918, the governorship of New York, then, two years hence, the presidency of the United States. By common agreement there were at least reasonable prospects that he could achieve his initial objective. Hearst, after all, had been a vital force behind John Hylan's recent election to the New York City mayoralty, and Hylan had been the "creature" of Charlie Murphy and his allies. Some even believed the rumor, widely circulating at the time, that Murphy and Hearst had sealed a hard-and-fast bargain for 1918. If nothing else the Hearst threat smoked out large numbers of Democrats in the state—mainly regulars but also the few independents still active—who freely pronounced their "dread" of the party's chances that fall with the controversial publisher as the gubernatorial standard-bearer. "Hearst is a political typhoid carrier," charged Thomas Mott Osborne's old ally Charles F. Rattigan. "The political party that beds him down," he added, "will have to hang the contagion card on its front door the next day." Aside from his usual liabilities, Hearst's major weaknesses in 1918 were his "pro-Germanism," which made him especially vulnerable in the upstate except perhaps in a few city organizations where he commanded minimal support, and the "character" of his services to the national Democracy in recent years, particularly his reluctant support of Wilson in 1912 and again in 1916. Hearst had also emerged as a dry in a wet party.[29]

It was good politics for the powerful Murphy, unquestionably the most influential figure in the New York Democratic organization, to allow others to take the initiative against the vulnerable Hearst. That the boss, in fact, had made a deal with the publisher was probably not the case. But the two had clashed so often in the past that yet another encounter might send Hearst off on the path of political independence, thus jeopardizing Democratic chances that fall. It was for this reason that Murphy turned over to his trusted upstate allies the task of letting their "threatened freshet" down easily and painlessly. The upstate leaders subsequently arranged two conferences in Syracuse, both hosted by Murphy's friend, Onondaga Boss "Will" Kelley—one in April and the other in July. In the first gathering, described by a sympathetic newspaper as a "tame affair," well over two hundred delegates representing every county outside of New York City elected a Committee of Forty-Two to sift through the names of prospective candidates "acceptable to the upstate Democracy." Conducting its initial canvass then and there at the conference, the newly formed committee discovered the obvious—that "hostility prevailed" against William Randolph Hearst. One delegate put well the nub of the opposition: "The great issue will be American patriotism in the war, and any man who has to explain that he is an American will not do as a candidate."[30] Less than three months later the Committee of Forty-Two met again, this time to ballot formally on "acceptable" candidates. In five ballots Hearst's name failed to appear once, nor, it was reported, did the publisher even receive mention in committee deliberations, despite the fact that he had recently announced his intention to run in the September primary with or without party designation. Seven prospects were forwarded to the "unofficial" Democratic convention scheduled to meet in Saratoga later in July. Heading the list was William Church Osborn, former state chairman. Al Smith, one of only two New York City men among the designees, finished fourth in the final ballot.[31]

Smith's unexpectedly "strong" support among the upstate leaders was probably the single most important factor that drew Charlie Murphy actively into the nominating process at the party conference in Saratoga. "Has Mr. Murphy passed the word?" was the question most commonly asked on convention eve. Already the boss had met twice with his upstate friends and pronounced Osborn unacceptable, for, said Murphy, "he is not a Democrat after Tammany's own heart." Osborn, in turn, withdrew his name from consideration, not in surrender to the leaders, but rather in protest of the gathering's "legal right to choose party candidates." Working behind the scenes mainly with Kelley and Fitzpatrick, Murphy relegated other prospects to the scrap heap as well. These events, together with Hearst's persistence as a contender, drove many of the convention delegates directly into Al Smith's camp: Smith had earlier emerged as the second choice of several delegations from the interior counties.[32] Before the balloting took place, however, the Democrats made their final move—a less gentle one than heretofore—against Hearst. On the opening day they adopted a resolution introduced by Samuel Seabury that repudiated "every truckler with our country's enemies." Next day the convention proceeded with the balloting, and Albany County began the steamroller that carried Smith to an easy, first-ballot victory. Only Seabury uttered a negative word. "I believe him [Smith] to be the best representative of the worst element in the Democratic party in this State," the judge exclaimed to a disapproving crowd. But it was also Seabury who, after the voting ended, moved that the convention unanimously endorse the gubernatorial designee. The motion carried, and the delegates named Mayor Harry Walker of Binghamton as Smith's running mate, selected the remainder of the ticket, and adopted a platform with little debate. Drafted principally by Robert Wagner, the 1918 Democratic platform pledged total support to the nation's war effort but insisted that "the world must be made safe for democracy at home as well as abroad." It then embraced "progressivism" and urged the adoption of specific reforms such as minimum wage legislation for women and children, the public development of waterpower sites in the state, and the proposed national woman suffrage amendment.[33]

Al Smith's impressive convention victory stemmed largely from the careful planning of the regular Democrats—and the manipulations of Boss Charlie Murphy. But the enthusiasm with which the nomination was greeted by all segments of the party was little less than phenomenal and surely unexpected. The *New York World,* longtime critic of Tammany Hall, could think of "no man in either party organization who has more of the qualities of progressive and constructive leadership than Mr. Smith."[34] Smith's record in the state assembly; his vice-chairmanship of the Factory Investigating Commission; his distinguished performance in the 1915 constitutional convention; and, generally, his fair-mindedness as a politician were rehearsed to show that he truly stood out as a Tammany man. Some recalled that in 1915 when he ran for sheriff of New York County and two years later when he was a candidate for president of the board of aldermen, he had obtained the backing of New York City's major reform organizations and much of the metropolitan press, including independent and Republican newspapers. These endorsements, especially that tendered by the Citizens Union, declared Judge Joseph Proskauer many years later, "gave Smith a sense of heightened responsibility" as well as "a new stature in the eyes of the public." Now, as he faced a statewide contest, opponents and rivals of the past—upstate independents like John Carlisle, Charles Rattigan, and Chester Platt—also fell into line. Later the old anti-Tammany war-horse, Thomas Mott Osborne, announced his support of Smith's candidacy. Although William C. Osborn did go on to challenge Smith in the Democratic primary, Osborn directed most of his barbs at the "Hearst menace." And when the publisher finally gave up his quest (ultimately to back Smith), he switched his attack principally to Tammany Hall, not Smith's "unimpeachable" record. In the September primary Al Smith, therefore, defeated Osborn handily all across the state, and Osborn's supporters, including Franklin Roosevelt, quickly jumped on the Smith bandwagon. Wilsonians McAdoo and Malone completed the roster of national administration politicos behind the Tammany-led New York ticket.[35]

The ensuing election campaign was brief but hardly quiet. A much-hailed Liberty loan drive followed by the worldwide influenza epidemic that reached its peak in late October cut politicking as usual to a mere two weeks. Such an abbreviated canvass, it was predicted, would benefit Governor Whitman, for Smith, the lesser-known candidate, had little time to carry his message into the upstate regions, where the Democrats were expected to be terribly vulnerable. Here the Republicans made the most of that old issue, "saving the State from Tammany." To newspaper attacks that Smith was a Murphy "puppet" Whitman added personal assaults on his opponent's integrity: Smith had "never made a dollar until he got it from politics"; and Smith, while speaker of the assembly, had toadied to underworld characters like "Philadelphia Slim," "Nigger Mike" Salta, and "Young" Reiddy.[36] Also, Whitman presented his *White Book* to the voters. This was a slim volume that rehearsed his administration's achievements, taking credit especially for woman suffrage and the prohibition gains, but ever returning to the themes of "patriotism" and "loyalty"—appeals that were tailor-made for the upstate Republican audience. The governor, however, was thrown on the defensive when, on October 25, President Wilson urged the election of a Democratic Congress in support of his war policies. "Loyalty to the war is at this time a secondary consideration," Whitman answered angrily. It was loyalty to Wilson's administration that was at issue, he insisted.[37]

Like Whitman, Smith and the Democrats mixed the transparent with the substantial in the fall campaign, though Smith's tone was far less vitriolic than Whitman's. He scored the governor for his vaulting political ambitions, replied brilliantly to the charge that his only "job" had been politics ("When Whitman was an Amherst College student, I was working at the Fulton Fish Market"), and declared his independence from any and all political organizations. The war issue brought little response from Smith; typical of all politicians of that day, he warmly endorsed the Liberty bond drive and sprinkled his addresses with expressions of patriotism. Democratic newspaper advertisements did liken Whitman to the Kaiser—"Kaiser Whitman" they called him—for seeking to impose prohibition upon the people. For his part, Smith wondered publicly why the governor had not denied the charge that liquor flowed freely in the executive mansion, and pressed hard for the statewide referendum on the prohibition question. But most of all, the Tammany candidate emphasized his record as a progressive and as a champion of the "little man" in his work on the FIC. Much of the press, including even the usually anti-Tammany *New York Times,* stressed the contrast between Whitman and Smith on the major progressive issues of recent times.[38]

Just as important as Al Smith's stance on the public questions in 1918 was the campaign apparatus he and his supporters constructed to give his candidacy the broadest possible appeal. It was in this area, indeed, that the Smith people were most innovative, for they chose as their organizational vehicle, not Tammany Hall or the Democratic state committee, but rather the Independent Citizens' Committee for Alfred E. Smith, a "reformist" group headed by the candidate's friends in Greater New York who were joined by independent Democrats and Wilsonians, former Roosevelt-Straus Progressives, and some Mitchel fusionists. The committee cast a wide net: much of its membership, drawn from contacts Smith had made and cultivated in his FIC days, included businessmen, lawyers, social workers, and intellectuals. Two key elements—Jews and women—were well represented, illustrating the importance in city and state politics these groups commanded for the Democracy. The Jewish contingent boasted Abram Elkus, who served as committee chairman; Jessie Straus; and Joseph Proskauer. The Women's Division attracted suffragists such as Harriet Stanton Blatch and was headed by Belle Moskowitz, who would soon be named to Smith's "board of strategy." Liaisons were worked out between the citizens' committee and the party organization, but even here Smith was careful in his use of the regulars. He selected Onondaga leader "Will" Kelley as his official campaign director with headquarters in Syracuse.[39] By careful design, then, Murphy and his Tammany minions were restricted in their activities to the district level in New York City, where they labored unobtrusively but effectively to deliver the vote for "Al" in November. From beginning to end, the Smith campaign effort was a superb blend of reformist and organizational politics, by far the best that the Democrats had mustered in the entire progressive era.

The superior canvass for Smith paid dividends when, on November 5, New Yorkers went to the polls and cast their ballots. The Republicans did win control of the legislature once again, captured a substantial majority of the state's congressional seats, and even elected several members of their state ticket. But Al Smith and Harry Walker grabbed the two top spots. Smith's plurality, which Whitman later challenged, was only about 15,000 in a total gubernatorial vote of 2,131,918. It came mainly on the strength of a relatively large New York City vote that fell in greater proportion than usual to the Democracy and a "disappointing" upstate total that, under the circumstances, went less solidly Republican than needed for a Whitman victory. While, therefore, the sectional patterns that traditionally characterized the state's politics persisted, for once the Democrats—and Al Smith in particular—wound up the beneficiary. Indeed, the gap between upstate and downstate turnout narrowed to such a degree in 1918 that future Republican successes in statewide elections would be placed in jeopardy. Furthermore, there continued in the Smith-Whitman contest the Democratic upswing in the larger interior cities that was first evident following the 1912 turmoil in the 1916 elections: although Smith actually carried only Utica and Troy, he scored higher percentages than Seabury two years earlier in five other urban centers and suffered a decline in two. In the largest upstate cities—Buffalo, Rochester, and Syracuse—the absolute Democratic vote rose sharply over that in key municipal contests in 1917. Whitman's best showing, on the other hand, came in hard-core Republican territory—the smaller cities, towns, villages, and rural New York where, contrary to earlier expectations, the vote aggregate fell below the registration levels relative to that cast in the cities; still, only two counties in the upstate failed to return a GOP plurality.[40]

A truly critical factor in Smith's solid performance in the cities was the support he obtained in heavily ethnic areas. A comparison of the average vote in such districts for the gubernatorial contests in 1910–1916 with that of 1918 illustrates the degree of Smith's success. Not surprisingly, he made his best showing in Irish-Catholic areas, where the Democratic mean for the earlier elections was substantially high. A student of the Syracuse Irish thus argues that this was the "critical election of the period." Smith also did extremely well in New York City's German neighborhoods, and in most of the upstate cities he ran somewhat better with these people on the average than his Democratic predecessors. Among new-stock voters—Jews, Italians, and Poles—he scored impressive gains even in traditional Republican strongholds like Albany, Rochester, and Syracuse. In Greater New York Smith built up larger than usual pluralities in Italian districts. While his increases in New York City's eastern European Jewish areas were less impressive, he was yet able to reverse the Democratic and Socialist percentages of the previous year, when Morris Hillquit captured so many of these districts in his bid for the mayoralty. Whereas the aggregate Socialist vote statewide, in 1918, did reach its highest point to date, Smith was instrumental in keeping that party's share in New York City at about the same level as in 1916. And Democratic-Republican fusion "to help win the war" in key congressional and assembly districts also contained the radical vote in legislative races. Socialists thus lost eight of their ten assemblymen, and Meyer London was defeated for reelection to his congressional seat.[41]

The close Democratic gubernatorial victory in an otherwise Republican sweep in New York State lent credence to the often expressed charge that Whitman's "personal" weaknesses represented the major factor in his defeat. The governor's "slipshod methods of administration"; "his hallucination that he is a serious candidate for the Republican nomination for President"; and especially "his zeal to force the Federal Prohibition Amendment upon the State," among other factors, argued the *New York Times*, accounted for the disparities in the election results.⁴² In county after county in the upstate where Republicanism was most powerful, the promise of a truly "magnificent" vote because of the heavy registration of women and because of the support the Prohibition party accorded Whitman never materialized: the heavy registration was itself chimerical; many of the enrollees never made it to the polls, due (it was said) in large part to the influenza epidemic that devastated the state's interior regions around election time; and the drys' influence was evidently offset by farmers' discontent over Whitman's foods and markets law that had been of little assistance to them.⁴³ But there was, too, the other side of the coin. That is, if Whitman failed, Smith succeeded: he exploited to the full his role as an urban progressive; he blended neatly organizational and reformist politics; and he struck precisely the right posture on prohibition. Democratic improvement in the cities' immigrant, lower-class neighborhoods may well have accrued principally from Smith's emphasis on "personal liberty," noted contemporary observers, although the party's upswing in the state's urban centers was, as already suggested, part of a larger pattern. And in Greater New York, prohibition meshed with other issues, with Smith's incredible personal popularity all through the city, and with his image as a politician projecting "the human side of Tammany" to give him an almost phenomenal vote. That Smith also won his share—probably a larger share than the Republicans—of the ballots of the newly enfranchised women who went to the polls seems likely given the increased vote totals relative to fall registration figures in areas where the Democracy did exceptionally well.⁴⁴

EPILOGUE

The long-range significance of Alfred E. Smith's gubernatorial victory in 1918—the first for the Democrats in what might be considered a normal two-party contest since Roswell Flower's election nearly three decades earlier—was not (indeed, could not be) apparent to contemporaries. The election was too close; the Republicans did very well otherwise; and the electoral patterns then taking shape were in the embryonic stage. But the Smith triumph did launch a trend, if not exactly a revolution, in New York State politics: with the exception of the one-term governorship of Nathan Miller, 1921–1922, this due mainly to the Harding-Coolidge landslide of 1920, Democrats would dominate the executive office in Albany until Thomas E. Dewey brought the Republicans back to power in 1943. The key factor behind this trend was the further development of the Democracy as the party of the cities, particularly New York City, which continued to grow in voting strength during the 1920s, and of ethnic minorities, who cast their ballots in larger and larger numbers in the years of Al Smith, Franklin Roosevelt, and Herbert Lehman.[45] Meanwhile, the Republicans, losing their strength proportionately in the major urban centers, nurtured themselves in the less populous regions of the upstate, where they monopolized local and county offices. Because of the "rotten borough" system of apportionment created way back in the 1890s, the Grand Old Party was also able to retain control of the state legislature and to hold a majority of the congressional delegation during much of this era of Democratic ascendancy. And in national politics New Yorkers' loyalties remained with the Republicans for a time—that is, until the Great Depression and FDR's election to the presidency in 1932.

In yet another vein Smith built for the future in 1918. His loose coalition of several elements—ethnic minorities, women, some labor representatives, progressive and citizens' societies, and even political independents—constituted the crowning arch of the new liberal Democratic party. The organizational base of that structure for the next several years continued to be Murphy's pragmatic Tammany Hall in New York City and its "satellite" machines in the upstate cities, most notably Buffalo and Syracuse. To these Smith would soon weld the Dan O'Connell organization in Albany. Ideologically, the Democracy would be left of center on state issues, later national issues as well—a kind of "market-basket" and cultural liberalism that carried over from the earlier era, then was tailored and refined to meet new needs and conditions. At the same time, the now provincial Republicans, having forsaken reform since the halcyon days of Charles Evans Hughes and boasting a far weaker organization in Greater New York than for many a year, languished in an unimaginative standpattism, which left them essentially with one state issue—antibossism and anti-Tammanyism— as they hobbled through the decade of the 1920s.[46]

9
Summary and Conclusions

The Smith election victory in November 1918—and equally important the program and coalition he forged to achieve it—symbolized the changes that the Democratic party had undergone in New York State since Charles F. Murphy's ascension to Tammany Hall leadership in 1902. Chased from power by the Republican "revolution" of the mid–1890s, the Democracy had become tentative, insecure, faction-ridden, and provincial-minded. If it embraced a program, that program, for the most part, was nineteenth century in scope and theme. Democrats basically stood for personal liberty, negative government, and local autonomy. While the Democracy boasted some strength in the upstate, it was primarily a New York City party, where it drew heavily upon the city's large Irish- and German-American population. Even here the "neighborhood politics" of Tammany Hall made for a less secure base than the critics of the day would dare admit. In fact, the organization that Murphy inherited was (and had been) wracked by powerful assaults from municipal clubs and fusion groups, by dissidence within the ranks, and by bitter crosstown rivalries. It also faced serious challenges from the Hearst forces and the Socialists, whose appeals were most persuasive among new-stock voters in districts that were traditional Democratic strongholds. Across the state the Democrats were badly divided between the Hall and its "machine" allies, on the one hand, and the growing phalanx of independents, on the other. Such divisions were deep and seemed unrelenting; they involved a veritable conflict in political cultures that would indeed prove difficult to mitigate.

By the conclusion of World War I, there was much about the New York Democracy that had changed. The party was now assertive, aggressive, unified, and possessed of a positive outlook and ideology. It had emerged from the shadows and moved to a position where it would serve as the main vehicle for political, economic, and social change in the state. While the party still did not—and could not—speak with one voice, it had developed and implemented a "program." Earlier historians were fundamentally correct in arguing that Tammany leaders—principally Charlie Murphy, Al Smith, and Robert Wagner—successfully transformed middle-class progressivism into an urban, working-class liberalism.[1] The major dimensions of that liberalism included labor and social reform as well as a broad advocacy and defense of the interests and values of immigrant groups and ethnic minorities. The Democrats also contributed political reforms and advanced the cause of economic regulation, but these were seldom central items on the politicians' agenda. Taken together, the Democratic performance and strategy in New York State markedly improved the party's image and made it a more attractive force to the many hesitant reformers and independents who had been identified with one or another progressive cause earlier in the era. For this and other reasons, intraparty tensions eased, and by 1918 the Democracy functioned rather cohesively as a state party.

But this programmatic transformation—important as it would be in the days ahead—was not accompanied in the progressive era by an equally dramatic change in the electoral base of the Democratic party. During most of the period, 1902–1918, the state's polity remained divided along sectional lines that, broadly speaking, corresponded with interparty divisions—that is: the upstate, which was highly Yankee-Protestant or at least dominated by a Yankee-Protestant ethos, was mainly the preserve of the Republicans; and heavily polyglot New York City was essentially Democratic. Down to 1910 the GOP held supremacy in state politics because the party was able to keep virtually intact its own domain, including most of the cities as well as the less populated areas, and yet deeply penetrate Greater New York. Profound Republican divisions modified this traditional pattern in 1910 and gave the Democracy its smashing statewide victory under John A. Dix. Two years later the Bull Moose rebellion further disturbed the old balance by decimating the Republicans in New York City and simultaneously weakening them in the upstate. Especially critical was the Roosevelt-Straus success in the larger interior urban centers, where the Progressives took the Republican measure, not only in many predominantly native-born districts, but also in heavily German-American and new-stock wards, a large number of which had been faithful to the GOP in the recent past. (It is noteworthy, too, that the Bull Moose also cut Democratic margins in the ethnic areas across the state.) But the consequent Democratic ascendancy was short-lived, and the Empire State, in 1914, returned to what was widely regarded as the "normal way." This judgment seemed confirmed two years hence with the resounding Hughes-Whitman triumph in which the GOP was able to combine the standard party doctrine with an Americanism and an anti-Tammany-ism that sent the Democrats reeling. In fact, the Republicans, by 1916, appeared to have regained all that they had lost since 1910 in both the upstate and Greater New York and, therefore, were once again as commanding a force in the state's politics as they had been at any time in the days before the Progressive challenge.

It was, indeed, not until the very end of the era under investigation that any meaningful shift in electoral support for the two parties began—and one must emphasize *began*—to take shape. Such a transformation was propelled during the war years by the Republican adoption of a narrow provincialism and a hard-line conservatism combined with continued Democratic pragmatism that allowed the party to move leftward in 1917 in Greater New York and to strike exactly the right posture in that year and the next on the new and critical statewide issues of woman suffrage and prohibition. The process was carried one step further in 1918 with the emergence of the popular and astute Al Smith. From the perspective of its full development under Smith in the 1920s, the dynamics of that transformation become manifest—an impressive enlargement and consolidation of the Democratic electoral base in New York City, particularly in the new-stock areas, with a corresponding shrinkage of Republican influence all through the city; and, coincidentally, a steady incursion by the Democrats in the larger upstate urban centers, again mostly in overwhelmingly ethnic, lower-class districts. One is thus tempted to conclude that, if it achieved little else, the earlier Bull Moose success in many of these same areas helped expose the principal weakness of the Yankee-led GOP county organizations that, under the proper circumstances, the Democrats could exploit. By 1918, then, the sectional balance was just beginning to tip in favor of the Democracy, which at last was putting together its future winning combination in the state.

The overall stability of the New York political system in the progressive era, despite the great turmoil and the wild voting fluctuations in the years 1910–1913, has been noted by other scholars.[2] Its foundation rested, not solely on the sectional-cultural underpinnings of the two-party system and the equilibrium that these underpinnings built into the general structure, but rather on a mix of this condition with lingering public attitudes and dispositions toward the Republicans and Democrats. The fact is that while Republican misfortunes followed by the party's disruption may have shaken considerably the GOP's once solid reputation among New Yorkers, the Democrats, when given the opportunity, simply could not muster enough goodwill and trust to make the most of the opposition's travails. To much of the citizenry the Democracy was still the party of "Tammanyism" and "bossism"— meaning corruption, incompetence, and unresponsive government— the very things, in short, that some of the most vocal, middle-class reformers sought to eradicate from politics in the state. The party's internal squabbling, which lasted through 1914, not only lent further credence to this perception but also obscured whatever achievements were made in the Dix-Sulzer-Glynn administrations. In 1911–1912, for example, public attention remained riveted on the Osborne-Roosevelt battle with the Tammany-led regulars over the U.S. senatorship, the patronage, and aspects of the Democratic legislative program at the expense of virtually everything else. There followed the bizarre Sulzer impeachment episode that pitted the much-maligned Charlie Murphy and his minions against the governor backed, if only reluctantly, by the independents. Further exacerbating party tensions was the persistent meddling by the Wilsonians in Washington spurred, in part, by the president himself, who deplored machine politics, yet, in the end, relented because he depended on Tammany support for his program and then for his reelection. Generally the perceived failure of the Democrats to govern and to administer wisely the affairs of New York was constantly played up by a powerful, articulate anti-Tammany press across the state that grasped every opportunity to expose the "shame" and "excess" of the boss system. That, therefore, the beleaguered Democracy sustained devastating defeats at the polls in 1913 and 1914, even as the leadership was shaping a positive legislative program, should have come as no surprise to anyone.

It is probably true that the poor image from which the Democrats suffered in the progressive era affected most segments of the voting public, including those people—the so-called urban masses—whom the party leaders considered their natural constituency. Actually, the multitudes of lower-class ethnic groups huddled in New York's larger cities remained a political question mark in these years. Among the older immigrants the Irish-Americans, to be sure, were most consistently supportive of the Democracy while German-Americans in New York City were fairly reliable. But otherwise the picture is less clear. For one thing, the new-stock elements did not vote in overwhelming numbers at this time. Since most of these poeple had only recently emigrated to America, and since the naturalization process consumed approximately ten years, the eastern European Jews, the Poles, and the Italians did not enter the electorate en masse until later.[3] For another, those who went to the polls, as far as can be gauged, expressed divided loyalties, or, perhaps for reasons of deference and preferment, went along with the predominant local organizations. In most of the upstate cities, except perhaps for Buffalo and Utica, this, of course, meant the Grand Old Party, whose national program, in any case, was more compelling than the Democrats'. Even in New York City, the Democracy had trouble with the new-stock groups, most notably the eastern European Jews. Indeed, much of the Democratic effort in 1917 and again in 1918 was directed at the strong attraction that the Socialists held for the big (and ever growing) Jewish vote in the city. In the main, Thomas Henderson's study of Tammany Hall and the immigrants corroborates these findings. For Henderson, the ethnic and geographic separateness of the new-stock groups, among other factors, constantly frustrated Tammany's attempts in Manhattan to expand the Democratic coalition all during the progressive era. It was really not until the early 1920s, Henderson concludes, that Italian-Americans and particularly Jewish-Americans swelled the Democratic ranks in such numbers as to refashion Greater New York's politics for at least the next decade.[4]

The Democratic problem with the state's voting public may have been a reflection, to some extent, of the general malaise that afflicted the New York citizenry in these years. As Richard L. McCormick has persuasively argued, the Empire State in the early twentieth century experienced important electoral changes that made up a vital component of the transformation in political participation and expression from nineteenth-century forms. One was a noteworthy and significant decline in voter turnout—from a level, McCormick tells us, of nearly 80 percent in presidential elections in the 1880s to that of about 55 percent in 1912 and 1916. While the figures that the present study has adduced for the post–1900 period are higher overall than his, the general pattern is no different. As fewer citizens cast ballots, McCormick also notes, more and more voters down through 1910 split their tickets. Doubtless, this trend continued during the next decade, though a good deal of ticket-splitting in the later era seems to have affected the top executive offices of the party ticket and evidently revolved about the charismatic quality (or lack of it) of the gubernatorial contenders—for example, William Sulzer in 1914 who drew away a healthy portion of the electorate from Martin Glynn, or Al Smith in 1918 who was much more popular than most of his Democratic running mates.[5] Just as revealing, certainly, was the dimension of anti–major party voting in 1910 and thereafter, as large numbers of New Yorkers abandoned both the Democrats and the Republicans for candidates of the Socialists, the Progressives, and other minor parties. The high point of this protest vote, naturally enough, came in 1912 with the appearance of Roosevelt's Bull Moosers; the percentage remained high two years later and then tailed off to the approximate levels of the period before 1910.[6]

The decline in voter turnout, the increase in ticket-splitting, and the rise and fall in anti–major party voting were not unique to New York State in either the progressive era or later. Rather, taken together, they have been shown to characterize the larger political universe in the twentieth century, as much of the nation's electorate has been alienated from the system, those who vote have been more independent-minded than their nineteenth-century ancestors, and many have exercised third- and fourth-party options when available. It is far easier to describe this phenomenon than to pinpoint the conditions that promoted it. But in the Empire State there are some identifiable factors and circumstances in the post–1900 period that evidently triggered the voter malaise. One factor may have been ballot law changes—especially the adoption of the Australian ballot—that, if little else, helped distance the parties from the electorate and made political participation a more formal act. Another perhaps was the passage of legislation that prohibited corporate contributions in political campaigns and thus limited the amount of money available to the politicians to get out the vote. More important probably was the general discontent among the public directed at the way government was responding—or was failing to respond—to the vast economic and social changes of the late nineteenth century. For over a decade independents and reformers had been struggling to soften the harshness, the misery, and the dislocation that accompanied industrialization, urbanization, and immigration. That by the early 1900s they had succeeded in casting into disrepute the old Republican system of Thomas C. Platt has been well documented elsewhere. Then, in 1905, came the shocking insurance investigation that brought to full view the evils of the corrupt politico-business alliance and dramatically exposed the weaknesses of nineteenth-century distributive government.[7] After four years of vigorous executive action and reform activity in the gubernatorial administrations of Charles Evans Hughes, the responsibilities of governing the state fell to the Democrats. But, as already noted, internecine warfare and Tammanyism—to which one might add the party's incapacity to bring forward truly effective leadership in the governor's office—spelled disaster. Put simply, the Democratic party for many New Yorkers remained an integral part of an entire system of politics that had been pilloried and discredited for the past decade or so. Thus it was that both major parties would continue to appeal to a proportionately smaller segment of the total electorate through 1918—and afterward.

The general political malaise that took root in the progressive era should not, however, obscure the innovations in policymaking offered first by the Republicans then by the Democrats in New York State. While Governor Hughes's most creative achievements may have been in the area of economic regulation where he utilized independent commissions to adjust clashing interests, his administration also introduced political reforms and backed measures in the broad field of social and public welfare. In one sense, the Democrats picked up on these themes as the party's pragmatic leadership, 1911–1915, devised policies that sought to respond to immediate exigencies and to accommodate specific demands issued by reform pressure groups, special-interest organizations (like the State Federation of Labor), independents, and political radicals. Thus during Glynn's brief tenure, they conceded a statewide direct primary law and a Massachusetts ballot bill that substituted the office-listed for the party ballot. Neither of these measures, it turned out, lived up to the expectations of the reformers, but their adoption underscores the degree to which the Murphy people were willing to give the progressives "everything" they wanted.[8] While placing somewhat less emphasis than Hughes on the regulation of corporations, the Democrats, nevertheless, did nothing to weaken or to undermine the public service commissions, and, in 1913, they passed a series of measures granting the state limited control over the stock markets. Furthermore, they themselves often resorted to the commission both as an investigative device and as a means of regulation or supervision, despite their reluctance to proclaim the virtues of such bodies and even their occasional denunciation of "commission government." On the first, there was, of course, the FIC and on the second the workmen's compensation commission together with those agencies under Sulzer—efficiency and economy, estimate, and contract and supply—that the governor extracted from the "uncooperative" Tammany legislature. And all three Democratic governors—Dix, Sulzer, and Glynn—drew upon the Moreland Act of 1907 to appoint commissions to scrutinize various agencies and boards lodged in the executive branch of state government.[9]

By far the most distinctive contribution made by the Democrats came in the realm of labor and social reform. Here the 1913 workmen's compensation law and especially the vast array of legislation growing out of the four-year effort of the Factory Investigating Commission not only helped lay the foundations of the welfare state in New York but also gave the Democracy new direction and purpose. No other single event in the period moved that party away from its nineteenth-century concept of negative government than did the shocking and tragic Triangle Shirtwaist Fire of 1911. Of great importance, too, the FIC investigation substantially enhanced the reputations of Tammany Hall's younger leaders, Al Smith and Robert Wagner, and aided immeasurably in broadening their horizons. "It was during . . . the investigation," Smith has testified in his autobiography, "that I got my first look at the State of New York." For Wagner the experience charted the course of his remaining years in the legislature and served as excellent training for his future career in the U.S. Senate where he became the foremost champion of FDR's New Deal.[10] Finally, the FIC investigation was highly instrumental in establishing a working relationship between the Democratic party regulars and spokesmen for progressive societies, labor groups, and others. Tentative and hesitant at first, this relationship would be consolidated and expanded in later years, when Republican traditionalism turned most reformers and proponents of change away from that party.

By the end of World War I, then, the New York Democrats stood on the brink of a new era in state politics. The party program and strategy concocted by the party leaders in the progressive period gave them a competitive advantage over the Republicans in accommodating what had become overall a highly skeptical, more sluggish, and less partisan voting public. At the same time, they were able to make a powerful case for themselves with the new and potentially large segments of the electorate—that is, the recently enfranchised women and particularly the emerging ethnic minorities. Certainly Democratic politicians acted and behaved as if they *could* attract such constituencies to their coalition. And not of least significance, the Democracy remained the only outlet for the self-proclaimed reform societies and civic improvement associations. The proliferation and professionalization of these bodies—and generally of the so-called special-interest groups—that historians have observed took place in the progressive generation continued apace in the next decade. Peopled usually by an educated, articulate elite and often self-consciously shunning the ballot box, these increasingly influential organizations perfected other forms of political expression: the shaping of legislative agenda; the pressuring of politicians and government agencies; and the molding of public opinion.[11] Beginning in 1919, they would have in Albany's executive mansion a sympathetic listener and a willing servant. For Al Smith understood, as they did, the changes that urbanization, industrialization, and immigration had wrought in American society and in American politics.

He had personally played a major role in adjusting his political organization and his party to these changes and, in the process, transformed both. It was now left to him to formulate the next phase of policy-making and administration for his fellow citizenry in the Empire State.

Appendix I

In all tables listed below the gubernatorial vote was gleaned from the *New York State Legislative Manual*.[1] For the upstate cities such figures are available by ward and, within wards, by election districts. For the counties constituting New York City vote totals are given by election districts within assembly districts; these are followed by a recapitulation that presents the aggregate vote within the county by assembly district.

Table 1: Percentage of the Republican Vote in Gubernatorial Elections in Selected Ethnic Wards

The ethnic wards delineated in this table were selected by using the *Thirteenth Census of the U.S. 1910 . . . New York* and, where appropriate, *The New York State Manuscript Census, 1905*.[2] The former makes it possible to identify those wards with the largest number of "foreign-born white" and "native white—foreign or mixed parentage," with numbers given for the country of origin. Although there is a five-year gap between the federal census and the New York census, the latter supplies more detailed and useful information: country of origin, age, and citizenship of each family member on an election-district and ward basis. Taken together these sources, sometimes supplemented with registration lists, afford a fairly accurate profile of those areas with the largest concentrations of particular ethnic groups. Vote percentages in the table were calculated on the basis of the two-party vote.

Table 2: Comparison of the Democratic Vote in Gubernatorial Elections, 1914–1918, in Selected Upstate Cities

Percentages in this table were calculated on the basis of the total vote recorded exclusive of blank and defective ballots.

Table 3: Comparison of the Democratic Vote in Selected Ethnic Areas in Gubernatorial Elections, 1910–1916 and 1918

This table is not merely an extrapolation of the percentages given in Appendix II, Table 4, for the years 1910–1916. Rather, an effort was made through the use of several sources to identify the most ethnically homogeneous election districts within wards in the upstate cities and within assembly districts in New York City for the years 1910, 1912, 1914, 1916, and 1918.[3] Especially useful for the upstate cities were the state census manuscripts for 1915 and 1925 that, in most cases, contain election district/ward maps.[4] These were supplemented by selected voter registration lists made available to the author for such cities as Albany and Buffalo. For New York City the state census manuscripts were also helpful, but two other works yielded considerable information. These were the volumes edited by Walter Laidlaw, one published in 1911, the other in 1922. Laidlaw's surveys were made in small units known as sanitary districts, and these have to be correlated with election districts by the use of maps and street descriptions. The pioneering work along these lines for the presidential elections of 1916 and 1928 in Manhattan was done by David Burner. Also, Thomas McInerney used the Burner analysis and the Laidlaw data to compute his ethnic vote percentages for the presidential election of 1912.[5] The present study has followed the methods and procedures employed by these students for the years 1910–1918 for most of the New York City districts.

For each year the total Democratic vote in these ethnically concentrated districts was averaged for each city, and the figures for 1910–1916 is the mean of the averages. The 1918 percentages were figured in the same manner, though in many instances the districts do not correspond with those for the earlier years because of a major statewide reapportionment in 1917. This was the only meaningful way that any comparison could be made between ethnic voting in the various cities in the years 1910–1916 and 1918.

TABLE I

Percentage of the Republican Vote in Gubernatorial
Elections in Selected Ethnic Wards

Year	1906	1908	1910
Older Groups			
Irish			
Albany 8th	48.3	37.7	40.1
Buffalo 1st	26	22	27
Syracuse 10th	43.4	47.4	42
Troy 10th	30.5	39.4	37.2
12th	16	20.9	20.4
German			
Albany 1st	57.9	51.1	50.1
Buffalo 12th	52	42	53
13th	47.4	39.7	45.6
14th	51.4	43.5	52.8
18th	45.6	46.6	47.1
19th	57.4	61.2	55.8
Rochester 17th	34	46	49
18th	54.8	60.4	62.1
20th	32.6	37.7	37.7
Syracuse 2nd	43	39	43
3rd	54	54	59
4th	57	61.8	62.6
Newer Groups			
Italian			
Albany 4th	54.5	49.9	58.4
Buffalo 25th	38.6	39.6	27.9
Rochester 2nd	51.9	48.6	65.5
9th	45	46.8	43.6
16th	47.7	56.8	54.3
Syracuse 7th	59.6	54.8	55.5
Utica 5th	40.7	46.4	36.3
8th	37.4	44.3	34.7

Jewish*

Rochester 7th	35.9	48.5	52.4
8th	40.4	47.6	50.2
Syracuse 15th	62.9	62.9	65.4
18th	61.1	54.4	54.7

Polish

Buffalo 8th	28	24	25
9th	47.5	41.3	45.1
10th	46	39	45
11th	38.3	36.8	36
Utica 2nd	46	43.5	26.8
9th	40.4	42.5	35.9

*These had substantial concentrations of Russian-born Jews.

TABLE 2
Comparison of the Democratic Vote in Gubernatorial Elections, 1914–1918, in Selected Upstate Cities

City	1914 Gub.		1916 Gub.		1918 Gub.	
	Total	%	Total	%	Total	%
Albany	8,493	31.9	9,999	37.2	15,609	39.5
Binghamton	3,378	40.7	4,571	41	6,815	41.2
Buffalo	26,099	36.5	34,759	44.6	39,031	42.8
Rochester	12,873	24	17,685	36.6	23,399	37
Schenectady	3,203	21.6	7,147	45.1	7,104	37
Syracuse	9,831	36.1	11,874	36.5	20,148	45.3
Troy	8,035	48.2	8,671	51.7	13,882	54.3
Utica	5,335	39.2	7,422	47	10,265	51.3
Yonkers	5,624	40.6	6,003	39.8	9,149	45

TABLE 3
Comparison of the Democratic Vote in Selected Ethnic Areas
in Gubernatorial Elections, 1910–1916 and 1918

Group	Avg. % 1910– 1916	1918%
Irish		
Albany	53	61.8
Buffalo	75.8	85.1
Syracuse	53.5	61.2
Troy	76.6	75.3
Yonkers	68.8	70.2
N.Y.C. (Man.)	66.4	80.3
German		
Albany	36.4	35
Buffalo	38.7	39.6
Rochester	38.7	45.4
Syracuse	34.5	46.1
N.Y.C. (Man.)	53.6	70.2
(Bkln.)	41.6	58
(Q.)	51.8	61.9
Jewish		
Rochester	35.9	42.9
Syracuse	33.5	44.7
N.Y.C. (Man.)	47.8	49.5
(Brx.)	45.7	50
(Bkln.)	40.4	48.4
Italian		
Albany	33.7	44.6
Buffalo	51.8	53.3
Rochester	36.6	43.8
Syracuse	41.5	53.5
Utica	48.6	61.7
N.Y.C. (Man.)	63.8	65.5
(Bkln.)	70.2	79.2
Polish		
Buffalo	50.4	59.3
Utica	53.9	68.5

Appendix II

References to the tables and figure that follow are made in various places in the body of this study. For the most part, the tables are self-explanatory, but a note or two concerning sources and methodology is in order.

Table 1: Gubernatorial and Presidential Vote, New York State, 1900–1918

The major sources for these figures were the *New York Red Book*, which lists election results for all gubernatorial and most presidential elections by county, and Edgar E. Robinson, *The Presidential Vote*, which in a few instances provided the total "other vote" that the *Red Book* failed to include.[1]

Table 2: New York City/Upstate Vote Breakdown, 1900–1918

These percentages were derived from the election statistics gleaned from the sources used in Table 1.

Figure 1: Turnout in Presidential and Gubernatorial Elections, 1900–1920

Determination of the eligible electorate in New York State was based mainly on population data available in the 1900, 1910, and 1920 federal censuses.[2] For the years up to 1918, the base figure used was the number of male citizens over twenty-one years of age. For 1920 and projecting back to 1918 (the first time women voted in the state), the figure used was the number of adult male and female citizens. Since it is impossible to know the actual size of the potential electorate in a particular year, except in the census years themselves, I have simply assumed a constant rate of increase in each two-year period.

Calculating the percentage turnout was a simple matter of dividing the total number who voted in a given election—in the state as a whole, in the upstate regions, or in New York City—by the estimated potential electorate.

Table 3: Non–Major Party Vote, New York State, 1908–1918

The figures and the percentages derived from them were gleaned from the sources used in Table 1.

Table 4: Democratic Percentage of Total Vote in Selected Ethnic Wards/ Assembly Districts, 1908–1916

As noted in the text of this study, any effort to gauge ethnic voting in the years through the era of World War I is, at best, a risky business. For one thing, the vast majority of new-stock peoples did not enter the electorate in large numbers till the decade of the 1920s. For another, even in wards or districts where a given ethnic group was predominant and where, it seems, a substantial portion of the group appeared to be eligible to vote, one cannot be sure what percentage of the total vote their ballots actually represented. No ward or district, as far as can be determined, was truly homogeneous. The problem for the older immigrant groups—the Irish and Germans, in particular—was somewhat different. Since these peoples were already well integrated into the general population by the twentieth century, they were sometimes difficult to identify. Here the state censuses of 1905 and 1915, together with available registration lists, were most useful, for they provided surnames by which reasonably informed guesses at ethnic background could be made. The alternative to employing these "questionable" data was to give up any effort at electoral analysis. But, in the final analysis, as other students have concluded, shedding a little light on the subject is preferable to total darkness.

The sources used to identify the most heavily ethnic wards and districts have already been mentioned. Of some help also were the studies of other scholars and writers on urban and ethnic history.[3] The election statistics from which percentages were calculated were taken from the *New York State Legislative Manual,* as noted in Appendix I, for all gubernatorial elections. Figures for the presidential elections were gleaned from the various county boards of supervisors proceedings, available in the New York State Library, and, in the few cases where these were not available, the local newspapers.

TABLE I
Gubernatorial and Presidential Vote, New York State, 1900–1918

1900 P.		Bryan (D)	McKinley (R)	Other
	N.Y.C.	309,524	280,343	17,715
	Ups.	368,938	541,670	29,853
	N.Y.S.	678,462	822,013	47,568
G.		Stanchfield (D)	Odell (R)	Other
	N.Y.C.	316,393	272,130	19,186
	Ups.	377,340	532,729	10,773
	N.Y.S.	693,733	804,859	29,959
1902 G.		Coler (D)	Odell (R)	Other
	N.Y.C.	327,132	304,499	24,367
	Ups.	329,215	360,651	37,303
	N.Y.S.	656,347	665,150	61,670
1904 P.		Parker (D)	Roosevelt (R)	Other
	N.Y.C.	326,900	289,345	35,829
	Ups.	357,081	570,188	38,422
	N.Y.S.	683,981	859,533	74,251
G.		Herrick (D)	Higgins (R)	Other
	N.Y.C.	348,493	268,322	35,181
	Ups.	384,211	544,942	36,637
	N.Y.S.	732,704	813,264	71,818
1906 G.		Hearst (D)	Hughes (D)	Other
	N.Y.C.	338,530	261,463	26,948
	Ups.	352,575	487,539	15,412
	N.Y.S.	691,105	749,002	42,360
1908 P.		Bryan (D)	Taft (R)	Other
	N.Y.C.	284,760	300,998	56,516
	Ups.	382,700	569,072	44,296
	N.Y.S.	667,460	870,070	100,812
G.		Chanler (D)	Hughes (R)	Other
	N.Y.C.	321,290	261,386	60,306
	Ups.	413,899	543,265	39,357
	N.Y.S.	735,189	804,651	99,663
1910 G.		Dix (D)	Stimson (R)	Other
	N.Y.C.	302,605	197,416	70,828
	Ups.	387,095	424,883	54,183
	N.Y.S.	689,700	622,299	125,011
1912 P.		Wilson (D)	Taft (R)	Other
	N.Y.C.	312,426	126,582	224,865
	Ups.	343,147	328,905	252,390
	N.Y.S.	655,573	455,487	477,255

G.		Sulzer (D)	Hedges (R)	Other
	N.Y.C.	306,000	111,630	223,687
	Ups.	343,559	332,475	249,864
	N.Y.S.	649,559	444,105	473,551
1914 G.		Glynn (D)	Whitman (R)	Other
	N.Y.C.	292,076	238,245	69,307
	Ups.	249,193	448,456	142,692
	N.Y.S.	541,269	686,701	211,999
1916 P.		Wilson (D)	Hughes (R)	Other
	N.Y.C.	353,435	313,813	37,266
	Ups.	405,991	555,253	40,547
	N.Y.S.	759,426	869,066	77,813
G.		Seabury (D)	Whitman (R)	Other
	N.Y.C.	326,199	305,890	42,760
	Ups.	360,663	544,130	33,314
	N.Y.S.	686,862	850,020	76,074
1918 G.		Smith (D)	Whitman (R)	Other
	N.Y.C.	559,284	290,708	89,175
	Ups.	450,652	704,386	37,713
	N.Y.S.	1,009,936	995,094	126,888

TABLE 2

New York City/Upstate Vote Breakdown, 1900–1918

Year & Office	New York City			Upstate		
	%D	%R	%Other	%D	%R	%Other
1900 P.	50.9	46.1	3	39.2	57.6	3.2
G.	52.1	44.8	3.1	41	57.9	1.1
1902 G.	49.9	46.4	3.7	45.3	49.6	5.1
1904 P.	50.1	44.4	5.5	37	59	4
G.	53.5	41.2	5.3	39.8	56.4	3.8
1906 G.	55	42.4	2.6	40.7	56.3	3
1908 P.	44.3	46.9	8.8	38.4	57.2	4.4
G.	50	40.7	9.3	41.5	54.5	4
1910 G.	53	34.6	12.4	44.7	49.2	6.1
1912 P.	47.1	19.1	33.8	37.1	35.6	27.3
G.	47.7	17.4	34.9	37.1	35.9	27
1914 G.	48.7	39.7	11.6	29.7	53.4	16.9
1916 P.	50.2	44.6	5.2	40.5	55.4	4.1
G.	48.3	45.3	6.4	38.4	58.2	3.4
1918 G.	59.6	31	9.4	37.8	59.1	3.1

FIGURE I

Turnout in Presidential and Gubernatorial Elections, 1900–1920

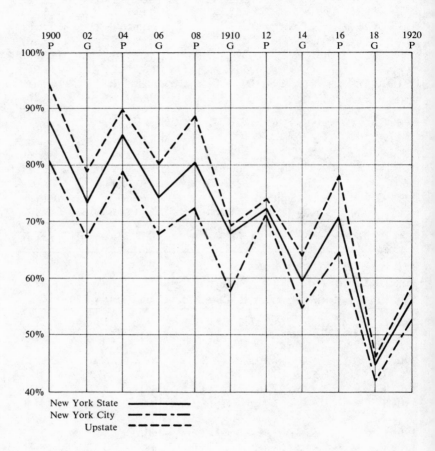

TABLE 3
Non–Major Party Vote, New York State, 1906–1918

Year & Office		Soc. Total	Total Non–Major Party Vote	% Non–Major Party Vote
1906 G.	N.Y.S.	21,751	42,360	2.9
	N.Y.C.	13,477	26,948	
	Ups.	8,274	15,412	
1908 P.	N.Y.S.	38,451	100,812	6.2
	N.Y.C.	25,965	56,516	
	Ups.	12,486	44,296	
1910 G.	N.Y.S.	48,529	125,011	8.7
	N.Y.C.	39,883	70,828	
	Ups.	8,646	54,183	
1912 P.	N.Y.S.	63,434	477,255	30
	N.Y.C.	33,423	224,865	
	Ups.	30,011	252,390	
1914 G.	N.Y.S.	37,793	211,999	14.7
	N.Y.C.	24,084	69,307	
	Ups.	13,709	142,692	
1916 P.	N.Y.S.	45,944	77,813	4.6
	N.Y.C.	31,788	37,266	
	Ups.	14,156	40,547	
1918 G.	N.Y.S.	121,705	126,888	6
	N.Y.C.	86,383	89,175	
	Ups.	35,322	37,713	

TABLE 4
Democratic Percentage of Total Vote in Selected Ethnic Wards/ Assembly Districts, 1908–1916

	1908 G.	1908 P.	1910 G.	1912 G.	1912 P.	1914 G.	1916 G.	1916 P.
Irish								
Albany 8th	61.5	54.6	58.6	50.6	49.9	45.3	48.6	52.1
Buffalo 1st	79.6	75.7	69.8	69.9	68.8	81.3	81.1	83.9
Syracuse 10th	50.5	48.8	51.5	47.4	44.5	57.8	51	54.4
Troy 10th	59.2	57.2	60.1	62.6	60.6	61.7	65.5	65.7
12th	78.2	77.4	77.8	77.8	68.9	80.7	82.1	83.4
Yonkers 6th	68.2	65	68.6	63.4	58.4	69.4	61.2	58.4
N.Y.C. M. 5th	64.4	60.5	68.1	69.6	67.5	74.2	71.7	73.1
M. 7th	59.3	54.3	63.8	63.6	60	64.4	64.1	58.2
M. 11th	62.7	58.4	61.2	67.6	63.8	68.6	65.3	66.3
M. 13th	57.9	56.8	59	60.6	58.5	67.8	62.1	63.1
M. 14th	60.3	55.7	61.6	62.7	58.9	66.4	63.8	64.7
M. 16th	62	57.1	62	61.2	57.8	64	63	62.8
German								
Albany 1st	48.1	44.1	47.4	41.6	40.6	30.8	30.2	31.3
Buffalo 12th	56	49	44.5	47.5	45.7	38.6	43	47.2
13th	57.3	49.7	52.4	39.3	38.2	29.1	36.5	36.9
14th	55.1	43.4	45.2	43.9	42.5	32.8	40.9	42.6
18th	52	47.4	48.5	32.9	32.4	26.3	35.1	36.1
19th	38.2	33.7	38.6	34.8	34.7	28.9	37	38.3
Rochester 17th	50.4	42.9	44.1	34.4	33.7	23	36.2	32.6
18th	37.9	35.8	35	29.5	26.2	20.4	34.5	33.1
20th	59.4	56	55.1	45	43.5	33.8	48.4	45.8
Syracuse 2nd	56.2	52.6	49.4	47.1	47.2	43.4	48.1	49.2
3rd	40.5	35.5	33.9	31.6	30.4	25.5	30.1	33.2
4th	34.1	31.5	30.8	25.4	26.3	30.9	26.3	31.3
N.Y.C. M. 22nd	52.6	46.6	50.7	57.5	49.9	53.7	52.5	47.4
Brk. 19th	48.7	43.1	48.3	48.4	46.4	40.7	36.4	37.1
Brk. 20th	38.4	31	41.8	46.4	43.8	34.6	36.4	36.5
Q. 3rd	52.2	47.5	50	57	52.6	51.8	48.5	41
Jewish								
Rochester 7th	48.5	43.4	42.4	32.7	36.4	22.8	48.2	45.1
8th	53	52.7	43.4	31.4	32.9	21.6	40.8	42.4
Syracuse 15th	36.1	32.2	32.9	28.7	32	30.9	40	41
18th	36.9	34.6	42.2	28.6	30.2	32.6	33.8	39.4
N.Y.C. M. 4th	63.7	62.3	62.6	46.6	52.3	54.3	66.3	68.1
M. 6th	44.5	42.6	40.5	25.4	30.5	29.3	38.7	37.8

M.	8th	53.7	50.7	56.2	28.9	38.1	44.3	57.7	61.8
M.	10th	53.5	50.8	48	38.3	35.4	41.1	46.5	45.4
M.	24th	57.3	54.7	57.3	52	54.2	58.3	53.5	52.7
M.	26th	46	40.9	41.6	31.7	37.7	31.6	44.8	50.4
M.*	32nd	52.3	47.5	50.4	47.6	47	47.4	49.9	50
M.*	33rd	52.9	47.7	49.8	49.3	46.2	50.1	48.4	46.7
M.*	34th	49.1	43.6	50	42	41.3	41.7	46.2	50.7
Brk.	14th	60.8	57.5	61.6	60.1	56.4	54.4	55.4	60.4
Brk.	21st	48.3	42.4	45.1	34.1	38.3	38	41.2	49.2
Brk.	22nd	39.3	34.5	38.5	40.4	37.7	35.6	36	39.8
Brk.	23rd	44.1	39.7	40.8	30.5	35.7	34.8	39.8	49.2

Italian

Albany 4th		49.8	44.3	41	33.9	34.2	23.6	37.1	40.1
Buffalo 25th		62.8	55.2	69.2	no longer heavily Italian				
26th		created in 1911			45.2	44.1	43.6	46.7	48.8
27th		created in 1911			40.2	39	42	49.3	49.6
Rochester 2nd		47.6	43.4	33.6	35.9	34.6	28.3	29.9	29
9th		51.9	50.3	53.5	41.5	37.3	36.4	41.9	41.4
16th		42.7	37.5	42.8	30.7	32.7	24	36.6	31.4
Syracuse 7th		44.2	48.7	42.5	38.6	36.5	42	31.4	38.8
Utica 5th		53.3	51.9	59.5	31.4	31.2	37.7	32.4	33.2
8th		54.4	50.9	53.4	45.2	44.9	45.9	51.1	49.2
N.Y.C. M.	1st	68.2	63.7	68.5	63.6	58.2	66.8	59.4	58.1
M.	3rd	75.2	72	78.9	70	65.3	71.1	65.5	63.9
M. 28th		57.6	53.5	56.2	45.4	45.2	49	49.9	50.7
Brk.	3rd	66.8	63.5	73.2	70.9	68.8	73.7	62.8	69.8

Polish

Buffalo 9th		56.7	48.6	48.7	46.6	37.3	48.1	54	58.3
10th		59.9	49.7	52	49.8	39.2	56.6	62.6	66.7
11th		63.2	55.6	61.4	no longer heavily Polish				
15th		not heavily Polish			46.9	43.8	45.1	48.2	51.2
Utica 2nd		54.7	51.9	67.6	45.1	46.7	58.4	54.2	56.9
9th		55.8	52.4	59.8	41.9	39.6	43.8	53.4	54.6

*Bronx districts beginning 1914.

Abbreviations

BECHSL	Buffalo and Erie County Historical Society Library
BECPL	Buffalo and Erie County Public Library
EPKC	Edwin P. Kilroe Collection, 1907–1911, 2 vols., and Edwin P. Kilroe Collection, 1911–1936, 28 vols.
FDRL	Franklin D. Roosevelt Library, Hyde Park, New York
LC	Library of Congress
LTR	Elting Morison et al., *The Letters of Theodore Roosevelt,* 8 vols. (Cambridge: Harvard University Press, 1951–1954)
N-YHSL	New-York Historical Society Library
NYPL	New York Public Library
NYSL	New York State Library
OHP	Oral History Project, Columbia University Library
OPL	Onondaga County Public Library, Syracuse, New York
RML	Rundel Memorial Library, Rochester, New York
UPL	Utica Public Library, Utica, New York

Notes

CHAPTER I

1. Everett S. Lee et al., *Population Redistribution and Economic Growth in the United States, 1870–1950*, 3 vols. (Philadelphia: American Philosophical Library, 1957), vol. 1, pp. 692, 697.
2. U.S. Department of Commerce, *The Statistical History of the United States from Colonial Times to the Present* (Stamford, Conn.: Fairfield Publishers, 1965), pp. 14, 56; U.S. Census Office, *Report on Population of the U.S. at the Eleventh Census* (Washington: Government Printing Office, 1895), part I, p. lxxx, and *Thirteenth Census of the U.S. 1910, Abstracts with Supplements for New York* (Washington: Government Printing Office, 1913), p. 218.
3. Leo Wolman, "The Extent of Labor Organization in the United States in 1910," *Quarterly Journal of Economics*, XXX (1916), 499; Marc Karson, *American Labor Unions and Politics, 1900–1918* (Boston: Beacon Press, 1958), pp. 27–28; James Weinstein, *The Decline of Socialism in America: 1912–1925* (New York: Vintage Books, 1969), p. 27.
4. Adna F. Weber, *The Growth of Industry in New York State* (Albany: State of New York Department of Labor, 1904), pp. 6, 31, 34, and 36; Walter Dunn, Jr., *History of Erie County, 1870–1970* (Buffalo: Buffalo and Erie County Historical Society, 1972), ch. I; Blake McKelvey, *Rochester: The Quest for Quality* (Cambridge: Harvard University Press, 1956), pp. 256–263, 275–276; W. Freeman Galpin, *Central New York: An Inland Empire*, 3 vols. (New York: Lewis Historical Publishing Company, Inc., 1941), vol. III, pp. 65–68.
5. The figure for 1880 represents the population of the territory included in New York City after consolidation in 1897.
6. *Thirteenth Census . . . New York*, pp. 620, 622, 624; and Lee, *Population Redistribution*, vol. 1, p. 359. Population in the rural areas can be checked in B. L. Melvin, *Rural Population of New York, 1855–1925* (Ithaca: Cornell University Agricultural Experiment Station, 1928), p. 25; and W. A.

Anderson, *Population Trends in New York State, 1900–1914* (Ithaca: Cornell University Agricultural Experiment Station, 1942), p. 6.

7. Irwin Yellowitz, *Labor and the Progressive Movement in New York State, 1897–1916* (Ithaca: Cornell University Press, 1965), pp. 26–28; Melvyn Dubofsky, *When Workers Organize: New York City in the Progressive Era* (Amherst: The University of Massachusetts Press, 1968), ch. 1.

8. Melvyn Dubofsky, "Organized Labor and the Immigrant in New York City, 1900–1918," *Labor History*, II (1961), 182–201, and "Success and Failure of Socialism in New York City, 1900–1918: A Case Study," *Labor History*, IX (1968), 361–375; David A. Shannon, *The Socialist Party of America: A History* (New York: The Macmillan Co., 1955), pp. 8–13; Svend Petersen, *A Statistical History of American Presidential Elections* (New York: Ungar, 1963), pp. 67–68; "Minutes, New York Socialist Party, Local, General Committee," February 23, 1907, "Minutes, Special Meeting of the State Committee," July 30, 1907, and "Minutes of the State Committee Meeting," December 19, 1909, in New York City Socialist Party Papers (Tamiment Institute); *New York Call*, November 5, 1908, November 10, 1910, and January 20, 1911; *Albany Times-Union*, November 8, 1911.

9. Herbert Bass, *"I AM A DEMOCRAT": The Political Career of David Bennett Hill* (Syracuse: Syracuse University Press, 1961), passim; Samuel T. McSeveney, *The Politics of Depression: Political Behavior in the Northeast, 1893–1896* (New York: Oxford University Press, 1972), ch. 1.

10. McSeveney, *Politics of Depression*, pp. 196–211; Eli Goldschmidt, "Labor and Populism: New York City, 1891–1897," *Labor History*, XIII (1972), 520–532.

11. The city of Buffalo went Democratic in four of the six gubernatorial contests from 1898 to 1908 but in none of the three presidential elections. Buffalo also elected Democratic mayors in 1897, 1905, and 1909. The exception was in 1901 when the Democrats were riddled with corruption (*Buffalo Courier*, November 6, 1901).

12. James M. Williams, *The Expansion of Rural Life: The Social Psychology of Rural Development* (Freeport, N.Y.: Books for Libraries Press, 1972), pp. 110–111; Richard L. McCormick, "Shaping Republican Strategy: Political Change in New York State, 1893–1910" (Ph.D. diss., Yale University, 1976), ch. 8. The appeal of the tariff to the New York farmer is argued in Roger Sipher, "Political Behavior in New York, 1890–1896: A Case Study of Two Counties" (Ph.D. diss., Syracuse University, 1971), esp. pp. 69–70.

13. Efforts in Rochester by George W. Aldridge are covered in McKelvey, *Rochester: The Quest for Quality*, pp. 82–85. In Syracuse, Republican leader Francis Hendricks made gestures even to the Irish community, and there remained strong Irish influence in the Onondaga County Republican

organization until 1914. See John A. Beadles, "The Syracuse Irish, 1812–1928: Immigration, Catholicism, Socio-Economic Status, Politics and Irish Nationalism" (Ph.D. diss., Syracuse University, 1974), pp. 184–191. In Albany accommodations by William E. Barnes are suggested in Robert E. O'Connor, "William Barnes, Jr.: A Conservative Encounters the Progressive Era" (Ph.D. diss., State University of New York at Albany, 1971), pp. 14–15, 36–38.

14. See Appendix I, Table 1.

15. Florence E. Gibson, *The Attitudes of the New York Irish Toward State and National Affairs, 1848–1892* (New York: Columbia University Press, 1951), pp. 321–322. The total Irish immigration to New York City from 1830 to 1899 has been estimated at 3,825,649. See H. J. Desmond, "A Century of Irish Immigration," *American Catholic Quarterly Review,* XXV (1900), 524.

16. Edward M. Levine, *The Irish and Irish Politicians: A Study of Cultural and Social Alienation* (Notre Dame: University of Notre Dame Press, 1966), pp. 111–112; John D. Buenker, *Urban Liberalism and Progressive Reform* (New York: Charles Scribner's Sons, 1973), p. 7; Dorothy Ross, "The Irish Catholic Immigrant, 1880–1900: A Study in Social Mobility" (M.A. essay, Columbia University, 1959), pp. 13–14.

17. *The Promised City: New York's Jews, 1870–1914* (New York: Harper and Row, 1962), p. 76.

18. Thomas Kessner, *The Golden Door: Italian and Jewish Immigrant Mobility in New York City, 1880–1915* (New York: Oxford University Press, 1977), passim; Henry Moskowitz, "New York's East Side as a Political Barometer," *The Outlook,* CXVIII (1918), 325–327; Frederick Davenport, "Human Nature in Politics: Al Smith and the Human Side of Tammany," ibid., CXIX (1918), 522; George E. Pozzetta, "The Italians of New York City, 1890–1914" (Ph.D. diss., University of North Carolina, 1971), passim; Irving Howe, *World of Our Fathers* (New York: Harcourt Brace Jovanovich, 1976), ch. 11.

19. Marvin G. Weinbaum, "New York County Republican Politics, 1897–1922: The Quarter Century After Municipal Consolidation," *New-York Historical Society Quarterly,* L (1966), 63–94; Charles Garrett, *The La Guardia Years: Machine and Reform Politics in New York City* (New Brunswick: Rutgers University Press, 1961), ch. 2. In one such fusion campaign, 1901, the reformers were particularly successful in winning over Democrats on the Lower East Side on the vice issue. See Jeremy P. Felt, "Vice Reform as a Political Technique: The Committee of Fifteen in New York, 1900–1901," *New York History,* LIV (1973), 24–51.

20. Dunn, *History of Erie County,* pp. 79–82; *Buffalo Evening Times,* September 8, 1913. Early attempts by Polish leadership to influence Buffalo's Poles to support the Democratic party are suggested in Brenda K.

Shelton, *Reformers in Search of Yesterday: Buffalo in the 1890's* (Albany: State University of New York Press, 1976), p. 8.

21. See Chapter 2.
22. Gerald W. McFarland, *Mugwumps, Morals, & Politics, 1884–1920* (Amherst: The University of Massachusetts Press, 1975), ch. 5; Richard L. McCormick, "Prelude to Progressivism: The Transformation of New York State Politics, 1890–1910," *New York History,* LIX (1978), 253–276.
23. Robert F. Wesser, *Charles Evans Hughes: Politics and Reform in New York, 1905–1910* (Ithaca: Cornell University Press, 1967), chs. I and II; Theodore Roosevelt to Nevada Stranahan, November 17, 1905, *LTR,* vol. V, pp. 78–79.
24. Wesser, *Charles Evans Hughes,* passim.
25. Information on these Republican reformers was obtained from biographical sketches in Edgar L. Murlin, *New York Red Book: An Illustrated Legislative Manual, 1907* (Albany: J. B. Lyon, 1907), pp. 64–97, 99–169. The Hughes program and its supporters are detailed in Wesser, *Charles Evans Hughes,* passim.
26. Theodore Roosevelt to Benjamin I. Wheeler, June 17, 1908, *LTR,* vol. VI, pp. 1082–1083.
27. Roosevelt's New York policy in the context of the broader needs of the Republican party in 1910 is analyzed in George E. Mowry, *Theodore Roosevelt and the Progressive Movement* (Madison: University of Wisconsin Press, 1947), ch. V. For revision on several key points, see Herbert H. Rosenthal, "The Cruise of the Tarpon," *New York History,* XXXIX (1958), 302–320.
28. Mowry, *Theodore Roosevelt,* p. 135; Lloyd C. Griscom, *Diplomatically Speaking* (Boston: Little Brown and Company, 1940), p. 342.
29. *The Literary Digest,* XLI (1910), 117–119; *New York World,* July 11, 1910; *New York Times,* July 13, 14, and 26, 1910; Timothy L. Woodruff to James S. Sherman, July 21, 1910, James S. Sherman Papers (NYPL).
30. Sherman to William Ward, July 25, 1910, Sherman Papers.
31. *Rochester Herald,* August 17, 1910, in "George W. Aldridge Scrapbooks," vol. 10, George W. Aldridge Papers (RML); Archie Butt to Clara Butt, August 17, 1910, in Archie Butt, *Taft and Roosevelt,* 2 vols. (New York: Doubleday, Doran and Co., 1930), vol. 2, pp. 479–482. For Taft's role in the New York Republican tangle, see Butt to Clara Butt, August 18, 20, and 23, 1910, in ibid., pp. 488–489, 491–492, 494–496. Taft's own version is given in Taft to Lloyd C. Griscom, August 20, 1910, William Howard Taft Papers (LC).
32. Sherman to William E. Barnes, August 18, 1910, Sherman Papers.
33. *New York Times,* August 23, 24, 1910; Theodore Roosevelt to William Allen White, August 22, 1910, *LTR,* vol. VII, p. 119; Oscar King Davis, *Released for Publication: Some Inside Political History of Theodore Roo-*

sevelt and His Times, 1898–1918 (Boston: Houghton Mifflin and Co., 1925), p. 196.

34. Mowry, *Theodore Roosevelt*, pp. 142–144, 147–148; Rosenthal, "Cruise of the Tarpon," 308.

35. Rosenthal, "Cruise of the Tarpon," 308–310; William Howard Taft to Horace Taft, September 16, 1910, Taft Papers.

36. Rosenthal, "Cruise of the Tarpon," 311, 314–315; William Howard Taft to Mrs. William Howard Taft, September 24, 1910, Taft Papers. It was after this conference that Taft reputedly remarked: "The fact of the matter is, if you were to remove Roosevelt's skull now, you would find written on his brain '1912.'" See Butt, *Taft and Roosevelt*, vol. 2, pp. 523–524. Roosevelt's version of the meeting is given in Theodore Roosevelt to Henry Cabot Lodge, September 21, 1910, *LTR*, vol. VII, pp. 134–137.

37. Quoted in *LTR*, vol. VII, p. 140.

38. *New York Times*, September 28, 29, 1910; Griscom, *Diplomatically Speaking*, pp. 349–350, "Personal Recollections of the Convention and Campaign of 1910," in *Henry L. Stimson Diary, 1910*, Henry L. Stimson Papers (Yale University Library).

39. See McCormick, "Prelude to Progressivism," esp. 254–255, and "Shaping Republican Strategy," ch. 8.

CHAPTER 2

1. Thomas Mott Osborne, "What Is the Democratic Party?" *National Monthly*, I (1909), 103, 105; Alfred B. Rollins, Jr., "The Political Education of Franklin D. Roosevelt: His Career in New York State Politics, 1910–1928" (Ph.D. diss., Harvard University, 1953), p. 5.

2. Robert Binkerd, "Reminiscences" (OHP, 1949), p. 59; Frances Perkins, "Reminiscences" (OHP, 1955), book 1, p. 426.

3. This sketch is drawn mainly from M. R. Werner, *Tammany Hall* (Garden City, N.Y.: Doubleday, Doran and Co., 1928), pp. 482–487; Alfred Connable and Edward Silberfarb, *Tigers of Tammany: Nine Men Who Ran New York* (New York: Holt, Rinehart and Winston, 1967), ch. 8; and Nancy Joan Weiss, *Charles Francis Murphy, 1858–1924: Respectability and Responsibility in Tammany Politics* (Northampton, Mass.: Smith College, 1968), chs. I and II.

4. "'Silent Charlie,' The Mayor Maker," *The Literary Digest*, LXXXI (1924), 42.

5. James J. Hoey, "Hon. Charles F. Murphy," *Journal of the American Irish Historical Society*, XXIII (1924), 237.

6. Connable and Silberfarb, *Tigers of Tammany*, p. 237.

7. Harold Zink, *City Bosses in the United States* (New York: AMS Press, 1968), p. 144; Isabel Paterson, "Murphy," *The American Mercury*, XIV

(1928), 349; Weiss, *Charles Francis Murphy,* pp. 26–27; " 'Silent Charlie,' " 42.

8. James W. Gerard, "Reminiscences" (OHP, 1949–1950), pp. 21–22; Jeremiah T. Mahoney, "Reminiscences" (OHP, 1949), p. 27; Edward J. Flynn, *You're the Boss* (New York: The Viking Press, 1947), p. 7; *New York World,* April 26, 1924, in Citizens Union Collection (Columbia University Library).

9. See Chapter 5.

10. Lawson Purdy, "Reminiscences" (OHP, 1948), p. 22; W. Axel Warn, "Charles Francis Murphy," *New York Times Magazine,* February 22, 1914, p. 2.

11. Weiss, *Charles Francis Murphy,* p. 27; Harold C. Syrett, ed., *The Gentleman and the Tiger: The Autobiography of George B. McClellan, Jr.* (Philadelphia: J. B. Lippincott Co., 1956), pp. 159, 185; Anna Lanahan, "The Attempt of Tammany Hall to Dominate the Brooklyn Democratic Party, 1903–1909" (M.A. essay, Columbia University, 1955), passim; John A. Heffernan, "Reminiscences" (OHP, 1950), p. 32.

12. Weiss, *Charles Francis Murphy,* p. 27; "Murphy's Victory Over Deveryism," ed., *Tammany Times,* XXI (September 19, 1903), 8, and ibid., XXI (May 9, 1903), 1, 8; Gerard, "Reminiscences," p. 19.

13. Werner, *Tammany Hall,* p. 495.

14. *Tammany Times,* XXII (April 23, 1904), 2; James A. Myatt, "William Randolph Hearst and the Progressive Era, 1900–1912" (Ph.D. diss., University of Florida, 1960), ch. 1; John Higham, *Strangers in the Land: Patterns of American Nativism, 1860–1925* (New Brunswick: Rutgers University Press, 1955), p. 127.

15. Students are in general agreement that but for Tammany malpractices Hearst would have won the election. See Myatt, "William Randolph Hearst," pp. 73–74; John J. Winkler, *William Randolph Hearst: A New Appraisal* (New York: Hastings, 1955), p. 143; and W. A. Swanberg, *Citizen Hearst: A Biography of William Randolph Hearst* (New York: Charles Scribner's Sons, 1961), pp. 237–238.

16. *New York Times,* November 8, 1905. Most of this vote analysis is based on election returns given in the *Times,* November 8 and 9, 1905. A similar analysis is made in Irwin Yellowitz, *Labor and the Progressive Movement in New York State, 1897–1916* (Ithaca: Cornell University Press, 1965), pp. 197–202.

17. *Buffalo Courier,* July 25, 1906; *New York Times,* November 7, 8, 1906; Robert F. Wesser, *Charles Evans Hughes: Politics and Reform in New York, 1905–1910* (Ithaca: Cornell University Press, 1967), ch. IV; Yellowitz, *Labor and the Progressive Movement,* pp. 212–213.

18. *New York Tribune,* November 19, 1906; Swanberg, *Citizen Hearst,* pp. 265–268; William R. Hochman, "William J. Gaynor: The Years of

Fruition" (Ph.D. diss., Columbia University, 1955), ch. IV; Mortimer Smith, *William Jay Gaynor* (Chicago: Henry Regnery Co., 1951), p. 61; Weiss, *Charles Francis Murphy*, pp. 44–45; *New York Times*, November 3, 4, 1909.

19. Shortly after the election Gaynor testified that Murphy had never asked anything of him. He added in reference to Murphy: "He fully realizes that a political organization cannot survive and grow broader on patronage alone, without ideas and virtue, but must shrivel up and die from worse than dry rot" (*Tammany Times*, XXXVI [January 8, 1910], 9).
20. October 1, 1909.
21. Richard Barry, "Mr. Murphy—the Politician's Politician," *The Outlook*, CXXXVII (1924), 55.
22. Weiss, *Charles Francis Murphy*, pp. 43–44; *New York World*, April 25, 1924, EPKC, vol. 15; Lanahan, "The Attempt of Tammany Hall," ch. IV; John A. Beadles, "The Syracuse Irish, 1812–1928: Immigration, Catholicism, Socio-Economic Status, Politics and Irish Nationalism" (Ph.D. diss., Syracuse University, 1974), p. 174; *Buffalo Evening News*, January 7, 1932, in "Local Biographies, Clippings," vol. II (BECPL); *Buffalo Evening Times*, September 8, 1913; *New York Times*, December 31, 1910; Wesser, *Charles Evans Hughes*, ch. IV and pp. 238–242; *Tammany Times*, ed., XXXII (April 18, 1908), 8.
23. The term is Rudolph W. Chamberlain's in *There Is No Truce: A Life of Thomas Mott Osborne* (New York: The Macmillan Co., 1935), p. 27. Most of this biographical sketch is drawn from Chamberlain. A shorter sketch can be found in Jack M. Holl, *Juvenile Reform in the Progressive Era: William R. George and the Junior Republic Movement* (Ithaca: Cornell University Press, 1971), pp. 21–28.
24. Holl, *Juvenile Reform*, p. 24.
25. Chamberlain, *There Is No Truce*, p. 119.
26. G. Wallace Chessman, *Governor Theodore Roosevelt: The Albany Apprenticeship, 1898–1900* (Cambridge: Harvard University Press, 1965), ch. II; Chamberlain, *There Is No Truce*, p. 141.
27. "An open letter addressed to every Democrat who wishes to act for the best interests of real Democracy," October 27, 1906, Chester C. Platt Papers (Cornell University Library); Thomas Mott Osborne to George F. Peabody, February 20, 1906, Thomas Mott Osborne Papers (Syracuse University Library); *New York Times*, September 5, 1906; Chamberlain, *There Is No Truce*, ch. VI and pp. 152–153.
28. Thomas Mott Osborne to Oswald Garrison Villard, n.d., Oswald Garrison Villard Papers (Harvard University Library). In 1908 Osborne did endorse Bryan's presidential bid but found it a "bitter pill." He was extremely critical of the Democratic nominee for governor that year and the state platform (Osborne to Villard, July 28, 1908, Villard Papers; and Osborne to George A. Ricker, September 22, 1908, Osborne Papers).

29. *Albany Times-Union,* September 9, 10, 1909; *New York World* in *The Literary Digest,* XXXIX (1909), 422; "New York State to Occupy Center Stage," *National Monthly,* I (1909), 193. Louis M. Howe's work with Osborne is analyzed in Alfred B. Rollins, Jr., *Roosevelt and Howe* (New York: Alfred A. Knopf, 1962), ch. I.

30. *New York Times,* January 28, 1910; Thomas Mott Osborne to Charles Evans Hughes, January 31, 1910; and to Leslie Hopkinson, February 1, 1910, Osborne Papers.

31. Wesser, *Charles Evans Hughes,* pp. 270–273; *Buffalo Courier* and *New York Times,* November 3, 1909; *Tammany Times,* XXXVI (March 5, 1910), 2.

32. Thomas Mott Osborne to *La Follette's Weekly Magazine,* March 17, 1910, Osborne Papers; Osborne to Oswald Garrison Villard, December 31, 1909, Villard Papers. The league's version of the primary was embodied in the Grady-Frisbie bill, a Democratic party measure, which was rejected by the state legislature in early 1910 (*New York Sun,* January 28, 1910; Wesser, *Charles Evans Hughes,* p. 292). An analysis of Democratic politics in 1910 from the league's point of view is given in Rollins, "The Political Education of Franklin D. Roosevelt," pp. 14–23.

33. *Albany Times-Union,* June 2, 1910; *Buffalo Courier,* June 3, 1910; *Tammany Times,* XXXVI (June 4, 1910), 1; Thomas Mott Osborne to M. J. Easley, June 11, 1910, Osborne Papers.

34. *Albany Times-Union,* August 9, 1909; *Tammany Times,* XXXVII (August 13, 1910), 7, and (September 10, 1910), 1. The Progressive Democrats of New York was also an upstate-oriented group. It prided itself in being more "radical" than the league but differed from Osborne's forces only on the primary issue. It manifested considerable support for the gubernatorial candidacies of William Jay Gaynor and William Sulzer (*New York Times,* August 9, 1910; Chester C. Platt to William Sulzer, August 5, September 19, 1910; Alexander S. Bacon to Platt, September 14, 1910; William Lustgarten to Progressive Democrats, September 17, 1910, Platt Papers; Rollins, "The Political Education of Franklin D. Roosevelt," pp. 18–19).

35. *New York Times,* September 29, 30, and October 1, 1910; *Albany Times-Union,* September 29, 30, 1910. Louis Antisdale's *Rochester Herald* (October 1, 1910) also lauded the Dix nomination and argued that his election would "meet the demand from the disturbed and alarmed business interests of the state for an orderly and capable business administration."

36. *Rochester Herald* and *New York Times,* October 1, 1910. The platform concentrated on national party principles and issues. It pledged the Democrats "anew to the old nationalism" and condemned "all attacks on the Supreme Court." It lauded the party's traditional states' rights doctrine and criticized "any usurpation by the Federal Government." It attacked

the Republican tariff and "gross extravagance in public expenditures." On state issues the platform called for a cleanup of the legislature, the direct election of U.S. senators, the income tax amendment, and a statewide primary. It concluded with another attack on Roosevelt's New Nationalism, charging: "Whatever advance its adoption would bring is advance toward Socialism" (*Tammany Times*, XXXVII [October 1, 1910], 4, 8). Osborne's complaint about the Rochester convention came soon afterward and was based not on the platform or the Dix nomination "but the rest of the ticket [which] is exceedingly weak" (Osborne to George A. Ricker, October 6, 1910, Osborne Papers; Osborne to Oswald Garrison Villard, October 19, 1910, Villard Papers).

37. *The Literary Digest*, XL (1910), 571–573; James W. Wadsworth, Jr., "Unpublished Autobiography," James W. Wadsworth, Jr., Papers (LC), p. 169; William Howard Taft to Myron T. Herrick, October 11, 1910, and to Elihu Root, October 12, 1910, William Howard Taft Papers (LC); Thomas Mott Osborne to Oswald Garrison Villard, October 10, 1910, Villard Papers; William Lustgarten to Chester C. Platt, October 10, 1910, Platt Papers.

38. *Albany Times-Union, Buffalo Courier, Rochester Herald*, and *New York Tribune*, November 9, 1910; *New York Times*, November 9, 10, 1910; *Tammany Times*, XXXVIII (November 12, 1910), 1. For greater details on the gubernatorial election returns and New York State—upstate percentage breakdowns, see Appendix II, Tables 1 and 2.

39. November 9, 1910.

40. *Rochester Herald, Rochester Evening Times*, and *Buffalo Courier*, November 9, 1910; Herbert H. Rosenthal, "The Cruise of the Tarpon," *New York History*, XXXIX (1958), 317; John L. O'Brian to Henry L. Stimson, and B. A. Sands to Stimson, October 21, 1910, Henry L. Stimson Papers (Yale University Library); William Loeb to George W. Aldridge, October 25, 1910, George W. Aldridge Papers (RML); Frederick M. Davenport to William E. Barnes, August 22, 1912, Frederick M. Davenport Papers (Syracuse University Library); George W. Perkins to William B. McKinley, April 29, 1912, George W. Perkins Papers (Columbia University Library). For the percentage voter turnout, see Appendix II, Figure 1.

41. The phrases and argument are Rosenthal's in "Cruise of the Tarpon," 317–318. Most contemporary observers cited the high cost of living as a major factor in the Republican defeat in New York City in 1910.

42. This survey of turnout, using total vote only, was based on some two-dozen carefully selected assembly districts in New York City and the nearly three dozen wards in Albany, Buffalo, Rochester, Syracuse, Utica, and Troy represented in Appendix I, Table 1. For Democratic percentages in the various ethnic areas, see Appendix II, Table 4.

43. Socialist Party, *State Platform*, 1910, and "How to Vote Intelligently,"

Socialist Party Pamphlet, 1910, in New York Socialist Party Papers (Tamiment Institute).

44. David A. Shannon, *The Socialist Party of America: A History* (New York: The Macmillan Co., 1955), p. 13; *New York Call,* November 11, 1910. For the Socialist vote, see Appendix II, Table 3.

45. The districts under examination were Manhattan's 4th, 6th, 8th, 10th, 24th, and 26th; Brooklyn's 14th, 21st, 22nd, 23rd, 32nd, 33rd, and 34th. Other analyses of the vote in the heavily Jewish districts can be found in Abram Lipsky, "The Political Mind of Foreign-Born Americans," *Popular Science Monthly,* LXXXV (1914), 399; and Melvyn Dubofsky, "Success and Failure of Socialism in New York City, 1900–1918: A Case Study," *Labor History,* IX (1968), 367. For the percentage Democratic vote, see also Appendix II, Table 4.

46. "In the East," ed., *The Outlook,* XCVI (1910), 608.

47. Norman E. Mack, "Roosevelt's New Nationalism," *National Monthly,* II (1910), 176–177.

CHAPTER 3

1. "Diary of FDR," January 1, 1911, Franklin D. Roosevelt Papers (FDRL); *New York Times,* November 9, 1910; *Albany Evening Journal,* January 2, 1911.

2. Edgar L. Murlin, *New York Red Book: An Illustrated Legislative Manual, 1911* (Albany: J. B. Lyon, 1911), pp. 25–28; *Rochester Herald,* October 1, 1910; John A. Dix to George W. Perkins, March 28, 1912, George W. Perkins Papers (Columbia University Library); Robert Binkerd, "Reminiscences" (OHP, 1949), p. 22.

3. Thomas Mott Osborne to John A. Dix, January 26, 1911, Thomas Mott Osborne Papers (Syracuse University Library); *Albany Times-Union,* January 3, 5, 1911; *New York Times,* January 6, 21, 1911.

4. *New York Times,* December 22, 1910; *Albany Times-Union,* January 4, 1911; "Diary of FDR," January 3, 1911, Roosevelt Papers. Frisbie's independent background is explored in *Albany Knickerbocker-Press,* August 15, 1915.

5. Thomas Mott Osborne to John A. Dix, November 13, 1910, to John K. Sague, November 14, 1910, and to George A. Ricker, December 31, 1910, Osborne Papers; *New York Times,* December 4, 26, 1910, January 9, 11, 1911; Alfred B. Rollins, Jr., *Roosevelt and Howe* (New York: Alfred A. Knopf, 1962), p. 24.

6. Unidentified newspaper clipping, December 1910, in EPKC, 1907–1911, vol. 2.

7. "Who Will Be the New U.S. Senator from New York?" in *New York Times Magazine,* December 4, 1910, p. 8; *New York Times,* December 31, 1910, January 2, 1911; *New York Tribune,* January 17, 1911; *Tam-*

many Times, XXIII (December 10, 1904), 6. The *Tammany Times,* in late 1904 and early 1905, carried several articles attacking Sheehan in an effort to prevent him from winning the Democratic state chairmanship upon the retirement of David B. Hill. In one such article (XXVI [January 28, 1905], 3, 11) the *Times* called him "King of Grafters" and "King of Lobbyists."

8. *New York Times,* December 1, 1910, January 3, and 12, 1911; *Tammany Times,* XXXVIII (January 14, 1911), 8; *New York American,* January 16, 1911; and unidentified newspaper clipping, 1911, in EPKC, 1907–1911, vol. 2.

9. Edmund R. Terry, "The Insurgents at Albany," *The Independent,* LXXI (1911), 534–540; *New York Tribune,* January 17, 1911. The caucus did vote overwhelmingly for Sheehen but fell short by 12 votes of winning a majority in the legislature for his candidacy (*Albany Times-Union,* January 17, 1911).

10. Roosevelt's entry into state politics is admirably covered in Frank Freidel, *Franklin D. Roosevelt: The Apprenticeship* (Boston: Little, Brown and Company, 1952), pp. 85–96, and Rollins, *Roosevelt and Howe,* pp. 16–22.

11. Terry, "The Insurgents at Albany," 538.

12. The term is Rollins's in *Roosevelt and Howe,* p. 26.

13. Freidel, *Franklin D. Roosevelt,* pp. 103–108; Rollins, *Roosevelt and Howe,* pp. 26–27; *New York Sun,* January 20, 1911; *New York Times* and *New York World,* March 17, 1911.

14. Franklin D. Roosevelt to Carter F. Harrison, February 17, 1911, Roosevelt Papers. Roosevelt made clear that the purpose of the insurgents was not necessarily to elect Shepard but to help name "someone who will not be a mere politician" (Roosevelt to George H. Knickerbocker, February 6, 1911, and Roosevelt to R. W. Bainbridge, February 1, 1911, and to Henry Hunter, February 10, 1911, Roosevelt Papers).

15. William E. Barnes to Edgar T. Brackett and E. A. Merritt, March 30, 1911, Roosevelt Papers. How serious was this effort to effect a Democratic-Republican alliance is difficult to ascertain. Brackett, a Republican leader, testifies that Barnes "pressed hard" for it, but Roosevelt insisted that "we could hope for little Republican support." (Edgar T. Brackett to Elihu Root, April 4, 1911, Elihu Root Papers [LC]; Roosevelt to Albert S. Vogan, April 4, 1911, Roosevelt Papers). Probably Roosevelt was correct when he recorded that "proposed aid from the Republicans served its purpose—it acted as a club to compel the withdrawal of Sheehan" (Roosevelt to J. B. Murray, April 18, 1911, Roosevelt Papers).

16. *New York Times,* March 28, 29, 30, April 1, 1911; *Buffalo Evening News,* March 28, 1911; *New York Evening Post,* April 1, 1911; Rollins, *Roosevelt and Howe,* pp. 29–31; Freidel, *Franklin D. Roosevelt,* pp. 109–115.

17. *New York Times,* April 1, 1911; "Sizing Up New York's New Senator," *The Literary Digest,* XLII (1911), 667–668.

18. Rollins, *Roosevelt and Howe*, p. 24.
19. Montgomery Hare to William Church Osborn, April 1, 1911, Roosevelt Papers. For Tammanyites the most important factor in the selection of a senator, so the reports went, was that the candidate be an organization man and an Irish Catholic. In a lengthy meeting at Delmonico's on the evening before O'Gorman's victory in the Democratic caucus, all participants agreed on this point. O'Gorman's views on the issues were not discussed or even mentioned to him when a telephone call was put through to the future senator (*Albany Times-Union*, May 2, 1911).
20. *Albany Times-Union*, February 7, May 5, 1911; *New York Tribune*, May 23, June 22, 1911.
21. Oswald Garrison Villard to Thomas Mott Osborne, May 16, 1911, Oswald Garrison Villard Papers (Harvard University Library); *New York Times*, February 11, May 8, 1911; "The Judiciary for Sale," ed., *The Outlook*, XCVIII (1911), 230–231.
22. *New York Times*, February 9, 1911; *Albany Times-Union*, May 8, 1911.
23. *New York Times*, May 9, 1912; "The New York Factory Bureau," *The Survey*, XXVIII (1912), 266. For other criticisms by the social progressives, see Paul Kennaday, "Labor Legislation in New York," *The Survey*, XXVII (1911), 1083–1084, and "Civil Service in New York," ibid., XXVIII (1912), 566.
24. Thomas Mott Osborne to John A. Dix, January 26, 1911, and to George A. Ricker, February 23, 1911, Osborne Papers. To Villard he wrote in disgust: "I have been consulted about nothing since I took office; and the 'cabinet' does not eventuate" (February 6, 1911, Villard Papers).
25. Rudolph W. Chamberlain, *There Is No Truce: A Life of Thomas Mott Osborne* (New York: The Macmillan Co., 1935), p. 168.
26. Thomas Mott Osborne to Oswald Garrison Villard, May 19, 1911, Villard Papers; to George A. Ricker, May 11, 1911, and to Joseph Scott, May 15, 1911, Osborne Papers.
27. Thomas Mott Osborne to John K. Sague, June 3, 1911, Osborne Papers.
28. *New York Tribune*, May 20, 1911. The *Tribune* added: "They offered no objection to bossism, but merely to a single act of the 'boss' " (in reference to Murphy's support of Sheehan). Roosevelt was personally aware of the unreliability of the insurgents when he decided to draw together a nucleus of ten or twelve legislators around whom "we can obtain . . . additional support" (Franklin D. Roosevelt to Montgomery Hare, April 13, 1911, Roosevelt Papers).
29. *New York Times*, January 28, May 23, 1911; Ernest Harvier to George F. Peabody, April 3, 1911, Osborne Papers; Alfred B. Rollins, Jr., "The Political Education of Franklin D. Roosevelt, 1909–1928" (Ph.D. diss., Harvard University, 1953), p. 197; *Tammany Times*, XXXIX (November 4, 1911), 1.

30. Quoted in J. Joseph Huthmacher, *Senator Robert F. Wagner and the Rise of Urban Liberalism* (New York: Atheneum, 1968), p. 12. A brief sketch of Wagner's early life and political beginnings is given here, pp. 12–18. See also Henry F. Pringle, "The Janitor's Boy," in *Big Frogs* (New York: Vanguard Press, 1928), pp. 211–213, and J. T. Salter, ed., *The American Politician* (Chapel Hill: University of North Carolina Press, 1938), pp. 116–118. Sketches of Smith's youth and early manhood are bountiful. Most useful are Matthew and Hannah Josephson, *Al Smith: Hero of the Cities* (Boston: Houghton Mifflin Co., 1969), pp. 8–69, and Smith's own *Up to Now: An Autobiography* (New York: The Viking Press, 1929), pp. 3–68.
31. The words are Smith's in reference to Foley's promise that if elected district leader over Patrick Divver he would reward supporters like Smith (*Up to Now*, p. 58).
32. Smith, *Up to Now*, p. 75; Huthmacher, *Senator Robert F. Wagner*, pp. 18–21; "Report of the Committee on Legislation of the Citizens Union for the Session of 1909" (New York: Citizens Union, 1909), pp. 30–31.
33. Smith, *Up to Now*, p. 80.
34. Ibid., pp. 81–83; *Albany Times-Union*, May 14, 15, 1907; *Tammany Times*, XXXI (July 6, 1907), 10; *New York Senate Journal*, 130th session (Albany: J. B. Lyon, 1907), p. 1773; and *New York Assembly Journal*, 130th session (Albany: J. B. Lyon, 1907), p. 3145.
35. Most of this information is gleaned from the *New York Senate Journal* and the *New York Assembly Journal*, 130th–133rd sessions (Albany: J. B. Lyon, 1907–1910).
36. January 6, 1910.
37. *New York World*, May 18, 1910.
38. *New York Times*, April 21, May 4, 18, 1910; *New York Tribune*, April 21, 1910. The vote in the senate was 26–20, with 13 of 14 Democrats voting for it and 19 of 32 Republicans voting against it. In the assembly the amendment actually carried those who voted, 74–66, but the vote in favor lacked the necessary majority (76) of the entire body. Forty-eight of 50 Democrats supported the amendment, while 64 of 90 Republicans recorded against it. A good analysis of the battle in the New York legislature is given in John D. Buenker, "Progressivism in Practice: New York State and the Federal Income Tax Amendment," *New-York Historical Society Quarterly*, LII (1968), 139–160. See also Buenker's *Urban Liberalism and Progressive Reform* (New York: Charles Scribner's Sons, 1973), pp. 111–112.
39. Quoted in Henry F. Pringle, *Alfred E. Smith: A Critical Study* (New York: Macy-Masius, 1927), p. 131.
40. June 27, 1911.
41. *Albany Times-Union*, April 20, 1911; *New York Times*, July 13, 1911.

The vote in the assembly was 91–42, with only one Democrat opposing the amendment; in the senate it was 35–16, again with only one Democrat in opposition. See also Buenker, "Progressivism in Practice," 157–158, and *Urban Liberalism,* pp. 112–113.

42. *Albany Times-Union,* April 20, 1911; *New York Times,* April 21, 26, 1911.

43. One provision authorized an advisory commission (made up of the conservation commissioner, the attorney general, the state engineer, the superintendent of the department of public works, and the state health commissioner) to purchase land for the state forest preserves and to make plans for the regulation of the flow of rivers and the construction of ditches, dams, and other public work deemed necessary for reclamation of swamps, bogs, meadows, and other lowlands. The other permitted the commission to make leases up to fifty years for electrical power purposes of canalized streams to municipalities and private corporations (*New York Times,* April 12, May 2, and June 29, 1911). Dix's role as well as his general views on conservation can be found in John Dix, "Conservation of Mankind," *The Survey,* XXVII (1912), 1880–1890.

44. *New York Times,* May 2, 1911; *Albany Times-Union,* June 29, 30, 1911; *New York Senate Journal,* 134th session (Albany: J. B. Lyon, 1911), p. 2023; and *New York Assembly Journal,* 134th session (Albany: J. B. Lyon, 1911), pp. 3524–3525.

45. Franklin D. Roosevelt to A. R. Conkling, June 22, 1911, Roosevelt Papers; *New York Senate Journal,* 134th session, p. 2047; and *New York Assembly Journal,* 134th session, pp. 3584–3585. The deal was evidently a complicated one in which Dix and the upstaters received quick approval by the legislature for the conservation bill and one other measure in return for their acceptance of the Levy bill (*New York Times,* June 30, 1911).

46. Franklin D. Roosevelt to Otis S. Beach, April 13, 1911, Roosevelt Papers; *New York Evening Post* and *New York Times,* October 2, 1911; *New York Senate Journal,* 134th session, p. 2536; and *New York Assembly Journal,* 134th session, p. 4523.

47. Rollins, *Roosevelt and Howe,* p. 37; *New York Tribune,* October 6, 1911. In brief the Ferris-Blauvelt bill provided for: (1) nomination by the direct method of all candidates for public office except those on the state ticket; (2) election of members of all party committees at the primaries; and (3) an official primary ballot with a modified system of party columns. Strong advocates of the direct primary like Harvey D. Hinman of Binghamton, who had coauthored the Hughes bill in 1910, objected to Ferris-Blauvelt because it did not extend the primary to statewide offices and did not abolish the state convention and the party emblem on the ballot.

48. The major criticisms of the charter bill were leveled against three provisions: first, a series of proposals enhancing executive authority in appoint-

ment-making; second, the substitution of a small, paid board of education for a large, unpaid one; and third, a strengthening of the mayor's final authority over franchise grants and contracts (*New York Times,* April 25, July 14, September 17, and 18, 1911; Frederic Coudert to Franklin D. Roosevelt, May 31, 1911, Roosevelt Papers; Binkerd, "Reminiscences," pp. 18–20; and Willilam Prendergast, "Reminiscences" [OHP, 1948–1951], pp. 337–344). Other criticisms are outlined in a memorandum issued jointly by the City Club, the Citizens Union, Greater New York Taxpayers' Conference, Public Education Association, and the Brooklyn League (The City Club of New York, *Bulletin,* June 1911 [NYPL]).

49. Lawrence A. Tanzer, "The Defeat of the Tammany-Gaynor Charter," *National Municipal Review,* I (1912), 61–68; The City Club of New York, *Bulletin,* September and October, 1911; "Report of the Committee on Legislation of the Citizens Union for the Session of 1911" (New York: Citizens Union, 1911), pp. 5–7; Binkerd, "Reminiscences," p. 32.

50. *New York Times,* September 30, and October 1, 1911; *New York American,* October 1, 1911; Rollins, *Roosevelt and Howe,* pp. 35–36.

51. *New York Evening Post,* March 29, 1912; *Tammany Times,* XXXIX (October 7, 1911), 15. Especially critical of the 1911 "Tammany" legislature were *New York Times,* July 22, 1911; "The Record of a Tammany Legislature: Intrenching the Machine," *The Outlook,* XCIX (1911), 391–393; "Report of the Committee on Legislation of the Citizens Union," passim; and City Club *Bulletin,* 1911, n.p.

52. *New York Times, New York Tribune,* and *Utica Daily Press,* November 8, 1911; Nelson Drummond to Franklin D. Roosevelt, November 9, 1911, Roosevelt Papers.

53. *Albany Times-Union, Syracuse Herald, Utica Herald-Dispatch, Rochester Evening Times, Buffalo Morning Express,* November 8, 1911; *Buffalo Courier,* November 9, 1911; *New York Times,* November 8, 9, 1911.

54. *Buffalo Evening News, Buffalo Courier,* November 8, 1911. For a similar opinion see "The Election," *The Outlook,* XCIX (1911), 646–647.

55. *Buffalo Morning Express,* November 8, 1911; *Utica Daily Press,* November 10, 1911; Ira Kipnis, *The American Socialist Movement, 1897–1912* (New York: Columbia University Press, 1952), p. 362. A good analysis of the Schenectady election is given in Henry F. Griffin, "The Rising Tide of Socialism," *The Outlook,* C (1912), 438–448, and Kenneth E. Hendrickson, Jr., "George R. Lunn and the Socialist Era in Schenectady, New York, 1909–1916," *New York History,* XLVII (1966), 22–39. Lunn's background and conversion to socialism are discussed in Livy S. Richard, "Democracy in Religion," *The Survey,* XXIV (1910), 535–540.

56. In New York county the three districts were the 26th, 32nd, and 33rd. In Brooklyn the four districts were the 9th, 13th, 22nd, and 23rd. In Queens the district was the 3rd.

57. *New York Sun,* December 5, 7, 19, 1911; Rollins, *Roosevelt and Howe,* p. 48; *New York American,* December 4, 1911; and *New York Journal,* December 5, 1911, January 4, 1912, in EPKC, 1911–1936, vol. 1.

CHAPTER 4

1. Roosevelt to Hiram Johnson, October 27, 1911, *LTR,* vol. VII, pp. 418–422. See also Roosevelt to Charles McCarthy, October 27, 1911, ibid., pp. 424–425.
2. Richard M. Abrams, *Conservatism in a Progressive Era: Massachusetts Politics, 1900–1912* (Cambridge: Harvard University Press, 1964), pp. 217–222.
3. Richard K. Fleischman, "Labor Unrest in Buffalo in 1913," *Social Science Research Notes,* II (1973), 1–35; Robert E. Snyder, "Women, Wobblies and Workers' Rights: The 1912 Textile Strike in Little Falls, New York," *New York History,* LX (1979), 29–57.
4. "High Rents Burden the Poor More than Food Prices," *New York Times Magazine,* July 21, 1912, p. 8; Melvyn Dubofsky, *When Workers Organize: New York City in the Progressive Era* (Amherst: The University of Massachusetts Press, 1968), chs. 3 and 4. The quotation appears in Dubofsky, pp. 72–73.
5. The terms are Dubofsky's in *When Workers Organize,* pp. 48, 85.
6. Leon Stein, *The Triangle Fire* (Philadelphia: J. B. Lippincott Co., 1962), passim; *New York Times,* March 26, 1911.
7. *New York Times,* March 27, 1911.
8. *New York Times,* April 3, 6, May 9, June 12, and July 15, 1911; "Committee on Safety: Outline of Work and Statement of Necessary Budget," May 26, 1911, in George W. Perkins Papers (Columbia University Library); Alfred E. Smith, *Up to Now: An Autobiography* (New York: The Viking Press, 1929), pp. 91–92; Thomas J. Kerr IV, "New York Factory Investigating Commission and the Progressives" (D.S.S. diss., Syracuse Universtiy, 1965), ch. I.
9. J. Joseph Huthmacher, *Senator Robert F. Wagner and the Rise of Urban Liberalism* (New York: Atheneum, 1968), p. 5.
10. Frances Perkins, *The Roosevelt I Knew* (New York: The Viking Press, 1946), p. 22.
11. Kerr, "New York Factory Investigating Commission," p. 94 and passim. The commission's work is also detailed in J. William Gillette, "Welfare State Trail Blazer: New York State Factory Investigating Commission, 1911–1915" (M.A. essay, Columbia University, 1956).
12. Henry Morgenthau, *All in a Life-Time* (Garden City, N.Y.: Doubleday, Page and Co., 1922), pp. 107–108; *New York Times,* February 20, March 10, 1913; Mornay Williams to Olivia E. Phelps Stokes, January 21, 1913, J. G. Phelps Stokes Papers (Columbia University Library); Consum-

ers' League of Buffalo, *Annual Report, 1912* (Buffalo, 1913), in Consumers' League Collection, Library of Industrial and Labor Relations (Cornell University); George A. Hall, "New Child Labor Legislation in New York," *The Survey*, XXXI (1913), 89–90; Consumers' League of the City of New York, *Report for the Year 1912* (New York, 1913), p. 9; Kerr, "New York Factory Investigating Commission," ch. III.

13. Nancy Joan Weiss, *Charles Francis Murphy, 1858–1924: Respectability and Responsibility in Tammany Politics* (Northampton, Mass.: Smith College, 1968), p. 87.

14. Philip C. Jessup, *Elihu Root*, 2 vols. (New York: Dodd, Mead and Company, 1938), vol. II, p. 170; "Minutes of the Republican State Committee, January 21, 1911" (Albany: Republican State Committee, 1911).

15. "Memorandum," May 13, 1911, William Howard Taft Papers (LC); William Barnes to Charles Evans Hughes, November 21, 1906, Charles Evans Hughes Papers (LC); Barnes to James S. Sherman, December 24, 1910, James S. Sherman Papers (NYPL); Barnes to Frederick M. Davenport, August 26, 1912, Frederick M. Davenport Papers (Syracuse University Library); James W. Wadsworth, Jr., "Unpublished Autobiography," pp. 197–198, in James W. Wadsworth Papers (LC); *New York Times*, May 17, 1912. A full analysis of Barnes's conservatism can be found in Robert E. O'Connor, "William Barnes, Jr.: A Conservative Encounters the Progressive Era" (Ph.D. diss., State University of New York at Albany, 1971), passim.

16. William Barnes to Elihu Root, May 10, 1911, Elihu Root Papers (LC); Barnes to Herbert Parsons, October 28, 1911, cited in Parsons to Charles D. Hilles, December 13, 1911, Taft Papers; *Albany Evening Journal*, January 27, 1911; Raymond A. Pearson to Elihu Root, February 15, 22, and 27, 1911, Charles J. Hewitt to Root, April 19, 1911, and Edgar T. Brackett to Root, December 30, 1911, Root Papers; O'Connor, "William Barnes, Jr.," ch. V.

17. *New York Times*, March 23, 27, 1912; Frederick C. Tanner, "Reminiscences" (OHP, 1950), p. 61; "The Verdict in New York and Indiana," *The Literary Digest*, XLIV (1912), 671–672; George E. Mowry, *Theodore Roosevelt and the Progressive Movement* (Madison: University of Wisconsin Press, 1947), ch. VII. For a comprehensive analysis of the New York Republican primary, see Thomas J. McInerney, "The Election of 1912 in New York State" (Ph.D. diss., University of Denver, 1977), pp. 36–45. In Manhattan and the Bronx Roosevelt lost all thirteen congressional districts to Taft with only about one third of the total vote.

18. *New York Times*, April 3, 8, 10, and 11, 1912; *Rochester Democrat and Chronicle*, April 8, 10, and 11, 1912; *New York Sun*, April 8, 1912, in EPKC, 1911–1936, vol. 1; William Barnes to William Howard Taft, May 28, 1912, Taft Papers; O'Connor, "William Barnes, Jr.," pp. 105–

106. O'Connor argues that Barnes did not make his final commitment to Taft until one week before the national convention opened (p. 109).

19. Jonathan M. Wainwright to F. C. Platt, August 20, 1912, Jonathan M. Wainwright Papers (N-YHSL); William Barnes to Elihu Root, August 7, 1912, Root Papers; Job Hedges to James S. Sherman, August 13, 1912, Sherman Papers; Henry L. Stimson to Felix Frankfurter, September 29, 1912, Henry L. Stimson Papers (Yale University Library).

20. *Albany Times-Union*, September 27, 1912. At least one Republican newspaper, the *Syracuse Post-Standard* (September 28, 1912), argued that the platform was "progressive." The convention is adequately covered in the *Albany Times-Union*, September 24–27, 1912. See also McInerney, "The Election of 1912," pp. 179–186.

21. William H. Hotchkiss to Clarence Parker, and to F. Tucker, July 22, 1912, Clarence Parker Papers (Lyall Squiar Private Collection, Syracuse); *New York Times*, July 29, 1912.

22. Henry Moskowitz to Lillian D. Wald, August 2, 1912, Lillian D. Wald Papers (NYPL); William H. Hotchkiss to Theodore Roosevelt, July 16, 1912, and Sylvester Viereck to Roosevelt, July 10, 1912, Theodore Roosevelt Papers (LC); Ernest Cawcroft to Henry Moskowitz, September 18, 1912, Arthur Brisbane to Oscar Straus, November 1, 1912, and Julius Kron to Straus, November 2, 1912, Oscar Straus Papers (LC); Darwin James, Jr., to Frederick M. Davenport, July 28, 1912, Davenport Papers; Paul Kellogg, "The Industrial Platform of the New Party," *The Survey*, XXVIII (1912), 668–670.

23. John M. Blum, *The Republican Roosevelt* (Cambridge: Harvard University Press, 1954), p. 149. For a similar assessment of the national party, see John A. Gable, *The Bull Moose Years: Theodore Roosevelt and the Progressive Party* (Port Washington, N.Y.: Kennikat Press, 1978), pp. 38–39. The presence of conservatives among the Bull Moosers was a source of deep concern to "advanced" progressives like Amos Pinchot, as evidenced in Pinchot to Medill McCormick, July 3, 1912, to Hiram Johnson, July 12, 18, 1912, and to Roosevelt, August 4, 1912, Amos Pinchot Papers (LC).

24. "The Progressive Party in New York," ed., *The Independent*, LXXIII (1912), 625; "The Syracuse Gathering," *Nation*, XCV (1912), 226; *New York Times*, September 4, 6, 1912.

25. *Syracuse Post-Standard*, September 4–7, 1912; Theodore Roosevelt to Oscar Straus, September 8, 1912, *LTR*, vol. VII, p. 625. The rivalry between Hotchkiss and Prendergast in its full dimension is covered in McInerney, "The Election of 1912," pp. 156–164.

26. "The Syracuse Gathering," 227. See also *New York Times*, September 7, 1912; *Syracuse Post-Standard*, September 9, 1912; and "State Elections, Primaries, and Conventions," *The Outlook*, CII (1912), 112–116.

27. Henry L. Stimson to Charles D. Hilles, October 16, 1912, Charles D. Hilles Papers (LC).

28. Thomas Mott Osborne to George A. Ricker, March 12, 1912, and to Francis Willard, April 9, 1912, Thomas Mott Osborne Papers (Syracuse University Library); *New York Times,* October 2, 1912.

29. *New York Times,* February 17, 18, and April 12, 1912; *Buffalo Courier,* February 17 and April 11, 1912; *New York Globe,* April 11, 1912, in EPKC, 1911–1936, vol. 1; *Tammany Times,* XL (April 13, 1912), 1.

30. Thomas Mott Osborne to Eleanor Roosevelt, April 19, 1912, Franklin D. Roosevelt Papers (FDRL); Osborne to Alonzo G. McLaughlin, June 11, 1913, Osborne Papers; Alfred B. Rollins, Jr., *Roosevelt and Howe* (New York: Alfred A. Knopf, 1962), p. 48.

31. For a thorough discussion of Wilson's presidential movement, see Arthur S. Link, *Wilson: The Road to the White House* (Princeton: Princeton University Press, 1947), chs. X–XII.

32. Thomas Mott Osborne to William G. McAdoo, April 6, 1912, Osborne to John N. Carlisle, April 17, 1912, to John E. Eastmond, April 22, 1912, and to Lawrence B. Dunham, May 1, 1912, Osborne Papers; "Call for Wilson Conference," n.d., Roosevelt Papers; *New York Times,* April 30, 1912; *Buffalo Courier,* May 1, 1912; Rollins, *Roosevelt and Howe,* pp. 49–50.

33. Thomas Mott Osborne to William G. McAdoo, May 28, 1912, Osborne Papers; Franklin D. Roosevelt to John K. Evans, June 14, 1912, Roosevelt Papers; *New York Times,* June 25, 1912; Rollins, *Roosevelt and Howe,* pp. 50–52.

34. *Albany Times-Union,* May 6, June 11, 22, 1912; William F. McCombs to Woodrow Wilson, April (?), 1912, quoted in Link, *Wilson,* pp. 405–406; W. A. Swanberg, *Citizen Hearst: A Biography of William Randolph Hearst* (New York: Charles Scribner's Sons, 1961), pp. 274–277; Roy Everett Littlefield III, *William Randolph Hearst: His Role in American Progressivism* (Lanham, Md.: University Press of America, 1980), pp. 283, 285; Link, *Wilson,* pp. 382–387; McInerney, "The Election of 1912," pp. 140–141.

35. *Albany Times-Union,* May 20, 1912; *New York Times,* July 1, 1912; *Buffalo Courier,* June 21, 1912; *Buffalo Evening Times,* June 21, 1912; John J. Broesamle, *William Gibbs McAdoo: A Passion for Change* (Port Washington, N.Y.: Kennikat Press, 1973), pp. 52–53.

36. Paolo E. Coletta, *William Jennings Bryan: Progressive Politician and Moral Statesman, 1909–1915* (Lincoln: University of Nebraska Press, 1969), pp. 56–57; *New York Times,* June 21, 23, 24, and 25, 1912; *Buffalo Evening Times,* June 21, 23, 1912. On June 27 the pro-organization *Albany Times-Union* declared that the "actual steering committee of the convention"—Murphy, Taggart, and Sullivan—"decided to fight the Bryan forces to a finish."

37. *New York Evening Telegram,* June 23, 1912, quoted in Weiss, *Charles F. Murphy,* p. 71.

38. William F. McCombs, *Making Woodrow Wilson President* (New York: Fairview Publishing Company, 1921), p. 123; Link, *Wilson*, p. 438; William Jennings Bryan, *A Tale of Two Conventions*, Rep. Ed. (New York: Arno Press, 1974), pp. 109–134. The best coverage of the Baltimore convention is found in Link, *Wilson*, ch. XIII, and Coletta, *Bryan*, ch. 3.
39. Coletta, *Bryan*, p. 61; William Jennings Bryan and Mary B. Bryan, *The Memoirs of William Jennings Bryan* (Philadelphia: The United Publishers of America, 1925), pp. 176–177; William G. McAdoo, *Crowded Years: The Reminiscences of William G. McAdoo* (Boston: Houghton Mifflin Company, 1931), pp. 148–149; Josephus Daniels, *The Wilson Era: Years of Peace—1910–1917* (Chapel Hill: The University of North Carolina Press, 1944), p. 57. As far as the platform was concerned, the New York delegation wrote a draft document of its own that, in most particulars, was as progressive as the convention's final product (*Buffalo Evening Times*, June 27, 1912).
40. Link, *Wilson*, p. 448; McAdoo, *Crowded Years*, p. 135; *Buffalo Evening Times*, June 27, 1912. The *New York American*, June 25, 1912, pointed out that two weeks before the Baltimore convention the New York delegation strongly supported a Clark nomination. See McInerney, "The Election of 1912," pp. 139–140.
41. James A. Myatt, "William Randolph Hearst and the Progressive Era, 1900–1912" (Ph.D. diss., University of Florida, 1960), pp. 149–150; *New York Times,* and *Albany Times-Union*, June 29, 1912; *Buffalo Evening Times*, June 28, 29, July 2, 1912; Norman E. Mack, "Wilson and Marshall—Mr. Bryan and New York," *National Monthly*, IV (1912), 65; Link, *Wilson*, pp. 448–449. Rumors persisted that Murphy remained terribly reluctant about Clark because of Hearst's influence and preferred either Harmon or Underwood (*New York Times*, June 26, 27, and 30, 1912; *Buffalo Evening Times*, June 30, 1912).
42. Link, *Wilson*, pp. 449–450, 455–456; Bryan, *Memoirs*, pp. 180–181; Bryan, *Two Conventions*, p. 195; *Buffalo Evening Times*, July 1, 1912; *New York Times*, July 2, 1912.
43. Link, *Wilson*, pp. 457–458; *New York Times*, July 1, 1912; *New York World* quoted in *Buffalo Evening Times*, July 1, 1912; *New York Journal*, April 26, 1924, in EPKC, 1911–1936, vol. 15; Broesamle, *McAdoo*, p. 63. For the last two days' balloting, see Link, *Wilson*, pp. 458–462, and Coletta, *Bryan*, pp. 72–73.
44. *Auburn Citizen*, quoted in *Buffalo Courier*, July 3, 1912, *Rochester Herald*, July 2, 1912; *New York World*, July 8, 1912, in EPKC, 1911–1936, vol. 1. The *Buffalo Courier*, July 3, 1912, made a survey of the "independent" press across the state and added its own bitter attack on Murphy.
45. "Packy" McCabe summed up the organization's attitude toward the Baltimore convention: "If we failed to nominate Clark we surely did eliminate

Bryan." See McInerney, "The Election of 1912," p. 147. Murphy's biographer comes very close to stating that Murphy actually engineered the Wilson nomination, an interpretation that held sway among some contemporary observers. See Weiss, *Charles F. Murphy*, p. 71. For a refutation, consult McInerney, "The Election of 1912," pp. 144–147. McInerney concludes sensibly that "Murphy reluctantly acquiesced in Wilson's nomination for the good of the party." See pp. 146–147.

46. Francis Willard to Thomas Mott Osborne, July 9, 1912, Osborne to Chester C. Platt, July 12, 1912, "To the People of the State of New York," n.d., Osborne to John N. Carlisle, July 22, 1912, Osborne Papers; *New York Times*, July 13, 18, and 30, 1912; *New York World* and *Buffalo Courier*, July 18, 1912; *New York Herald*, July 30, 1912. Osborne's threat was made once again after Straus received the Progressive nomination for governor (Osborne to E. R. L. Gould, September 23, 1912, Osborne Papers; and *New York Sun*, September 21, 1912). The development of the Empire State Democracy is discussed in Rollins, *Roosevelt and Howe*, p. 53.

47. Thomas Mott Osborne to Franklin D. Roosevelt, August 19, 1912, Roosevelt Papers; Frank J. Hoyle to William Sulzer, August 16, 1912, William Sulzer Papers (Cornell University Library); *Buffalo Courier*, August 3, 4, and 13, 1912; *New York American*, August 3, 1912, in EPKC, 1911–1936, vol. 1; *New York Times*, July 14, August 4, 5, 13, 25, and September 25, 1912; Osborne to William Lustgarten, September 12, 1912, to E. R. L. Gould, September 23, 1912 to Milo Maltbie, September 24, 1912, and to R. A. Widenmann, September 25, 1912, Osborne Papers; Rollins, *Roosevelt and Howe*, p. 54.

48. "New York in the Campaign," ed., XL (July 13, 1912), 4.

49. Alexander S. Bacon to Anson L. Gardiner, August 20, 1912, in Sulzer Papers; *Buffalo Evening Times*, July 13, 1912; *New York World*, July 11, 21, and 25, 1912, in EPKC, 1911–1936, vol. 1; *Tammany Times*, XLI (August 3, 1912), 3; John B. Stanchfield to Woodrow Wilson, July 22, 1912, Woodrow Wilson Papers (LC); Daniels, *The Wilson Era*, p. 80; Link, *Wilson*, pp. 470, 481; *New York Times*, August 2, 1912. Some Tammany critics seized upon James O'Gorman's close relationship with the Wilson campaign to boom the senator for Murphy's replacement as leader of the New York State Democratic party.

50. *New York Times*, August 12, September 13, 14, and 30, 1912; *New York Telegram*, September 8, 1913, in EPKC, 1911–1936, vol. 1; Link, *Wilson*, pp. 495–496; *New York World*, in "Newspaper Clippings," vol. 34, Sulzer Papers; *Syracuse Post-Standard*, September 30, 1912; M. F. Collins to Charles F. Murphy, September 13, 1912, in Sulzer Papers.

51. Morgenthau, *All in a Life-Time*, p. 157; Broesamle, *McAdoo*, p. 71; McAdoo, *Crowded Hours*, pp. 168–169; "Diary of Edward M. House,"

September 25, 1912, vol. 1, p. 1, Edward M. House Papers (Yale University Library). For an interpretation of these events that argues Murphy thus capitulated to Wilson, see Link, *Wilson*, p. 497. A different interpretation can be found in McInerney, "The Election of 1912," pp. 212–214.

52. *New York Times*, September 30, October 1, 3, 1912; *New York World*, September 27 and October 1, 1912, in "Newspaper Clippings," vol. 34, Sulzer Papers; *Tammany Times*, XLI (September 28, 1912), 9–10; *Buffalo Evening Times*, October 1, 1912; *Syracuse Post-Standard*, September 30, October 2, 1912; *Syracuse Herald*, October 1, 2, 1912; Jacob A. Friedman, *The Impeachment of Governor William Sulzer* (New York: Columbia University Press, 1939), pp. 28–29.

53. *New York Times*, October 3, 1912; *Buffalo Evening Times* and *Syracuse Post-Standard*, October 3, 1912. The platform reiterated Wilson's pledge on a lower tariff and mildly endorsed the record of the Dix administration, pointing to the income tax amendment, direct election of U.S. senators, home rule, and (with reference to the work of the FIC) "the most advanced labor legislation in the history of the State." It pledged a host of labor and social reforms, including a workmen's compensation law and a measure regulating more effectively tenement house manufacturing; a referendum on woman suffrage; and a statewide direct primary. It even called for a state constitutional convention that would consider such reforms as the initiative and referendum and the short ballot.

54. *New York American*, October 4, 1913, *Buffalo Enquirer*, n.d., in "Newspaper Clippings," vol. 35, Sulzer Papers; *New York American*, October 6, 1912, ibid., vol. 36; *Buffalo Evening Times*, October 4, 5, 1912; R. A. Widenmann to Thomas Mott Osborne, October 8, 1912, Osborne Papers; *Albany Times-Union*, October 7, 1912; *New York Times*, October 4, 1912.

55. *Syracuse Post-Standard*, October 3, 1912; Thomas Mott Osborne to Oswald Garrison Villard, October 5, 1912, Oswald Garrison Villard Papers (Harvard University Library); John T. Hettrick, "Reminiscences" (OHP, 1949), p. 191. Osborne himself continued to register disgust during the campaign and tendered only a weak endorsement of the Sulzer ticket. He remained especially critical of McAdoo and O'Gorman for their work at the Syracuse convention (Osborne to R. A. Widenmann, October 14, 1912, and to D. J. Van Aucken, October 29, 1912, Osborne Papers).

56. Frederick M. Davenport, "Reminiscences" (OHP, 1952), p. 60; *New York World*, September 5, 1912. For other aspects of the Wilson effort, see Link, *Wilson*, pp. 499–500; McInerney, "The Election of 1912," pp. 295–298, and Daniels, *The Wilson Era*, p. 86. The Wilson campaign in New York is narrated in Link, *Wilson*, pp. 489–491, 494–496, 521–522.

57. *Rochester Democrat and Chronicle,* October 30, 1912; *Buffalo Evening Times,* October 11, 20, 23, 27, and 30, 1912; *Buffalo Evening News,* October 25, 1912; *New York Times,* September 29, October 1, 3–6, 11, 18, 20, 22, 24, 31, and November 1, 1912; Oscar Straus to Elmer C. Adams, October 19, 1912, Straus Papers. The Straus campaign is also summarized in Naomi Cohen, *A Dual Heritage: The Public Career of Oscar S. Straus* (Philadelphia: The Jewish Publication Society of America, 1969), pp. 212–217.

58. *New York Times,* November 6, 7, 1912. For details on election returns, voter turnout, and New York City-upstate percentage breakdowns, see Appendix II.

59. *Buffalo Evening Times,* November 7, 1912; *Buffalo Courier, Rochester Herald, Syracuse Post-Standard,* and *Utica Daily Press,* November 6, 1912. The wards with a high proportion of native-born voters that witnessed a heavy Progressive vote were: in Buffalo, the 17th, 20th, 23rd, 24th, and 25th; in Rochester, the 12th and 19th; in Syracuse, the 13th, 16th, 17th, and 19th; and in Utica, the 7th and 15th. The ethnic wards mentioned here can be identified by referring to Appendix II, Table 4, for which only Democratic percentages are given. The average Progressive vote in each category, however, exceeded 25 percent.

60. Samuel Koenig, "Reminiscences" (OHP, 1950), p. 14; *New York Times* and *New York Tribune,* November 7, 1912; unidentified author to George W. Aldridge, November 7, 1912, George W. Aldridge Papers (RML).

61. *New York Tribune,* November 6, 1912. The Progressive assembly victories came in the 8th, 10th, and 31st assembly districts of Manhattan, and the senate victory came in the 27th district, where A. J. Parker ran with Republican support.

62. *New York Call,* November 6, 1912. The Socialist increase in New York City over 1910 ran from approximately 3,000 votes in the gubernatorial election to 6,000 in the presidential contest. Statewide the Socialists did even better, scoring a 52 percent increase over their vote two years earlier. Many of these gains were made in upstate cities like Buffalo, Rochester, Schenectady, Troy, and Utica (*Albany Times-Union,* November 6, 1912, and *New York Call,* November 10, 1912). For the comparative Socialist vote, see Appendix II, Table 3.

63. *New York Call,* November 7, 1912; Melvyn Dubofsky, "Success and Failure of Socialism in New York City, 1900–1918: A Case Study," *Labor History,* IX (1968), 365–367; "Report of the Executive Secretary of Local New York for the Year 1912," n.d., in the Julius Gerber Collection (Cornell University Microfilm).

64. *Buffalo Evening News,* November 7, 1912.

CHAPTER 5

1. *New York Tribune,* November 6, 1912.
2. See especially Arthur S. Link, *Woodrow Wilson and the Progressive Era, 1910–1917* (New York: Harper and Brothers, 1954), chs. 3 and 9.
3. Thomas Mott Osborne to John E. Eastmond, April 12, 1913, Osborne to R. A. Widenmann, February 12, April 12, 1913, Thomas Mott Osborne Papers (Syracuse University Library); Frank Freidel, *Franklin D. Roosevelt: The Apprenticeship* (Boston: Little, Brown and Company, 1952), p. 174.
4. William S. Bennet, "Reminiscences" (OHP, 1951), p. 123. This biographical sketch is drawn from Jacob A. Friedman, *The Impeachment of Governor William Sulzer* (New York: Columbia University Press, 1939), ch. I; Edgar L. Murlin, *New York Red Book: An Illustrated Legislative Manual, 1913* (Albany: J. B. Lyon, 1913), pp. 33–38; and *New York Times,* October 18, 1913.
5. William Sulzer to Chester C. Platt, October 6, 1910, William Sulzer Papers (Cornell University Library); *Tammany Times,* XXIX (September 18, 1906), 6; XXXIII (September 12, 1908), 7; XXXVII (September 3, 1910), 6; and (September 24, 1910), 8. Much of the information in this paragraph is gleaned from the Sulzer Papers and the Platt Papers, also housed in the Cornell University Library. For a similar interpretation, see Friedman, *The Impeachment,* pp. 24–26.
6. Norman Hapgood, "The Dr. Cook of Politics," *Harper's Weekly,* LVIII (August 23, 1913), 25; John Lord O'Brian, "Reminiscences" (OHP, 1972), p. 124; Robert Binkerd, "Reminiscences" (OHP, 1949), p. 33; *New York Evening Mail,* January 4, 1913, in EPKC, 1911–1936, vol. 1; *New York Evening Post,* October 4, 1912.
7. *Public Papers of Governor William Sulzer, 1913* (Albany: J. B. Lyon, 1913), pp. 6–7, 21–39; *Albany Times-Union,* January 3, 1913; *New York Times,* January 3, 5, 1913; *New York World,* January 4, 1913, in "Newspaper Clippings, 1913–1914," Sulzer Papers.
8. *New York Sun,* February 4, 1913; *New York Times,* February 12, 1913; Chester C. Platt to Thomas Mott Osborne, January 6, 1913, Sulzer Papers. One of Sulzer's key appointments, that of Judge Edward E. McCall, as chairman of the New York City Public Service Commission, was reportedly very pleasing to Charlie Murphy (*New York Times,* February 5, 1913).
9. Amasa Thornton to William Sulzer, February 1, 1913, Sulzer Papers; *New York Press,* January 8, 1913, in "Newspaper Clippings, 1913–1914," Sulzer Papers.
10. *New York Times,* January 23, February 12, 1913; *Buffalo Courier,* March 5, 1913; Friedman, *The Impeachment,* pp. 45–47; Samuel Bell

Thomas, *The Boss or the Governor* (New York: The Truth Publishing Co., 1914), pp. 98–99.

11. *Public Papers of Sulzer,* pp. 832–834; *Buffalo Courier,* March 8, 1913; *New York Times,* January 22, 1914.

12. Thomas Mott Osborne to William Sulzer, February 17, 1913, and Sulzer to Osborne, February 19, 1913, Osborne Papers; Franklin D. Roosevelt to William G. Rice, January 10, 1913, Franklin D. Roosevelt Papers (FDRL); Rudolph W. Chamberlain, *There Is No Truce: A Life of Thomas Mott Osborne* (New York: The Macmillan Co., 1935), pp. 187–188.

13. *Buffalo Courier,* March 10, 12, 13, and 14, 1913; *New York Times,* March 10–13, 1913; *Public Papers of Sulzer,* pp. 848, 855–856; *New York Senate Journal,* 136th session (Albany: J. B. Lyon, 1913), p. 575.

14. *Buffalo Evening News,* January 6, 1913, in "Newspaper Clippings, 1913–1914," Sulzer Papers; *New York Times,* February 4, 5, 1913; *New York World, New York Sun,* and *Buffalo Morning Express,* February 4, 1913; *New York Evening Mail,* February 4, 1913, in EPKC, 1911–1936, vol. 1; *New York Journal,* February 7, 1913. The Sulzer "Newspaper Clippings" at Cornell and the Kilroe Collection at Columbia contain a wealth of material on the press' critical attitude toward Sulzer in the early days of his administration.

15. Anthony J. Schreiber to William Sulzer, February 7, 1913; Samuel Bell Thomas to Sulzer, February 19, March 8, 1913, Sulzer Papers. See also Henry Morgenthau, *All in a Life-Time* (Garden City, N.Y.: Doubleday, Page and Co., 1922), p. 169.

16. William Sulzer to Ralph Pulitzer, February 17, 1913, to Don C. Seitz, February 20, 1913, and to Frank Cobb, March 10, 1913, Sulzer Papers; *New York Times,* February 6, March 21, 1913; *Albany Times-Union,* March 26, 1913; *New York Senate Journal,* 136th session, appendix I, p. 107; Friedman, *The Impeachment,* pp. 52, 55–56.

17. *New York Times,* March 29, April 18, 22, and 23, 1913; Friedman, *The Impeachment,* pp. 65–70.

18. *New York Times,* March 12, April 7, 1913; Thomas Mott Osborne to William Sulzer, March 14, 1913, Sulzer Papers.

19. Friedman, *The Impeachment,* p. 58; *Albany Knickerbocker-Press,* February 3, 1913, in "Newspaper Clippings, 1913–1914," Sulzer Papers; *New York Times,* March 13, 1913; *Albany Evening Journal,* March 25, 1913.

20. *New York Times,* February 14, May 4, 1913; Paul C. Wilson, "Governor Sulzer's Financial Program," *The Survey,* XXIX (1913), 857–858. On the health department, see Walter I. Trattner, *Homer Folks: Pioneer in Social Welfare* (New York: Columbia University Press, 1968), pp. 168–172. The Public Health Law of 1913, concludes Trattner, "still remains the basis of health administration in New York State" (p. 172).

21. *New York World,* December 23, 1912, and *New York Herald,* February 6, 1913, in "Newspaper Clippings, 1913–1914," Sulzer Papers; *New York Times,* February 1, 6, and 13, 1913.
22. *New York Times,* February 13, 14, 27, and May 3, 1913; *New York Sun,* April 23, 1913, in "Newspaper Clippings, 1913–1914," Sulzer Papers; William Sulzer to W. P. Hamilton, January 30, 1913, to A. P. Pujo, February 15, 1913, to Henry Clews, February 17, 1913, to Ralph Pulitzer, February 17, 1913, and to Don C. Seitz, February 20, 1913, Sulzer Papers.
23. Lawrence A. Tanzer, "Legislative Interference in Municipal Affairs and the Home Rule Program in New York," *National Municipal Review,* II (1913), 597–604; *New York Times,* April 11, 18, and May 4, 1913.
24. "New Laws for Social Justice," *The Outlook,* CIV (1913), 84–85; *New York World,* April 3, 1913, in EPKC, 1911–1936, vol. 2; Frank I. Cobb to William Sulzer, April 4, 1913, Sulzer Papers.
25. Robert F. Wesser, *Charles Evans Hughes: Politics and Reform in New York, 1905–1910* (Ithaca: Cornell University Press, 1967), chs. XI and XII. The disagreement among Democrats took place on the question of whether statewide primaries meant automatically the elimination of the state nominating convention. Many supporters of the primary wanted to retain the principle of party responsibility and proposed devices like party nominating committees.
26. Frank M. Loomis to Franklin D. Roosevelt, January 25, 1913, Roosevelt Papers; *New York Times,* January 25, February 18, 1913; *Public Papers of Sulzer,* p. 106.
27. *New York Tribune,* April 6, 1913, in "Newspaper Clippings, 1913–1914," Sulzer Papers; *Buffalo Courier,* April 11, 15, 1913. Lustgarten had prodded Sulzer only a few days earlier (Lustgarten to Sulzer, April 2, 1913, Sulzer Papers).
28. *New York Herald,* May 30, 1913, in EPKC, 1911–1936, vol. 2. The arguments against the Sulzer primary are outlined in Friedman, *The Impeachment,* pp. 85–86.
29. "Governor Sulzer's Primary Campaign," *The Outlook,* CIV (1913), 85; *New York Times,* April 11, May 8, and June 1, 1913; Friedman, *The Impeachment,* p. 99; W. A. Swanberg, *Citizen Hearst: A Biography of William Randolph Hearst* (New York: Charles Scribner's Sons, 1961), p. 288. Hearst had earlier recommended to Sulzer that the Democrats pass the measures to which they were pledged and "some other measures to which they are not pledged" to stave off fusion of progressive Democrats (Hearst to Sulzer, April 16, 1913, Sulzer Papers).
30. *New York World,* April 28, 30, 1913; Theodore Roosevelt to William Sulzer, June 12, 1913; Chester C. Platt to Warner W. Sweet, June 10, 1913, and to St. Clair McKelway, July 15, 1913, Sulzer Papers; *New York Times,* June 11, 1913.

31. "Governor Sulzer's Fight on Tammany," *The Literary Digest*, LV (1913), 1164–1165. See also "Governor Sulzer's Primary Campaign," *The Outlook*, CIV (1913), 85; "Governor Sulzer's Fight," *The Independent*, LXXIV (1913), 1120–1121; and "Governor Sulzer and the Fight for Direct Primaries," *Review of Reviews*, XLVII (1913), 682–686. That the Sulzer campaign captured enormous attention in the state is witnessed by the large number of press clippings from both New York City and the upstate in "Newspaper Clippings," Sulzer Papers.

32. "Report of the Committee on Legislation of the Citizens Union for the Sessions of 1913," p. 14, Citizens Union Collection (NYPL).

33. *Public Papers of Sulzer*, pp. 190–196; *New York Times*, April 30, 1913; *Albany Times-Union*, May 1, 1913.

34. Friedman, *The Impeachment*, pp. 90–91; "Memorandum *in re* situation in Westchester County," n.d., Sulzer Papers. The most flagrant example of a major bill that Sulzer vetoed for "political" reasons was the Murtaugh electric power bill that would have established a publicly owned generating plant on the Mohawk River to serve the Albany area. Most critical of the veto were Lieutenant Governor Glynn (of Albany) and his allies (*Albany Times-Union*, May 28, 1913, and *New York World*, May 29, 1913). Robert Wagner also insisted that Sulzer vetoed the bill calling for a state constitutional convention in return for support of his primary measure (*Albany Times-Union*, June 18, 1913).

35. William Sulzer to Norman Mack, April 23, 1913; Chester C. Platt to Edward Murphy, June 2, 1913, Sulzer Papers; *Public Papers of Sulzer*, p. 1312; *New York Times*, May 17, 20, 1913. Sulzer often went public with his threats. To Mike Walsh, Democratic leader of Westchester County, he said: "You have four assemblymen and a senator from your county who recognize you as leader. If one of them votes against the people on this [direct primary] bill you will have the hardest fight of your life right at home, for I will go after you there" (*Buffalo Courier*, April 25, 1913).

36. *New York Sun*, April 29, 1913, in *EPKC, 1911–1936, vol. 2*; *New York Times*, April 25, 30, May 1, 23, 1913; *Albany Times-Union*, June 17, 1913.

37. *Albany Times-Union*, April 30, May 1, 1913; *New York Times*, May 1, 22, 1913; *New York Senate Journal*, 136th session, p. 1825; *New York Assembly Journal*, 136th session, p. 3300; Anthony Griffin to William Sulzer, May 21, 1913, Anthony Griffin Papers (NYPL).

38. George C. Thompson to Chester C. Platt, June 20, 1913; Frederick Ulrich to Chester C. Platt, June 20, 1913; and Ransom L. Richardson to Chester C. Platt, June 21, 1913, Sulzer Papers; *New York Globe*, June 25, 1913, in "Newspaper Clippings, 1913–1914," Sulzer Papers; *New York Senate Journal*, 136th session, appendix II, p. 69; *New York Assembly*

Journal, 136th session, vol. IV, pp. 35–36; *New York Times,* June 25, 1913. Sulzer's campaign for the primary yielded him 7 votes in the assembly and 2 votes in the senate.

39. *New York Senate Journal,* 136th session, appendix II, p. 72; *New York Assembly Journal,* 136th session, vol. IV, p. 48.

40. *New York Times,* May 18, 1913. Sulzer's friends maintain that at a Tammany conference at Delmonico's in New York City on May 20, Murphy and his advisors decreed Sulzer's removal from office if he did not refrain from attacking the organization and call a halt to the investigations of the prison and highway departments. See Jay W. Forrest and James Malcolm, *Tammany's Treason: Impeachment of Governor William Sulzer* (Albany: The Fort Orange Press, 1913), pp. 76–77. Murphy denied that such a conference ever took place, and Jacob Friedman adduces evidence to show that if it occurred it could not have been on May 20. See Friedman, *The Impeachment,* pp. 257–259.

41. One rumor was that, in mid-July, Murphy and his people decided to impeach Sulzer if the governor "did not come to terms with the Tammany leaders by August 1" (*New York Tribune,* October 18, 1913). See Friedman, *The Impeachment,* p. 135. This discussion of Murphy's strategy is based, not on information accruing from specific party conferences, but rather on subsequent events in the unfolding impeachment drama.

42. *New York Times,* June 12, 1913; *Albany Times-Union,* June 14, 26, 1913; *New York Senate Journal,* 136th session, appendix II, p. 78; *New York Assembly Journal,* vol. IV, p. 55.

43. *New York Times,* June 12, October 18, 1913; Friedman, *The Impeachment,* pp. 127–129, 131–132; *Albany Times-Union,* July 17, 1913. It is interesting to note that in the early part of the hearings the committee subpoenaed documents on Sulzer's probe of the prison department but was told that some of them could not be made available, since they contained privileged communications within the executive department (*Albany Times-Union,* July 3, 5, 1913).

44. *Albany Times-Union,* July 30, August 6, 7, and 8, 1913; Friedman, *The Impeachment,* pp. 143–146; *The Outlook,* CV (1913), p. 357. A full transcript of the Frawley hearings containing testimony on these and other charges can be found in the *New York Assembly Journal,* 136th session, vol. IV, appendix, pp. 310–438.

45. *Albany Evening Journal,* August 8, 1913; *Albany Times-Union,* August 8, 13, 1913; *New York Assembly Journal,* 136th session, vol. IV, pp. 102–103. The vote was 79–45, with 72 Democrats and 7 Republicans in favor of the resolution and 26 Democrats, 16 Republicans, and 3 Progressives against it.

46. William Sulzer to John Purroy Mitchel, July 15, 1913, Sulzer Papers. The Sulzer Papers contain scores of letters like this one to independent Democrats and others all over the state.

47. "The Impeachment of Governor Sulzer," *The Literary Digest*, XLVII (1913), 267–270; *New York Times*, August 9, 1913; *New York World*, August 11, 1913, in EPKC, 1911–1936, vol. 2; Friedman, *The Impeachment*, pp. 150–151.

48. B. S. Price to William Sulzer, August 19, 1913, Sulzer Papers; *New York Times*, August 11, 1913;; *Albany Times-Union*, August 11, 1913, in "Newspaper Clippings, 1913–1914," Sulzer Papers; *New York World*, August 14, 1913. Evidence was later introduced at the impeachment trial showing that Sulzer tried to appeal to Murphy through DeLancey Nicoll to halt the case against him. In return, Sulzer supposedly promised "to do whatever was right." See *Proceedings of the Court for the Trial of Impeachments: The People of the State of New York by the Assembly thereof against William Sulzer, as Governor*, 2 vols. (Albany: J. B. Lyon, 1913), vol. II, pp. 1105–1106, and *New York Herald*, October 8, 1913.

49. Thomas Mott Osborne to Oswald Garrison Villard, August 15, 1913, Oswald Garrison Villard Papers (Harvard University Library); *New York Times*, August 12, 1913. The Progressives were probably Sulzer's most consistent supporters all through the Frawley committee hearings and later during the impeachment proceedings.

50. *Albany Times-Union*, September 26, October 7, 1913; *Proceedings of the Court*, vol. II, pp. 1094–1095; Friedman, *The Impeachment*, ch. VI.

51. *Albany Times-Union*, October 3, 4, and 6, 1913; *New York World*, October 1, 1913, quoted in Friedman, *The Impeachment*, p. 217. Sulzer's defenders argue that he did not take the stand because one of his own witnesses, special investigator John A. Hennessy, was not allowed to testify on "what he found in some of the departments and the relation between his work and the activity of the Frawley committee." See Forrest and Malcolm, *Tammany's Treason*, p. 167. Another story had it that Sulzer battled his own attorneys up to the end, arguing that he would come clean "even though I pull the entire temple down upon my head." See *Albany Times-Union*, October 8, 1913.

52. *New York Times*, October 18, 1913; *Proceedings of the Court*, vol. II, pp. 1621–1622, 1748, 1759.

53. *Rochester Herald*, October 17, 1913. The *New York Times*, October 19, 1913, carried a summary of the attitude of the upstate press on the Sulzer removal.

54. Friedman, *The Impeachment*, p. 270.

55. See especially Thomas, *The Boss or the Governor*; Forrest and Malcolm, *Tammany's Treason*; Alexander C. Flick, ed., *History of the State of New York*, 10 vols. (New York: Columbia University Press, 1933–1937), vol. 7, pp. 194–195; and David M. Ellis et al., *A Short History of New York State* (Ithaca: Cornell University Press, 1967), p. 388. For a more recent version of the older interpretation, see Jacob I. Hotchkiss, "The Fall of William Sulzer," *NAHO*, IX (Fall 1976), 13–15.

56. *New York American,* September 18, 1913, in EPKC, 1911–1936, vol. 2; *New York Times* and *New York Tribune,* September 18, 1913; George W. Perkins to Hiram Johnson, September 19, 1913, George W. Perkins Papers (Columbia University Library); unidentified newspaper clippings, September 17, 27, 1913, in William Samson Scrapbooks, vol. 23 (RML). In Albany County several days passed before the McCabe forces were known to be clear-cut winners (*Albany Times-Union,* September 27, 1913).

57. *Buffalo Courier,* September 17 (the quotation), 18, 24, 1913; *Buffalo Evening Times,* September 8, 1913; *Buffalo Morning Express,* September 17, 1913.

58. "The Struggle in New York," *The Literary Digest,* XLVII (1913), 303–305; *New York Times,* January 26, 1913; William Hotchkiss to Theodore Roosevelt, June 20, 1913, Theodore Roosevelt Papers (LC); Herbert Parsons to Frederick C. Stevens, June 20, 1913, Herbert Parsons Papers (Columbia University Library).

59. *New York Times,* April 25, May 2, 11, 1913.

60. "Diary of Edward M. House," March 9, 1913, vol. 1, p. 130, in Edward M. House Papers (Yale University Library); Arthur S. Link, *Wilson: The New Freedom* (Princeton: Princeton University Press, 1956), p. 165. For a different view, see John J. Broesamle, *William Gibbs McAdoo: A Passion for Change, 1863–1917* (Port Washington, N.Y.: Kennikat Press, 1973), pp. 84–85.

61. William G. McAdoo to Joseph P. Tumulty, August 1, 1913, William Gibbs McAdoo Papers (LC). Osborne's complaint on this score was registered in Thomas Mott Osborne to R. A. Widenmann, July 16, 1913, Osborne Papers.

62. William G. McAdoo to Woodrow Wilson, April 11, 1913, McAdoo Papers; *New York Times,* April 15, 18, 1913; *New York Evening Post,* April 18, 1913; *New York Evening Mail,* April 19, 1913; and *New York Press,* April 24, 1913, in "Newspaper Clippings, 1913–1920" (FDRL); James Kerney, *The Political Education of Woodrow Wilson* (New York: The Century Company, 1926), p. 320. This entire episode is covered in detail in Link, *Wilson,* pp. 164–167; Broesamle, *McAdoo,* pp. 86–87; and Freidel, *Roosevelt,* pp. 176–177. For documents on Wilson's role, see Arthur S. Link, ed., *The Papers of Woodrow Wilson* (Princeton: Princeton University Press, 1978), vol. 27, pp. 407–408.

63. Kerney, *The Political Education,* p. 320; *New York Times,* May 8, 9, 1913. Some Tammanyites thought that Mitchel's appointment removed him from consideration for the mayoralty nomination. Nor was Tammany left out by the administration: Wilson named James W. Gerard, Murphy's confidant, as ambassador to Germany, and several positions in Mitchel's customs house went to Tammany. See Freidel, *Roosevelt,* p. 177.

64. *New York Sun,* July 18, 1913, in EPKC, 1911–1936, vol. 2; John Pur-

roy Mitchel to William L. Ransom, July 29, 1913, John Purroy Mitchel Papers (LC); William Prendergast, "Reminiscences" (OHP, 1948–1951), pp. 504–509; Edwin R. Lewinson, *John Purroy Mitchel: The Boy Mayor of New York* (New York: Astra Books, 1965), pp. 82–86.

65. *New York Times*, August 1, 1913; George McAneny, "Reminiscences" (OHP, 1949), p. 6; "The New York City Mayoralty," *The Outlook*, CIV (1913), 779; Lewinson, *Mitchel*, p. 86. The fusionist platform gained much publicity because it did not emphasize only honest, efficient, and economical government. It also maintained that the authority of city government extended to strict regulation of public utilities—municipal ownership if necessary; development of a system of parks and playgrounds as well as transportation facilities; socialization of entertainment and cultural facilities; and equalization of taxation for the sake of economic justice. See "The Progressive Municipal Platform," *National Municipal Review*, II (1913), 699.

66. *New York Times*, August 2, 1913; Samuel Koenig, "Reminiscences" (OHP, 1950), pp. 18–19; *New York American*, August 24, 1913, quoted in Lewinson, *Mitchel*, p. 92. For other editorial opinion on the Mitchel nomination, see "Mr. Mitchel's Chances against Tammany," *The Literary Digest*, XLVII (1913), 229–231.

67. John Purroy Mitchel to William J. Taylor, August 25, 1913, Mitchel Papers; Lewinson, *Mitchel*, p. 92. Later Mitchel, threatened by an independent Hearst candidacy, relented and accepted the league's endorsement but only after the executive committee of the fusion committee tendered its approval (*New York World*, September 27, 1913).

68. Amos Pinchot to Gifford Pinchot, January 27, 1913, Amos Pinchot Papers (LC); Prendergast, "Reminiscences," p. 518; *New York World*, June 4, 1913, in EPKC, 1911–1936, vol. 2; *New York Times*, August 23, 24, 1913; Lewinson, *Mitchel*, pp. 89–90; Mortimer Smith, *William Jay Gaynor: Mayor of New York* (Chicago: Henry Regnery, 1951), pp. 177–178.

69. Prendergast, "Reminiscences," pp. 521–522; *New York Sun* and *New York Press*, September 2, 1913, in EPKC, 1911–1936, vol. 2; *New York Times*, September 1, 5, and 7, 1913; *New York Tribune*, September 7, 1913; *New York American*, September 12, 1913, quoted in Lewinson, *Mitchel*, p. 93.

70. *New York Press*, quoted in "Death of Mayor Gaynor," *The Literary Digest*, XLVII (1913), 458–459; George W. Perkins to Theodore Roosevelt, January 6, 1914, Perkins Papers; *New York Times*, October 21, 26, 1913; *New York American*, October 21, 1913, in EPKC, 1911–1936, vol. 2.

71. *New York Tribune*, October 21, 1913; "Sulzer and Tammany," *The Literary Digest*, XLVII (1913), 797–799; *New York American*, October 26, 1913; and *New York World*, November 4, 1913, in EPKC, 1911–1936, vol. 2.

72. *Tammany Times,* XLIII (November 8, 1913), 1; *New York Times,* November 5, 6, 1913; "Tammany's Waterloo," *The Literary Digest,* XLVII (1913), 927–929; *New York Sun,* November 6, 1913, in EPKC, 1911–1936, vol. 3.
73. Unidentified newspaper clipping, August 26, 1913, in Samson Scrapbooks, vol. 23; *Rochester Herald,* November 5, 6, 1913; *New York Times, New York Tribune, Albany-Times Union, Rochester Evening Times, Buffalo Courier,* and *Syracuse Herald,* November 5, 1913.
74. *New York Times,* November 5, 1913; "The Elections," *The Outlook,* CV (1913), 555–557.
75. *New York Call* and *New York Tribune,* November 5, 1913. The progressive *New York Evening Post* commented that "there are signs of that steady advance which the Socialists profess to accept as indicative of ultimate success." See "Tammany's Waterloo," 927–929.
76. *Utica Herald-Dispatch* and *Buffalo Courier* (the quotation), November 6, 1913; *Buffalo Morning Express,* November 5, 1913, in "John Lord O'Brian Scrapbooks," vol. 4 (BECHSL); *New York Tribune,* November 7, 1913; *Buffalo Evening News,* November 5, 1913; *New York Times,* November 5, 6, 1913.

CHAPTER 6

1. Quoted in "Democracy Holding Its Own," *The Literary Digest,* XLVII (1913), 930–931.
2. William Barnes to Elihu Root, May 19, 1913, and Root to Barnes, May 20, 1913, Elihu Root Papers (LC); Robert E. O'Connor, "William Barnes, Jr.: A Conservative Encounters the Progressive Era" (Ph.D. diss., State University of New York at Albany, 1971), pp. 94–133; *Albany Evening Journal,* December 5, 6, 1913; *New York Times,* December 6, 1913.
3. *Tammany Times,* XLIII (November 8, 1913), p. 1.
4. *New York World,* November 16, 17, 1913; and *New York Evening Post,* November 12, 13, 1913, in EPKC, 1911–1936, vol. 3; *New York Times,* November 23–25, 1913; *Tammany Times,* XLIII (November 15, 1913), p. 2.
5. "New Democratic Party to Fight Tammany Hall," *New York Times Magazine,* November 16, 1913, p. 4; *New York Times,* November 25, December 1, 1913; *New York World,* November 6, 7, 1913; *New York Sun,* December 11, 1913; *New York Evening Post,* November 20, 28, 1913, in EPKC, 1911–1936, vol. 3; J. Joseph Huthmacher, "Charles Evans Hughes and Charles Francis Murphy: The Metamorphosis of Progressivism," *New York History,* XLVI (1965), 25–40.
6. This sketch is based on "Glynn, Whom Sulzer's Impeachment Makes Governor," *New York Times Magazine,* August 17, 1913, p. 2; "Governor Martin H. Glynn," in Edgar L. Murlin, *New York Red Book: An Il-*

lustrated Legislative Manual, 1914 (Albany: J. B. Lyon, 1914), pp. 29–44; James J. Walsh, "Martin H. Glynn, First Catholic Governor of New York," *Catholic World,* CXX (February 1926), 646–654; and "Martin H. Glynn," *Journal of the Irish-American Historical Society,* XXIV (1925), 279–281.

7. *Albany Times-Union,* September 30, October 1–3, 1906; *New York Tribune,* October 18, 1913; *New York Times,* November 13, 1913.

8. Robert Binkerd, "Reminiscences" (OHP, 1949), p. 40; *New York Times,* November 21, 1913.

9. Jacob A. Friedman, *The Impeachment of Governor William Sulzer* (New York: Columbia University Press, 1939), p. 91; *New York Times,* May 29, August 14, 1913; *New York World,* July 26, 1913.

10. *Albany Times-Union,* October 17, 1913.

11. "Glynn, Whom Sulzer's Impeachment Makes Governor," p. 2; *New York Times,* December 19, 1913.

12. *Public Papers of Martin Glynn, Governor* (Albany: J. B. Lyon, 1925), pp. 43–53.

13. Charles W. Thompson, "Why Glynn and Murphy Made Osborn Chairman," *New York Times Magazine,* March 8, 1914, p. 2; *New York World,* November 10, 1913; and *New York American,* November 11, 26, 1913, in EPKC, 1911–1936, vol. 3; *New York Times,* December 10, 1913.

14. *New York Senate Journal,* extra session, 136th session (Albany: J. B. Lyon, 1913), pp. 229–230, 242; *New York Assembly Journal,* extra session, 136th session (Albany: J. B. Lyon, 1913), pp. 239, 255–256, 262; Robert F. Wesser, "Conflict and Compromise: The Workmen's Compensation Movement in New York, 1890's–1913," *Labor History,* XII (1971), 345–372.

15. *New York Times,* December 13, 1913; *Albany Times-Union,* December 13, 1913, August 27, 1914; editorial, *The Survey,* XXXI (1913), 332–333; E. A. Bates to Martin Glynn, December 18, 1913, in N.Y.S. Federation of Labor, *Proceedings, Fifty-first Annual Convention* (Schenectady, 1914), n.p.

16. *Public Papers of Glynn,* pp. 9–25; *New York Tribune,* January 8, 1914; *New York Times,* March 18, April 28, and May 21, 1914; Martin H. Glynn, "Efficiency Methods in Government," *The Outlook,* CVI (1914), 234–236; "Governor Glynn's Fight for the Taxpayer," *Tammany Times,* XLIV (August 8, 15, 1914), 1.

17. "The War on Murphy," *The Literary Digest,* XLVIII (1914), 361–363; "Diary of Edward M. House," December 3, 1913, vol. 3, p. 382, and January 16, 1914, vol. 4, p. 14, in Edward M. House Papers (Yale University Library); *New York American,* January 9, 1914, in EPKC, 1911–1936, vol. 3; *New York Sun,* January 29, 1914, ibid., vol. 4; John J. Broesamle, *William Gibbs McAdoo: A Passion for Change, 1863–1917*

(Port Washington, N.Y.: Kennikat Press, 1973), p. 87; Arthur S. Link, *Wilson: The New Freedom* (Princeton: Princeton University Press, 1956), pp. 168–169.

18. *Albany Times-Union* and *New York Times,* February 10, 11, 1914; *New York Herald,* February 10, 1914, in "Newspaper Clippings, 1913–1920" (FDRL).

19. *New York World,* February 7, 1914; *New York American,* February 11, 1914, in EPKC, 1911–1936, vol. 4; *New York Times,* February 11, 15, 1914; "Why Glynn and Murphy," p. 2; *Albany Times-Union,* March 2, 1914.

20. Link, *Wilson,* p. 169; *New York World,* February 11, 1914, in EPKC, 1911–1936, vol. 4; Chester C. Platt to William Sulzer, January 27, 1914, William Sulzer Papers (Cornell University Library); Louis Antisdale to Montgomery Hare, February 13, 1914, House Papers.

21. William Gibbs McAdoo to Edward M. House, February 22, June 28, 1914, House Papers. For Wilson's "lid of silence," see Woodrow Wilson to Franklin D. Roosevelt, April 1, 1914, Woodrow Wilson Papers (LC), and Link, *Wilson,* p. 170.

22. Frank Polk to Franklin D. Roosevelt, March 16, 1914; Roosevelt to Montgomery Hare, August 31, 1914; and to Lawrence B. Dunham, August 14, 1914, Franklin D. Roosevelt Papers (FDRL); *New York Tribune,* August 13, 14, 1914; *New York Herald,* August 14, 1914, in "Newspaper Clippings, 1913–1920" (FDRL); Frank Freidel, *Franklin D. Roosevelt: The Apprenticeship* (Boston: Little, Brown and Company, 1952), pp. 179–180, 183. Wilson's clarification of his support of the Glynn-McCombs group would come as a result of cross-pressures, one set deriving from Roosevelt and his people and the other from Tammany congressmen who bridled at charges presumably made by administration spokesmen that they were "the representatives of crooks and grafters, and political buccaneers." In a series of conferences in late July, the president refused to come out for Roosevelt and repudiated the attacks on Tammany. (See Freidel, *Roosevelt,* pp. 182–183; *New York Times,* July 22, 23, and 24, 1914; and *New York World,* July 30, 1914, in EPKC, 1911–1936, vol. 5.)

23. *Albany Times-Union,* August 17, 24, 26, and 27, 1914; *New York World,* August 26, 27, 1914; *New York Evening Post,* August 27, 1914, in EPKC, 1911–1936, vol. 5.

24. *Albany Times-Union,* August 22, 26, 1914; *New York World,* August 21, 1914; and *New York American,* August 26, 1914, in EPKC, 1911–1936, vol. 5; Franklin D. Roosevelt to Louis M. Howe, August 22, 1914, and Howe to Roosevelt, August 24, 1914, Louis M. Howe Papers (FDRL); Freidel, *Roosevelt,* pp. 184–185; Alfred B. Rollins, Jr., *Roosevelt and Howe* (New York: Alfred A. Knopf, 1962), 105–106.

25. Louis M. Howe to Lathrop Brown, September 21, 1915, Howe Papers;

Albany Times-Union, August 18, 26, and 28, September 1, 4 and 21, 1914; *New York Times,* September 29, 30 and October 3, 1914. The Roosevelt campaign is well covered in Freidel, *Roosevelt,* pp. 185–188, and Rollins, *Roosevelt and Howe,* pp. 106–107. Glynn's campaigning was limited mainly to the county (and state) fairs.

26. *New York Times,* October 16, 1914; *New York Sun,* October 2, 1914, in EPKC, 1911–1936, vol. 5; *Albany Times-Union,* September 29, 1914; Broesamle, *William Gibbs McAdoo,* p. 89; Link, *Wilson,* pp. 171–172.

27. *New York Times,* May 31, 1914.

28. George E. Mowry, *Theodore Roosevelt and the Progressive Movement* (Madison: University of Wisconsin Press, 1947), p. 291; William A. Prendergast, "Reminiscences" (OHP, 1948–1951), p. 648. The Progressive troubles of 1913–1914 are analyzed in Mowry, ch. 11. See also John A. Garraty, *Right-Hand Man: The Life of George W. Perkins* (New York: Harper and Brothers, 1957), ch. XV, and John A. Gable, *The Bull Moose Years: Theodore Roosevelt and the Progressive Party* (Port Washington, N.Y.: Kennikat Press, 1978), chs. 7 and 8.

29. *Tammany Times,* XLIV (February 7, 1914), 1; *New York Times,* February 13, 1914. In April 1914, Amos Pinchat wrote to his brother Gifford: "In New York . . . the Progressive Party is simply melting away like snow" (April 7, 1914, Amos Pinchot Papers [LC]).

30. Theodore Douglas Robinson to Frederick M. Davenport, May 1914, Frederick M. Davenport Papers (Syracuse University Library); Oscar S. Straus, "Diary, 1914–1919," June 7, 1914, Oscar S. Straus Papers (LC); *New York Times,* May 25, 29, 31, and June 3, 1914.

31. George W. Perkins to Theodore Roosevelt, June 8, 1914, George W. Perkins Papers (Columbia University Library); Herbert Parsons to William Calder, January 26, 1914, and Parsons to Charles S. Whitman, May 26, 1914, Herbert Parsons Papers (Columbia University Library); William Barnes to Elihu Root, April 24, 1914, Root Papers; O'Connor, "William Barnes, Jr.," p. 136; *New York Times,* May 29, 1914.

32. Ogden Mills to Herbert Parsons, August 3, 1914, Parsons Papers; *Albany Times-Union,* July 21, 1914; *New York Times,* May 6, 29, June 3, 16, 18, 24, 26, and July 19, 1914; Theodore Roosevelt to Arthur H. Lee, June 29, 1914, in *LTR,* vol. VII, p. 769; Roosevelt to Lyman Abbott, June 29, 1914, in "Abbott-Roosevelt Papers," Theodore Roosevelt Collection (Harvard University Library). The Progressive charge against Whitman was based on the fact that as a fusionist in 1913 he also accepted the Tammany nomination for district attorney.

33. Frederick M. Davenport to Theodore Roosevelt, July 3, 1914, Davenport Papers; Theodore Roosevelt to William Loeb, July 22, 1914, William Loeb Microfilm (Harvard University Library); George W. Perkins to Progressives, July 22, 1914, in Davenport Papers; O'Connor, "William

Barnes, Jr.," pp. 136–137; *Albany Times-Union,* July 21–23, 1914; "New Alignments at Armageddon," *The Literary Digest,* XLIX (1914), 219–220; *New York World,* August 20, 1914, in EPKC, 1911–1936, vol. 5.

34. *New York Tribune,* August 22, 1914; Theodore Roosevelt to John C. O'Laughlin, August 27, 1914, *LTR,* vol. VII, pp. 813–815; *New York Times,* August 28, 1914; Ernest Harvier to William Bourke Cockran, September 23, 1914, William Bourke Cockran Papers (NYPL); *Albany Times-Union,* September 30, October 1, 1914. After the Sulzer-Roosevelt conference, Sulzer behaved as if Roosevelt promised not to interfere in the Progressive primary (William Sulzer to Theodore Roosevelt, August 25, 29, 1914, Sulzer Papers). Roosevelt categorically denied that he made such a promise (Roosevelt to Sulzer, August 31, 1914, Sulzer Papers).

35. *New York World,* September 1, 1914; Henry L. Stimson to Elihu Root, September 14, 1914, Root Papers; *New York Times,* September 30, 1914; *Albany Times-Union,* October 2, 1914; Frederick C. Tanner, "Reminiscences" (OHP, 1950), p. 82.

36. *Buffalo Courier,* October 17, 24, 1914; *Tammany Times,* XLIV (October 31, 1914), p. 4; *New York American,* October 29, 1914, in EPKC, 1911–1936, vol. 6; *Buffalo Evening Times,* October 27, 1914; *Albany Times-Union,* October 1, 3, 6–8, 14–16, 21, 23, 26–30, and November 2, 1914; *New York Times,* October 13, 1914.

37. For the general background of the anti-Catholicism in 1914, see John Higham, *Strangers in the Land: Patterns of American Nativism, 1865–1920* (New Brunswick: Rutgers University Press, 1955), pp. 175–184, and Edward M. Levine, *The Irish and Irish Politicians: A Study of Cultural and Social Alienation* (Notre Dame: University of Notre Dame Press, 1966), pp. 73–82.

38. *Albany Times-Union,* October 22, 1914; *Utica Daily Observer* and *Buffalo Courier,* October 21, 1914; "Villainous Campaigning," ed. (Syracuse) *Catholic Sun,* October 30, 1914. In a statewide canvass the *New York World* (October 27, 1914) reported that these documents were mainly the publications of evangelical Protestantism such as *The Menace* out of Aurora, Missouri; *The Peril* from Pennsylvania; the *Protestant Magazine* from Washington, D.C.; and the *Reform Bulletin,* published in Albany, New York, by the Reverend O. R. Miller, a civic crusader.

39. *Buffalo Evening Times* and *Albany Times-Union,* October 28, 1914; *New York Times,* October 27, 1914. James W. Gerard later charged that "Wadsworth supporters flooded the western part of New York State, always strongly Protestant, with circulars stating that I was a Roman Catholic." See *My First Eighty-three Years in America* (Garden City, N.Y.: Doubleday and Co., 1951), p. 216. Wadsworth's biographer rejects this charge out of hand. See Martin L. Fausold, *James W. Wadsworth, Jr.: The Gentleman from New York* (Syracuse: Syracuse University Press, 1975), 90–91.

40. *Buffalo Evening Times,* October 29, 1914; *Buffalo Morning Express,* October 30, 1914; *Rochester Herald,* November 3, 1914; *New York Times,* April 14, 1914; Platt to William Sulzer, April 27, 1914, William Sulzer Papers (Cornell University Library). Platt insisted later that he urged Sulzer "to repudiate the efforts made by many of his friends to stir up religious prejudice" (Platt to Franklin D. Roosevelt, November 19, 1914 [FDRL]).

41. Unsigned letter to William Sulzer, July 9, 1914; O. R. Miller to Frederick M. Davenport, August 10, 1914; Secretary of State Committee to Charles Whitman, October 10, 1914; A. J. Bourdeau to Samuel Bell Thomas, October 9, 1914; and Thomas to Bourdeau, October 13, 1914, Sulzer Papers.

42. William Sulzer to William C. Osborn, October 28, 1914, Sulzer Papers.

43. Highlighting the Sulzer campaign was the resignation, on October 27, of P. J. Quinn from Sulzer's staff. Quinn accused Sulzer and his allies of "endeavoring to create fanatical and irreligious doctrines, through hatred of a certain creed of which they are not familiar" and urged voters to support any of the other candidates (*Buffalo Evening Times,* October 28, 1914).

44. *Buffalo Evening Times,* November 4, 1914; *New York Tribune,* November 4, 5, 1914; *New York Times,* November 5, 1914. For the upstate-downstate percentage breakdown, see Appendix II, Table 2.

45. *Rochester Democrat and Chronicle,* November 4, 1914. The Polish 2nd ward in Utica and Buffalo's East Side wards (9th and 10th) showed an increased Democratic percentage and vote total over 1912. However, six of ten upstate Italian wards showed a decline in the Democratic vote from 1912, as did most of the German areas in Albany, Rochester, Syracuse, and Buffalo. The results in Jewish wards in Rochester and Syracuse were mixed. For Democratic percentages in the ethnic wards, see Appendix II, Table 4.

46. *New York Tribune* and *New York Times,* November 4, 5, 1914. For voter turnout and Democratic voting percentages in New York City's heavily ethnic districts, see Appendix II.

47. *New York Tribune,* November 4, 1914; *New York Call,* November 4, 5, 1914; "Some Other Election Results Last Week," *The Survey,* XXXIII (1914), 167; "The Socialist Congressman," *The Outlook,* CVIII (1914), 617; Melvyn Dubofsky, "Success and Failure of Socialism in New York City, 1900–1918: A Case Study," *Labor History,* IX (1968), 361–375. For the comparative Socialist vote, see Appendix II, Table 3.

48. These districts were the Bronx 32nd, 34th, and 35th and Brooklyn's 22nd. The eastern European Jewish districts where the 1914 Socialist vote surpassed the 1910 vote were Manhattan's 26th and Brooklyn's 23rd.

49. Link, *Wilson,* pp. 468–469; *Buffalo Evening Times,* November 5, 1914;

"The Republican Revival," *The Literary Digest*, XLIX (1914), 937–938; *Utica Daily Observer*, November 5, 1914. On the "depression," see also *Syracuse Post-Standard*, November 2, 1914. A series of articles appeared in the *Albany Times-Union* (July 20, August 14, 17, 1914) on the rise in food prices due in large part to shortages created by processors and farmers taking advantage of the war in Europe.

50. *Utica Daily Press*, November 4, 1914; *Rochester Democrat and Chronicle*, October 23, November 6, 1914; *Syracuse Post-Standard*, November 2, 1914; *New York Tribune*, November 4, 1914; Theodore Roosevelt to Meyer Lissner, November 16, 1914, *LTR*, vol. VIII, pp. 843–845; Frederick M. Davenport to unidentifiable correspondent, November 8, 1914, Davenport Papers.

51. *New York Tribune*, November 4, 1914. A summary of New York City press opinion is given in the *New York Times*, November 4, 1914, and a good sampling appears in EPKC, 1911–1936, vol. 5, and in the "Chauncey J. Hamlin Scrapbooks," vol. 2, 1914 (BECHSL). Other opinion is found in *The Outlook*, CVIII (1914), 562–563, *Buffalo Courier*, *Rochester Herald*, *Syracuse Herald*, and *Utica Daily Observer*, November 4, 1914.

52. *New York Times*, *New York Tribune*, November 4, 1914. Sulzer's own correspondence shows that he and his supporters truly believed that many of "his" votes went to Whitman to prevent Glynn's election (John B. Neily to William Sulzer, November 4, 1914; Sulzer to Isidore Rosenberg, and Chester C. Platt to Sulzer, November 5, 1914, Sulzer Papers).

53. *New York Times*, November 4, 1914; *Rochester Herald*, November 4, 1914; *Buffalo Evening Times*, August 24, 1914; and *Brooklyn Times*, August 29, 1914, in "Hamlin Scrapbooks," vol. 2, 1914.

54. *New York Times*, November 7, 1914; *Utica Daily Press*, October 23, 1914.

CHAPTER 7

1. *New York Call*, November 5, 1914.
2. The term "cultural liberalism" has been used to signify this extension of Democratic progressivism. See especially J. Joseph Huthmacher, *Senator Robert F. Wagner and the Rise of Urban Liberalism* (New York: Atheneum, 1968), p. 42. See also John D. Buenker, *Urban Liberalism and Progressive Reform* (New York: Charles Scribner's Sons, 1973), ch. 5.
3. *New York World*, April 2, 1915, in EPKC, 1911–1936, vol. 7; "A Lost Opportunity," *World's Work*, XXX (1915), 16–17; Henry L. Stimson to Frank B. Kellogg, November 8, 1915, Henry L. Stimson Papers (Yale University Library).
4. *New York Times*, March 17, 1915; *New York Tribune*, April 28, 1915, in EPKC, 1911–1936, vol. 7; "Senator Brown Would Repeal Labor

Laws," *Legislative Labor News and Labor Advocate,* IV (February 15, 1915), 1, 4. Whitman's approval of Brown's position is quoted in *New York Evening Post,* April 14, 1915, in EPKC, 1911–1936, vol. 7.

5. *Revised Record of the Constitutional Convention of the State of New York, 1915,* 4 vols. (Albany: J. B. Lyon, 1916), IV, 4212; Frederick M. Davenport, "The Prenomination Campaign: Popular Government Still on Trial," *The Outlook,* CXII (1916), 911–915; "Health Insurance Argued at Albany," *The Survey,* XL (1918), 18–20.

6. "New York and National Politics," ed., *The Outlook,* CIX (1915), 2–3; Walter I. Trattner, *Homer Folks: Pioneer in Social Welfare* (New York: Columbia University Press, 1968), pp. 174–176; Tenement House Department Officers to Robert deForest, May 3, 1915, Lawrence Veiller Papers (Columbia University Library); Lawrence Veiller to J. G. Phelps Stokes, March 8, 1915, J. G. Phelps Stokes Papers (Columbia University Library); "Saving the Labor, Safety, Health and Housing Codes of New York," *The Survey,* XXXIV (1915), 142–144; "Labor Opposes Consolidation," *Legislative Labor News and Labor Advocate,* IV (April 9, 1915), 1.

7. "The Republican Exhibit at Albany," ed., *Nation,* C (1915), 376–377; Henry F. Pringle, *Alfred E. Smith: A Critical Study* (New York: Macy-Masius, 1927), p. 176; *New York Times,* April 17, 25, 1915; *New York World,* April 2, 10, 1915; *New York Evening Post,* April 2, 14, 1915. On the Republican "failure" in Albany, see also "A Poor Beginning," ed., *The Outlook,* CIX (1915), 848. In some instances Governor Whitman did use the veto power to retain FIC legislation. See Thomas J. Kerr IV, "New York Factory Investigating Commission and the Progressives" (D.S.S. diss., Syracuse University, 1965), pp. 118–119.

8. Elting Morison, *Turmoil and Tradition: A Study of the Life and Times of Henry L. Stimson* (Boston: Houghton Mifflin, 1960), p. 218; Gerald D. McKnight, "The Perils of Reform Politics: The Abortive New York State Constitutional Reform Movement of 1915," *New-York Historical Society Quarterly,* LXIII (1979), 215–216. Some of the press did not miss the connection between the record of the legislature and prospects for constitution-making. See *New York World,* April 3, 1915, in EPKC, 1911–1936, vol. 7.

9. *New York Times,* March 23, 1913, December 2, 1913, February 17, and March 18, 1914; *New York World,* May 16, 1913, in "Newspaper Clippings, 1913–1914," William Sulzer Papers (Cornell University Library); *New York Tribune,* May 15, 1913, April 8, May 1, 1914. Support for the convention was heavy in several of the strongly Democratic wards in Buffalo (*Buffalo Morning Express,* April 8, 1914), and in the Democratic and Progressive wards in Syracuse (*Syracuse Herald,* April 7, 1914, and *Syracuse Post-Standard,* April 8, 1914).

10. *Albany Times-Union,* August 26, October 30, 1914; *New York World,* August 27, 1914, in EPKC, 1911–1936, vol. 7; *New York Times,* August 28, October 25, and November 14, 1914; *New York Tribune,* October 31, 1914.

11. Henry L. Stimson to Elihu Root, n.d., Elihu Root Papers (LC); Seth Low to Stimson, July 14, 1914, Stimson Papers; John Lord O'Brian, "Reminiscences" (OHP, 1972), pp. 136–141; Morison, *Turmoil and Tradition,* pp. 214–215; Philip C. Jessup, *Elihu Root,* 2 vols. (New York: Dodd, Mead and Company, 1938), vol. II, pp. 291–292; *New York Tribune* and *New York Times,* August 20, 1914. For a full treatment of the relationship between constitutional reorganization and the feud between the progressive and conservative wings of the Republican party, consult McKnight, "The Perils of Reform Politics," 203–212. A good summary of the progressive Republican position on the needed constitutional changes can be found in *New York Evening Post,* November 5, 1914, in EPKC, 1911–1936, vol. 6.

12. *Syracuse Post-Standard,* October 28, 1914. See also *Rochester Democrat and Chronicle,* November 5, 1914, and *Utica Daily Press,* October 30, November 7, 1914. An excellent representation of the anti-Tammany campaign can be found in "Chauncey J. Hamlin Scrapbooks," 2 vols. (BECHSL), vol. 2.

13. *New York Times,* January 14, 1915; Jessup, *Elihu Root,* vol. II, pp. 291–292. Stimson's influence over Root on specific aspects of constitutional revision is stated in Thomas Schick, *The New York State Constitutional Convention of 1915 and the Modern State Governor* (New York: National Municipal League, 1978), p. 55.

14. William Barnes to Elihu Root, April 10, 1915, Root Papers; *New York Evening Post,* November 2, 1914, in EPKC, 1911–1936, vol. 6; "Making a Constitution," *New Republic,* II (1915), 278–279; John Lord O'Brian, "Local Politics" (OHP: Buffalo and Erie County Historical Society, 1970), p. 21.

15. *New York Times,* April 7, 1915.

16. *Revised Record,* I, 342, 478; *New York Times,* March 28, April 6, 1915; William Barnes to Elihu Root, April 10, 1915, Root Papers. Barnes's role at the convention is outlined in Robert E. O'Connor, "William Barnes, Jr.: A Conservative Encounters the Progressive Era" (Ph.D. diss., State University of New York at Albany, 1971), pp. 144–146. The 1894 apportionment formula provided that no county could have more than one third of all the senators and that no two contiguous counties could have more than one half of all the senators. This provision, of course, was directed against New York City.

17. The last two were adopted. See *Revised Record,* IV, 4115, 4120. The minimum wage amendment, however, was allowed to die in the convention.

18. *New York Times,* May 7, June 9, 1915; *New York Tribune,* June 25, 1915; *New York World,* July 2, 1915, in EPKC, 1911–1936, vol. 7; *Revised Record,* I, 429. The Brackett move, it was widely believed, was also meant to give fair warning to the leadership as to the upstate position regarding the short ballot, the attempt to increase gubernatorial power, the executive budget, and the proposal for an appointive rather than an elective judiciary.

19. *Revised Record,* I, 627–634, 625; *New York Sun,* July 1, 1915, in EPKC, 1911–1936, vol. 7; *New York Times,* July 1, 1915.

20. Henry L. Stimson to Mabel Stimson, June 30, 1915; Stimson to DeLancey Verplanck, July 2, 1915, Stimson Papers; *New York Times* and *New York Tribune,* September 4, 1915; *Revised Record,* IV, 4015, 4036 Actually, the final vote on senate apportionment came on a compromise version of Brackett's amendment, which would have lumped together all the counties in New York City under the one-half clause of the 1894 constitution.

21. *New York Times,* August 11, 19, 1915; *Revised Record,* II, 1635, 1657–1659, 1672; Henry L. Stimson to William Howard Taft, August 25, 1915, Stimson Papers. For a good summary of the debate on the executive budget, see Schick, *The New York State Constitutional Convention,* pp. 88–91.

22. *New York Times,* August 25, September 3, 1915; Elihu Root to William J. Schieffelin, August 12, 1915, Root Papers; *Revised Record,* III, 2935; IV, 3885. Low's compromise home rule measure granted to each municipality the general right to "control its property, affairs and municipal government" as well as the power to alter its own charter within this area. It also prohibited the legislature from passing any but general laws "applying alike to all cities." Smith's amendments would have permitted a municipality to *adopt* and *change* its own charter and would have given constitutional backing to a statutory right of firemen and policemen to carry dismissals to the courts. A summary of the debate on the short ballot is given in Schick, *The New York State Constitutional Convention,* pp. 92–100.

23. *New York Times,* September 11, 1915; *New York Sun,* September 10, 1915, in EPKC, 1911–1936, vol. 7; O'Brian, "Reminiscences," p. 194. The final vote on the proposed revisions was 118–133 (*Revised Record,* IV, 4300–4301).

24. *Revised Record,* IV, 4324, 4301, 4305–4306, 4309; *New York American,* July 1, 1915, in EPKC, 1911–1936, vol. 7; Alfred E. Smith, *Up to Now: An Autobiography* (New York: The Viking Press, 1929), pp. 145–146.

25. *New York Times,* October 5, 1915; Henry L. Stimson to A. J. Hemphill, September 9, 1915, to Samuel H. Beach, October 8, 1915, and to Paul S. Andrews, October 18, 1915, Stimson Papers. The campaign is well covered in EPKC, 1911–1936, vol. 8.

26. Henry L. Stimson to Herbert Parsons, n.d., and October 19, 1915, Herbert Parsons Papers (Columbia University Library); Edgar T. Brackett to George W. Perkins, September 14, 1915, George W. Perkins Papers (Columbia University Library); Henry L. Stimson to Paul S. Andrews, September 27, 1915, to Samuel Koenig, October 20, 1915, and to Elihu Root, October 20, 1915, Stimson Papers; unidentified newspaper clipping, October 23, 1915, in EPKC, 1911–1936, vol. 8; *New York Herald,* October 31, 1915; *New York Times,* October 7, 22, 24, and November 4, 1915. This possibility—and especially Root's prospects—prompted George Perkins to launch a statewide letter-writing and advertising campaign that cost him over $45,000. This campaign was not really waged under the auspices of the Progressive party, such as it was in 1915, though Perkins did make use of the staff at Progressive headquarters in New York City. See George W. Perkins to Hiram Johnson, November 8, 1915, and to Francis M. Hugo, December 31, 1915, Perkins Papers; "Open Letter to Progressives," November 17, 1915, in Elon Hooker Papers, Theodore Roosevelt Collection (Harvard University Library); and John A. Garraty, *Right-Hand Man: The Life of George W. Perkins* (New York: Harper, 1957), pp. 320–326. Perkins's campaign is also thoroughly analyzed in McKnight, "The Perils of Reform Politics," 203–227.

27. *New York Times,* October 7, 8, 1915; *New York World,* September 16, 22, October 30, 1915; and *New York Evening Post,* October 11, 1915, in EPKC, 1911–1936, vol. 7. Stimson, of course, blamed Tammany Hall for the partisan nature of the campaign (Henry L. Stimson to John B. Rose, October 25, 1915, Stimson Papers).

28. Unidentified newspaper clipping, October 22, 1915, in EPKC, 1911–1936, vol. 7; *New York Times,* November 1, 1915.

29. "Labor Opposition to New York Constitution," *The Survey,* XXXV (1915), 81; "Labor Unites Effectively at the Ballot Box," *Legislative Labor News and Labor Advocate,* IV (December, 1915), 5; Samuel Gompers, "Mr. Root's Government Rejected," *American Federationist,* XXII (1915), 1051–1055. Labor's campaign is examined in Irwin Yellowitz, *Labor and the Progressive Movement in New York State, 1897–1916* (Ithaca: Cornell University Press, 1965), pp. 240–244.

30. *Official Proceedings, Fifty-third Annual Convention* (Glens Fall, N.Y.: 1916), 57, 59; *New York Call,* October 5, 23, 31, November 1, 3, and 4, 1915; *New York Times,* October 5, 6, 10, and 22, 1915; "Vote 'No' on New Constitution Nov. 2," *Legislative Labor News and Labor Advocate,* IV (December, 1915), 1, 16.

31. November 5, 1915. The official tally was 400,423 for the revised constitution and 910,462 against it (Francis M. Hugo, *Manual for the Use of the Legislature of the State of New York, 1916* [Albany: J. B. Lyon, 1916], p. 857).

32. *New York Tribune,* November 3, 1915; *New York American,* November 4, 1915, in EPKC, 1911–1936, vol. 8. Even a recent student of the 1915 convention considers the failure to divide up the proposed changes as the "foremost of the reasons" for the document's ultimate defeat. See Schick, *The New York State Constitutional Convention,* p. 119.

33. *New York Tribune,* November 3, 1915; Morison, *Turmoil and Tradition,* p. 224.

34. Alexander C. Flick, ed., *History of the State of New York,* 10 vols. (New York: Columbia University Press, 1933–1937), vol. 7, pp. 292–293; Francis Russell, *The Great Interlude: Neglected Events and Persons from the First World War to the Depression* (New York: McGraw-Hill, 1964), pp. 7–20; Robert D. Ward, "The Origin and Activities of the National Security League, 1914–1919," *Mississippi Valley Historical Review,* XLVII (1960), 51–65; Howard D. Wheeler, "Plattsburg—What Is It?" *Harper's Weekly,* LXI (1916), 202; Winthrop Lane, "The 'Militarist' Laws of New York," *The Survey,* XXXVI (1916), 313–314.

35. "Statement of New York State County Chairmen of the Progressive Party," February 19, 1916; and George W. Perkins to Progressives, February 17, 1916, in Hooker Papers.

36. *New York Times,* August 3, 7, 1915; George E. Mowry, *Theodore Roosevelt and the Progressive Movement* (Madison: University of Wisconsin Press, 1947), pp. 332–333; William H. Harbaugh, *Power and Responsibility: The Life and Times of Theodore Roosevelt* (New York: Farrar, Straus and Cudahy, 1961), p. 486.

37. "The Public Eye and the People in It," *National Monthly,* VII (1915), 87; Frank B. Lord, "Political Comment," ibid., VII (1916), 221, 233; *New York Tribune* and *Albany Evening Journal,* February 16, 1916; S. D. Lovell, *The Presidential Election of 1916* (Carbondale and Edwardsville: Southern Illinois University Press, 1980), p. 21. Lovell argues that the Republican state conclave, which sent unpledged delegates to the national convention (with three of four delegates at large meeting and endorsing Root) meant "that Roosevelt was through in New York since Root had been instrumental in driving Roosevelt from the national convention four years before." Theodore Roosevelt later credited Root's speech with having placed the Republican party on just the right track as far as preparedness was concerned (Roosevelt to Henry L. Stimson, June 19, 1916, *LTR,* vol. VIII, p. 1065).

38. *New York Times,* September 15, 21, and 29, 1916; Horace Wilkinson et al., to Charles S. Whitman, August 11, 1916, and John Gerdes to Progressives, September 7, 1916, in Hooker Papers; O'Connor, "William Barnes, Jr.," pp. 151–152. The platform forged in the Saratoga convention did call for the resubmission of the woman suffrage question to the elec-

torate. But it excoriated Wilson's preparedness policy, attacked the administration's Mexico policy, denounced the Underwood tariff, blasted the Adamson Act, and went on record for the arbitration of industrial disputes. It appealed to "patriotism," "honor," and "prestige." The Republicans almost included a plank calling for the repeal of the direct primary but decided against it in part for fear that the Progressives would consider the document "reactionary."

39. John J. Broesamle, *William Gibbs McAdoo: A Passion for Change, 1863–1917* (Port Washington, N.Y.: Kennikat Press, 1973), pp. 90–91; *New York Times*, November 14, 1915; *New York World*, March 13, 1916, in EPKC, 1911–1936, vol. 10. For the Wilsonians' determination to carry New York, see "House's Plan of Campaign" in Charles Seymour, *The Intimate Papers of Colonel House*, 2 vols. (Boston: Houghton Mifflin Company, 1926), vol. II, p. 361. See also Lovell, *The Presidential Election*, p. 121.

40. *Buffalo Evening Times*, January 7, 1932, in "Local Biographies, Clippings," vol. II (BECPL); *Buffalo Courier*, April 11, 1916; *Buffalo Evening News*, April 12, 1916; *Albany Times-Union*, January 27, March 1, 2, 1916; *Syracuse Herald*, March 2, 1916; "Baffled in Finding an Issue," *National Monthly*, VII (1916), 242; "Memorandum," April 4, 1916; and William C. Osborn to Woodrow Wilson, April 10, 1916, William C. Osborn Papers (privately held); *New York Times*, March 1, 1916; unidentified newspaper clipping, April 16, 1916, in EPKC, 1911–1936, vol. 10. Osborn had become unacceptable to Tammany because of his constant carping against federal appointments to Murphy's allies and his open support of the 1915 constitutional changes. On the Buffalo situation, Fitzpatrick himself did not assume the duties of chairman of the Erie County Democratic Committee but turned it over to Daniel Riordan in a "harmony" move.

41. Broesamle, *William Gibbs McAdoo*, pp. 91–92; unidentified newspaper clipping, April 23, 1916, in EPKC, 1911–1936, vol. 10; Nancy Joan Weiss, *Charles Francis Murphy, 1858–1924: Respectability and Responsibility in Tammany Politics* (Northhampton, Mass.: Smith College, 1968), p. 71. During the campaign a further deal was made between Wilson and Tammany. Murphy promised to commit the organization's full resources to Wilson's reelection in return for which the Wilson administration would keep hands off the 1917 municipal elections in New York City (*Syracuse Herald*, September 24, 1916; *New York Journal*, September 24, 1916, in EPKC, 1911–1936, vol. 10).

42. *Albany Times-Union*, March 1, 1916; A. J. Elias to Chester C. Platt, March 3, 1916, Chester C. Platt Papers (Cornell University Library). The spring Democratic primaries made the question all the more poignant, for the regulars emerged triumphant all across the state. See *Buffalo Courier* and *New York Times*, April 5, 1916.

43. *Syracuse Herald,* August 12, 1916; "The Democratic Situation in New York," *Nation,* CIII (1916), 100–101.
44. Yellowitz, *Labor and the Progressive Movement,* pp. 244–245; *New York Times,* June 12, 25, July 5, 6, August 2, 8, 1916; *New York World,* August 3, 1916, in EPKC, 1911–1936, vol. 10.
45. "Memorandum," August 4, 1916, in Osborn Papers; *New York Sun,* August 3, 5, 1916; *New York American,* August 2, 3, 11, 1916; and *New York Tribune,* August 11, 1916, in EPKC, 1911–1936, vol. 10; *Albany Times-Union,* August 11, 1916; Franklin D. Roosevelt to Eleanor Roosevelt, August 14, 1916, in Elliot Roosevelt, ed., *F.D.R.: His Personal Letters, 1905–1928,* 4 vols. (New York: Duell, Sloan and Pearce, 1947–1950), vol. 2, pp. 320–321.
46. *Albany Times-Union* and *Rochester Herald,* August 12, 1916; Walter Chambers, *Samuel Seabury: A Challenge* (New York: Century Co., 1932), p. 188. Two weeks later Seabury resigned his judgeship and outlined his progressive program for New York: order and economy in state government; "popular government" in Albany; conservation of natural resources; regulation of monopoly and special privilege; and the promotion of just relations between employees and employers. See *New York Times,* August 29, 1916.
47. *Rochester Evening Times,* October 25, 1916; *Buffalo Morning Express,* October 26, 27, 29, November 2, 7, 1916; *Buffalo Evening News,* November 3, 1916; *Syracuse Post-Standard,* November 3, 1916. Illustrations of Republican press comment can be found especially in the *Buffalo Morning Express,* October 31, November 7, 1916; *Buffalo Evening News,* October 26, 27, 31, November 1, 3, 7, and 8, 1916; and *Rochester Evening Times,* October 27, November 6, 1916. The quotation is taken from the *Syracuse Post-Standard,* November 4, 1916. The success of such Republican appeals in Buffalo and Rochester is covered, respectively, in John T. Horton et al., *History of Northeastern New York,* 5 vols. (New York: Lewis Historical Publishing Co., Inc., 1947), vol. I, pp. 374–375; and Blake McKelvey, *Rochester: The Quest for Quality, 1890–1925* (Cambridge: Harvard University Press, 1956), pp. 294–295.
48. *Buffalo Morning Express,* October 24, 1916. For a friendly opinion from labor on Hughes's contributions to social and labor reforms, see *Legislative Labor News,* V (October 27, 1916), 3.
49. *New York Times,* September 24, October 11, 13, 15, and 19, 1916. Some of these quotations are taken from Herbert Mitgang, *The Man Who Rode the Tiger: The Life and Times of Judge Samuel Seabury* (Philadelphia: J. B. Lippincott Company, 1963), pp. 116–121.
50. *New York Sun,* August 21, 1916, in EPKC, 1911–1936, vol. 10. Seabury was especially bitter about the Progressive endorsement of Whitman because he believed he had extracted a commitment from Theodore Roo-

sevelt. See Mitgang, *The Man Who Rode the Tiger,* pp. 112–114, 118; and Chambers, *Samuel Seabury,* pp. 180–181, 183.

51. Thomas M. Henderson, "Tammany Hall and the New Immigrants, 1910–1921" (Ph.D. diss., University of Virginia, 1973), pp. 141–146. See also William M. Leary, Jr., "Woodrow Wilson, Irish-Americans, and the Election of 1916," *Journal of American History,* LIV (1967), 58–64; Clifton J. Child, *The German-Americans in Politics, 1914–1917* (Madison: The University of Wisconsin Press, 1939), esp. chap. IV; and Thomas J. Kerr IV, "German-Americans and Neutrality in the 1916 Election," *Mid-America,* XLIII (1961), 102–103.

52. *New York Tribune,* September 19, 1916; *Syracuse Herald,* September 20, 1916; *New York Times,* September 21, 1916. What was astonishing about the strong Bacon bid was that he had entered the race late and most of the Republican leaders supported Calder. Bacon ran very well in the up-state, particularly in the rural areas where military preparedness had a great appeal (*Syracuse Herald,* September 21, 1916). It was New York City that turned the tables on Bacon; here the more moderate Calder, a congressman from Brooklyn, won by a margin of over two to one.

53. "The President and the Hyphen," *The Literary Digest,* LIII (1916), 935; *New York World,* August 26, October 18, 25, and 26, 1916; and *New York Evening Post,* October 24, 1916, in EPKC, 1911–1936, vol. 10; Philip Gleason, *The Conservative Reformers: German-American Catholics and the Social Order* (Notre Dame: University of Notre Dame Press, 1968), p. 168; Norman Hapgood to Edward M. House, October 9, 1916, Edward M. House Papers (Yale University Library). For the anti-Catholicism theme, see Arthur S. Link, *Wilson: Campaigns for Progressivism and Peace, 1916–1917* (Princeton: Princeton University Press, 1965), pp. 130–134. Link's Chapter IV deals thoroughly with the last part of the 1916 campaign.

54. Leary, "Woodrow Wilson," 64–65; John A. Beadles, "The Syracuse Irish, 1812–1928: Immigration, Catholicism, Socio-Economic Status, Politics and Irish Nationalism" (Ph.D. diss., Syracuse University, 1974), pp. 259–260; Seymour, *The Intimate Papers,* vol. II, pp. 374–375; "The Diary of Edward M. House," November 2, 1916, in House Papers; *New York Times,* November 5, 1916. For Wilson's New York State campaign tour, see Lovell, *The Presidential Election,* pp. 121–122.

55. November 8, 1916; *Syracuse Post-Standard,* November 8, 9, 1916. For details on election returns and voter turnout, see Appendix II, Table 1 and Figure 1.

56. For Democratic percentages in the heavily ethnic wards, see Appendix II, Table 4.

57. *New York Tribune,* November 9, 1916; *Albany Times-Union,* November 8, 9, 1916; *New York Evening Post,* November 8, 1916, in

EPKC, 1911–1936, vol. 10. The *New York Times* (November 9) compared Wilson's vote total in New York City with that of the Tammany candidate for president of the board of aldermen and concluded that there was no substance to the charge of Tammany knifing.

58. For the Irish vote in Manhattan, see Leary, "Wilson and the Election of 1916," 70; for the Irish, German, and Italian vote, see Henderson, "Tammany Hall and the New Immigrants," pp. 157–159. Henderson's sample Italian election districts in Manhattan's 1st, 28th, and 30th assembly districts show that Wilson lost the Italian vote in 1916 (see pp. 261, 267–268). Note that the analysis given here agrees with David Burner's in *The Politics of Provincialism: The Democratic Party in Transition, 1918–1932* (New York: Alfred A. Knopf, 1968), p. 236.

59. Henderson's sample Jewish areas show similar trends. See "Tammany Hall and the New Immigrants," pp. 159, 262–264, 266. The average increase in the Brooklyn districts was 7.6 percent and came largely on the strength of a 10.9 percent increase in the 21st and a 13.5 percent increase in the 23rd. In Manhattan the average increase per assembly district was 11.3 percent, whereas the total vote in the county declined 20 percent. The figures are based on the turnout in the presidential election.

60. October 26, 1916. For the campaign in these districts, see the *Call*, October 27, 28, 29, and 31, 1916.

61. *New York Call*, October 24, 31, November 9, 10, 1916; *New York Evening Post*, September 19, 1916, in EPKC, 1911–1936, vol. 10; Morris Hillquit, *Loose Leaves from a Busy Life* (New York: Macmillan, 1934), p. 118.

62. *Syracuse Post-Standard* and *New York Tribune*, November 8, 1916.

63. The nonmajor party vote statewide in 1916 was only 4.6 percent, the lowest in a presidential election since 1900. See Table 3 in Appendix II.

CHAPTER 8

1. Alexander C. Flick, ed., *History of the State of New York,* 10 vols. (New York: Columbia University Press, 1933–1937), vol. 7, pp. 283–303, 323–357. For Whitman and the 1918 legislature, see "Meager Work of New York Legislature," *The Survey,* XL (1918), 73; and *New York Times,* April 14, 1918.

2. David A. Shannon, *The Socialist Party of America: A History* (New York: Macmillan, 1955), p. 95; Maurice Isserman, "Inheritance Lost: Socialism in Rochester, 1917–1919," *Rochester History,* XXXIX (1977), passim; Julian Jaffe, *Crusade against Radicalism: New York during the Red Scare, 1914–1924* (Port Washington, N.Y.: Kennikat Press, 1972). For the changing attitude of the needle trades unions on the war question, see Melvyn Dubofsky, "Organized Labor and the Immigrant in New York City, 1900–1918," *Labor History,* II (1961), 182–210, and "Organized

Labor in New York City and the First World War, 1914–1918," *New York History*, XLII (1961), 3–23.

3. Edwin R. Lewinson, *John Purroy Mitchel: Boy Mayor of New York* (New York: Astra Books, 1965), chs. VIII–IX; Thomas M. Henderson, "Tammany Hall and the New Immigrants, 1910–1921" (Ph.D. diss., University of Virginia, 1973), pp. 169–171. An unusually good analysis of Mitchel's troubles and the election itself is provided in Kenneth S. Chern, "The Politics of Patriotism: War, Ethnicity, and the New York Mayoral Campaign, 1917," *New-York Historical Society Quarterly*, LXIII (1979), 291–313. The problems of price inflation and unemployment in New York City are treated, respectively, in Bruno Lasker, "The Food Riots," *The Survey*, XXXVII (1917), 638–641, and Donald S. Ritchie, "The Gary Committee: Businessmen, Progressives and Unemployment in New York City, 1914–1915," *New-York Historical Society Quarterly*, LVII (1973), 327–347. For an excellent discussion of the Gary school plan and its impact on the Mitchel administration, see Ronald D. Cohen and Raymond A. Mohl, *The Paradox of Progressive Education: The Gary Plan and Urban Schooling* (Port Washington, N.Y.: Kennikat Press, 1979), ch. 2. Wilson's disillusionment with Mitchel on preparedness is discussed in Henry Morgenthau, *All in a Life-Time* (Garden City, N.Y.: Doubleday, Page and Co., 1922), p. 238.

4. Lewinson, *John Purroy Mitchel*, ch. XII; *New York Times*, March 4, August 16, 1917; *New York World*, September 1, 1917; Ernest Harvier to William B. Cockran, September 12, 1917, William B. Cockran Papers (NYPL); Marvin Weinbaum, "New York County Republican Politics, 1897–1922, "The Quarter Century After Municipal Consolidation," *New-York Historical Society Quarterly*, L (1966), 63–94. In spite of Bennett's victory in the Republican primary, several GOP leaders, most notably in Brooklyn, continued to support Mitchel (*New York Times*, October 23, 1917).

5. James Weinstein, *The Decline of Socialism in America: 1912–1925* (New York: Vintage Books, 1969), pp. 152–153; Oswald Garrison Villard, "The New York City Mayoralty Election," *Nation*, CV (1917), 448–449; *New York Times*, July 24, 26, August 8, 15, September 22, October 2, 19, 21, 22, 23, 24, and November 7, 1917; "Hearst, Tammany, Mitchel, and America," *The Literary Digest*, LV (1917), 11–13. The campaign is treated in Weinstein, *The Decline*, pp. 159–164; Lewinson, *John Purroy Mitchel*, ch. XIII, and Zosa Szajkowski, *Jews, War, and Communism*, 2 vols. (New York: Ktav Publishing House, 1972), vol. I, ch. XI.

6. "New York's Return to Tammany," *The Literary Digest*, LV (1917), 12–13; *New York Times* and *New York Tribune*, November 8, 1917; Lewinson, *John Purroy Mitchel*, p. 245; "Common Welfare," *The Survey*, XXXIX (1917), 144–145. The vote totals were: Hylan, 313,956; Mitchel,

155,497; Hillquit, 145,332; and Bennett, 55,438. Outside Manhattan, Hillquit carried the Bronx 3rd, 4th, and 5th districts and Brooklyn's 6th, 14th, and 23rd districts. Interestingly, Hillquit did not do exceptionally well in the city's German districts: Manhattan's 16th, Brooklyn's 20th, and Queens's 2nd and 6th. Apparently the reason was that he made it clear to German leaders that his position on the war could not be considered pro-German. See Allen Ricker, "Victory for New York's Socialists," *Pearson's Magazine* (1918), 21–22; and Chern, "The Politics of Patriotism," esp. 301.

7. "New York's Return to Tammany," 12–13. On the Buffalo primary and general elections, see *Buffalo Morning Express*, October 17, November 7, 1917; *Buffalo Evening News*, October 17, 1917; *Buffalo Courier*, November 7, 1917; and (Buffalo) *New Age*, October 20, November 10, 1917. On Rochester, see *Rochester Herald*, November 7, 1917; *Rochester Union and Advertiser*, November 7, 8, 1917; and Isserman, "Inheritance Lost," 3–12. On Syracuse, see *Syracuse Herald*, October 24, 28, 31, November 4, 5, and 7, 1917. In the only statewide election in 1917, that of attorney general, Merton Lewis won easily; he did so on a sharply sectional division of the electorate, with an unusually strong upstate vote (*New York Tribune*, November 9, 1917).

8. Alan P. Grimes, *The Puritan Ethic and Woman Suffrage* (New York: Oxford University Press, 1967), chs. II, III, and V; Aileen S. Kraditor, *The Ideas of the Woman Suffrage Movement, 1890–1920* (Garden City, N.Y.: Doubleday and Co., 1971), passim; Norman H. Clark, *Deliver Us from Evil: An Interpretation of American Prohibition* (New York: W. W. Norton and Company, Inc., 1976), ch. 6.

9. Vira B. Whitehouse to Glenolen Bens, February 15, 1917, New York State Woman Suffrage Party Papers (NYPL); Harriet Stanton Blatch, "Woman Suffrage in New York," *National Monthly*, VI (1914), 80, 94; Doris Daniels, "Building a Winning Coalition: The Suffrage Fight in New York State," *New York History*, LX (1979), 59–80; Ronald Schaffer, "The New York City Woman Suffrage Party, 1909–1919," ibid., XLIII (1962), 269–287; Kraditor, *The Ideas*, p. 121.

10. Julius Gerber to Members of Locals in New York, November 7, 1911, New York City Socialist Party Papers (Cornell University Microfilm); Harriet Stanton Blatch and Alma Lutz, *Challenging Years: The Memoirs of Harriet Stanton Blatch* (New York: G. P. Putnam's Sons, 1940), pp. 125, 186–187, 189–190; *Albany Times-Union*, January 23, 1913; Ida Husted Harper, *History of Woman Suffrage, 1900–1920* (New York: Arno, 1969), vol. VI, pp. 458–459; Carrie Chapman Catt and Nettie R. Shuler, *Woman Suffrage and Politics: The Inner Story of the Suffrage Movement* (Seattle: University of Washington Press, 1969), p. 287.

11. Carrie Chapman Catt to Campaign District Chairmen, February 4, 1915,

Carrie Chapman Catt Papers (NYPL); *Buffalo Courier, Rochester Evening Times,* and *Syracuse Post-Standard,* November 3, 1915; *New York Times,* November 4, 1915; Blatch, *Challenging Years,* pp. 238–239. The statewide vote was 553,384 for and 748,332 against the referendum.

12. Carrie Chapman Catt to Leaders [Empire State Campaign Committee], November 17, 1915, Catt Papers; Abram Lipsky, "The Foreign Vote on Suffrage," *The American Hebrew,* November 26, 1915, in Lillian D. Wald Papers (NYPL); *Buffalo Morning Express,* October 25, 1915; *New York Times,* October 27–31, 1915; *New York Tribune,* November 5, 1915; Schaffer, "The New York Woman Suffrage Party," 282.

13. National Association for the Woman Suffrage Amendment, *Victory: How Women Won It* (New York: H. W. Wilson Co., 1940), pp. 115–118; Harper, *History of Woman Suffrage,* pp. 465, 476–478; 482; unidentified newspaper clipping, July 17, 1917, in "Syracuse in the World War, 1917–1919" (OPL); *New York Tribune,* October 27, 1917; *Buffalo Evening Times,* November 2, 1917; *Syracuse Herald,* November 4, 1917; *Albany Times-Union,* November 5, 1917; *Buffalo Courier,* November 6, 7, 1917.

14. *New York Tribune,* October 26, 27, 1917; *Syracuse Herald,* October 26, 1917. Similar statements by other supporters were quoted in *New York Times,* October 26, 1917, and *Buffalo Courier,* November 6, 1917.

15. Blatch, "Woman Suffrage," 80, 94; Mary K. Simkovitch, "Casual Reflections on the Election," *The Survey,* XXXIX (1917), 160–161, and "As to How the Vote Was Won," 176; National Association for the Woman Suffrage Amendment," *Victory,* p. 120.

16. *New York Times,* November 8, 1917; *Buffalo Courier* and *Syracuse Herald,* November 7, 1917. The final statewide vote on the referendum was 703,129 in favor and 600,776 opposed. The Buffalo ward-by-ward vote for the two referendums are given in *Buffalo Courier,* November 3, 1915, and November 7, 1917.

17. *Rochester Herald,* November 7, 1917; *New York Times,* November 8, 1917; "Suffragists Take New York," *The Literary Digest,* LV (1917), 14–15. Simkovitch, "Casual Reflections," 161; Barry Richard, "Mr. Murphy—The Politicians' Politician," *The Outlook,* CXXXVII (1924), 54–55. The Socialists did lay claim to the referendum victory ("Suffragists Take New York," 14–15; (Buffalo) *New Age,* November 10, 24, 1917; and *New York Call,* November 8, 1917).

18. *Albany Times-Union,* November 7, 1917; Harper, *History of Woman Suffrage,* p. 483. It is true that Republican State Chairman George Glynn issued orders to the upstate leaders to get out the vote for suffrage on Election Day. Doubtless, some did, but Barnes in Albany and Aldridge in Monroe balked, and the referendum lost in these counties (*New York Times,* November 13, 1917).

19. *New York Tribune,* January 20, 1918; *New York American,* February 22,

April 5, and May 18, 1918; *Brooklyn Standard-Union,* March 6, 1918; and *New York World,* June 17, 1918, in EPKC, 1911–1936, vol. 14. Democrats expressed delight at the registration for the fall primaries. While "Republican" women would probably outnumber "Democratic" women statewide, the percentage of women voters relative to New York City's total registration was higher than that in the upstate (32.5 percent to 30.9 percent). State Republican Chairman Glynn thus announced his displeasure with the Republican plight in the state (*New York Times,* May 26, 27, 1918).

20. Edward Marshall, "Is National Prohibition Actually Close at Hand?" *New York Times Magazine,* April 19, 1914, sec. 6, p. 10. For an excellent analysis of the prohibition movement, see James H. Timberlake, *Prohibition and the Progressive Movement, 1900–1920* (New York: Atheneum, 1970), and Clark, *Deliver Us from Evil,* esp. chs. 5–7.

21. Peter H. Odegard, *Pressure Politics: The Story of the Anti-Saloon League* (New York: Octagon Books, 1966), pp. 228, 231–233; *New York Times,* February 6, 25, March 1, 30, 1915; Thomas M. Coffey, *The Long Thirst: Prohibition in America, 1920–1933* (New York: W. W. Norton Co., 1975), p. 13; Marshall, "Is National Prohibition Close?"

22. *Rochester Evening Times,* November 3, 1915; *New York Times,* March 23, December 1, 1916; January 4, February 21, April 12, and May 8, 1917; *Albany Times-Union,* May 7, 8, 1917; Marshall, "Is National Prohibition Close?" William H. Anderson, "Reminiscences" (OHP, 1950), p. 9. The bill provided that all cities in New York State were local option "territory." In each instance, except for New York City, a petition carrying the signatures of one fourth of the votes cast in the last mayoralty election would place local option—divided into separate votes for the licensing of saloons, stores, drugstores, and hotels—before that city's electorate in April 1918. For New York City a double referendum was required on local option—the first asking for submission of the petition, the second on the question itself. A local option vote in New York City could not take place before 1919.

23. *New York Times,* June 3, 1917; January 27, April 15, 18, and 19, 1918; *Syracuse Post-Standard* and *Buffalo Evening Times,* April 18, 1918; *Syracuse Journal,* April 18, 1918, in Prohibition File (Onondaga County Historical Association). In one city, Amsterdam, separate voting machines, reported the *Utica Daily Observer* (May 1, 1918), recorded the vote by sex on the four license questions. The results showed that women were only slightly less in favor of licensing—that is, remaining wet—than men.

24. *New York Tribune,* November 12, 1916; *New York Times,* March 21, 1918.

25. *New York Times,* April 12, May 5, 15, 1917; *Albany Times-Union,* May 7, 8, 1918.

26. *New York Times,* February 21, March 18, 1918; *Albany Times-Union,* March 18, 1918. This conclusion rests on the legislative history of the 1918 session. On March 12, the assembly, refusing to bring out the federal amendment, passed a referendum resolution. The vote was 84–64, with 35 Republicans joining the 40 Democrats and 9 Socialists to constitute the majority. See *New York Assembly Journal,* 141st session (Albany: J. B. Lyon, 1918), pp. 707–708. Under pressure from Whitman the assembly later reversed this action. The senate in a close vote also refused to take up the federal amendment, then on March 21 voted 27–22 to advance a state constitutional amendment on prohibition. This, too, would ultimately require a referendum. In this vote 13 Democrats lined up with 14 Republicans to make up the majority. See *New York Senate Journal,* 141st session (Albany: J. B. Lyon, 1918), p. 611.
27. Merton Lewis to George W. Aldridge, April 19, 1918, George W. Aldridge Papers (RML); *New York Times,* May 8, 14, 20, and June 21, 1918; Anderson, "Reminiscences," p. 18; Ferdinand Pecora, "Reminiscences" (OHP, 1962), p. 160.
28. Robert E. O'Connor, "William Barnes, Jr.: A Conservative Encounters the Progressive Era" (Ph.D. diss., State University of New York at Albany, 1971), pp. 161–162; *New York Times,* June 11, July 20, September 1, 4, 5, and 8, 1918. When, in 1919, the New York legislature approved the federal prohibition amendment, some Republicans continued to balk. In the assembly eleven Republicans, six from New York City, bolted, and the final vote was 81–66. See *New York Assembly Journal,* 142nd session (Albany: J. B. Lyon, 1919), pp. 122–123. In the senate two Republicans bolted, and the final vote was 27–24. See *New York Senate Journal,* 142nd session (Albany: J. B. Lyon, 1919), p. 113. The senate vote came on the very day that the U.S. State Department declared that the proposed Eighteenth Amendment had been ratified by three quarters of the state legislatures (*New York Times,* January 30, 1919).
29. William Swanberg, *Citizen Hearst* (New York: Charles Scribner's Sons, 1961), pp. 311–312; "Issues in the Coming Election," *The Outlook,* CIX (1918), 508; *New York Times,* February 24, July 10, 1918; *New York Tribune,* April 24, 25, 1918; *New York World,* June 28, 1918, in EPKC, 1911–1936, vol. 14.
30. *New York Times,* March 26, 1918; *Albany Times-Union,* April 24, 25, 1918; *Syracuse Post-Standard,* April 24, 1918; *New York Tribune* and *Buffalo Courier,* April 25, 1918.
31. *Syracuse Post-Standard,* July 9, 10, 1918; *New York Times,* July 10, 1918; William Adams, "The 1918 Gubernatorial Election in New York State" (M.A. essay, SUNY at Albany, 1965), pp. 14–16.
32. *Buffalo Morning Express,* July 24, 1918; *New York Times,* July 14, 1918; William C. Osborn to William H. Kelley, July 22, 1918, William C. Os-

born Papers (privately held); *Syracuse Post-Standard* and *Buffalo Courier,* July 23, 1918; *Syracuse Herald,* July 25, 1918.

33. "Eliminating Hearst," *The Outlook,* CIX (1918), 539; *New York World,* July 25, 1918; *Rochester Herald,* July 24, 25, 1918; *New York Times,* July 24, 26, 1918.

34. July 26, 1918. Some believe that Murphy and his New York City friends had been working to create sentiment for Smith as early as June (Winfield Huppuch to Franklin D. Roosevelt, June 17, 1918, Franklin D. Roosevelt Papers [FDRL]). Others, by their accounts, intimate that this was not the case. See esp. Alfred E. Smith, *Up to Now: An Autobiography* (New York: The Viking Press, 1929), p. 159; and James W. Gerard, *My First Eighty-three Years in America: The Memoirs of James W. Gerard* (Garden City, N.Y.: Doubleday and Co., Inc., 1951), p. 287. Gerard and Binghamton Mayor Harry Walker were both ahead of Smith on the upstaters' list. Gerard claims that he was actually offered the gubernatorial nomination by Kelley but lost out because of a delay in obtaining "a release from Hearst" whom he had told earlier that he was not in the running.

35. William C. Youker to Alfred E. Smith, October 9, 1915, Citizens Union Collection (Columbia University Library); Norman Hapgood and Henry Moskowitz, *Up from the City Streets: Alfred E. Smith* (New York: Harcourt, Brace and Co., 1927), pp. 132–137; Joseph M. Proskauer, "Reminiscences" (OHP, 1961), p. 132; *Albany Times-Union,* October 28, 1918; *New York Times,* July 26, September 4, October 20, 21, and 30, 1918; Paula Eldot, "Alfred E. Smith: The Politician as Reformer" (Ph.D. diss., Yale University, 1961), pp. 13–14. Smith's victory over Osborn statewide was six to one (199,752 to 32,761). In New York City it was "phenomenal," averaging fifteen to one in Manhattan, ten to one in Brooklyn, twelve to one in Queens, and ten to one in the Bronx. All across the state, reported the *New York Times* (September 6, 1918), the results showed "a practically unbroken line of organization victories."

36. *Buffalo Morning Express,* September 5, 6, November 1, 3, 1918; *Rochester Democrat and Chronicle,* November 4, 1918; *New York Times,* September 23, October 23, 25, and 31, 1918. For Democratic unity after the primaries, see *Buffalo Evening Times,* November 2, 3, and 4, 1918.

37. *New York Times,* September 28, October 23, 1918; *Buffalo Morning Express,* October 31, 1918.

38. Walter B. Hayward, "Whitman versus Smith," *Nation,* CVII (1918), 482–483; Henry F. Pringle, *Alfred E. Smith: A Critical Study* (New York: Macy-Masius, 1927), p. 232; *New York Times,* October 21, November 3, 1918; *New York Telegram,* September 27, 1918; and *New York American,* October 19, 22, 1918, in EPKC, 1911–1936, vol. 14.

39. Frances Perkins, "Reminiscences" (OHP, 1955), book 2, pp. 208–219; *New York Times,* October 17, 1918; Smith, *Up to Now,* pp. 162–163;

Pringle, *Smith,* pp. 65–68; Matthew and Hannah Josephson, *Al Smith: Hero of the Cities* (Boston: Houghton Mifflin Co., 1969), pp. 191–192.

40. *Buffalo Courier,* November 6, 1918; *Rochester Democrat and Chronicle,* November 6, 7, 1918. The dramatic slippage in the Republican vote in Syracuse may have stemmed, in part at least, from an intraparty battle on the prohibition issue that had resulted in the resignation of Thomas Hendricks as chairman of the GOP county committee (*Syracuse Herald,* August 28, 29, September 4, 1918). For the comparative Democratic vote in the upstate cities, see Appendix I, Table 2. The turnout figure for 1918, as represented in Appendix II, Figure 1, is somewhat misleading. It is unusually low because it takes into account the total number of eligible voters—male *and* female—and this, of course, was the first time that women voted in a statewide gubernatorial election.

41. John A. Beadles, "The Syracuse Irish, 1812–1928: Immigration, Catholicism, Socio-Economic Status, Politics and Irish Nationalism" (Ph.D. diss., Syracuse University, 1974), p. 211; Melvyn Dubofsky, "Success and Failure of Socialism in New York City, 1900–1918: A Case Study," *Labor History,* IX (1968), 371–372; *New York Call,* November 6, 1918; *New York Times,* November 7, 1918. The Democratic-Republican fusion is covered in *New York American,* July 16, 1918; and *New York World,* August 1, 1918, in EPKC, 1911–1936, vol. 14. For a comparison of the Democratic vote in heavily ethnic areas in 1918 with that of the average for 1910–1916, see Appendix I, Table 3.

42. *New York Times,* November 6, 1918. See also *New York World* and *Rochester Herald,* November 9, 1918; and "The Republican Opportunity," *The Literary Digest,* LVI (1918), 14–15.

43. Discontent in essentially Republican districts was discussed in *New York Times,* October 3, 15, 1918; *Albany Times-Union,* October 30, 1918; and *Buffalo Courier,* November 3, 1918. The enrollment figures in the upstate outside the cities appeared to be large because enrollment was done, not by personal registration as in the cities, but by merely writing the names of eligible women in the poll books. See *New York Times,* October 27, 1918. Comparison of registration figures in the less populous upstate counties with actual vote totals thus shows a proportionately small percentage of the electorate going to the polls relative to Greater New York and the larger upstate cities.

44. *Syracuse Herald,* November 5, 6, and 7, 1918; *New York Times,* November 6, 1918; Warren Moscow, *Politics in the Empire State* (New York: Alfred A. Knopf, 1948), p. 93. In Syracuse and Brooklyn the women's vote was reported to be very heavy. In Brooklyn, also, a local tragedy—the Brighton train wreck killing ninety and injuring over one hundred people—made Whitman's "incompetent" public service commission vulnerable to strong Democratic attacks in the last days of the cam-

paign. In addition, Republican factionalism evidently helped produce an unusually heavy Democratic plurality in Kings County. For these factors, see Josephson, *Al Smith*, pp. 206–207; *Brooklyn Daily Eagle*, November 2, 5, and 6, 1918; *New York World*, November 7, 1918; and Pecora, "Reminiscences," pp. 157–159.

45. Moscow, *Politics*, p. 94. For the development of Smith's Democratic party as the party of the cities in New York State, see James Malcolm, *New York Red Book: An Illustrated State Manual, 1928* (Albany: J. B. Lyon, 1928), p. 379. See also Ralph J. Papaled, "The Democratic Party in Urban Politics in New York State: 1933–1938" (Ph.D. diss., St. John's University, 1978), pp. 17–20.

46. Republican standpattism in the 1920s is discussed in Moscow, *Politics*, pp. 72–73, and Marvin G. Weinbaum, "A Minority's Survival: The Republican Party of New York County, 1897–1960" (Ph.D. diss., Columbia University, 1965), p. 53. Speaking of New York City Republicanism in that decade, Moscow states that GOP district leaders in Manhattan "lived all during national prohibition on the pickings they got from dry-law corruption, plus a little federal patronage" (p. 129).

CHAPTER 9

1. See especially J. Joseph Huthmacher, "Urban Liberalism and the Age of Reform," *Mississippi Valley Historical Review*, XLIX (1962), 231–241; Huthmacher, "Charles Evans Hughes and Charles Francis Murphy: The Metamorphosis of Progressivism," *New York History*, XLVI (1965), 25–40; Huthmacher, *Senator Robert F. Wagner and the Rise of Urban Liberalism* (New York: Atheneum, 1968), chs. 1–3; John D. Buenker, *Urban Liberalism and Progressive Reform* (New York: Charles Scribner's Sons, 1973), passim; and Nancy Joan Weiss, *Charles Francis Murphy, 1858–1924: Respectability and Responsibility in Tammany Politics* (Northampton, Mass.: Smith College, 1968), ch. V.

2. Lee Benson, Joel Silbey, and Phyllis F. Field, "Toward a Theory of Stability and Change in American Voting Patterns: New York State, 1792–1970," in Joel Silbey et al., *The History of American Electoral Behavior* (Princeton: Princeton University Press, 1978), pp. 96–97. For the role of major party gubernatorial candidates in achieving political stability in such states as New York, see V. O. Key, Jr., *American State Politics: An Introduction* (New York: Alfred A. Knopf, 1956), pp. 233–234.

3. The ten-year estimate for naturalization in the period comes from Harold F. Gosnell, "The Chicago Black Belt as a Political Battleground," *American Journal of Sociology*, XXXIX (1933), 329–341. This estimate, however, is probably a conservative one. For estimates on specific groups that average out somewhat longer than ten years, see John P. Gavit, *Americans by Choice* (New York: Harper and Brothers, 1922), pp. 241, 245.

The slowness with which Italian and Jewish immigrants became citizens and voters is suggested in Thomas M. Henderson, "Tammany Hall and the New Immigrants, 1910–1921" (Ph.D. diss., University of Virginia, 1973), p. 113. Henderson cites a study that purports to show that in the period of World War I, 40 percent of these immigrants in the United States from six to nine years had not even yet registered their "first papers."

4. Henderson, "Tammany Hall and the New Immigrants," ch. VI, pp. 230–236, and Conclusion.

5. Richard L. McCormick, *From Realignment to Reform: Political Change in New York State: 1893–1910* (Ithaca and London: Cornell University Press, 1981), esp. ch. 9. A shorter version of this analysis can be found in McCormick, "Prelude to Progressivism: The Transformation of New York State Politics, 1890–1910," *New York History,* LIX (1978), 253–276. That even prior to 1910 ticket-splitting in New York was often most evident in the top executive offices in a given election is a point made in a yet unpublished paper authored by John F. Reynolds, entitled, "An Honest and Straight Party Vote: Ballot Reform and Split Ticket Voting in New Jersey and New York, 1880–1910."

6. For percentages of anti–major party voting, see Appendix II, Table 3.

7. The probable causes of the electoral malaise in New York State are brilliantly analyzed in McCormick, *From Realignment to Reform,* passim.

8. That the Massachusetts ballot had little real effect on straight-ticket voting is argued in Howard A. Scarrow, *Parties, Elections, and Representation in the State of New York* (New York and London: New York University Press, 1983), pp. 61, 57. On the direct primary see H. Feldman, "The Direct Primary in New York State," *American Political Science Review,* XI (1917), 494–518, and Scarrow, *Parties, Elections,* pp. 34–42. The primary did not work well because the 1913 law placed obstacles in the way of challenge contests; parties were still able to choose "preferred" candidates for statewide offices in the so-called unofficial conferences, as was done in 1914, 1916, and 1918; and the cost of mounting challenges was usually too high for independent contenders. In 1921 the state legislature repealed that section of the law which extended the primary to statewide offices, and New York State returned to the convention system. It was not until 1967 that the statewide direct primary was reenacted.

9. J. Ellswerth Missall, *The Moreland Act: Executive Inquiry in the State of New York* (New York: King's Crown Press, 1946), pp. 41, 45–47, 66, 75–76, and table on 137–138. The three Sulzer agencies were terminated in 1915. See Robert P. Kerker, *The Executive Budget in New York State: A Half-Century Perspective* (Albany: New York State Division of the Budget, 1981), pp. 15–16, for a brief history of the commission of efficiency and economy.

10. Alfred E. Smith, *Up to Now: An Autobiography* (New York: The Viking Press, 1929), p. 96; Huthmacher, *Senator Robert F. Wagner,* passim.

11. The general development of professional, economic, and other interest organizations and groups are presented in Robert H. Wiebe, *The Search for Order, 1877–1920* (New York: Hill and Wang, 1967), ch. 5, and Samuel P. Hays, *The Response to Industrialism, 1885–1914* (Chicago: University of Chicago Press, 1957), pp. 48–70. Some of these concepts applied to New York State can be found in McCormick, *From Realignment to Reform,* esp. pp. 264–267, 269–271. On the reform and progressive societies as well as organized labor, see Irwin Yellowitz, *Labor and the Progressive Movement in New York State, 1897–1916* (Ithaca: Cornell University Press, 1965), passim; and on civic associations in New York City, see Richard Skolnik, "Civic Group Progressivism in New York City," *New York History,* LI (1970), 411–439. Suggestive of the continuation and functioning of the social progressive groups in the decade of the 1920s is the excellent study by Clarke Chambers, *Seedtime of Reform: American Social Service and Social Action, 1918–1933* (Minneapolis: University of Minnesota Press, 1963).

APPENDIX I

1. *Manual for the Use of the Legislature of the State of New York* (Albany: J. B. Lyon, 1907, 1909, 1911, 1913, 1915, 1917, and 1919).
2. *Thirteenth Census of the U.S. 1910, Abstracts with Supplements for New York* (Washington: Government Printing Office, 1913), pp. 633–645; *New York State Manuscript Census, 1905* (Albany: New York State Library Microfilm, 1967). Many of the county reports are not available on this microfilm and must be checked in county clerks' offices across New York State.
3. In brief, the federal census for 1910, as noted above, and *Fourteenth Census of the U.S. Taken in the Year 1920* (Washington: Government Printing Office, 1922), vol. III, pp. 705–727.
4. *New York State Manuscript Census, 1915* (Albany: New York State Library Microfilm, 1967), and *New York State Manuscript Census, 1925* (Albany: New York State Library Microfilm, 1967).
5. Walter Laidlaw, ed., *Statistical Sources for Demographic Studies for Greater New York, 1910* (New York: The New York City 1910 Census Committee, 1911), and *Statistical Sources for Demographic Studies for Greater New York, 1920* (New York: The New York City 1920 Census Committee, 1922); David Burner, *The Politics of Provincialism: The Democratic Party in Transition, 1918–1932* (New York: Alfred A. Knopf, 1968), pp. 231–233; Thomas J. McInerney, "The Election of 1912 in New York State" (Ph.D. diss., University of Denver, 1977), p. 346.

APPENDIX II

1. *New York Red Book: An Illustrated Legislative Manual* (Albany: J. B. Lyon, 1901, 1903, 1905, 1907, 1909, 1911, 1913, 1915, 1917, and 1919); Edgar Eugene Robinson, *The Presidential Vote, 1896–1932* (New York: Octagon Books, 1970), pp. 275–280.

2. For 1900 and 1910, see *Twelfth Census of the United States Taken in the Year 1900* (Washington: U.S. Census Office, 1901), vol. 1, pp. cxcix, and ccxi; and *Thirteenth Census of the U.S. 1910, Abstracts with Supplements for New York* (Washington: Government Printing Office, 1913), pp. 110–111, 117, 594–595, and 623. For 1920, see *Fourteenth Census of the U.S. Taken in the Year 1920* (Washington: Government Printing Office, 1922), vol. III, pp. 678, 710.

3. Especially useful were the following: Walter A. Borowiec, "Politics and Buffalo's Polish American," in Angela T. Pienkos, ed., *Ethnic Politics in Urban America: The Polish Experience in Four Cities* (Chicago: Polish American Historical Association, 1978), pp. 16–17; John Daniels, "Americanizing Eighty Thousand Poles," *The Survey*, XXIV (1910), 373–385; John W. Briggs, *An Italian Passage: Immigrants to Three American Cities, 1890–1920* (New Haven: Yale University Press, 1978), pp. 98, 100–104, 107–108, 119, 172–177; Stuart E. Rosenberg, *The Jewish Community in Rochester, 1843–1925* (New York: Columbia University Press, 1954), passim; John A. Beadles, "The Syracuse Irish, 1812–1928: Immigration, Catholicism, Socio-Economic Status, Politics and Irish Nationalism" (Ph.D. diss., Syracuse University, 1974), pp. 207–219; Thomas M. Henderson, "Tammany Hall and the New Immigrants, 1910–1921" (Ph.D. diss., University of Virginia, 1973), passim; Alter F. Landesman, *Brownsville: The Birth, Development, and Passing of a Jewish Community in New York* (New York: Bloch, 1969), ch. XVII; Jeffrey S. Gurock, *When Harlem Was Jewish, 1870–1930* (New York: Columbia University Press, 1979), ch. 3; Abram Lipsky, "The Political Mind of Foreign-Born Americans," *Popular Science Monthly*, LXXXV (1914), 397–403. For ethnic districts in the major cities across the state, see Thomas J. McInerney, "The Election of 1912 in New York State" (Ph.D. diss., University of Denver, 1977), chs. IX and X.

Bibliographical Essay

UNPUBLISHED MANUSCRIPT COLLECTIONS

As the notes to this study indicate, a large number of private and organizational manuscript collections were consulted for all aspects of the politics of New York State, 1902–1918. Some collections proved to be far more valuable than others in providing insights into the plans, strategies, and responses of the major political leaders. The most revealing papers are discussed below; following this discussion is a list of others that were read but used less frequently.

Among the Democratic politicians of the period, the fullest and most complete collections were those of the independents. The Franklin D. Roosevelt Papers at Hyde Park, New York, and the Thomas Mott Osborne Papers in the Syracuse University Library adequately document the battle that these upstaters waged against Tammany Hall and the other regular organizations through 1914. Supplementing these collections were the manuscripts of Oswald Garrison Villard (Harvard University Library); a few items were also found in the William C. Osborn Papers, which are privately held. The maneuverings of the Wilsonians, 1912–1918, were traced through the Papers of William Gibbs McAdoo (LC), John Purroy Mitchel (LC), Edward M. House (including the "Diary of Edward M. House") at Yale, and Woodrow Wilson himself (LC). One of the bulkiest sets of manuscripts consulted for this study was the William Sulzer Papers in the Cornell University Library. The Sulzer materials, containing newspaper scrapbooks as well as correspondence and memoranda, supplied information about both the independent and the regular Democrats in the different phases of Sulzer's career and afforded good coverage of the post-gubernatorial years, especially Sulzer's role in the 1914 political campaign in the state. A companion collection at Cornell is the Chester C. Platt Papers, which gave a glimpse at upstate antiorganizational politics in 1910 and again in 1915 and 1916. While personal manuscripts of the principal organization leaders—Charlie Murphy, Al Smith, and Robert Wagner—are nonexistent for these years, two smaller collections in the New York Public Library offered an occasional insight: The Papers of Anthony Griffin, a Bronx state senator and a severe critic of Sulzer; and the Papers of William Bourke Cockran, who was both a regular and independent (joining the Progressives in 1912) in the period under investigation.

Republican politics in New York State can be better documented by use of personal manuscript collections than Democratic politics. The Papers of James S. Sherman (NYPL), James W. Wadsworth, Jr. (LC), and George W. Aldridge (RML) were good on aspects of upstate conservatism. The Papers of Herbert Parsons and Seth Low, both in the Columbia University Library, and those of Henry L. Stimson at Yale proved to be equally useful for the progressive wing of the GOP headquartered in New York City. Also helpful for understanding the progressives who remained loyal to the Republican party were the Jonathan M. Wainwright Papers (N-YHSL). The large Elihu Root Collection (LC) shed light on the party turmoil of 1912; included much correspondence with William Barnes, Jr.; contained a number of items on the federal crowd in the 1915 state constitutional convention; and yielded some information on the politics of 1916 in the state. To these collections should be added the William Howard Taft Papers (LC), which gave the president's view on the tangled New York situation in 1910 and 1912.

There is no better source for the history of the Progressive party (or, for that matter, the Republican party before 1912 and after 1915) than the voluminous Papers of Theodore Roosevelt (LC). A smaller but solid set of manuscripts on the Bull Moose is the Roosevelt Collection in the Harvard University Library. The impact of progressivism on the Empire State was traced in several collections: the Amos Pinchot Papers (LC), the Oscar Straus Papers (LC), and the George W. Perkins Papers (Columbia University Library). Upstate progressivism was covered in the Clarence Parker Papers, held by Lyall Squiar in Syracuse; the Frederick M. Davenport Papers (Syracuse University Library); and the Chauncey J. Hamlin Papers (BECHSL).

Several organizational collections were consulted for this study. On socialism, there were the New York City Socialist Party Papers, housed in the Tamiment Institute at the Bobst Library (New York University). Of limited use but containing a few items were the Julius Gerber Socialist Collection and the New York County Socialist Party Papers, 1907–1914, available on microfilm in the Cornell University Library. The woman suffrage movement in the Empire State is documented by the New York City Woman Suffrage Party Papers (Columbia University Library) and the New York State Woman Suffrage Party Papers (NYPL). Used in conjunction with the Carrie Chapman Catt Papers (NYPL), these collections helped outline the movement's strategy in city and state and its relationship with the politicians, particularly the Democrats.

OTHER MANUSCRIPT COLLECTIONS USED

John B. Andrews (Library of Industrial and Labor Relations, Cornell University)

Citizens Union (Columbia University Library and NYPL)
Consumers' League (Library of Industrial and Labor Relations, Cornell University)
Gherardi Davis (NYPL)
Charles D. Hilles (LC)
Louis M. Howe (FDRL)
Norman Mack (BECHSL)
John Mitchell (Catholic University Library)
Rose Schneiderman (Tamiment Institute, Bobst Library, New York University)
Jacob Gould Schurman (Cornell University Library)
J. G. Phelps Stokes (Columbia University Library)
Lawrence Veiller (Columbia University Library)
Lillian Wald (NYPL)
Women's Trade Union League of New York (New York State Department of Labor, New York City)

ORAL HISTORY COLLECTIONS

The Oral History Project at Columbia University has on file the unpublished reminiscences of many people who were active in the politics of New York City and New York State during the period that this study examines. Of special relevance were the reminiscences of the following:

George W. Alger (1951–1952)
William H. Allen (1949–1950)
William H. Anderson (1950)
William S. Bennet (1951)
Robert S. Binkerd (1949)
Henry Bruere (1949)
Frederick M. Davenport (1952)
Edward J. Flynn (1950)
James W. Gerard (1949–1950)
Jonah Goldstein (1966)
Lloyd C. Griscom (1951)
John A. Heffernan (1950)
John T. Hettrick (1949)
Samuel Koenig (1950)
Herbert Lehman (1961)
George McAneny (1949)

Jeremiah T. Mahoney (1949)
John Lord O'Brian (1952)
Ferdinand Pecora (1962)
Herbert C. Pell (1951)
Frances Perkins (1955)
Louis Pink (1949)
William A. Prendergast (1948–1951)
Joseph M. Proskauer (1961)
Lawson Purdy (1948)
Beverly R. Robinson (1949)
William J. Schieffelin (1949)
Francis Stoddard (1949)
Frederick C. Tanner (1950)
Lawrence A. Tanzer (1949)
Lawrence Veiller (1949)
James W. Wadsworth, Jr. (1952)

Two other brief recollections of John Lord O'Brian—"Interview" (1969) and "Local Politics" (1970)—on deposit in the Buffalo and Erie County Historical Society Library were also consulted.

AUTOBIOGRAPHIES, MEMOIRS, AND LETTER COLLECTIONS

Although a large number of volumes in this category were checked, few yielded much information, particularly about Democratic politics. Among the autobiographies and memoirs, Alfred E. Smith's *Up to Now: An Autobiography* (New York: The Viking Press, 1929) provides a good account of Smith's background together with some materials on Tammany Hall from the insider's point of view. It is sketchy, however, on most of the major events that took place during the progressive era. Some few items were unearthed in the works of William McCombs, William Gibbs McAdoo, William Jennings Bryan, Frances Perkins, Edward J. Flynn, George B. McClellan, Jr., Josephus Daniels, Henry Morgenthau, and James W. Gerard, as cited in the Notes. Two letter collections proved to be of some value. One was Arthur S. Link's excellent collection of Wilson letters, entitled *The Papers of Woodrow Wilson* (Princeton: Princeton University Press, 1978–1983), especially vols. 27 (on 1913), 29 (on 1914), and 31 (also on 1914). The other was Elliot Roosevelt, ed., *F.D.R. His Personal Letters, 1905–1928* (New York: Duell, Sloan, and Pearce, 1947–1950), vol. 2, which contained an occasional letter of importance. Charles Seymour's *The Intimate Papers of Colonel House,* 2 vols. (Boston and New York: Houghton Mifflin, 1926) documented certain efforts made by the Wilsonians to reconstruct New York Democratic politics in 1913 and 1914.

The Republicans and the Progressives wrote numerous accounts of their activities in the first two decades of the twentieth century. However, the single most important source of information on GOP–Bull Moose politics and strategy is Elting Morison et al., eds., *The Letters of Theodore Roosevelt* (Cambridge: Harvard University Press, 1951–1954), especially vols. V–VIII. Read in conjunction with the Roosevelt collections in the Library of Congress and Harvard University, these letters were particularly enlightening on the Colonel's attitudes toward the entrenched leadership of the two major parties, 1909–1916. Volumes by Archie Butt and Lloyd C. Griscom, as cited in the Notes, helped round out the story of Republican politics in 1910.

DOCUMENTS AND REPORTS

Documents used for the purpose of electoral analysis have already been mentioned in Appendix I and Appendix II and need not be outlined here. Of considerable value in appraising the performance of the governors were the published volumes: *Public Papers of John A. Dix* (Albany: J. B. Lyon, 1912–1913); *Public Papers of William Sulzer* (Albany: J. B. Lyon, 1913); and *Public Papers of Martin H. Glynn* (Albany: J. B. Lyon, 1925). The history of key legislation was followed in the *New York Assembly Journal,* 134th–142nd sessions (Albany: J. B. Lyon, 1911–1919) and the *New York Senate Journal,* 134th–142nd sessions (Albany: J. B. Lyon, 1911–1919). Although debates are not recorded in the journals, these documents can be read along with newspapers to obtain a full account of specific bills and resolutions. While a host of other state documents were checked, two proved to be of special value for this study: *Proceedings of the Court for the Trial of Impeachments: The People of the State of New York by the Assembly thereof against William Sulzer, as Governor,* 2 vols. (Albany: J. B. Lyon, 1913) for the Sulzer impeachment episode of 1913, which was also detailed in the newspapers; and *Revised Record of the Constitutional Convention of the State of New York, 1915,* 4 vols. (Albany: J. B. Lyon, 1916) for the debates, resolutions, and roll-call votes at the ill-fated Albany conclave.

The reports and proceedings of private organizations filled in certain gaps with regard to support for, and opposition to, policies and programs advanced by the politicians. The reports of the Consumers' League of New York City, 1912–1917; the Consumers' League of New York State, 1910–1914; the City Club of New York, 1911 and 1914; and the Citizens Union in New York City, 1911–1915, were particularly helpful on some of the reform bills that came before the legislature during the years of Democratic control of the state. The *Official Proceedings* of the New York State Federation of Labor, 1913 and 1916, gave indications of that body's perspective on labor and social reform and on the constitutional convention of 1915.

NEWSPAPERS

Newspapers and newspaper collections formed perhaps the single most important source for an investigation of New York politics in the decade and a half before 1918. Dailies in both New York City and the major upstate urban centers yielded information about day-to-day activities of the politicians; strategies and plans concocted in meetings and conferences; and, broadly speaking, public support for, and opposition to, specific policies and programs. Indeed, the newspapers of that era were especially effective at molding as well as mirroring public opinion, the more so because prominent leaders like William Randolph Hearst, Oswald Garrison Villard, William Barnes, Martin H. Glynn, Norman Mack, William J. Conners, and Louis Antisdale were owners or publishers of dailies in their respective cities.

A starting point for all students of this period is the *New York Times* (independent Democratic), which was read on a day-to-day basis through 1918. Key news stories and important legislative debates were corroborated by selective but careful use of the *New York Tribune* (Republican), the *New York World* (independent Democratic), and the *New York Sun* (Republican). Occasional use was also made of the *New York Evening Post,* the *New York Herald,* and the *Brooklyn Daily Eagle* (mainly in 1918). Socialist activities together with radical commentary on major party politics were gleaned from the *New York Call.* A host of other dailies in Greater New York were sampled through a close reading of the two excellent newspaper scrapbook collections compiled by Edwin P. Kilroe, which are on deposit in the Columbia University Library.

One collection, 2 volumes, covers the years 1907–1911; the other, comprising 28 volumes, spans the period 1911–1936. The first 14 volumes of the latter, representing virtually every major daily in New York City, provided an unusually rich coverage of the nuts-and-bolts operations of the Democratic party in the state as well as in New York City. Only occasionally was it not possible to identify newspapers or dates in this exceptional collection.

Several upstate newspapers were consulted extensively both for local Democratic politics and state-national affairs. Especially helpful was Martin Glynn's *Albany Times-Union* (1906, 1909–1918; NYSL); William Conners's *Buffalo Courier* (1909–1918; BECPL); Norman Mack's *Buffalo Evening Times* (1911–1917; BECPL); Louis Antisdale's *Rochester Herald* (1906, 1908, 1910–1918; RML); and the *Utica Observer* (1911–1914, 1918; UPL). The last two were particularly critical of the Democratic state organization led by Charlie Murphy.

In some instances, upstate Republican newspapers supplied considerable information about Democratic politics as they did about the GOP and the Bull Moose. These included: William Barnes's *Albany Evening Journal* (1911, 1913–1915; NYSL); *Buffalo Evening News* (1912–1914, 1916–1918; BECPL): *Buffalo Morning Express* (1910, 1912–1918; BECPL); *Rochester Democrat and Chronicle* (1912, 1914, 1918; RML); *Rochester Evening Times* (1910–1917; RML); *Syracuse Herald* (1911–1918; OPL); *Syracuse Post-Standard* (1911–1918; OPL); *Utica Daily Press* (1911–1914; UPL); and *Utica Herald-Dispatch* (1911–1913; UPL).

Other newspapers and newspaper collections were of value for specific events or background on individual political leaders: *Albany Knickerbocker-Press* (1915; NYSL) on Schoharie County Democrats; (Buffalo) *New Age* (1917; BECPL) on socialism in the Buffalo municipal election; "Chauncey J. Hamlin Scrapbooks" (2 vols.; BECHSL) on the upstate anti-Tammany campaign of 1914; "Local Biographies, Clippings" (BECPL), a large collection with sketches of prominent Buffalo and state Democratic leaders; Howard T. Mosher's "Politics, 1915" (RML), on local Rochester politics with some information on the state situation; "Newspaper Clippings, 1910–1913" (FDRL) on Roosevelt's years in the state senate and related activities; John Lord O'Brian Scrapbooks (5 vols.; BECHSL) on O'Brian's early career, Buffalo politics, and the constitutional convention of 1915; Prohibition File (Onondaga County Historical Association), containing some items on the 1918 local option campaign in Syracuse; William Samson Scrapbooks (RML) on the impact of Sulzerism on Rochester politics; "William Sulzer Newspaper Clippings, 1913–1914" (Cornell University Library) on the Sulzer governorship and impeachment, with items from both the New York City and upstate press; and (Syracuse) *Catholic Sun* (1914; OPL) on nativism and the Guardians of Liberty in the 1914 campaign.

For a sampling of editorial opinion on state and national politics, *The Literary Digest*, vols. XXXIX–LVI (1909–1918) was of value.

CONTEMPORARY MAGAZINES AND PERIODICALS

A great variety of contemporary magazines and periodicals gave information and commentary on politics and the politicians of the progressive era. Unlike other students of the Democracy, I found the weekly *Tammany Times* most revealing and instructive on details of party management, attitudes toward certain personalities, and aspects of political strategy. The largest collection of the *Times* is housed in the Cornell University Library. Reading it for the years immediately after the turn of the twentieth century into the era of World War I gives the historian a flavor for the organizational side of Democratic politics that is offered by few other sources. In a similar vein, the *National Monthly* (1909–1916) presented a sympathetic view of key aspects of state and national party affairs. A nearly complete file is available in the BECHSL. From the perspective of the social progressives, *The Survey* (1910–1918) carried articles on labor legislation and enforcement, detailed efforts to undermine FIC-related laws, and defined the parameters of social reform through World War I. Also useful along these lines was the *American Labor Legislation Review* (1911–1917). Other magazines that were consulted, albeit less frequently, were: *Review of Reviews* (1906, 1910, 1913); *Nation* (1910–1913, 1915–1917); *New Republic* (1914–1917); *Independent* (1910–1913); *Harper's Weekly* (1913); *Atlantic Monthly* (1908); *World's Work* (1915); and *Pearson's Magazine* (1918).

Excellent signed articles on all phases of New York politics appeared in the Sunday *New York Times Magazine* (1911–1918).

UNPUBLISHED ESSAYS, THESES, AND DISSERTATIONS

Among the two dozen unpublished works read in connection with New York political and social history, 1900–1918, several deserve special mention. John A. Beadles, "The Syracuse Irish, 1812–1928: Immigration, Catholicism, Socio-Economic Status, Politics and Irish Nationalism" (Ph.D. diss., Syracuse University, 1974), ably traces the manifold influences of Irish-Americans on the history of Syracuse and includes a valuable interpretation of the plight of the Democratic party in the progressive era. Thomas J. Kerr IV, "New York Factory Investigating Commission and the Progressives" (D.S.S. diss., Syracuse University, 1965), presents the most complete analysis of the background and workings of the FIC. While Kerr overstates the importance of the so-called FIC political coalition in the progressive years, he is quite correct in his overall appraisal of the commission's performance under the tutelage of Smith and Wagner. Thomas M. Henderson, "Tammany Hall and the New Immigrants, 1910–1921" (Ph.D. diss., University of Virginia, 1973), is a perceptive study of the problems Charlie Murphy's organization faced in dealing with the new-stock groups in New York County. The author argues his case persuasively and backs up his conclusions with election analyses on the district level. Anna

Lanahan, "The Attempt of Tammany Hall to Dominate the Brooklyn Democratic Party, 1903–1909" (M.A. essay, Columbia University, 1955), is one of the few studies that deals with the nuts-and-bolts operations of the Democratic party in New York City in the years when Murphy was consolidating his power. Richard L. McCormick, "Shaping Republican Strategy: Political Change in New York State, 1893–1910" (Ph.D. diss., Yale University, 1976), affords a brilliant interpretation of the transformation that the Republican party underwent down through the gubernatorial administrations of Charles Evans Hughes. By focusing on such electoral changes as the decline in voter turnout and partisanship, the author projects his analysis beyond New York State and beyond the progressive period. Thomas J. McInerney, "The Election of 1912 in New York State" (Ph.D. diss., University of Denver, 1977), covers every major feature of this event, including a regional as well as a local vote breakdown. McInerney is somewhat more critical than my study on the negative impact of Wilson's presidential nomination on the Democracy's ability to attract the immigrant vote. Robert E. O'Connor, "William Barnes, Jr.: A Conservative Encounters the Progressive Era" (Ph.D. diss., State University of New York at Albany, 1971), treats of the Albany boss' rise to power in the late nineteenth century; his maneuverings to insulate the New York Republican party from Rooseveltian progressivism; and his ventures in national politics, especially his work on behalf of Taft's reelection in 1912. Alfred B. Rollins, Jr., "The Political Education of Franklin D. Roosevelt: His Career in New York State Politics, 1910–1928" (Ph.D. diss., Harvard University, 1953), offers the most thorough discussion of the Osborne-Roosevelt relationship and the several organizations they formed to reconstruct Democratic politics in the Empire State. Herbert H. Rosenthal, "The Progressive Movement in New York State, 1906–1914" (Ph.D. diss., Harvard University, 1955), analyzes the foundations of the Progressive party in New York State and its checkered history. Marvin G. Weinbaum, "A Minority's Survival: The Republican Party of New York County, 1897–1960" (Ph.D. diss., Columbia University, 1965), details in its opening chapter the plight of Republicans in Manhattan during the Platt, Parsons, and Koenig era.

SECONDARY BOOKS AND SCHOLARLY ARTICLES

The general histories of New York State yielded little information for this study. A few items were gleaned from Alexander C. Flick, ed., *History of the State of New York,* 10 vols. (New York: Columbia University Press, 1933–1937), especially vol. 7, which contains some materials on the constitutional convention of 1915 and on general conditions in the state during World War I. Ray B. Smith, ed., *History of the State of New York: Political and Governmental,* 6 vols. (Syracuse: Syracuse Press, 1922), vol. IV, presents a standard political narrative of the period under examination. David M. Ellis et al., *A Short History of New York State* (Ithaca: Cornell University Press, 1967), ch. 29, provides a convenient summary of the progressive era, including a tribute to the record of Smith and Wagner in the state legislature.

A number of volumes supplied background information of one kind or another. They were: Herbert J. Bass, *"I AM A DEMOCRAT": The Political Career of David Bennett Hill* (Syracuse: Syracuse University Press, 1961) on the Hill leadership of the Democratic party into the 1890s; Samuel T. McSeveney, *The Politics of Depression: Political Behavior in the Northeast, 1893–1896* (New York: Oxford University Press, 1972), a first-rate behavioral study covering several states in this era of political realignment; Richard L. McCormick, *From Realignment to Reform: Political Change in New York State, 1893–1910* (New York and London: Cornell University Press, 1981), a revision of the dissertation noted above, which superbly studies the Republican party and its leaders in these years; Gerald W. McFarland, *Mugwumps, Morals, and Politics, 1884–1920* (Amherst: The University of Massachusetts Press, 1975), dealing with the "best men" reformers of the late nineteenth century and their continuing influence through the first two decades of the twentieth century; and John Higham, *Strangers in the Land: Patterns of American Nativism, 1865–1920* (New Brunswick: Rutgers University Press, 1955), for background on nativistic patterns in 1914 and during World War I.

Histories of various cities or reform within cities proved useful. On Buffalo there were Walter Dunn, Jr., *History of Erie County, 1870–1970* (Buffalo: BECHSL, 1962), a general study with information on the economic and political developments in that city; and Brenda K. Shelton, *Reformers in Search of Yesterday: Buffalo in the 1890's* (Albany: State University of New York Press, 1976), a well-written monograph on both the successes and the failures of the preprogressives in the depression decade. On Rochester, Blake McKelvey's volumes admirably tell the story of that city. Especially helpful was *Rochester: Quest for Quality, 1890–1925* (Cambridge: Harvard University Press, 1956), which included a great deal on the leadership of Republican George W. Aldridge and on the ins and outs of Flower City politics. W. Freeman Galpin, *Central New York: An Inland Empire*, 3 vols. (New York: Lewis Historical Publishing Company, 1941), vol. III, had some information on Syracuse.

The historian who first drew attention to the development of urban liberalism in the progressive era was J. Joseph Huthmacher in the essay, "Urban Liberalism and the Age of Reform," *Mississippi Valley Historical Review*, XLIV (1962), 231–241. Huthmacher's "Charles Evans Hughes and Charles Francis Murphy: The Metamorphosis of Progressivism," *New York History*, XLVI (1965), 25–40, further details the concept with reference to New York State and contrasts this version of reform with middle-class progressivism. The most ambitious statement of urban liberalism and cultural liberalism is John D. Buenker, *Urban Liberalism and Progressive Reform* (New York: Charles Scribner's Sons, 1973), which, in addition to New York, covers the states of Illinois,

Massachusetts, Michigan, New Jersey, Pennsylvania, and Rhode Island. In an engaging concluding chapter the author relates the idea of urban liberalism to the historiography of the progressive era. While both Huthmacher and Buenker have done a service to the profession by opening the closed door of progressivism, neither fully explores the context of New York politics in which Democratic reform efforts developed or the electoral impact of the leaders' strategies and programs. Two articles by Buenker were also useful in understanding Democratic reformism in the Empire State: "Progressivism in Practice: New York State and the Federal Income Tax Amendment," *New-York Historical Society Quarterly,* LII (1968), 139–160; and "The Urban Political Masses and Woman Suffrage: A Study in Political Adaptability," *The Historian,* XXXIII (1971), 264–279.

Among the biographies of Democrats, two frame the lives of their subjects in the context of urban liberalism. J. Joseph Huthmacher's excellent *Senator Robert F. Wagner and the Rise of Urban Liberalism* (New York: Atheneum, 1968) shows the influence of this politician's apprenticeship in New York State during the progressive era on his later career as an avid New Dealer. Nancy Joan Weiss, *Charles Francis Murphy, 1858–1924: Respectability and Responsibility in Tammany Politics* (Northampton, Mass.: Smith College, 1968), presents a sympathetic treatment of this unusual political boss whose enlightened approach to politics played a major role in the Hall's transformation through the early years of the 1920s. Appropriately, Weiss pays greater attention to Murphy's activities in New York City than in the state as a whole. Other briefer yet perceptive sketches of Murphy can be found in Alfred Connable and Edward Silberfarb, *Tigers of Tammany: Nine Men Who Ran New York* (New York: Holt, Rinehart and Winston, 1967), and Harold Zink, *City Bosses in the United States* (New York: AMS Press, 1968). Al Smith has been the subject of several studies. The most complete biography to date is Matthew and Hannah Josephson, *Al Smith: Hero of the Cities* (Boston: Houghton Mifflin Company, 1969), which is based in part on Frances Perkins's uncompleted manuscript on Smith. An admirable shorter work is Oscar Handlin, *Al Smith and His America* (Boston: Little, Brown and Company, 1958). Some insights into Smith's character and politics can be gleaned from Norman Hapgood and Henry Moskowitz, *Up from the City Streets: Alfred E. Smith* (New York: Harcourt, Brace and Co., 1927), and Henry F. Pringle, *Alfred E. Smith: A Critical Study* (New York: Macy-Masius, 1927). For an interpretation of Smith and the 1918 election campaign somewhat different from mine, see Paula Eldot, *Governor Alfred E. Smith: The Politician as Reformer* (New York and London: Garland Publishing, Inc., 1983), ch. 1.

Biographies and political studies of the antiorganization Democrats abound. Frank Freidel, *Franklin D. Roosevelt: The Apprenticeship* (Boston: Little, Brown and Company, 1952), thoroughly surveys its subject's entry into politics, his career in the state senate, and his battle against Tammany into the

Wilson years. For the Osborne-Roosevelt relationship and the several organizations these independents formed to rejuvenate Democratic politics, see Alfred B. Rollins, Jr., *Roosevelt and Howe* (New York: Alfred A. Knopf, 1962), which incorporates much of the material from Rollins's dissertation cited above. Rudolph W. Chamberlain, *There Is No Truce: A Life of Thomas Mott Osborne* (New York: The Macmillan Company, 1935), is a sympathetic yet not totally uncritical biography of the Auburn independent. There is need for a modern study of this important upstate politician and penal reformer. William Randolph Hearst has been the subject of several tracts. The best among the lot for my purpose was W. A. Swanberg, *Citizen Hearst* (New York: Charles Scribner's Sons, 1961), but a few items were found in Roy Everett Littlefield III, *William Randolph Hearst: His Role in American Progressivism* (Lanham, Md.: University Press of America, 1980). Samuel Seabury's role as an anti-Tammanyite is best analyzed in Herbert Mitgang, *The Man Who Rode the Tiger: The Life and Times of Samuel Seabury* (Philadelphia: J. B. Lippincott Company, 1963). Although the impeachment trial of William Sulzer has elicited much attention from commentators and historians, only one book has stood the test of time. This is Jacob A. Friedman's *The Impeachment of Governor William Sulzer* (New York: Columbia University Press, 1939), which actually covers the man's entire life. Friedman apparently had only limited access (if any at all) to the massive Sulzer Papers at Cornell, but by and large his conclusions are borne out by the research I have done.

Biographies of Wilson and the Wilsonians helped round out the picture of New York Democratic politics, 1912–1918. Most helpful were those by Arthur S. Link of Wilson, John Blum of Joseph Tumulty, John J. Broesamle of William Gibbs McAdoo, and Edwin R. Lewinson of John Purroy Mitchel. Paolo Coletta, *William Jennings Bryan: Progressive Politician and Moral Statesman, 1909–1915* (Lincoln: University of Nebraska Press, 1969), was packed with information on Bryan in the 1912 presidential contest.

Important for what they say about their subjects, biographies of Republicans active in New York politics also shed some light on Democratic activities and strategies in the state. William Harbaugh's *Power and Responsibility: The Life and Times of Theodore Roosevelt* (New York: Farrar, Straus and Cudahy, 1961) is the best of the one-volume biographies of the Colonel. Specifically on the Roosevelt governorship there is G. Wallace Chessman, *Governor Theodore Roosevelt: The Albany Apprenticeship* (Cambridge: Harvard University Press, 1965). Philip C. Jessup's *Elihu Root*, 2 vols. (New York: Dodd, Mead and Company, 1938) is a mine of information on Root and several aspects of the state's politics, including the constitutional convention of 1915. Martin L. Fausold, *James W. Wadsworth, Jr.: The Gentleman from New York* (Syracuse: Syracuse University Press, 1975), ably traces the Geneseo politician's career through the Albany and (later) the Washington years. Fausold gives perspectives on Al Smith from the vantage point of a Republican friend. Elting Morison,

Turmoil and Tradition: A Study of the Life and Times of Henry L. Stimson (Boston: Houghton Mifflin Company, 1960), does a superb job of outlining Stimson's entire career, placing the man in the context of the gentlemanly traditions of the late nineteenth century. My earlier study, *Charles Evans Hughes: Politics and Reform in New York: 1905–1910* (Ithaca: Cornell University Press, 1967), contains some material on the Democrats in the Hughes years. Two books that treat of Republicans who became Progressives are: John A. Garraty, *Right-Hand Man: The Life of George W. Perkins* (New York: Harper and Brothers, Publishers, 1957), which has an engaging chapter on New York City and state politics, 1914–1915; and Naomi Cohen, *A Dual Heritage: The Public Career of Oscar S. Straus* (Philadelphia: The Jewish Publication Society of America, 1969), which presents a good summary of the 1912 state campaign from Straus's point of view.

Other works dealing with Republican and Progressive politics that have a bearing on New York State are: George E. Mowry, *Theodore Roosevelt and the Progressive Movement* (Madison: University of Wisconsin Press, 1947), the standard account of the Roosevelt-Taft feud, the split in the Republican party, and TR's Progressives; and John A. Gable, *The Bull Moose Years: Theodore Roosevelt and the Progressive Party* (Port Washington, N.Y.: Kennikat Press, 1978), the most recent treatment of the Bull Moosers, with an intelligent profile of the 1912 vote breakdown.

A miscellany of other studies proved helpful on a variety of topics particularly relevant to New York City. Jeremy P. Felt, "Vice Reform as a Political Technique: The Committee of Fifteen in New York, 1900–1901," *New York History,* LIV (1973), 24–51, points to the Republican penetration of Democratic districts on the vice issue. Richard Skolnik, "Civic Group Progressivism in New York City," *New York History,* LI (1970), 411–439, shows how reformers relinquished partisan politics and found other means to press for change. Leon Stein's *The Triangle Fire* (Philadelphia: J. B. Lippincott Co., 1962) is the best account of that tragedy. Donald S. Ritchie, "The Gary Committee: Businessmen, Progressives and Unemployment in New York City, 1914–1915," *New-York Historical Society Quarterly,* LVII (1973), 327–347, is a critical study of the ill-fated school "reform." But the definitive work on this subject is Ronald D. Cohen and Raymond A. Mohl, *The Paradox of Progressive Education: The Gary Plan and Urban Schooling* (Port Washington, N.Y: Kennikat Press, 1979). Kenneth S. Chern, "The Politics of Patriotism: War, Ethnicity, and the New York Mayoral Campaign, 1917," *New-York Historical Society Quarterly,* LXIII (1979), 290–313, gives a fine analysis of this bitter election campaign and contains an enlightening breakdown of the vote in the city's various ethnic and native American districts. Melvyn Dubofsky's studies of New York City labor, cited individually in the Notes, are encapsulated in his excellent book, *When Workers Organize: New York City in the Progressive Era* (Amherst: The University of Massachusetts Press, 1968). Deserving special mention, however, is Dubofsky's "Success and Failure of Socialism in New York City, 1900–1918: A Case Study," *Labor History,* IX (1968), 361–375, which argues the appeal of the left-wing to eastern European Jews and shows the degree of Jewish support for the Socialist party during the progressive era.

A large number of works, some general and others specific in nature, illuminated particular events in New York State. Herbert H. Rosenthal, "The Cruise of the Tarpon," *New York History,* XXXIX (1958), 302–320, adds a dimension to George Mowry's coverage of Republican factionalism that helped elect Democrats in the 1910 elections. My article, "Conflict and Compromise: The Workmen's Compensation Movement in New York, 1890's–1913," *Labor History,* XII (1971), 347–372, has information on the role of labor, social progressives, and businessmen in the 1910 and 1913 compensation bills. Howard A. Scarrow, *Parties, Elections, and Representation in the State of New York* (New York and London: New York University Press, 1983), offers a critique of primary reform and the Massachusetts ballot legislation. Thomas Schick, *The New York State Constitutional Convention of 1915 and the Modern State Governor* (New York: National Municipal League, 1978), explores the major aspects of reform at the convention, the campaign for the revision's adoption, and its electoral defeat in November. Also enlightening is Gerald D. McKnight, "The Perils of Reform Politics: The Abortive New York State Constitutional Reform Movement of 1915," *New-York Historical Society Quarterly,* LXIII (1979), 203–227, which emphasizes the division within the Republican party before, during, and after the convention but concentrates on the role played by George W. Perkins in defeating the revision. In addition to detailing the relationship generally between labor and the social progressives, Irwin Yellowitz's *Labor and the Progressive Movement in New York State, 1897–1916* (Ithaca: Cornell University Press, 1965) has a sound chapter on the campaign waged by the State Federation of Labor and other groups to defeat the 1915 constitution. S. D.Lovell, *The Presidential Election of 1916* (Carbondale and Edwardsville: University of Southern Illinois Press, 1980), provides the most thorough treatment of this subject, including part of a chapter on hyphenism in the campaign. Information on the Irish-Americans and the German-Americans can be checked in William M. Leary, Jr., "Woodrow Wilson, Irish-Americans, and the Election of 1916," *Journal of American History,* LIV (1967), 57–72; Clifton J. Child, *The German-Americans in Politics, 1914–1917* (Madison: University of Wisconsin Press, 1939); and Thomas Jefferson Kerr IV, "German-Americans and Neutrality in the 1916 Election," *Mid-America,* XLII (1961), 95–105. Most useful for a vote analysis in the heavily ethnic areas of New York County is David Burner, *The Politics of Provincialism: The Democratic Party in Transition, 1918–1932* (New York: Alfred A. Knopf, 1968), which compares the 1916 and 1928 results. The best coverage of Wilson's campaign is Arthur S. Link, *Wilson: Campaigns for Pro-*

gressivism and Peace, 1916–1917 (Princeton: Princeton University Press, 1965).

Although the general studies of woman suffrage and prohibition had little of great value on the New York experience, books by Alan P. Grimes and Aileen S. Kraditor on the first and Norman H. Clark, Peter H. Odegard, and James H. Timberlake on the second supplied good background materials. Two scholarly articles on woman suffrage were helpful: Ronald Schaffer, "The New York City Woman Suffrage Party, 1909–1919," *New York History*, XLIII (1962), 269–287, which chronicles that party's struggles up through the 1919 victory; and Doris Daniels, "Building a Winning Coalition: The Suffrage Fight in New York State," *New York History*, LX (1979), 59–80, which highlights the role of the social progressives.

Writings on radicalism abound. The classic account of the Socialist party is David A. Shannon, *The Socialist Party of America: A History* (New York: The Macmillan Company, 1955), which contains a good amount of material on New York. Supplementing Shannon is James Weinstein's *The Decline of Socialism in America, 1912–1925* (New York: Vintage Books, 1969), which challenges the argument advanced by both "liberal" and "Communist" historians on the party's decline in the period of World War I. Students of this topic, however, should not overlook the highly critical chapters on the Socialist party in Bernard K. and Lillian Johnpoll, *The Impossible Dream: The Rise and Demise of the American Left* (Westport, Conn.: Greenwood Press, 1981). On the Lunn experience in Schenectady, see Kenneth E. Hendrickson, Jr., "George R. Lunn and the Socialist Era in Schenectady, New York, 1909–1918," *New York History*, XLVII (1966), 22–39, which is based in part on Lunn's own paper, *The Citizen*. Julian Jaffe, *Crusade against Radicalism: New York during the Red Scare* (Port Washington, N.Y.: Kennikat Press, 1972), has a background chapter on the radical movement in New York State and the foundation of the Red Scare in the days of World War I. Maurice Isserman, "Inheritance Lost: Socialism in Rochester, 1917–1919," *Rochester History*, XXXIX (1977), 1–24, outlines the travails of socialists in the Flower City.

Full references to secondary works used in connection with Appendix I and Appendix II, the concluding chapter, and (in a few instances) the body of this study are given in the Notes.

Index

preparations for, 168–69; and campaign for delegates, 169–70; and Root's election as president, 170; and political groupings in, 170–72; and Democratic priorities, 172; and apportionment issue, 172–74; and home rule, 174–75; approves package of revisions, 175–76; and labor opposition to, 177–78; defeated at the polls, 178–79; and reasons for defeat of, 179, 285n32. See also Stimson, Henry L.

Consumers' League, 166; critical of Dix's spoilsmanship, 54; and FIC, 73, 74

Cosgrove, Mike: Tammany leader, 58

Cram, J. Sergeant: as Murphy's social mentor, 27; appointed to public service commission, 53

Crane, Murray, 75, 76

Creel, George: and committee on public information, 193, 194

Creelman, James, 130

Croker, Richard, 25–26, 46, 47, 51, 102, 136; boss of Tammany Hall, 24; and retirement, 24

Cullen, Edgar T.: abstains on Sulzer impeachment, 122–23

Davenport, Frederick M., 79, 152, 153, 158, 165, 181; wins 1914 Progressive gubernatorial nomination, 151; loses election, 155

Debs, Eugene V., 5

Democratic League of New York State, 44, 46, 47, 48, 53, 102; formed, 34–35; FDR a coleader of, 51; incorporates a New York County chapter, 56; weakened in 1912, 67, 80; abandoned by Osborne, 82. See also Dix, John A.; Osborne, Thomas Mott; Roosevelt, Franklin D.

Democratic party (national), ix–x, 6–7; Bryan's capture of, 33; and 1910 gains, 43; captured by Wilson, 80; and Baltimore convention, 84–88; and St. Louis convention, 183–84. See also Wilson, Woodrow

Democratic party (New York State), ix; in Cleveland-Hill years, 6–7; strength in

New York City, 9–10; nature of in upstate, 11–12; and independents, 11–12; weaknesses in to 1910, 21; and factionalism, 22, 67; and Rochester convention, 37–38; and campaign of 1910, 38; sectional-cultural divisions in, 44, 52, 80; damaged by U.S. Senate fight, 52; and 1911 legislative successes and failures, 64–65; importance of FIC in, 74, 225–26; and 1912 Syracuse convention, 91–92; and campaign of 1912, 93–94; and fragile harmony, 98; and promise of Wilson, 99–100; and 1913 legislature, 110–12; and meaning of primary, 114; devastated in 1913 elections, 132–34; plight in 1914, 136; undergoes reorganization, 141–43; and reasons for 1914 defeat, 157–59; record of from 1911–1914, 159–60; and expanded progressivism, 161–62; pushes for constitutional convention, 167–68; and priorities in constitutional convention, 171–72; opposes constitutional revisions, 177; and 1916 campaign, 185–88; and postmortem on defeat, 190–92; and 1918 harmony, 207–8; future of, 216, 226–27; and changes in Murphy era, 218–19; record of in progressive era, 225–26. See also Elections (New York State); Murphy, Charles F.; Osborne, Thomas Mott; Roosevelt, Franklin D.; Tammany Hall

Depew, Chauncey M., 46

Devery, William ("Big Bill"): is ousted by Murphy, 27

Direct election of U.S. senators, 35, 45, 76, 103, 109; Democratic support of, 61

Dix, John A., 46, 49, 56, 63, 64, 80, 88, 90, 98, 104, 133, 136, 143, 159, 163, 219, 221, 225; as member of Democratic League of New York State, 36–37; Democratic state chairman, 37; is nominated for governor, 37–38; campaign and election of, 38–41; background and views of, 43–45; and patronage troubles, 53–54; and Osborne departure, 54–55; on conservation, 45, 61–62; is dumped in 1912, 91